Learning

Nineteen Scenarios from Everyday Life

This book is a systematic introduction to the psychology of learning. It describes, analyzes, and explains learning by means of 19 scenarios from everyday situations. The reader may therefore connect theoretical considerations with experiences he or she can easily follow. Several scenarios stem from family situations, others from school and business, and still others refer to individual learning processes: modification of one's own behavior, acquisition of motor skills, or elaboration of one's knowledge structures or problem-solving abilities. By working through the 19 scenarios the reader will become acquainted with the important learning theories: behavioristic, cognitive, sociocognitive as well as Gestalt.

Gerhard Steiner is Chairman of the Department of Psychology at the University of Basel, Switzerland.

Learning

Nineteen Scenarios from Everyday Life

GERHARD STEINER

Department of Psychology, University of Basel, Switzerland

Translated by Joseph A. Smith

PUBLISHED BY THE PRESS SYNDICATE OF THE UNIVERSITY OF CAMBRIDGE
The Pitt Building, Trumpington Street, Cambridge, United Kingdom

CAMBRIDGE UNIVERSITY PRESS
The Edinburgh Building, Cambridge, United Kingdom   http: //www.cup.cam.ac.uk
40 West 20th Street, New York, NY 10011–4211, USA   http: //www.cup.org
10 Stamford Road, Oakleigh, Melbourne 3166, Australia
Ruiz de Alarcón 13, 28014 Madrid, Spain

First published in English in 1999 by Cambridge University Press. This edition of
Gerhard Steiner, *Lernen – 20 Szenarien aus dem Alltag,* is published by arrangement
with Verlag Hans Huber, © Verlag Hans Huber, Bern 1988, 1996

Printed in the United States of America

Typeface Times Roman [au]

A catalogue record for this book is available from the British Library.

Library of Congress Cataloguing-in-Publication Data
Steiner, Gerhard.
    [Lernen. English]
    Learning : nineteen scenarios from everyday life / Gerhard Steiner ; translated by
Joseph A. Smith.
        p.   cm.
    Includes bibliographical references and index.
    ISBN 0 521 47220 2 (hardback). – ISBN 0 521 47800-6 (paperback)
    1. Learning. 2. Learning, Psychology of. 3. Cognitive learning. I. Title.
LB1060.S84   1999
370.15'23 – dc21   99-26136
                                            CIP

ISBN 0 521 47220 2 hardback
ISBN 0 521 47800 6 paperback

Contents

Preface

In the years since the appearance of the first German edition of this book I have received extensive feedback, both positive and negative, some of great relevance, some more trivial in nature. Together, however, all have shown me that the book was in great need of a revision. Particularly productive were the comments of my colleagues Urs Aeschbacher (Basel), Kurt Reusser (Zurich), and Jean-Luc Gurtner (Fribourg) and of others who had used it in their seminars and courses as a textbook. For their collective breath of fresh air I thank them all, even if it at times did give me a slight chill.

One of my staunchest critics I have since made my "coauthor": Dr. Joachim Hermann of the University of Lüneburg. In some of the early chapters he has succeeded in drawing a fine line between the behavioral and the cognitive moments in the learning situations being discussed. I have worked into the text many of his ideas and phrases, which have heightened the precision of my interpretation of many learning aspects. In other chapters, particularly in the second part of the book, I have integrated new findings into the text, though this should not imply that the text has been thoroughly updated in all respects. The greatest amount of revision was certainly done in the chapters on the various forms of knowledge acquisition and motor learning, i.e., in areas that have experienced the most progress in the last 10 years. Here, I am indebted to my earlier mentor, Gordon H. Bower of Stanford University, as well as to my colleagues Robert A. Bjork (University of California, Los Angeles) and Walter Kintsch (University of Colorado, Boulder), whose publications and occasional personal discussions with me have helped me hone many of the sections included in this edition. I am also thankful to Walter Kintsch for giving me the idea of having the second German edition appear as a first English edition.

I am very grateful to Irmela Erckenbrecht for adapting the geography of my hometown, Basel, to New York, and above all, to my translator, Joseph Smith, for both his expertise and his patience.

I hope this English edition will be as well received as the first German one among the readers: May they experience the joy of learning about learning.

Basel, Summer 1998

vii

Introduction:
What This Book Intends and
What It Does Not

My adding yet another volume to the already large collection of books on learning is in need of some explanation. In the following I attempt to observe and analyze learning not in a laboratory setting, but in real life, under everyday conditions. I hope to impart to the reader, on the basis of individual examples, the theoretical knowledge gathered through the studies of learning psychology during this century as well as the vocabulary necessary to its understanding and to enable the reader to use this theoretical knowledge analytically in the respective everyday situations in his or her own learning surroundings. Thus, the object of this book is to apply (and extend) laboratory-oriented descriptions of theories of learning (e.g., Bower & Hilgard, 1981).

Through the study of everyday situations from a learning psychology vantage point the reader will quickly discover just how complex such ordinary processes are and realize that it is virtually impossible to explain real human behavior via a single theory of learning. Nevertheless, a certain convergence of interpretations toward a cognitive view of things will emerge for a number of cases.

This book deals with 19 cases taken from everyday life. The choice of these cases was guided by my goal of presenting the theories of learning psychology as completely and as encompassingly as possible up to the present day. Thus, the cases reported do follow a clear historical trail, with Chapters 1 to 6 covering the classical theories of learning. Chapter 1 deals with classically conditioned fear, Chapter 2 with its extinction and the associated reactions; Chapter 3 treats the behavioristic theory of learning by trial and error. Here, it becomes clear, for the first time, that today one cannot explain learning processes solely on the basis of the behavioristic tradition, but must also take cognitive considerations as well as a cybernetic model into account. Chapter 4 has as its theme a child's unlearning of undesirable habits and the learning of desirable habits. Here, too, we see that behavioristic theory can explain a great deal quite plausibly, but that modern demands call for a modification of this regimen.

This forms the background for Chapters 6 and 7: These chapters take an in-depth look at the phenomenon of reinforcement from many different vantage points, among others from a cognitive point of view. This reveals one major intent of this book: While walking along the historical path of learning psychology, we want always to be observing other, newer interpretations that have sprung up. It is thus not our aim to discredit the "old" theories – quite the opposite: We want to reveal their revered place in modern cognitive learning theory.

The next group of chapters (7 through 11) demonstrate this even more clearly: The five examples discussed there show how behavior can be established which is not so easily explained via standard stimulus–response links; rather, we experience the establishment of encompassing behavioral plans – thought systems – that regulate behavior. Most of these examples place a stronger emphasis than the previous ones on learning in a social environment: Children must learn to wait or learn to do without; they must learn to control their own behavior and participate in a larger society, thus the behavioral plans. Similarly, behavior-regulating thought systems must be established in order to learn helping or prosocial behavior. This is perhaps best seen in the way executives learn to deal with job stress: Setting up behavior-controlling cognitive systems also means creating a representation of the entire social situation at hand as well as dealing with one's own emotions.

Chapters 9 and 11 play a special role in this group of chapters. Both deal with how we cope with personal problems – in one example with the fear of taking exams, in the other with failure or helplessness in mastering difficult tasks in school. The coping strategies necessary to both situations (and to coping with job stress, too, for that matter) cannot (or only partially can) be grasped in terms of behavioristic learning theory, that is, in terms of simple reinforcement mechanisms. Rather, cognitive models become indispensable to this end.

Chapter 12, with the example of juggling, shows how learning motor skills (something traditional behavioristic theory would simply call "habits") can, in the end, be explained plausibly only with newer models of cognitive theories of learning. The third set of chapters, encompassing Chapters 13 through 19, turns our attention toward the so-called higher processes of learning, particularly how knowledge is acquired.

With every chapter it should become clearer what the psychology of learning proposed in this book is aiming at: the construction of dynamic systems of thinking that, despite their broad differences in content, reveal great similarities in the way they go about establishing behavior. The focus lies on the linking of elements to other elements of a higher order, in the compression of knowledge to the point that we humans can deal with it – in other words, creating a format that corresponds to the human information processing system, to human memory and its limited capacity. The emphasis lies on the construction of thought systems with their manifold names (semantic, numeric, or spatial networks; mental models; thought or operational systems) – and specifically on the construction of hierarchically organized systems that are extended, modified or differentiated, compressed and unfolded at will, searched and queried during the act of learning.

All of the above is true regardless of whether the person doing the learning is drawing upon knowledge from written texts or illustrations, whether one is striving to learn a foreign language, whether the problem at hand is mathematical or is complex, like learning to play chess.

Historically seen, Chapter 18, which deals with solving a set of problems involving figures built with matches, may seem like a fish out of water. But the Gestalt psychologists, whose learning theory we introduce in that chapter for solving the problems at hand, were the most important forerunners of modern cognitive psychology, and they thus rightly have a place in this volume.

Many of the learning processes introduced in the early chapters are relatively simple conditioning processes that impinge from without: i. e., parents, teachers, and others can employ them and have relative assurance of their effectiveness in certain situations. The so-called higher processes, on the other hand, demand much more effort. They must adhere to a set of criteria and are based on a differentiated evaluation of the particular situation; they can be very complex, imply more heuristic than algorithmic methods, and have a certain amount of uncertainty as to their outcome, which in turn can lead to a number of different solutions (cf. Resnick, 1987). Whereas elementary learning processes can be sufficiently explained on the basis of stimulus–response connections, higher learning processes are characterized by the construction of meaning, for meaningful content. If I were to formulate the goal of this book in a single sentence, I would say it is the attempt to gain an understanding of the complexity of learning processes on the basis of everyday situations in terms of the characteristics of elementary and higher-level learning processes mentioned above.

My choice of themes for the cases introduced in the individual chapters occurred in accordance with this goal of presenting learning psychology from a cognitive point of view, albeit along a historical line. The emphasis is on more or less typical, everyday situations that do not exclusively demonstrate the point at hand, but can be understood by everyone. Five of the 19 cases derive from the family (Chapters 1, 4, 6, 7, 8), four from the school (Chapters 5, 14, 15, 16); four belong to the sphere of acquiring personal skills (in the sense of improving one's self-management or, if you will, mental health: Chapters 2, 9, 10, 11); four cases deal with the acquisition of intellectual competence (Chapters 13, 17, 18, 19); and, finally, two chapters (3 and 12) concern motor skills.

The book also integrates a few didactic ideas that serve to ease learning a prose text (as exemplified in Chapter 13). The introduction to each chapter attempts to present enough of the contents of the respective chapter to stimulate the reader's prior knowledge. Some sort of knowledge is always present, even if one is entering a completely new field. Ausubel (1968) alluded to this fact when he coined the term advance organizers. The most important terminology is also mentioned in this early section of each chapter, though no reader can be expected to be aware of or understand immediately the terms presented. The goal, rather, is that the reader become aware of what he or she must be on the lookout for – the final state of understanding that will develop throughout the chapter. It may further be of some help if the readers quite literally imagine the situation being described and formulate their own questions in advance.

At the end of each chapter there follows a "Memo" section, which summarizes the most important learning psychology facts given in the chapter. It serves to present a concise recapitulation of the entire contents, to spur one's memory and to allow comparison with one's own conclusions, a very helpful sort of feedback.

That some themes are repeated throughout the book should not be a source of irritation. An example is the theory of learning through modeling (Bandura, 1977). A network of recurring concepts has been spread quite systematically over 19 chapters to allow the purposeful repetition of certain information in order to implant it in the reader's memory. I am of the opinion that learning, even learning from a prose text, cannot succeed without repetition, and that repetition is not just an "old-fashioned" method of learning, especially when the information is repeated in a slightly different manner and form.

I will admit that the Memo sections are sometimes a little long, and that the reader may feel the need to compress them somewhat. This should particularly be tried at the end of Chapters 13 and 14!

A few chapters contain thoughts on what the best conditions are for better or even optimal learning. We cannot avoid discussing this topic, particularly in association with the question of the optimal *teaching* conditions under which knowledge transfer can best take place. Such discussions make clearly evident the educational or didactic relevance of statements about learning. But it is not the main goal of this book to deal with the optimization of learning/teaching conditions; rather, we will focus on the learning processes themselves, as the title already suggests.

Once in a while learning is dealt with in a clearly developmental scope. This cannot be avoided. After all, learning depends directly on the subject's respective developmental stage, and what we call development is at least partially influenced by learning processes. Thus, development is sometimes considered the sum of all successful learning processes – a somewhat simplistic view, however, that ignores aspects of organic maturation. Though the findings of developmental psychology are certainly relevant here, it is not the intent of this book to present an overview of developmental psychology.

By no means do I presume to present an exhaustive study of motivational or cognitive psychology, though both areas will (and must) be touched on quite often: Much of what can be said about higher learning processes is part of a theory of cognition. The newest results from both research areas cannot be presented here and must be drawn directly from the respective sources.

This book was conceived as a textbook for courses on learning theory. It can be employed as an introductory text under competent tutorial supervision (e.g., in undergraduate courses, in teacher education, but also in courses for students of the social professions). But it can also be introduced at a much higher level, for example, as the basis for discussions of the newest findings in learning psychology or with regard to classical systematic or applied aspects of learning. The didactic concept of the book also allows students to read through it on their own. It is not, however, intended to be a practical how-to volume for tortured parents, teachers, or managers.

1. The Fear of White Lab Coats: Classical Conditioning

[handwritten: stresses the stimulus response]

In Cooperation with Joachim Hermann

[handwritten: guilty w/ association. (lab coat) (no more simplicity) lost it's neutrality]

1.1 Introduction

In this chapter we recount and analyze the story of how a young child comes to be afraid of white lab coats. We will learn how environmental stimuli that were originally neutral came to trigger behavior – and what the phrase "conditioned to (white lab coats)" means. The key concepts of this chapter are *unconditioned stimulus, unconditioned response, neutral stimulus, conditioned stimulus*, and *conditioned response*. Also of importance are the terms *stimulus generalization* and *stimulus substitution*.

The theme of *classical conditioning* leads us back to the beginnings of research in learning theory, to the first quarter of the 20th century. The theories of that era can even today explain a number of behavioral patterns, though their powers of interpretation are limited.

1.2 Classical Conditioning: Pavlov's Discovery

The Russian neurophysiologist Ivan P. Pavlov (1849–1936) knew that his dogs always salivated every time he gave them something to eat (meat powder). He then paired a bell sound several times with the presentation of the food, the bell sound occurring half a second earlier than presentation of the food, so that eventually the dogs learned to salivate at the sound of the bell without being fed. That, in short, is the basic mechanism of classical conditioning: An *elementary response* (in this case, the innate *reflex* of salivation) caused by a certain stimulus is later provoked under certain conditions by a hitherto *neutral stimulus* (in this case, the sound of a bell ringing) (Pavlov, 1927, 1928).

Now let us take a look at a situation *outside the laboratory*, in real life.

[handwritten: (associate a bell w/ food)]

1.3 The Classical Conditioning of Emotions

The Situation (Child associated the nurse w/ fear)

A young mother is sitting with her 18-month-old child on her lap in the waiting room of an ophthalmologist. At the last visit, the child's tear ducts had to be cleaned out; today's visit is only a control of the last treatment. But the child is more disquieted than usual, and the mother tries to calm him down with storytelling. When the doctor's assistant enters the room, the child immediately begins to scream and cry: This is the child's response to the new stimulus situation caused by the assistant – whom the child has never seen before – when she entered the room. The reaction is clear: the expression of a *strong emotion*, of a *fear* of something, an utter *horror* in the face of something. A characteristic stimulus causes a characteristic response. Let's go further.

Fear Responses as an Elementary Behavior

Fear belongs to the very basic, early human emotions. Between the ages of 3 and 6 months, it develops together with *anger* and *reluctance* from a common early form, namely, an uneasiness called *distress*, which in turn is a derivative of a more *general state of excitation* (after Allport, 1961, and Bridges, 1932). This reaction belongs to the most basic and natural means of behavior humans have at their disposal, and it is part of our innate repertoire of behavior.

That we are dealing here with highly *elementary, natural forms of behavior* is of great importance to classical conditioning: Such behavior is found only where *already existing elementary forms of behavior* (e.g., reflexes such as salivating) that can be triggered by new stimuli are present.

But first the simple question: What is the stimulus that caused the child to scream and cry? The fact is, we don't really know for sure! We can only say that the assistant's appearance changed the entire *stimulus situation* in many ways. The assistant is a complex visual stimulus: a human being in a white lab coat, with a head of certain proportions, diverse body movements, and perhaps even a way of moving toward one. This person is also the source of acoustic stimuli.

Selecting Stimuli in Complex Daily Situations

The situation at hand is much more complex than the one in Pavlov's laboratory. Exactly *what part* of the stimulus situation caused the child's reaction of fear is hard to say. The early learning theorists of this century were also concerned with such problems. They had observed that only rarely do *simple, individual stimuli* that occur in everyday life clearly cause a certain response. The learning theorist Edwin R. Guthrie (1886–1959) was well aware of the complexity of everyday stimulus situations and spoke of how an organism actively "selects" certain stimuli; what the organism experiences becomes a signal for how he reacts (Guthrie, 1959, 186). In other words, not the entire situation stimulates a response, but rather what the person "gets" from it. That is the signal, and that causes the response.

person is proactive

As early as 1931, another American learning theorist, Edward L. Thorndike (1874–1949), formulated learning principles and laws, one of which touched on the *differential salience of stimuli in a situation.* A correlate to one of those principles concerns the *prevalence of elements* (cf. Bower & Hilgard, 1981, 27). In short, a learner can respond selectively to particular (i.e., particularly prepotent or salient) elements of the stimulus situation. The salient features of the situation present themselves, as it were, to the organism to be grasped. There is an important difference, however, between the theories of Thorndike (1931) and those of Guthrie: In Thorndike's opinion, the salient features present themselves to – force themselves upon – an otherwise passive organism; Guthrie, on the other hand, speaks of the *activity of the organism* toward elements of the situation to be grasped. Thus, Guthrie ascribes to the active organism a special position vis-à-vis the characteristics of the respective stimulus situation. Yet, Guthrie does not reveal any more precise details about such characteristics, nor does he mention that identical parts of any one situation can have a different meaning for different people – and thus cause very different responses! Neither Pavlov's theory of conditioning nor the learning theories of the early behaviorists such as Thorndike and Guthrie allow us to make precise predictions about the selection of stimulus elements in any particular situation. For that purpose, we need theories that cover the way attention becomes directed toward stimulus elements. It is these *newer theories of cognitive psychology* that will guide us in upcoming chapters (cf. Neisser, 1967, 1976; Eysenck & Keane, 1990).

environment prominent

The Child's Original Conditioning

The previous act of cleaning out the child's tear ducts created a *stimulus* for the child to which he responded with natural patterns of behavior. He turned his head away, withdrew, stamped his feet, cried out. The child did not have to *learn* to respond this way; this reaction is perhaps the most elementary, biologically founded reaction available. Rather, we can only assume that the previous treatment had caused this innate reflex to be activated. What is new is the fact that this time the child responded to seeing the *assistant*, something that didn't happen during the first visit to the doctor's office, when the assistant was still a *neutral stimulus*.

We may assume that during the first visit to the doctor's office a certain stimulus (say, the doctor's white lab coat) was created out of the multitude of stimuli present in the complex situation and became connected to the reflex caused by the treatment. In fact, it could have been any other stimulus, for example, the doctor's glasses. Within the overall stimulus situation, the white lab coat became a partial stimulus associated with the reflex as something occurring *simultaneously and at the same place*, and from now on it stimulates the reflex even in the absence of the original stimulus (the treatment). White lab coats, even those of persons other than the doctor, now cause the child to cry out.

UCS – UCR – CS – CR

To reiterate: In the beginning there was a stimulus acting upon someone's body (his eye) causing a reflex to be triggered. This stimulus is called the *unconditioned stimulus* (UCS), which causes an equally *unconditioned response* (UCR) – the child's crying. Later another, originally *neutral stimulus* will cause this same response. This stimulus, now a trigger (it is our assumption that it is the white lab coat that attracts the child's attention), is called a *conditioned stimulus* (CS), the child's reaction of crying out the *conditioned response* (CR).

white lab coat (neutral stimulus)	→	orientation response
tear duct treatment (UCS)	→	crying (UCR)
white lab coat, treatment	→	crying
white lab coat (CS)	→	crying (CR)

In everyday life, there are other characteristics of the doctor's office besides the doctor and the white lab coat which can become the conditioned stimuli, even if we can't pinpoint them all as individual stimuli. That it is not *only* the lab coat that later on causes the child's crying, but also specific parts of the office environment, may be seen by observing that the mother's wearing of such a white coat (e.g., while washing the child) does not lead to a similar outburst. White lab coats and other characteristics of the doctor's office are all parts of the initially neutral stimulus situation that later on, through their association with the tear-duct treatment, will come to represent to the child the entire situation – and thus become the conditioned stimulus of the child's conditioned response (crying).

This process by which the child learns to show a reflex response (the crying) to a new triggering stimulus is the essence of *classical conditioning* after Pavlov. Here, we are dealing with a basically biological theory about temporary (transient) neural connections. How the conditioned stimulus loses its trigger function is discussed below.

Besides reflex responses Pavlov later included in his theory the realm of speech (his so-called second signal system) as a conditioned stimulus. More on that later.

The cognitive approach to the learning situation in question would describe more exactly the *psychological processes* active in the person doing the learning. It would assume that the child has consciously experienced the pain of the treatment, and that the white lab coat becomes a signal of impending pain – that the pain is *anticipated*, and that the cognitive processes are accompanied by fear.

1.4 A Classical Experiment on the Conditioning of Emotions: Little Albert

Emotional responses like those observed in the child described earlier and the way in which they are triggered were the subject of very early research in learning psychology. An example may be found in Watson and Rayner's (1920) study on "Little Albert." This is such a famous chapter in the history of psychology – and in many respects such a poignant piece of experimental evidence for the example at hand – that we would like to share it with the reader here.

Watson and Rayner (1920) were studying the source or presence of expressions of the most (in their opinion) important nonlearned (i.e., innate) emotions, such as fear, anger, or love. To Watson and Rayner, envy and guilt were examples of more elaborated emotions they did not intend to study. They assumed that emotions in small children can be triggered by relatively simple physical means – anger, for example, by limiting their field of movement to prevent them from being able to reach a toy; fear by presenting them with a high level of noise.

Watson and Rayner were searching for the answer to the following three questions:

1. Can a baby or a small child learn (= be conditioned) to fear a particular animal that appears simultaneously with loud, terrifying noises?

2. Can such fears be transferred to other animals or even to inanimate objects?
3. How long does such a conditioned fear last?

Little Albert, chosen by these authors for their experiment, was 9 months old at the time, a healthy, happy, and certainly not overly sensitive child. (He was in any case *not* the child of the authors, as some have stated; cf. Harris, 1979.) He had no fear of rats, rabbits, dogs, or monkeys, nor of cotton swabs and human masks – he wasn't even afraid of a burning newspaper. He did, however, clearly respond to loud noises with fear.

The authors first observed Albert's natural responses and behavior over a period of two months before starting to condition him. Initially, he responded positively to a rat, which as a stimulus had no negative effects on his behavior: a *neutral stimulus*. Similar, though negative, was his reaction to loud noises: The sudden sound of a hammer hitting a piece of metal directly behind him produced great anxiety, causing him to topple over backward, cover his face with his hands (to protect himself), and cry. The noise was a stimulus that triggered both a bodily response (falling over backward) and an emotional response, namely, the fear of a loud noise of unknown origin. Such a response can be seen as a natural and *unconditioned response* (UCR).

Later, whenever Albert was playing with the rat – previously a *neutral stimulus* – the experimenters sounded the loud noise of a hammer hitting metal every time Albert touched the animal; that is, they coupled the *neutral* with the *unconditioned stimulus* (UCS). The simultaneous occurrence of these two stimuli, repeated seven times in two sessions at a one-week interval, subsequently caused the fear response in Albert whenever the rat alone was presented. The neutral stimulus had now assumed the effect of the unconditioned stimulus of causing anxiety. The rat had become the *conditioned stimulus* (CS), the child's anxiety the *conditioned response* (CR).

A Comparison with Everyday Life

If we compare Watson and Rayner's experimental situation with our everyday situation in the doctor's office, the following questions occur: Why did the experimenters have to repeat the stimulus coupling *seven times* before Albert was properly conditioned? And why did the conditioning in the doctor's office occur after only a single visit? Connections between stimuli and reactions arise after only a single occurrence (so-called one-trial learning) whenever the conditioned stimulus (let us assume here the white lab coat) becomes closely associated with a very strong *unconditioned*, painful stimulus. We must as-

sume that the pain the child felt during the treatment was considerably stronger, perhaps even more life-threatening, than the noise Little Albert reacted to.
Further, the child's level of excitement in the doctor's office was probably
very high, so that the pain he felt was felt very intensely, leading to the one-
trial learning effect. Little Albert's level of excitement in the experimental
situation, on the other hand, was clearly lower in intensity.

Both children, in any case, learned to adapt to new stimuli, be they white
lab coats or rats. Cognitively speaking, the stimuli point toward something
that is about to occur – pain or a loud noise. In other words, both children have
learned something about the *relationships of things* present in their environment and react accordingly (cf. Rescorla, 1988). At this juncture, a behaviorist
would critically remark that the children's responses would be predictable
even without our knowing more about their cognitive processes, and that in
the case of conditioned responses their anticipation of coming events is irrational and not based on any real-life conditions.

1.5 Extensions of the Triggering Stimulus Situation

Stimulus Substitution and Higher-Level Conditioning

The future of our 18-month-old child holds, besides a fear of white lab coats,
something else in store: He may very well begin to cry upon seeing the house
in which the doctor's office is located or upon entering the hallway to the
office. Perhaps even the mother's *verbal* announcement of an impending visit
to the doctor's office will suffice as trigger.

What has happened? First, the white lab coat replaced (= was a substitute
for) the pain-producing stimulus. Through subsequent visits, in which the
sight of a white lab coat is preceded by the sight of the building housing the
doctor's office, the building itself becomes the stimulus for the child's crying
response. The conditioned stimulus is thus replaced by yet another stimulus,
the house, which becomes a second-order conditioned stimulus; the corresponding act of learning is called *second-order conditioning*. Even *higher-order conditioning* is possible. Such repeated substitution of stimuli was observed even by Pavlov: Following the initial conditioning, his dogs salivated
not only at the sound of the bell, but soon after hearing the sounds of the
researcher's footsteps in the hallway.

Everyone has experienced such substitution. A well-illustrated (or perhaps
even an unillustrated) menu in a restaurant often suffices to make a hungry
person's mouth water long before any food has reached the table. This, too, is

higher-order conditioning: The unconditioned stimulus is the food in one's mouth, the first-order conditioning lies in the designation of that food item and one's imagination thereof, the second-order conditioning in the printed text and illustration of such food. The higher the order of a stimulus, the weaker the conditioned response.

This phenomenon of *repeated substitution of stimuli* can be introduced deliberately into learning processes. Words can function as *substitute stimuli* triggering originally unconditioned responses. With respect to such *linguistic stimuli*, in his theory of the second signal system (namely, language) Pavlov pointed out that there is a major difference between the conditioned responses of humans and those of other animals. Stimuli and associated signals influence the respective organism; these are the perceptions, feelings, and ideas we have of our environment – the *first signal system of reality*, which we share with the animal world. Language, be it written or spoken, forms a *second signal system inherent only to humans*. According to Pavlov (1927, 1928) these are signals for the primary signals, which, however, are governed by the same laws as the first signal system. Today, we would probably add that besides words any concrete or abstract symbol such as a traffic sign or hand sign can function as a signal for the primary reality.

Stimulus Generalization

In classical conditioning, nothing new is learned; that is, *no new behaviors*, rather only the *connections between existing responses and new triggering stimuli*. The coupling of neutral stimuli with unconditioned stimuli raises the *excitation level* of an organism, who in turn learns to anticipate the reappearance of the unconditioned stimuli (food, noise, pain, etc.) with the corresponding unconditioned responses (salivation, fear, etc.).

Because such situations cause a rise in the overall level of excitation of the organism, it is not surprising that a conditioned response can be triggered by stimuli that are only *similar* to the original stimulus. Thus, theoretically, our 18-month-old child might react similarly at some other place that only bears a certain resemblance to the conditioned stimulus situation – a hospital, nursing home, government building, etc. Such responses are evidence of *stimulus generalization*. We know, for example, that Little Albert reacted not only to rats with anxiety, but as a result of stimulus generalization also to rabbits, a short-haired dog, and sealskin.

1.6 The Extinction of a Conditioned Response

The conditioned response is *weakened* if, after the conditioning of a response to a particular conditioned stimulus, the unconditioned stimulus is no longer present. If the conditioned stimulus continues to be presented, the conditioned response will occur ever more rarely and finally disappear altogether. This is the phenomenon of *extinction* – the extinguishing of a conditioned response. (We will study this phenomenon more closely in Chapter 2.)

To come back to the child in the doctor's office: Can we rescind his fears with the help of extinction? Remember that he learned this behavior through a *single event*, and that the connection between the UCS and the UCR is very strong indeed. Extinguishing his anxiety would certainly take more than one session, that is, more than one confrontation with white lab coats, in complex stimulus situations and in the absence of the UCS (the tear-duct treatment). Theoretically, it could work; practically, it is not so easy to realize. The number of extinction trials necessary to extinguish the anxiety response would serve as the *measure of the intensity of the conditioned response.*

In Little Albert's case, the experimenters had to repeat the conditioning to the rat periodically by coupling the loud noise and touching the rat in order to produce the conditioned response. In some cases, however, even presenting the conditioned stimulus after a longer period of time without the presentation of the unconditioned stimulus can still produce a hefty conditioned response. This is so-called *spontaneous recovery.* In the light of such spontaneous recovery, it is assumed that the extinction of a conditioned response does not in fact completely eradicate the response as the term might suggest, or that it simply becomes "lost" or "forgotten," but rather that it does not reappear as a result of the subject's active inhibition (with corresponding physiological correlates in the brain; cf. Pavlov 1927; also Bower & Hilgard, 1981, 49 f.).

1.7 The Meaning of the Subjective Interpretation of Stimuli

But extinction is not the only way to relieve the child's anxiety. (Chapters 9 and 10 deal further with the concept of fear.) Most mothers know how to react in such situations – taking the small child in their arms and calming him, preparing the older child in advance of any visit to the doctor's office, etc.

That such *preparatory calming* by the mother actually reduces the child's later anxiety in the doctor's office is not foreseen in the classical theory of conditioning, at least not on the level of the primary signal system. Cognitively speaking, because of the mother's soothing words in advance, the child perceives and processes the stimuli in the doctor's office differently than during the first visit. Thus, the *stimulus-controlled automatic information processing* in the central nervous system does not trigger the anxiety response, but rather the child's *subjective interpretation* of the situation at hand, based on complex cognitive processes over which the child has at least partial control. And it is these cognitive processes that begin during the preparatory talk with the mother. This once again points toward the importance of linguistic cognitive processes in the explanation of the child's behavior and learning experience.

1.8 Further Learning Processes

The Verbalization of Internal States

The use of verbal means is not something cognitive psychologists only recently landed upon: Even Skinner pointed out their importance (cf. also Bower & Hilgard, 1981, 169f.). Yet, if the child is to be influenced verbally, he must be able to understand what the mother is saying, for example, when she says, "Today it won't hurt." She directs her words to the child's *internal state* – the pain previously suffered. That the child can understand the mother presumes he has learned to verbalize internal states or at least to understand what the mother means. The child can do this both before and during the visit to the doctor's office: The mother comforts the child with words; she is cautious, not pressing his head tightly to her own body, but stroking him lightly, cuddling him, whatever is necessary – all the time speaking to him: "Now, now, everything will be all right." The child learns that some things "hurt" and that this feeling is called "pain."

Similarly, the child learns to call his fear "fear." Statements such as "You don't have to be afraid today" concern the child's response part ("It won't hurt" refers to the stimulus) and helps the child to understand that the awful feeling he has is called "fear." It is interesting to note how exactly we can describe the open behavior of others – and how inexact and undifferentiated our vocabulary is for describing *inner states* such as emotions. We have only limited ways of describing the various levels of emotions (in connection with pain); localizing our pain is a game of rough guesses at best. Yet it is an important step for any child to learn to talk about his or her inner states. In Chapter 10, which concerns how adults deal with their feelings and inner states, we will see that we are dealing here with a learning process that extends far into the adult age.

Another Kind of Conditioning: Instrumental Conditioning

So why did the child really start to cry at the doctor's office? This reaction was most certainly part of an unintentional reflex response. On the basis of his previous learning experiences, the child was probably also using crying in this specific situation to bring about a change in the (uncomfortable) situation he was having to go through. Perhaps he had earlier learned that crying under such circumstances has the best chance of causing reactions in the environment that lead to the desired change – that he can in this manner *control* his environment in a certain way.

In everyday terms, we say that a child, by showing such a behavior, has a certain intention; or that the child's behavior has a certain goal in mind; and that the child will learn and retain these behaviors if they lead to "satisfying" or "pleasant" final states. Early behaviorally oriented theoreticians of learning also assumed that the connections between certain stimuli and responses are best learned if the *result* of the reaction is a "pleasant state," though in their striving for objectivity they did not refer to described or assumed experiences. For example, they tried to judge how "thirsty" someone was by measuring the time since the last drink and described "pleasant" states as those states that someone often or repeatedly instigated (and did not cause flight or avoidance behavior). This type of learning of stimulus–response connections as the *effect of response consequence* is what Thorndike called *instrumental conditioning* (learning by success); we will touch on this more again later. One difference from Pavlov's theory is important, though: With respect to the first signal system, Pavlov is concerned with the connection of environmental stimuli to "involuntary" behavior, whereas Thorndike is concerned with the connection between environmental stimuli and "voluntary" responses (movements of the skeletal muscular system).

Memo

1. In classical conditioning, the triggering of elementary, natural reactions (innate or acquired very early in life) is learned. In short, there are no new behaviors under the sun, rather many connections with new stimuli.
2. In classical conditioning, (1) a natural stimulus (e.g., a painful experience) is presumed that reliably triggers a response (such as crying); (2) there must first be a neutral stimulus that does not trigger the response; (3) because of the systematic way in which it is presented together with the naturally occurring stimulus, the neutral stimulus assumes the triggering function for the response in question.
3. Responses can also be triggered by stimuli that are only similar to the conditioned stimulus. Such triggering is based on a stimulus generalization.

4. Triggering stimuli can be replaced by other stimuli through their (repeated) coupling with those stimuli. This is called stimulus substitution. If conditioned stimuli are replaced by other stimuli, this is called higher-level conditioning.
5. Classical conditioning began with the work of Pavlov (1849–1936).
6. The studies done by Watson and Rayner (1920) with Little Albert prove experimentally that emotions too can be classically conditioned.
7. Reflexes are triggered by stimuli of a certain physical quality. This is true also for elementary emotional responses such as fear if the stimuli are intense enough. Conditioned stimuli can be not only physical stimuli, but also words, verbal expressions, and signs (signals) – Pavlov's so-called second signal system. Conditioned emotions can be both triggered and influenced by cognitive processes (interpretations of particular situations, memories, etc.).
8. For more information on the physiological foundations of classical conditioning, see Pavlov (1927, 1928) as well as Bower and Hilgard (1981, 54f.).
9. A further kind of conditioning is instrumental conditioning, in which the origin of the stimulus–response connection depends on the consequence of the behavior in question. The frequency of a certain type of behavior increases if that behavior is reinforced (= leads to a "satisfying" situation). This concerns voluntary behavior (responses of the skeletal muscular system).

2. A Learned Heart Attack? The Problem of Extinction

In Cooperation with Joachim Hermann

2.1 Introduction

The reader may ask, What does having a heart attack have to do with learning? Though the association may not be immediately clear, we will see in the following that there is indeed a connection between learned behavior and this medical problem. In a certain sense this chapter is a continuation of the previous one, though here we are concerned not so much with *learning* as with *unlearning* certain behavior. Conditioned behavior is not a simple phenomenon; it has both observable and nonobservable (e.g., physiological) components – a matter of some consequence to the extinction of such behavior. Thus, the most important term in this chapter will be *extinction*.

2.2 Prerequisites

Most likely no one to date has based a learning-theoretical study on a case that occurred a few years ago, in which a guard in a prison was attacked by an inmate and beaten with a water pot the guard was carrying. Such dangerous situations can occur almost anywhere. The natural reaction to such a *stimulus situation* that poses a threat to one's life is *flight* coupled with feelings of *fear*, or *escape* from situations in which flight is not necessary. If the local situation does not permit flight, or if one's own ability to flee is not given (due to individual reasons), the natural response is more or less fear, depending on the nature and extent of the threat, expressed in the usual (including physiological) forms known. This brings us back to the situation discussed in the previous chapter at the doctor's office.

2.3 The Learning Situation – with a View toward Cognitive Psychology

Upon being attacked, the prison guard wanted to flee and get help. That at least is what he remembers thinking. But things went so fast that he never actually got that far. What exactly the stimulus was that triggered the guard's flight is unknown; what we can be sure of is that the prisoner played a major role. The prisoner's physical appearance, the expression on his face, his aggressive stance, or perhaps even direct threats all were part of the stimulus situation. The prisoner was originally a neutral stimulus, who then became a threat and thus now represents a conditioned stimulus for an unconditioned stimulus (the attack) causing the flight response (or fear, if flight is not possible).

According to classical conditioning, fear slowly subsides through *extinction* if no further attack follows. But this is not a very satisfactory approach. Besides extinction, the guard's *knowledge* is decisive to whether he feels fear at seeing the prisoner. The guard may consider the prisoner aggressive, and that may or may not be true; or he may judge the situation to have been an exceptional case, leading to less fear. Thus, *not the conditioned stimulus alone,* as an isolated fact, triggers a certain behavior; rather, cognitive processes are active that influence the way in which the guard perceives and reacts to the situation. In other words, the (conditioned) stimulus is not *judged on its own* as a single piece of data (as the stimulus–response theories suggest), but rather in the *scope of stimulus-independent cognitive processes*. This is the explanation for the situation from the vantage point of cognitive psychology. But let us remain for a while within the theoretical realm of *conditioning* as discussed in the first chapter.

Stimulus Generalization

On the basis of what we have learned from the first case, we can imagine that any subsequent meeting with the prisoner will result in the same or a similar reaction by the guard. The prisoner has become a stimulus that will most likely, if not certainly, lead to responses of flight and fear. If we see flight and fear as elementary, natural behaviors that guarantee survival, we are in effect saying that they are unconditioned responses (UCRs) to the respective threatening stimuli. On the basis of the original, very complex stimulus situation (the corridor in which the incident took place, the exact spot, the time, etc.), stimuli other than the prisoner will now result in the guard's feeling fear. Whenever he enters the corridor, he feels afraid – more so when he reaches the exact place of the attack, even if he knows that the prisoner in question is no longer there. Perhaps even the key chain he held in his hand on that day suffices to produce the original feelings. Thus, we may assume that besides the prisoner other stimuli from the earlier situation have become *conditioned stimuli.* Even if no further confrontation with the prisoner is possible (say, the prisoner has been transferred to some other prison), there are still enough stimuli available to trigger responses similar to those felt in the original situation.

But the number of stimuli is in fact even greater: Because of *stimulus generalization* – in this case – all other prisoners, all prison corridors and doors, can become triggering stimuli.

2.4 Extinction: A Complex Process

Most likely, for some time following the incident, the guard will not have a flight response to conditioned stimuli (CS) amenable to *stimulus generalization*. After a few days' time he will probably also no longer feel fear – at least there will be no perceptible signs of such feelings (e.g., becoming pale). This, of course, does not mean that the *extinction of such feelings* has occurred completely. We should recall that fear is accompanied by a number of physiological responses, for example, increased pulse and blood pressure, stricture of the blood vessels (leading to that pale look on one's face), spontaneous incontinence or diarrhea, heavy breathing, change in galvanic skin resistance. In other words, the conditioned response the guard (like the child of Chapter 1) has *learned* in a single confrontation is a very complex phenomenon with a series of consequences that we shall now focus on.

It would be ideal if the guard could *unlearn* his feelings of fear. The extinction or eradication of his reactions according to classical conditioning theory would proceed by presenting the *conditioned stimuli* to the guard under other circumstances so that the unconditioned response, namely, the accompanying fear, was not triggered. On the one hand, the prisoner's transfer to another prison now means that the original stimulus generating the response is absent. Yet, we also know that there were a number of other stimuli present in the original situation (the cell door, the water container, the key chain). Let us assume, though, that the guard quickly learned that these objects are in fact harmless and extinguished his fear of them in due time.

Stimulus generalization, however, means that any other prisoner or any other circumstance similar to the original situation can trigger feelings of flight or fear. Complete extinction will thus be a difficult matter, to be approached with care. Perhaps the guard should preferably be sent in the near future to better adapted, less aggressive prisoners; he should not have to do his rounds alone. Every time nothing happens will *weaken* the connection of the conditioned response to the conditioned stimuli (as well as to the generalized ones). Yet all of this will still not extinguish the fear of the original prisoner, since he is no longer present.

From a cognitive point of view, we should add that another guard accompanying our subject on his rounds might serve as a *model* for overcoming the situation. (We shall later on return to the theme of *learning by observing models* according to Bandura [1977].) The two can talk about their work, their *expectations*, perhaps even their fears; that can help the guard to *work through the incident mentally.* Thus, the guard becomes aware of the fact that the present situation is no longer like the past incident and that he can return to his proper work. Above all, the past situation does not continue to be an objective stimulus situation; rather, the guard's conscious reflection reveals it as embedded in a complex cognitive context.

Freud's analysis= talking cure."

Turning Our Sights from the Stimulus Situation to the Response

If we take a closer look at the process of the guard's *unlearning* his response, we can see the problem does not lie in the stimulus and the guard's working through it mentally, but rather in his *conditioned response* to that stimulus! The CR consists of several individual *components* whose fate we do not know: Were they truly eradicated through extinction or did they *resist extinction successfully* and now slumber, as it were, unrecognized from without?

We know that conditioned responses (CRs) can be very similar to unconditioned responses (UCRs), though they *need not be identical* to them. The blinking reflex as a response to a puff of air (the *unconditioned* closing of the eyelid) as opposed to *conditioned* blinking as a response to a buzzer noise occurs more quickly and is shorter (from 0.05 to 0.1 vs. 0.25 to 0.5 second).

Even in Pavlov's dogs, with their unconditioned response (UCR) of salivation, the conditioned response had other characteristics that had nothing to do with salivation. In sheep conditioned to withdraw the leg in response to the stimulus of electroshock (Liddell, 1934) there also occurred changes in breathing, heart rate, and overall activity (in contrast to the situation with unconditioned responses).

In humans, extinction carries with it the danger that, although more clear and observable responses such as flight, avoidance, or fear may disappear and everyone has the feeling that the behaviors in question have been extinguished, other components of the conditioned response were not amenable to extinction and continue, unknown even to the person concerned. Thus, the following: The fact that it is so difficult to extinguish conditioned responses makes one, as one grows older, a veritable antiquary full of ancient remnants of past behaviors – laden with useless or even now dangerous reactions. This is true especially for the cardiovascular domain, where old conditioned responses may prove to be particularly robust. People continue to react to past defeats and other long-lost situations without ever truly realizing where their high pulse rate or high blood pressure comes from. The result is a chronic state, which further predisposes to heart failure (Gantt, 1966). That, finally, closes the gap between our thoughts on learning theory and having a heart attack!

The guard's life history clearly shows that no one ever purposefully tried to extinguish his fears. At the most someone took the time to talk with him about the incident. Similarly, it is clear that he never unlearned his emotional responses to the stimuli that occurred in the situation described; on the contrary, he continued to reinforce them over and over again. That is, many a stimulus occurring in his daily work routine served to trigger hidden fears and uncertainties. Later interviews with the guard clearly showed that he had been *unable to improve his coping with the stress* particular to his profession.

The Various Levels of Conditioned Responses

Conditioned responses have many different levels – behavioral, physiological, emotional, cognitive. Thus, we are always dealing with *multiple reactions,* even if not explicitly addressed. Gantt (1966) called such multiple reactions, manifested in conditioned responses and divisible into components, *schizo-kinesis,* meaning moving separately. This means that the acquired *components* of a conditioned response can have a life of their own (with all the respective dangers to the organism) even when no signs remain of other components of the response to a conditioned stimulus. If extinction is equal to the *inhibition* of a learned behavior (this is what Pavlov thought; cf. Bower & Hilgard, 1981, 58 f.), then it is safe to assume on the basis of our present knowledge that this inhibition is *usually* (and not *exceptionally*) only partial and incomplete (Gantt, 1966, 63): One must always reckon with unextinguished remnants of the original response.

An example from the literature to show that these thoughts are not just theoretical constructs but measurable phenomena of learning theory (Edwards & Acker, 1962, 462): World War II veterans of the army and navy were presented with a series of 20 different acoustic stimuli, and their psychogalvanic skin response was measured. There were significant differences in the skin reactions of the army and navy personnel when the (warship) battle station signal, i. e., a repetitive gong with approximately 100 percussions per minute, was presented. More than 20 years after the war this stimulus still elicited an autonomic response to an aversive situation with the navy veterans, but not with the army veterans (Edwards & Acker, 1962).

Components remaining from the original conditioned response, for example, physiological reactions to the original conditioned stimuli, may eventually reappear in response to a number of similar stimuli (stimulus generalization) or even to completely different stimuli (higher-level conditioning), to the point of impairing the proper functioning of the organism. With this we approach the topic of psychosomatic diseases as well as the phenomenon of stress, which we will deal with in more detail in Chapter 10.

The Consequences for an Extinction

The reduction of or, in the terminology of learning theory, extinction of fear responses may be (and practically speaking also is) attained by linking inescapable stimuli or stimulus situations (e.g., the cell door or some necessary action such as bringing meals) with new responses incompatible with earlier responses (fear responses) and reinforcing them thereafter. This could, for example, be reached by having the guard make his rounds together with a colleague, having him open the door, but not deliver the meal directly, so that the experience of the earlier stimulus situation could through repetition become associated with a new, more relaxed response.

This, in short, is the standpoint of Edwin R. Guthrie (1886–1959), one of the leading American learning theorists: Extinction occurs by learning a new response, incompatible with the earlier response on the conditioned stimulus. Interference results as well as a retroactive inhibition (i.e., affecting what had previously been learned) of the original conditioned response (cf. Chapter 4 for more). We might also be inclined to assume that the guard's new behavior is being *reinforced* by his colleague's repeated confirmation that things are working out well. Reinforcement, however, does not in and of itself increase the probability of the new behavior; rather, it only serves to prevent a connection between the original fear-producing signals and any other reactions than the new behavior from being made.

In order for the guard to create an acceptable work atmosphere, one could try (à la Guthrie) to replace the fear response with *new, incompatible respons-*

es. Or one could (à la Pavlov) expose the guard repeatedly to the fear-producing signals (but without being attacked by the prisoner), thus slowly but surely lowering the fear response (extinction). These two methods differ less in practice than they do in theory in explaining how extinction works. (Refer also to Chapter 9, in which the problem of coping with fear may be seen in a different context.)

The guard could also have been put through a completely different type of therapy – biofeedback training – in which he would have learned to control certain physiological responses (e.g., pulse) on his own (cf. for details Bower & Hilgard, 1981, 259 f.). Perhaps this would have enabled him to control at least some of his physical reactions to some extent during critical situations such as those he was afraid of encountering. These are speculations, to be sure, but they lie clearly within the realm of the learning theory we have studied up to now.

Memo

1. Extinction, generally speaking, means the gradual decrease or complete reduction of a conditioned stimulus–response connection. In classical conditioning, extinction occurs if the UCS does not regularly follow the CS. With Pavlov's dogs, the *unconditioned* stimulus was the food; in the absence of occasionally presented food, salivation eventually subsided.
2. The guard's fear response can be extinguished, albeit not quickly or easily, when substitution stimuli (e.g., other prisoners) do not threaten him.
3. Conditioned behaviors and their extinction form complex processes, with both behavioral and physiological components. One cannot be sure whether complete extinction would in fact cause all components to be decreased or eradicated.
4. After Pavlov, extinction is the inhibition of learned responses or behaviors. One may safely assume that such inhibition normally remains incomplete.
5. The heart attack mentioned in this chapter can be associated with learning processes inasmuch as physiological components of the learned (conditioned) fear were not extinguished and thus maintained their negative effect on the cardiovascular system.

3. The World Fair's Nails: Learning by Trial and Error?

In Cooperation with Joachim Hermann

3.1 Introduction

In this chapter we discuss how a person learns the solution to the motor problem of untangling two nails that have been twisted together (a highlight of the Paris World Fair before World War II). This serves to illustrate the theory of trial-and-error learning as developed by the behavioristic learning theorist Edward L. Thorndike (1874–1949). In contrast, we will also be looking at a cognitive interpretation of the same situation. An important factor in solving the problem at hand is how the problem solver codes each individual step of the learning process. The reader will have the opportunity to compare the different approaches, behavioristic and cognitive, in explaining this specific learning situation.

Keywords will be *trial-and-error learning* or *learning by selecting and connecting*, the *law of effect (law of success), reinforcement, stimulus–response connections, proprioceptive stimuli*; also *plan of action* or *behavior plan, TOTE unit, enactive, iconic*, and *symbolic representations*.

Learning to untangle the two nails by trial and error does not consist of purposeless trials; nor does it entail only motor activities. Rather, the process of solving this problem follows a systematic course involving motor, visual, and in part even verbal processes.

Figure 1: The "hit" at the 1937 World's Fair in Paris – the World Fair's Nails.

25

The playful subject matter may initially lead the reader to assume that this chapter is a lighthearted one. This is not the case! It will quickly become apparent that we are in fact concerned with a complicated analysis of complex learning processes.

3.2 Trial and Error

When a person first takes hold of the two entwined nails (cf. Figure 1), it does not seem possible that they can ever be separated from one another. But the more convincing the challenge, the more determined one is to try it anyway. The first reaction may be to take hold of one nail and shake the other, then push both of them up a little to see whether this kind of movement has any effect; then one takes hold of the heads of both nails and begins pushing them toward each other (Figure 2) – no luck! "But it can be done!" Now we take hold of the tips of the nails and begin to move them again. Anyone who reaches this point without immediate success will certainly be tempted at some point to use force. "It must be possible, if only there were a little more space!"

Figure 2: The nails cannot be separated in this way, as the nail heads are blocking the way.

It is tempting to regard this kind of experimentation as a typical example of *trial-and-error learning*. If people (not only children!) behave in this way, it certainly appears they are experimenting more or less blindly. Perhaps even the nails will unexpectedly, *by chance*, fall into the position that allows them to be drawn apart or even actually fall apart on their own (Figure 3). The task has certainly been solved – but *not learned*!

Such an outcome is indeed a *chance result*. The test subject cannot clearly remember the last position the nails were in and is thus unable to reproduce

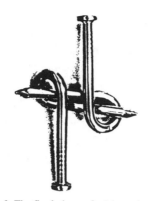

Figure 3: The final phase of a (chance) solution.

the position and repeat the solution at will. But still he or she is delighted with this unexpected *success.* At least one thing has been learned: It is in fact *possible!*

Let us break down the components of the situation in terms of the learning theory we have been concerned with up to now. The nails are the *given stimulus situation* that triggers all kinds of responses, from gently pushing the nails back and forth to trying to bend them apart by force. These responses are selected from a vast behavioral *repertoire of motor movements* (according to Thorndike there is no need for a conscious act). Thus, a *selection of responses* takes place. The unexpected solution leads to a new situation that increases the probability of the person's making further attempts to solve the problem. It therefore has the role of a reinforcer or reward.

Thorndike's Classical Experiments

The concept of learning by trial and error goes back to Thorndike's *cats in a puzzle box.* This box, with its many levers and cords, represented the stimulus situation to which the cats responded by trying out various tactics from their repertoire of behavior until they eventually pushed or released the correct lever by chance, thus freeing themselves from the box to get to the food. The cat coupled the stimulus situation with a large variety of responses, one of which led to success or *reinforcement through food.* According to Thorndike, the reaction most closely connected with the reward will be strengthened the most. If the procedure is continually repeated, the time needed to solve the problem gradually becomes shorter. Precisely because there is no dramatic decrease in the solution time does Thorndike conclude that the cat in fact does not truly "understand" how it has solved the problem.

Untangling Nails vs. Thorndike's Cats

The situation in which a person tries to disentangle two nails differs from that of Thorndike's cats in several ways. The cat has a definite state of drive to escape the cage: It is *hungry*. Furthermore, it can see the food sitting in front of the cage, which acts as a strong *incentive*. Humans involved with solving the nails task do not suffer any *organic deprivation*; thus there is no corresponding *motivating impulse*, nor is there any other incentive present comparable with food for the cat. For some individuals, however, the challenge of solving the tricky problem suffices as an *incentive*.

Not Just Blind Experimentation – A Subtle, Purposeful Testing Process

In the cat (as Thorndike sees it), the selection of appropriate responses and the "elimination" of inappropriate responses entailed a gradual process that required the whole procedure to be repeated several times. In human beings, however, from a cognitive point of view, a change in the solution process already takes place even after the first attempt.

The human immediately *restricts* the number of trial activities made, scratching the forceful method altogether and no longer holding the nails by their heads – that led only to a dead end! Rather, humans will concentrate on recognizing the critical phases, trying to remember exactly what happened in the final phase of the trial run, trying to adapt the movements more closely to the structure of the nails. The method used is still a sort of experimentation, but it will be purposefully applied and not be restricted to motor processes.

3.3 The Behavioristic Interpretation

The Problem of Reinforcement: Thorndike's Law of Effect

The nail puzzle described above is far more complex than the puzzle box. It involves learning a methodical sequence of steps: Beginning from an explicit start situation, appropriate reactions lead to a series of interim states that eventually produce the situation shown in Figure 3, from which in turn the solution is reached by simply pulling or pushing the nails apart. Thorndike recognized that human beings are capable of recognizing such interim states. From Thorndike's point of view, each interim goal that is reached reinforces the corresponding response – the learning process starts at the end of the chain: First, the final solution reinforces the response of pulling the nails apart from the last interim position shown in Figure 3, which in turn reinforces the response necessary to reach that interim position, and so on. In this way, then, each interim state has two functions: It reinforces the action necessary to its own realization and acts as a cue for the resultant action that follows.

Thorndike does not resort to conscious events in his explanation of the reinforcement processes. Otherwise, we could say that *associations* become stronger the more they are recognized as being necessary for progressing toward the solution, and the more rewarding or liberating they are felt to be, that is, the better they make the person feel during the experience. In other words, the experience of success reinforces the association, making it more likely to recur.

In his *law of effect*, Thorndike explains that the learning of stimulus–response associations depends on the ensuing consequences of the behavior:

> Of several responses made to the same situation those which are accompanied or closely followed by satisfaction to the animal will, other things being equal, be more firmly connected with the situation . . . ; those which are accompanied or closely followed by discomfort to the animal will, other things being equal, have their connections with that situation weakened. (Thorndike, 1911, 244; cf. Chapter 1, Memo 9)

This has obvious parallels with the selection mechanisms Charles Darwin (1859) described in his famous book *The Origin of the Species*. The words *accompanied by satisfaction* and *pleasurable* (similarly *unpleasurable*) do not refer to subjective experience:

> By a satisfying state of affairs is meant one which the animal does nothing to avoid, often doing things which maintain or renew it. By an annoying state of affairs is meant one which the animal does nothing to preserve, often doing things which put an end to it. (Thorndike, 1913, 2)

Thorndike explained stimulus–response associations in a purely physiological way, without recourse to experience. If we study the wording of the law of effect, it becomes clear why Thorndike later spoke of *learning by selecting and connecting* rather than learning by trial and error (Bower & Hilgard, 1981, 22).

Thorndike's law of effect was an important supplement to the widely held view of that era that habits are formed through *repetition*. This law, initially also accepted by Thorndike, quite simply stated that a connection is strengthened *by use alone*, i.e., by its *repetition*, and is weakened by lack of use. Later, however, he wrote the following:

But practice without zeal – with equal comfort at success and failure – does *not* make perfect, and the nervous system grows *away* from the modes in which it is *exercised with resulting discomfort*. When the law of effect is omitted – when habit-formation is reduced to the supposed effect of mere repetition – two results are almost certain. By the resulting theory, little in human behavior can be explained by the law of habit; and by the resulting practice, unproductive or extremely wasteful forms of drill are encouraged. (Thorndike, 1913, 22)

Thorndike drew conclusions from observations he had made in his animal experiments to make this statement relating to human learning. He defended his point of view defiantly, often taking aim at what we would now call *cognitive learning theory*. Although intellectually far ahead of his contemporaries, Thorndike was still a man of his time. He writes:

Both theory and practice need emphatic and frequent reminders that man's learning is fundamentally the action of the laws of readiness, exercise, and effect. He is first of all an associative mechanism working to avoid what disturbs the life-processes of the neurons. If we begin by fabricating imaginary powers and faculties, or if we avoid thought by loose and empty terms, or if we stay lost in wonder at the extraordinary versatility and inventiveness of the higher forms of learning, we shall never understand man's progress or control his education. (Thorndike, 1913, 23)

Critical Observations

Before we leave the subject of reinforcement in Thorndike's theory, we should mention another theoretical problem arising from his views. As the test subject gradually discovers the correct sequence of fine-motor movements necessary to complete the task successfully, at some point in time he becomes able to predict that success. Maybe he will even say, "That's it!" before he actually reaches the goal a second later. The pleasant feeling of having reached the goal is *anticipated* by the test subject. What does this mean? Presumably, the test subject *imagines* the imminent success at the end of the journey. That is to say, a mental image mediates the reinforcement. Thorndike did acknowledge the existence of such *anticipatory activity*, but at that time it was not considered appropriate to speak of such mental phenomena as imagination. The behaviorists, after all, only acknowledged externally observable behavior as being worthy of psychological research.

Clark L. Hull (1884–1952), the most systematic of the American behaviorist learning theorists, introduced the term *fractional anticipatory goal response* in 1943 to describe the type of reactions mentioned above. Of course, effectively he was also acknowledging the phenomenon of the mental image (though without ever expressly mentioning the term), so scorned by the behaviorists at that time, since anticipation cannot take place without some sort of mental image (see also Bower & Hilgard, 1981, 103).

Still, we must acknowledge that Thorndike did consider the process of reinforcement to be a highly complicated one involving far more than principles of pleasure and displeasure, or simple hedonism.

3.4 A Cognitive Interpretation of Learning How to Untangle the Nails

The Informative Function of Reinforcement

To achieve the goal, in this case pushing the nails apart, a problem-solving learning process has to take place. Reinforcement plays a part in arriving at the solution and in mastering the sequence of movements leading up to the solution. From the point of view of cognitive psychology, reinforcement has not only a *selective* function (as Thorndike believed), but rather an *informative function* that guides the learner and shows him *what* he should do and *how* he should do it. In other words, the "good" or "bad" feelings experienced at the various points of the solution process contain *information* and thus provide *feedback* on changes in the learning situation.

Such a learning situation is characterized by various *sources of information*: the trigger stimuli, i.e., the various states along the course of solving the problem, as well as the *feedback* contained in the reactions and their corresponding *reinforcements* (see also Adams, 1984). How this happens is explained below in detail.

Perceptual Feedback and Correction

Learning to solve the nail puzzle involves both *movements* and *control perceptions* that give feedback on the movements made thus far – and how they must be corrected or modified by repetition to achieve success. The problem at hand clearly shows that the solution depends on the nails' being moved into a position that allows them to be easily pulled apart (cf. Figure 4d). This, however, is possible only if they are first rotated appropriately in several different directions (Figure 4b and 4c) until they are in the correct "preparatory" position. At some stage, the correct rotation will be made from the plane where the nails were last turned (starting from a point somewhere between Figure 4b and 4c). Then, only a last rotation is required, more or less perpendicular to the previous one, before the pushing motion resulting in the final solution can be made.

The most intensive trial-and-error behavior is likely to be observed during the mastering of the important rotations leading from the situation in Figure 4b to that in Figure 4c. The problem solver searches for the *critical moment* in a continual sequence of movements when the solution can be "grasped." This is the point at which the direction of the rotation is no longer from right to left (from Figure 4a and Figure 4b), but more complexly, in an almost indescribable way, cuts through space, as it were, directly toward the problem solver. There is, to be sure, within certain limits, room for individual variations in these rotational movements; the important thing is that they eventually lead out of the original working plane through space.

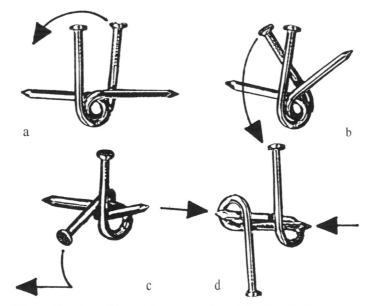

Figure 4: Scenes from the problem-solving process of untwisting the nails. The arrows show the respective next movement of the nail head. This does not, however, depict *all* the hand or finger movements necessary. (a) The starting position. (b) Situation after the right nail has been turned toward the left in the working plane such that the right nail head comes to lie behind the head of the left nail. This very same rotation must be carried out smoothly. (c) Situation immediately after the rotation of the nail head (now on the left-hand side) from the working plane toward the upright nail (originally on the left-hand side) to the front and downwards. (d) Situation immediately before the solution is found.

Miller, Galanter, and Pribram's Behavior Plans and the TOTE Action Units

Miller, Galanter, and Pribram (1960) put forward a model to explain movements such as those shown in Figure 4a–4d within their context. They were of the opinion that the actions of the problem solver are directed by his or her *knowledge* and by the *plans* prepared on the basis of this knowledge. Figure 5 shows a schematic diagram of this. The most important factor is the constant *repetition of test and operation phases at various levels of action organization*, first and foremost at the level of movements that prepare the way for the correct rotation. Before larger movements such as rotations and finally translations (pushing motions) can be made, a series of smaller, preparatory movements may become necessary. Each individual movement is observed and its further usefulness tested. Or, to use Miller, Galanter, and Pribram's (1960) words, each *test phase* (T) is followed by an *operation phase* (O), which in turn is succeeded by a new test phase (T), until the *solution* or the *conclusion* (E for exit) is reached. The *basic unit* of this procedure thus consists of a test–operation–test sequence, followed either by further operation–test phases or by the conclusion. This unit of activity is called the TOTE unit (Test–

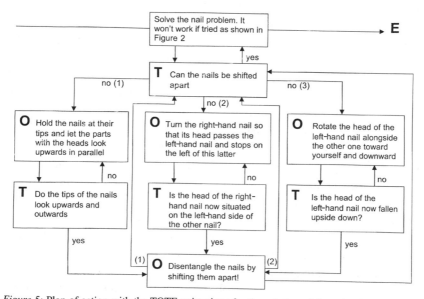

Figure 5: Plan of action with the TOTE units given for the solution of the twisted-nail problem (after Miller, Galanter, & Pribram, 1960). T = Test, O = Operation, E = Exit (solution). The figure shows the basic steps involved in the solution to the problem. It is assumed that the learner has already gathered the experience depicted in Figure 2. The codings important to learning problem-solving behavior in the individual steps are not shown in this figure (see text, especially Section 3.5).

Operation–Test–Exit). It is a simple organizational structure that reveals nothing about the individual contents and how they are represented in the memory of the learner. Therefore, we must investigate how the test subject stores the individual steps of the learning process so that he or she can recall them and later retrieve and reapply them when making a further attempt to solve the same problem.

3.5 Coding the Correct Sequence of Movements

Anyone who tries to solve the puzzle will have difficulty storing and remembering the various positions the nails were in and the sequence in which the positions were changed. Because of the similarity of the different positions at the beginning of the learning process, *visual coding* is difficult indeed. *Verbal coding* is also difficult as no precise terminology is available. The only remaining possibility is to *store the movements directly* in memory, without the help of images or words. The behaviorist learning theorists had already recognized the significance of movements in the learning process. At least two of them, John B. Watson (1878–1958), the so-called Father of Behaviorism, and Edwin R. Guthrie (1886–1959), expressly referred to the importance of movements. According to Watson, it is not the visual stimuli that trigger a further response, but rather the previous kinesthetic or *proprioceptive stimuli*, that is, complex muscular or movement sensations, that release the responses that follow. Guthrie also stresses the function and role of the latter in relation to the (proprioceptive) stimuli for the coordination of complex movement sequences. Guthrie's system particularly emphasizes that stimuli caused by movements represent *the true conditioning events* (Bower & Hilgard, 1981, 77).

It is evident, then, that the coding of movements plays a part in learning how to disentangle the nails. Some people clearly recognize that their successful movements consisted of rotating their right hand while slightly moving their right thumb and forefinger. Following an initial trial period, children are able to complete the successful movements quite simply – "Like that!" – although they cannot explain exactly how they did it. Nevertheless, they can repeat the same movements quite exactly. In other words, they must have a representation available to them somewhere in their memory that allows them to reconstruct the entire problem-solving process. Presumably, this is what J. S. Bruner (1964; Bruner et al., 1971; see also Steiner, 1973) called an *enactive representation*: a representation based on action-related codings. (Most people have this kind of *enactive representation* for tying their shoelaces, for example.)

Yet, children who succeed in solving the nail puzzle are able to say how it is *not* to be done. They must have an "image" of the right way to go about solving the task, even when they are not holding the nails in front of them. As Bruner would say, they have an *iconic representation*, an "image" of how the solution *ought* to look, at least for certain stages of the process. This does not necessarily mean that they would be able to draw the important configurations of the nails; rather, their representation would allow them to recognize a right configuration from a wrong one. Thus, their representation does not consist only of motor codings; it is *not a purely enactive representation*.

The *chaining* of movements caused by proprioceptive *(response–produced)* stimuli, as postulated by the behavioristic learning theorists, therefore does not provide us with a full explanation of the situation: Pictorial, *iconic representations* which contain information on how the sequence of motions has to be carried out, corrected or modified in order to succeed in solving the problem must also be present. These pictorial representations act as a kind of visual or perceptual guide for the fine-motor activities. The inner representations and the respective external situations are continually being compared with one another, providing constant feedback on how things are progressing toward the "ideal" sequence of movements. At this point we shall not discuss whether there are connections between this type of learning and the modern concept of *implicit* learning (see Berry & Dienes, 1993; Cleeremans, 1993; Reber, 1993).

One question has yet to be answered – how does the problem solver learn the correct overall sequence of movements that leads to untangling the two nails? Does one movement lead to the next one, as the behaviorists suggested? In view of what we discussed above concerning the information contained in the reinforcements, this approach would appear to be insufficient. Learning the correct procedure is not simply a matter of coupling response-produced stimuli with new movement responses, which in turn represent response-produced stimuli – there is more to it. Do some kind of characteristic pictures or visual patterns trigger the continuation of the sequence of movements? It is conceivable that patterns such as those shown in Figure 4b and 4c trigger whole segments of the sequence of movements. It is also probable, on the basis of the spontaneous comments of some learning subjects, that the verbal coding of typical sections is also responsible for the continuing succession of movements. This type of verbal coding is what Bruner calls *symbolic representation* (for Bruner, symbolic generally means "in natural language"). Such symbolic representation may contain complete sentences, but it may also remain quite rudimentary. The important thing is that the person using the symbolic representations understand them and apply them appropriately. They do not have to be communicable. For example, the person learning could say to himself or herself, "Turn it around toward the back, then to me!" No one else would be able to make any sense of this representation; representations are always idiosyncratic.

Someone wanting to master the puzzle, that is, to be able to take hold of the nails time and time again and disentangle them at will, must learn to represent the solution procedure enactively, iconically, and, having mastered the skill to a certain degree, also symbolically. These representations complement the structural learning organization of the TOTE units. The cognitive interpretation of the solution to the nail puzzle, then, consists of coordination of learning organization (*sensu* Miller et al., 1960), with the representation of the individual steps of the solution process (*sensu* Bruner, 1964). (We will return to the problem of how single action segments are "chained" to form whole action sequences in Chapter 12.)

Many Problem Solvers Display Strange Reversibility in Their Behavior

We can now understand why many people who try to separate the two nails repeat certain segments of their movements several times, running through them backward and forward: They are adding new test phases to their learning process, following them up with operation phases. The test phases provide the feedback information necessary for continuing or correcting a movement or a larger element of the whole sequence; the repeated operation phases lead to the development of various representations – enactive, iconic, or symbolic. These representations, in turn, are necessary to the test phases in order to make comparisons between the current and the ideal situation. Running through segments of movements in various directions allows the purposeful use of test and operational phases, and the development or employment of codings or representations. Furthermore, the *reversibility* of certain segments of movements leads to their eventual integration, anchoring them, as it were, within the wider context of the sequence of movements as a whole.

In other words, we may assume that the forward and backward movements are not merely playful in nature; rather, they are accompanied by considerable *visual control (monitoring)* and verbalization. *Visual control* plays a major role in the *test phases* (T) as described by Miller, Galanter, and Pribram (1960), providing the basis for feedback. Indeed, many problem solvers say that they are simply trying to find out whether the way they have done it is right or not. That is to say, even if a certain situation cannot be accurately *described*, it can be *recognized as a pattern*. As for *verbalization*, even Thorndike (!) noted that while repeating a movement the learning subject can give extra reinforcement verbally, for example, by saying, "Yes, exactly!" or "Here we go!" Reinforcement à la Thorndike – and this again points to the informational character of reinforcement – is similar to the kind of recognition procedure we all use for spelling a difficult word (*rhythm*, for example): We search for the correct spelling (is it *rythm* or *rhithm* or ...) by writing down the word several times, thus generating patterns that help us to *recognize* the correct spelling form.

Someone trying to solve the nail puzzle creates his or her own opportunities to recognize certain situations in the same way (test phase, "Is that it?"), resulting in either the continuation or the modification of the sequence of movements. If a configuration is not recognized, the nails are moved backward or forward until a *recognizable configuration is reached*. Of course, we must not assume that only static configurations can be coded and recognized; characteristic movements as well, such as the one immediately preceding the rotation leading out of the working plane, may also be coded and recognized. As we mentioned above, Watson's *proprioceptive* and Guthrie's *movement-induced* stimuli probably play a larger part at the beginning of the learning process, along with visual coding. Later, the critical points are coded using more or less detailed verbal representations.

Of course, this process of initially concentrating on experimenting with certain tentative movements, then *correcting*, *modifying*, and *anticipating* suitable or unsuitable ways of continuing the movement sequences, no longer corresponds to trial-and-error learning. Countless conscious feedbacks of one's perceptions and modifications of one's movements in terms of TOTE units gradually turn the course of action into the *structure of the problem* (and of the material). In other words, the behavioral course is integrated into a system of *visual monitoring* with *feedback loops* (TOTE units). Further, the association of fine-motor processes should not be considered to be one-directional: The reversibility of movements in certain sections of the solution process results in *anticipatory* and *retrospective* processes that serve to integrate individual elements into the movement sequence as a whole. This is the deciding factor for a true *"understanding" of the entire sequence*.

Memo

1. Thorndike (1874–1949) carried out research on trial-and-error learning. Later he spoke of learning by selection and connection.

2. Other important behaviorist learning theorists are Watson (the "Father of Behaviorism"), Guthrie, and Hull (the system builder of the behaviorists).

3. Thorndike's law of effect and success says that stimulus–response associations are learned when they are brought into association with "satisfaction," or when the reaction is immediately followed by a satisfying experience. An association is weakened, on the other hand, when connected to displeasure or followed by displeasure. Thorndike later retracted (or at least limited the importance of) the latter part of his law of effect.

4. Pleasurable states in the context of stimulus–response associations serve as reinforcements. Reinforcements are not defined via subjective experience, but by observable behavior (not avoiding a situation, but seeking it out frequently).

5. During the disentangling of the two nails, perceptual controls lead to reinforcements; their most important function is not to strengthen stimulus–response associations, but to provide information; they give the problem solver feedback.

6. The actions and perceptual controls that occur during the learning of the task follow certain plans of action that – according to the theory of Miller, Galanter, and Pribram (1960) – are organized into TOTE units.

7. TOTE units are the basic elements of behavior plans, characterized by a series of action or operation phases and test phases. Test phases are followed by operation phases until the goal is reached – or given up.

8. While learning to solve the nail puzzle, a person will code certain positions and segments of movement along the way (i.e., convert them into codes that can be stored in memory) and represent them enactively, iconically, and verbally (symbolically). Such representations complement the structural organization of TOTE units.

9. Behaviorists believe that proprioceptive stimuli are responsible for the smooth course of a succession of movements; that is, a linear chain of stimuli and responses forms the basis of a movement sequence. This explanation, however, does not suffice: The visual control processes and verbal representations that control actions rather demand a hierarchical organization. According to the cognitive theory of Miller, Galanter, and Pribram, plans of action and TOTE units provide this kind of organization (cf. Chapter 12).

4. An Untidy Child Learns to be Neat: Signals for New Habits

In Cooperation with Joachim Hermann

4.1 Introduction

The learning processes introduced in this chapter lie within the realm of the behavioristic tradition we have studied up to now. We will be studying which stimuli trigger certain undesirable responses, what reinforces the formation of corresponding habits (stimulus–response connections), and why desirable reactions cannot be reinforced under certain conditions. Further, we show how *desirable behavior patterns* can be established with the help of new signals, how these patterns can be sustained, and how they come to be *new habits*. At the same time, we will get to know the different *theoretical interpretations of reinforcement* according to Thorndike and Guthrie.

The term *signal* has the same meaning as *trigger stimulus*; other important terms are *contiguity, tolerance method, method of incompatible responses,* and *exhaustion method.*

4.2 Habits, Signals, and Reinforcing Effects

The Situation

A 10-year-old girl comes home, throws her coat and hat on the floor, and goes on her way, either to the refrigerator in the kitchen or into her room. She has been annoying her mother with this behavior for a long time (the mother tells the psychologist; cf. Guthrie, 1935, 21; Bower & Hilgard, 1981, 87–88).

Analysis

The situation may at first seem simple, but in fact it is quite complex – at least in the scope of a psychological analysis of the learning processes involved! We are clearly concerned here with a long-established *habit*, i.e., a complex

39

behavior pattern triggered, according to Guthrie, by certain stimuli present in the situation.

But which stimulus–response associations actually produce the *undesirable* behavior? What do the stimulus situations and the individual responses actually consist of? Which *reinforcers* might have played an important part in the establishment of these associations? Further, what possibilities are there of *breaking such habits* or learning *desirable* behavior?

Throwing one's clothing on the floor may be viewed as a response. If so, which stimulus situation or signal is it linked with? It is difficult to find an immediately plausible external stimulus that could result in the response of throwing clothing on the floor. It is conceivable that – at least at the very beginning – a full coatrack led to the reaction. Yet, the behavior is clearly evasive: The child avoids the task of rearranging other pieces of clothing to make room for her own. No obvious reinforcer can be found; according to Thorndike we would have to presume that the action of throwing clothes down is satisfying. Following his *law of effect*, this would increase the probability of the established association's recurring – in our case, the association of the stimulus "full coatrack" with the response "throw clothes on floor." A *stimulus generalization* may also be at work, so that an *almost full* coatrack or even the absence of a completely empty peg could produce the reaction, particularly if the action of throwing down the clothes is a satisfying one. Another contributing factor could be that her clothes have been neatly hung up the next time the child walks past the coatrack – not by her, of course, but by her mother! This could function as a reinforcer, even if it is not a *direct and immediate* consequence of her action. We can assume that this is how such a habit has come to be formed – at least, the mother described the recurring situation in this way.

The mother also affirms that, time and time again, she has asked the daughter to hang up her clothing properly. This introduces a *new stimulus situation*: the mother's insistence. Although the daughter eventually hangs up her things each time she is scolded, it is easy to imagine that the scolding itself has an unsatisfying, unpleasant aftertaste for both parties. Following Thorndike's law of effect, it is easy to see that the association between the new stimulus situation (the mother's scolding, nagging, or simply ordering) and the new response (the child's hanging up her coat and hat) is not a strong and enduring one. This would not even necessarily have been desirable: The daughter should learn to hang up her things without being grumbled at in the first place. On the other hand, the mother seems to have had no other choice than to force the child to hang up the clothes by scolding her.

4.3 Effective New Signals and Various Interpretations of Reinforcer

Evidently the given stimuli (the full coatrack – or other stimuli we are n
aware of!) produce *undesired behavior*, whereas an *unpleasant stimulus* such
as scolding produces *desired behavior*. As is usually the case outside the laboratory, the stimulus situation here is complex; any new stimulus or signal
introduced to achieve a change in behavior must be clearly recognizable. In
other words, first an empty, attractive hook must be made visible. Guthrie's
advice to the mother is not to scold the child, but to send her back out again
with her hat and coat and let her reenter the house. However, this will be
effective only if *behavior-regulating stimuli* (here: empty hook) are present.
Perhaps the mother must also quite simply learn to keep the coatrack in order
herself. According to the theory of modeling or imitation learning (Bandura,
1977), this could be a promising way of tackling the problem! Of course,
sending the child out again *instead of scolding* has an extremely important
signal function: It is the new stimulus for a response; i.e., it is an activity that
in the future will precede the neat hanging up of hat and coat. "Coming home
again" now simply precedes the neat hanging up of clothes. Now the mother
herself – together with the empty peg – becomes a stimulus that triggers the
child's memory (an internal response): You get sent out again if you fail to
complete the task of "putting outdoor clothing away" properly.

The learning process, i.e., the establishment of *new associations* or of desired behavior that is to become a habit, can be *reinforced* by the mother by
rewarding her daughter for neatness. She can smile at her *(social reinforcement)* or offer her something to drink *(consummatory reinforcement)*. That
would all correspond with Thorndike's *law of effect*.

Guthrie would certainly also have no disagreement with giving this kind of
reward, though he would give a *completely different theoretical interpretation*
of its effect. For Guthrie the reward – the smile as *social* or the drink as
material reinforcement – would not have a stabilizing effect on a physiological basis (as Thorndike claims). Rather, Guthrie claims that any kind of reinforcement represents a *new stimulus*, which in turn leads to its own reaction.
One response to her mother's smile as a reinforcement stimulus would perhaps
be the daughter's smiling back; her response to the offer of a drink would be
the action of drinking. To Guthrie, this is the deciding factor: The last response
does not interfere with the previous response (i.e., hanging up the clothes);
this habit remains unchanged. This is how the desired behavior is *learned*.
The empty hook (or other parts of the overall stimulus situation) is the stimulus that becomes associated with the desired response. The same stimulus

...ion and its corresponding response remain untouched by the completely ...erent activity that follows it when the reward is given (e. g., drinking as a ...action to the offering of a drink). This is why the previous learned behavior *is not unlearned*. According to Guthrie, then, a reward does *not* reinforce an association, but *protects it from interference*, from being unlearned! That is Guthrie's very interesting point of view on the effects of reinforcement.

Guthrie's answer to the question of what actually brings about the coupling of a stimulus to a response is *contiguity*: i.e., their closeness or proximity in space and time. Stimuli that are effective in the situation (including the proprioceptive, movement-induced stimuli within the person in question) are, when they become conditioned stimuli, able to produce the same reaction even when introduced in a new context (Guthrie, 1935, 1960). The intensity and stability of the stimulus–response association depend on just how many stimuli from the situation become connected to the response, and how often the coupling of stimulus and response is repeated.

4.4 Stabilizing the Newly Learned Reaction

Let us assume that the desired behavior of hanging up one's clothes has now been learned through clear behavior-regulating signals and reinforcement.

The next task is to generalize this behavior for everyday situations. This is done by modifying the trigger stimulus – in this case, the empty hook. First, the mother could hang a light, unobtrusive scarf (preferably one belonging to the child) on the hook, later possibly a piece of clothing that has to be moved to another place. Here we are making use of the *generalization effect* – the reaction is a response to stimuli *similar* to the original conditioned stimulus. Changes to the trigger stimulus are made step by step.

Of course, the learning situation must be repeated many times. Following Guthrie's frequency law, new stimuli from the complex situation, for example, the cloakroom mirror, become associated each time the procedure is repeated. *The more stimuli that become coupled with the desired reaction, the more likely it is to appear*, because it can now be triggered by various stimuli. At the same time, an undesired response to these (other) stimuli becomes less likely to occur.

Basically, then, various signals from a complex stimulus situation can lead to a child's putting away clothing correctly. In our example we selected one of many possibilities – the empty hook!

4.5 Breaking Old Habits

The starting point in our case study was that the child had already acquired the undesired response of throwing her clothes on the floor upon entering the house. Why is it so difficult to change such responses? According to Guthrie, habits consist of complex patterns of movement. Each movement produces *proprioceptive* stimuli, which in turn work as conditioned stimuli to trigger the next movement. The whole sequence of movements making up a habit thus becomes an integrated behavior pattern, more or less independent of the original stimuli (Guthrie, 1960, 106). One of the many conditioned stimuli is enough to set the complete sequence of movements in motion. To break a fixed and well-integrated habit, it is necessary not only to extinguish each single stimulus–response association within the movement sequence, but also to break up the integration of the responses. Guthrie uses the term *inhibitory conditioning*, meaning that a conditioned stimulus can be made ineffective by learning an incompatible response to it, thus inhibiting the old reaction. He suggested three techniques of inhibitory conditioning (Smith & Guthrie, 1921).

In the first method, the stimulus is introduced in a situation in which the undesired response cannot be produced *(method of incompatible stimuli)*. The stimulus situation is extended to contain additional stimuli that prevent the appearance of the undesired reaction. Obviously, this method is difficult to carry out in our example. One possibility would be for the mother to help her daughter to take off her outdoor clothing when she enters the house and then hand the clothes directly to the girl. The hope is that this situation would be incompatible with the child's throwing her things on the floor, so that she could learn the desired reaction.

The second method that can be used to break a habit, the *toleration method*, can be illustrated using the example of the small child's fear of white lab coats in Chapter 1. We assumed that this fear had become broadly generalized, already appearing at the sight of the doctor's office building. Using the *toleration method*, one introduces the stimulus so faintly that it does not produce the undesired response. Gradually, then, the intensity is increased; for example, the mother can go past the ophthalmologist's office building several times, getting closer each time. Of course, this technique too cannot be used on our untidy child, as the triggering stimulus – the hook – is a clear signal that cannot be weakened so as to become unnoticeable to the child.

The third way of canceling undesired behavior patterns is the *exhaustion method*, which is controversial even in animals. It is used, for example, to tame wild horses for rodeo purposes. The horse is exposed to the full stimulus, i.e., the saddle and rider, until it is exhausted, no longer displays the undesired behavior, and is thus ready to learn a new response. The application of this method to the problem of dropping clothes on the floor would consist of the mother's allowing her daughter to throw her things down until she gets tired of it and is ready to learn to hang them up. Few people would seriously consider using this method.

Common to all three methods is that the original stimulus becomes conditioned to produce new reactions, thus inhibiting the original response. The conditional stimulus loses its effect because it has become linked with another kind of behavior. This is why we speak of *counterconditioning* (see Guthrie, 1935, 70f.).

When we try to break an unwanted habit, we aim for it to be replaced by a *new habit*. The most effective way of dealing with the child in our example would probably be to change the stimulus situation, introducing clear additional signals such as a helpful mother to encourage the child to display the desired behavior – and subsequently to reinforce this behavior, for example, by having the mother smile at her child. The next time, much of this procedure is reactivated in the child in the form of a memory, possibly a mental image, which in its turn works as an internal stimulus (besides the mother and the hook). Even the behaviorist Guthrie would agree that memories can function as stimuli; he explains such phenomena, however, as visual imagination and thoughts in the context of his theory of contiguity.

Guthrie introduces an amusing example of the problems involved in replacing unwanted habits with desirable ones in connection with the method of incompatible stimuli:

> Drinking or smoking after years of practice are action systems which can be started by thousands of reminders. … I had once a caller to whom I was explaining that the apple I had just finished was a splendid device for avoiding a smoke. The caller pointed out that I was at that moment smoking. The habit of lighting a cigarette was so attached to the finish of eating that smoking had started automatically. (Guthrie, 1935, 139)

The new response (eating an apple) had indeed interrupted and repressed the old habit of smoking – for the moment. But the old stimulus, the end of a meal or the final movement of throwing the apple core away (though it could just as easily have been the putting down of knife and fork, pushing one's plate to the side, wiping the mouth, or folding up the napkin!), then triggered the next reaction, namely, reaching for cigarettes and matches. Truly to stop smoking, *counterconditioning* would have to be carried out on many different stimuli. For example, the end of a meal could be coupled with reactions such as inhaling deeply, reaching for the newspaper, or clearing away the dishes. But as every smoker knows, there are countless other cues for smoking, and incompatible reactions would have to be practiced for each one of them. Certain stimuli, of course, can be eliminated more easily than others: If cigarettes, ashtray, etc., are put out of sight, their presence as trigger stimuli can be avoided from the beginning.

Memo

1. A habit is a stabilized automatic sequence of movements that can be activated by many different external stimuli or by movement-induced, internal (proprioceptive) stimuli.

2. Desirable habits can be developed as responses to new signals by introducing the signal stimulus at the beginning of the activity and ensuring that no other (undesirable) response to the signal occurs.

3. Sometimes a new habit can be acquired by taking a particularly salient signal for the desired behavior and successively changing it until it resembles the normal stimulus situation (generalization by stimulus modification).

4. Reinforcement stabilizes new habits. Thorndike explains the effect of reinforcement in terms of "satisfying states," for the most part physiological. Guthrie, on the other hand, claims that reinforcement works as a new stimulus that evokes a further response. This change in the stimulus situation prevents other responses from becoming associated with the old stimulus situation. In this way reinforcement protects the stimulus–response connection from disturbance, so that it remains intact, learned.

5. Undesirable habits can be broken by using inhibitory conditioning (counterconditioning), whereby the response to a stimulus is replaced by another, incompatible response.

6. In the method of incompatible stimuli, inhibitory conditioning ensures that the old signals, in combination with other signals, evoke new (desirable) responses that are incompatible with the undesirable responses; i.e., it is impossible for them both to be displayed at the same time.

7. In the toleration method, the trigger stimulus is introduced, but in such a weak form that the undesirable response does not occur. The intensity of the stimulus is then successively increased in tiny steps so that the undesirable reaction does not appear.

8. In the exhaustion method, the subject is exposed to the trigger stimulus until the undesired reaction ceases to appear because of fatigue, at which point a new response can be learned.

9. Someone wanting to give up smoking must make sure to have no cigarettes in the house, as even the sight of them can trigger the reaction of lighting up. One must also learn to respond to a large number of stimuli with behaviors incompatible with smoking.

5. Michael the Troublemaker: Operant Conditioning and Sociocognitive Learning

In Cooperation with Joachim Hermann

5.1 Introduction

This chapter introduces us to a particularly complex learning situation: a lesson in school. We will look at two further learning theories to demonstrate how a certain behavior arises and how it can be influenced. Skinner's *operant conditioning* is a radically behavioristic theory, whereas Bandura's theory of *sociocognitive learning* takes cognitive processes and the possibility of self-regulation into account. Other key words in this chapter are *operant behavior, respondent behavior, positive reinforcement, negative reinforcement, extinction, differential reinforcement, discrimination, discriminating stimulus, stimulus control, successive approximation, self-control, resistance to extinction, continual reinforcement, intermittent reinforcement, interval reinforcement, ratio reinforcement, reinforcement schedule, random contingency, punishment, aversive stimulus, sociocognitive theory of learning, modeling, substitute reinforcement, expectation of self-efficacy.*

5.2 Scenes from a Lesson

"Stop talking, Michael!" the teacher admonishes during a lesson. Michael takes little notice. "Michael, how many times do I have to tell you to stop talking to your neighbors?" The pencils used for writing have to be sharpened every so often. Michael drops his pencil-sharpener, it bursts open and the shavings fall all over the floor. "For Heaven's sake, Michael! What have you done now? Go and get a broom and dustpan and clear that away!" Trailing his feet, Michael goes off, to return after a while empty-handed. "You can't be trusted with anything!" The other pupils' attention has long since strayed from the grammar exercises they were supposed to be doing; the interruption is complete. Twenty more minutes until break time, a long 20 minutes for pupils and teacher alike! Time for an oral vocabulary test!

46

"To enjoy?" asks the teacher. The pupils raise their hands. *"Geniessen!"* one pupil calls out. "To sip?" is the next question. The exercise runs along perfectly smoothly, until Michael raises his hand to answer a question. He snaps his fingers and waves his hand around in the air, making groaning noises with each movement. The teacher immediately calls out his name: "Michael!" "Ah, what was the word again?" Laughter! "Why weren't you paying attention? To chew!" "To chew, oh, that's right! Ah! *Kauen!"* "To lick?"

This scene contains a sequence of behavior patterns that, according to Thorndike and Guthrie, are elicited by the preceding stimulus situation. These authors believe that reinforcement is responsible for the learning of stimulus–response associations. In this chapter, we introduce a theory in which less importance is attached to stimuli; rather, we concentrate more on the *ensuing consequences* of behavior than on its association with preceding stimuli.

5.3 Operant Conditioning – Reinforcement within the Range of Interest

According to Thorndike, we could interpret Michael's behavior during the lesson quite simply as a satisfying activity, whereas Guthrie would deem it necessary to look for some trigger stimulus. The American psychologist and learning theorist Burrhus F. Skinner (1904–1991), probably the most well-known behaviorist of all, believes that behavior such as Michael's talking is controlled not directly by the stimuli preceding it, but rather by the consequences following it. He calls such behavior patterns (as Michael's) *operant behavior.* He states that all modes of behavior that have not been learned by means of Pavlov's classical conditioning (cf. Chapters 1 and 2) belong to this behavior category. This kind of behavior, which corresponds to classical conditioning, he calls *respondent behavior.* One example of this would be the conditioned fear of white lab coats studied in Chapter 1; Skinner (1938, 1953) agrees that this response is triggered by a conditioned stimulus. In everyday language, operant behavior is seen as "voluntary," respondent behavior as "involuntary" behavior.

The consequence of Michael's talking to his neighbors is the teacher's scolding. If, upon observing several lessons, we were to discover that Michael talks all the more when he is scolded, then we might conclude that scolding is a *positive reinforcer* for his behavior. Putting behavioristic theories aside for a moment, we would say that Michael evidently receives too little social attention, so that even being grumbled at by his teacher has a positive value for him. But Skinner, the radical behaviorist, is not interested in whether the

[handwritten annotation: By yelling at Michael, the teacher does it more.]

consequence of a mode of behavior is experienced as being pleasant or unpleasant. He considers a stimulus to be a reinforcer if it causes the behavior preceding it to occur more often. The sad thing about this situation is that the teacher is actually *reinforcing undesirable behavior.*

Skinner differentiates between *positive reinforcers* and *negative reinforcers*. A positive reinforcer results in the behavior's occurring more often, as in the example of the teacher's scolding (positive reinforcer) after the boy's chattering (reinforced behavior). A negative reinforcer also causes the behavior to occur more often, though because an unpleasant or aversive stimulus is subsequently *removed* (an example of this will be given in the following section).

Skinner calls the forming of an association between a particular behavior and a subsequent reinforcing event *operant conditioning*, regardless whether the reinforcing event is a positive or a negative reinforcer. The theory of operant conditioning presented here is based on the studies of Holland and Skinner (1961).

5.4 The Wrong and Right Places for Reinforcement

Let us look now, from Skinner's point of view, at the second learning sequence in this lesson, the vocabulary test. Michael apparently does not know much vocabulary. Every now and then he knows a word, and he tries to draw attention to himself through a great deal of additional noise and movement. For most teachers, this annoying behavior is likely to lead to a response that stops it; stopping that undesired behavior is therefore a negative reinforcer for the teacher. The teacher calls out Michael's name, thus making him stop snapping his fingers, waving his arms around, and groaning; i.e., her behavior (calling out Michael's name) is being *negatively reinforced*. On the other hand, having his name called out is a *positive reinforcer* for Michael as it encourages him to continue his method of drawing attention to himself. Such forms of mutual reinforcement are commonly found in social relationships. In this particular case, the *mutual reinforcement* results in the disturbing behavior's being terminated for the time being, though Michael is encouraged to adopt the behavior more and more. The situation becomes a vicious circle.

We may assume that at least a dozen other pupils also raised their hands quietly, but were not called on. Later, we will look at Skinner's so-called reinforcement schedules, which explain why it is important for all pupils to take regular turns answering questions. In any case the teacher made the mistake of reinforcing undesirable behavior and of *not reinforcing* desirable behavior (active participation in the lesson).

5.5 The Extinction of Undesirable Behavior

Let us again assume that attention – even in the form of grumbling – is a positive reinforcer for Michael. We would be correct in this assumption if Michael were to display this behavior with other teachers when he received attention for it, be it in the form of scolding, a smile or praise. The teacher in our example always acknowledges Michael's disturbing behavior. What would happen *if she didn't react* to Michael's disruptive activities – not a word, not a glance? It is possible that he would continue being disruptive because of the presence of other reinforcers – applause from his schoolmates, etc. The teacher could, of course, ask the class not to pay any attention to Michael when he was being disruptive. But what would happen then, if no reinforcement at all were given to his behavior? According to Skinner, reinforcement not only makes operant behavior more likely to arise, but also sustains it. If reinforcement is no longer given in response to a particular behavior, that particular behavior will become less and less frequent. Skinner calls this *extinction*.

We could also interpret the process of extinction in terms of *cognitive* theories. Here, we might assume that Michael needs attention and has certain expectations regarding the consequences of his (disruptive) behavior. If in fact his behavior fails to produce the expected consequences, i.e., reaction from the teacher, this experience would result in his abandoning the behavior. Skinner, however, would not agree with this explanation: He confines himself to establishing regular patterns in the relationships between observed behavior and environmental circumstances and conditions.

5.6 The Adaptation of Behavior to Different Situations – Learning to Discriminate

Let us turn our attention to the teacher. On observing her behavior, we notice that she reacts much more calmly to the disruptive behavior of other pupils. If they begin to chatter in the middle of the lesson, she simply stops talking for a moment, something she doesn't do with Michael. Her short silence actually stops the other children from talking. Why doesn't the teacher react to Michael's interruptions in the same way? We must assume that she has already tried using this tactic on him, but without success. When a response is reinforced in the presence of one stimulus, but not in the presence of another, the response becomes *partially extinguished*; that is, when the nonreinforcing stimulus is present, the response becomes less and less frequent and finally disappears altogether. A *discrimination* has been established, and the response is now controlled by the stimulus situation preceding the response: The behavior is now displayed only in the presence of the *discriminating stimulus*. In our example, all pupils except Michael would be discriminating stimuli for modes of behavior such as the teacher's short silence when the lesson is disrupted. This kind of *stimulus control* always ensues when a response is reinforced only under certain stimulus conditions.

5.7 Supplying Alternatives for Undesirable Behavior – Shaping New Behavior

Many teachers and parents have to come to terms with the fact that extinction attempts are usually not particularly successful. If no attention were paid to Michael's disruptive behavior and annoying way of raising his hand, he could easily adopt other modes of behavior that simply could not be ignored. First, he would probably disrupt the lesson more often if the teacher completely ignored him. He could force the teacher to take notice, for example, by shouting loudly, making it impossible for the lesson to continue. Practically speaking, a strict refusal to give reinforcement is often impossible to carry through with. In order to extinguish the undesirable behavior, it would be advisable, besides withholding reinforcement, to encourage an incompatible, desirable behavior to take its place. If the teacher in our example knows that attention is a positive reinforcer for Michael, that is her chance of helping him to adopt desirable behavior. She made a first step in this direction by calling out his name immediately when he signaled the wish to answer a question. Unfortunately, she also reinforced his unpleasant way of drawing attention to himself. It is important that the teacher give Michael reinforcement only when his behavior conforms with normal requirements.

A further possibility of dealing with the problem is *behavior shaping*. Here, the teacher could follow two of Skinner's principles: First, she could offer Michael *differential reinforcement*, i.e., reward desirable behavior while ignoring undesirable behavior (see above); second, she could gradually bring the desired final behavior into shape using *successive approximation*. In successive approximation, the most elementary components of the desired final behavior are reinforced. In Michael's case, the final aim would be for him to pay attention in the lesson without interrupting and to participate actively, putting his hand up in a normal way. An elementary component of this behavior would be for him to succeed in sitting still in his chair for five minutes. In the beginning, then, Michael would be praised every time he managed to sit still for five minutes (providing that praise had been shown to be an effective reinforcer for him). Following the principle of successive approximation *(shaping)*, the criterion for the reinforcer would be gradually shifted toward the desired final behavior: Praise would be given for maintaining longer periods of self-discipline, for putting his hand up correctly, and so on.

Yet this marks a major difference from how people actually behave in everyday situations. Teachers and educators usually tend only to criticize when a child's behavior is unsatisfactory. This could be asking far too much from the child, especially if the child is expected to conform to several different criteria at the same time. It further disregards the possibility of reinforcing the small fragments of an approximation toward the desired behavior that are always present. For Skinner, this kind of reinforcement is crucial to the process of developing desirable behavior. The principle of successive approximation allows for reinforcement to be given on many occasions, thus continually making a positive contribution to the behavioral development or change. This is far more effective than waiting until the desired final behavior is present in its ideal form.

It is important to note that the replacement of undesirable behavior with desirable behavior here is *not counterconditioning*. Skinner's form of shaping a certain behavior is based on processes of extinction and the development of new *response–consequence associations* using operant reinforcement instead – not on stimulus–response associations. In contrast, counterconditioning (as in Pavlov's classical conditioning and Guthrie's theory of contiguity) is based on the coupling of a trigger stimulus with a new, incompatible response, i.e., the learning of a new stimulus–response association whereby the stimulus remains unchanged.

5.8 Emotional Responses

Let us take another look at the teacher, who finds it so difficult to cope with Michael's disruptive behavior. We notice that she almost always responds to his interruptions and attempts to stop them with various different methods. Stopping interruptions, then, is a negative reinforcement for her. Michael's interruptions occur frequently and massively, but none of the measures the teacher takes to stop them is in fact successful. Under these circumstances we must assume that the teacher is clearly reacting in an emotional way, with anger or even with fear. Emotions are always accompanied by a number of physiological reactions (reflexes). The so-called activation syndrome is at work here: Epinephrine (adrenaline) production is increased, the pupils become enlarged, the smooth muscular system and digestion stop working, and there is an acceleration in breathing and transpiration. The activation syndrome is triggered by certain stimuli, namely, *emotional stimuli*. Michael is presumably an emotional stimulus for the teacher, triggering the response of anger or fear. This is heightened when her various attempts to end his interruptions (aversive stimuli) meet with no success. We can understand how difficult the situation is for the teacher: She is unable to put an end to the aversive stimuli and reacts emotionally. Following the principles of classical conditioning (cf. Chapters 1 and 2), the teacher will very likely also react emotionally to other stimuli present at the same time as Michael, for example, the sight of the classroom. If the sight of the classroom comes to trigger anger and fear, we would say that through classical conditioning the classroom has become a conditioned stimulus, in exactly the same way as the child's fear of white lab coats in Chapter 1.

How can the teacher be helped? From the point of view of classical conditioning, this would be a clear-cut case for *counterconditioning,* with the aim of extinguishing her responses to stimuli that produce anger or fear. Step by step, anger or fear reactions would be replaced by those of relaxation, found in the so-called process of systematic desensitization (see also Chapter 9, Section 9.4). First, the teacher would learn a relaxation technique using autogenic training or more modern biofeedback methods. Once she had learned to relax completely, she would be asked to establish a hierarchy of the stimuli that trigger anger or fear, starting with the weakest and ending with the strongest stimulus. The weakest would perhaps be imagining an empty classroom, the strongest Michael standing up in the lesson, calling out, "I've had enough!" and walking out of the classroom amid the laughter of the other pupils. She would then, while in a state of relaxation, imagine the empty classroom time and time again until she could manage to call up the image without reactions of fear or anger. One by one the stimuli would similarly be brought into association with the relaxation response, until the teacher could imagine even the strongest stimulus without experiencing feelings of anger or fear.

This method would most certainly be helpful to the teacher. However, in the classroom she would still need to use additional techniques to cope with Michael's disruptive behavior, for example, the behavior-shaping methods discussed above. Skinner would again describe the teacher's learning of such methods as operant conditioning; the resulting decrease in Michael's disruptive behavior and increase in his active participation would raise the probability of the teacher's continuing to use behavior-shaping methods.

5.9 Self-Control

Even if Michael's behavior were to improve, some disruptions are still bound to occur in the beginning. The teacher could deal with these by additionally learning to control her ensuing responses of anger and fear. For example, she could take a deep breath when she was interrupted, thus allowing time for her emotional excitation to die down. Deep breathing is the *controlling response;* the emotional response is the *controlled response.* The controlling response is learned through operant conditioning, through *negative reinforcement,* because it has the effect of weakening the emotional response. By toning down her emotional response with the help of self-control, our teacher would be able to respond in a more "laid-back," "level-headed" way. She would probably speak more calmly and choose her words more carefully, resisting the temptation to attack and degrade Michael personally with such comments as "You can't be trusted with anything!" This calmer way of reacting would probably result in the interruptions' becoming less frequent.

According to Skinner this form of *self-control,* in which one response is controlled by another, can be learned to influence all kinds of operant behavior patterns, smoking, for example. One of various *controlling responses* could be that a smoker would put cigarettes, lighter, and ashtray out of his or her field of vision, thus eliminating discriminating stimuli that might prompt smoking and reducing the probability of the occurrence of the *controlled response.*

Clearly, Skinner's *theoretical* explanation of how to give up smoking is quite different from Guthrie's (cf. Chapter 4), although the *practical* advice given is identical.

We will return to this theme in Chapter 7, in which we discuss the *cognitive* aspects of self-control.

5.10 Reinforcement Schedules and Their Specific Effects

An increase in the probability of a response's occurring is generally achieved only by repeatedly coupling it with a reinforcer. The speed of learning and *resistance to extinction* of a particular response (i.e., the number of nonreinforced responses necessary before extinction takes place) depend on whether the response is always or only sporadically reinforced. Specific effects of reinforcement depend on the type of reinforcement given. Skinner studied this intensively in animal experiments (mostly on pigeons and rats), systematically varying the conditions for reinforcement.

It could be argued that behavioral laws observed in such animals cannot be applied to humans. This is a valid objection, especially considering that the human being has a far more advanced nervous system. On the other hand, why should we not carry out control experiments on humans to test whether the same behavioral laws can be used to understand and predict human behavior? Skinner himself used many examples from human experience and behavior to demonstrate the validity of his behavioral laws. Even if we today have newer theories at our disposal as well as a completely different conception of human life (thus clearly recognizing the limitations of Skinner's radically behavioristic point of view), we must still acknowledge the relevance of his findings on the conditions for the effectiveness of reinforcement.

Continual Reinforcement

Skinner speaks of *continual reinforcement* when every response is reinforced; this form of reinforcement leads to a rapid increase in the appearance of the response, though it also has clear disadvantages. Most importantly, the response is also *quickly extinguished* when reinforcement ceases to be given. Children know that chewing gum comes out of a vending machine when they put a coin in the slot. If the coin remains in the machine and no chewing gum appears, only a few children will react by putting another coin into the machine – and even fewer children will insert a third coin after a second fruitless attempt. Continual reinforcement offers the advantage of rapid development of behavior coupled with the disadvantage of *extremely low resistance to extinction.*

Intermittent Reinforcement

In *intermittent reinforcement,* not every response is reinforced. Yet reinforcement can be given systematically by reinforcing the first response after a set period of time *(fixed-interval reinforcement)* or by reinforcing a response after a set number of nonreinforced responses *(fixed-ratio reinforcement).*

In fixed-interval reinforcement, a pigeon is rewarded with a grain of food when it pecks at a small disk on the wall of the experimental box (desired behavior) for the first time after a period of, say, three minutes. Reinforcement is again given when it pecks at the disk for the first time after a further interval of three minutes, regardless of how many times it pecked at the disk in the intervening time. Skinner also speaks of *reinforcement schedules* or *reinforcement programs*, since he was able to program the feeding machines to carry out the experiment. Under this type of reinforcement, the response rate slows down considerably immediately after reinforcement (fixed interval), gradually increases again, and reaches its peak just before it is time for the next reinforcement to be given. An example of this type of behavior would be that of "seasonal workers" at school who work harder when report cards become imminent, intensifying their efforts even more the nearer report card time comes.

In fixed-ratio reinforcement, the pigeon is rewarded with a grain of corn for, say, every 20th peck at the disk. This form of reinforcement is used in manufacturing when workers are given piece-rate wages, for example, a certain amount of money for every 30 units of a particular item they are producing. This kind of reinforcement leads to high response rates, although a lapse also occurs immediately after reinforcement has been given.

The drawback of response intermissions that follow reinforcement in the above-mentioned reinforcement schedules (with a *fixed* interval or a *fixed* ratio) is much less likely to occur if *variable-interval reinforcement* or *variable-ratio reinforcement* is used. In *variable-interval reinforcement*, the period of time that elapses before reinforcement is given is varied. If a teacher were to give a class a surprise written test once a month, but vary the actual number of days between tests each time, the aim would be to encourage the pupils to work steadily all the time. This would be an example of variable-interval reinforcement, with an average interval of one month. This kind of reinforcement offers an extremely high resistance to extinction. An even greater rate of response as well as the highest possible resistance to extinction can be achieved by using variable-ratio reinforcement. In slot machines, the average winning quota is fixed (to the advantage of the house, of course), but the number of games a player loses before each win is variable. The persistence of gamblers in playing these machines is an example of the high resistance to extinction achieved with this reinforcement program.

Intermittent reinforcement increases the probability of a response's occurring more slowly than *continual reinforcement*; on the other hand, *resistance to extinction is raised considerably*. In order to profit from both reinforcement programs, one can allow behavior to develop using continual reinforcement and then switch over to variable-ratio reinforcement, gradually increasing the average number of responses per reinforcement. After an initial continual reinforcement, one continues with an average ratio of, say, 3:1, then 6:1, finally ending up at 20:1. It is extremely important to continue giving occasional reinforcement in order to maintain the desired behavior, which will otherwise eventually be extinguished.

Random Contingencies and Superstitious Behavior

Skinner also did experiments on other reinforcement programs and program combinations. He described one curious phenomenon observed in pigeons as "superstitious" behavior.

The researcher placed several pigeons in separate experimental boxes. A programmed dispenser gave each pigeon a small amount of food every 15 seconds, regardless of what the pigeon was doing at the time. This reinforcement program thus differs from interval reinforcement in that no attention is paid to whether a particular response is displayed or not before reinforcement is given. When the researcher later returned to the laboratory, he found one bird sitting still, one hopping around on one leg, and a third turning around in circles. Each one of the pigeons was repeating its own "behavior ritual" between feeds. Skinner called this kind of behavior *superstitious* because the relationship between behavior and reinforcement was based on a *random contingency*. Superstitious behavior sometimes develops after a single random reinforcement; the way the pigeon was behaving immediately before receiving food was reinforced.

Skinner believed that superstitious behavior in humans develops in exactly the same way: If you scratch your head before finding the solution to a problem, your behavior is reinforced and a habit is formed (providing the behavior is reinforced again from time to time). Similarly, random negative reinforcers explain why some people stop what they are doing when a black cat crosses their path or avoid all important activities on the 13th day of the month. Many prejudices not learned by modeling (Bandura, 1977) also have their origins in random contingencies and intermittent reinforcement.

Reinforcement Programs in Everyday Situations and in Our Classroom Situation

A knowledge of the specific effects of reinforcement programs can help us to avoid common educational problems. If a father *sometimes* gives in to his three-year-old son's insistent begging for candy in the supermarket, he is giving *intermittent reinforcement*. The same holds true if parents give in and fulfill a wish they would normally ignore when a child behaves in a particularly *annoying* or a particularly *loving* way. We know that intermittent reinforcement leads to a gradual increase in the child's "successful" behavior, which is subsequently extremely resistant to extinction. This gives strong support to the view of education experts that *consistency* is the crux of bringing up children. Knowledge of the theory of operant conditioning can also prevent us from unknowingly encouraging the development of undesirable behavior by giving reinforcement in the wrong place.

As far as Michael is concerned, we discussed above (Section 5.7) how he might be encouraged to participate constructively in the lesson by ignoring his disruptive behavior and using *behavior shaping* with *differential reinforcement* and *successive approximation* to achieve an increase in desirable behavior.

Now we can recognize the importance of successive approximation. In the beginning, the criteria for reinforcement are at a low level, allowing considerable opportunities for reinforcement. When the teacher gradually increases her demands for behavioral changes, she should continue to give reinforcement as continually as possible. She will find it worthwhile to devote this much attention to a single pupil if she knows that it will be necessary only for a limited time. However, it is then important – for Michael's sake as well as for the teacher's – to change over to intermittent reinforcement, reinforcing his desirable behavior only from time to time.

5.11 Aversive Stimuli: Punishment

Anyone who plays around with an electrical socket and receives a shock experiences an *aversive stimulus* as a direct consequence of a previous activity. This is the phenomenon of *punishment*; the corresponding activity will most likely not be repeated.

But let us put punishment into the context of learning psychology: Skinner defined a reinforcer (positive or negative) as an event that increases the probability that a previous behavior will occur again. Punishment according to Skinner entails (1) the introduction of an aversive stimulus as a *direct and immediate consequence of behavior* (in contrast to negative reinforcement, in which the aversive stimulus disappears after the response), or (2) the *removal of a positive reinforcer* (in contrast to the realization of positive reinforcement, in which the reinforced event takes place). Punishment, then, is the direct consequence of behavior and the exact opposite of (positive or negative) reinforcement. But because of negative reinforcement aversive stimuli can lead to the development of avoidance behavior that is incompatible with the punished behavior. In other words, punishment can indirectly bring about a reduction in the occurrence of undesirable behavior by reinforcing avoidance behavior.

In Michael's case, if he were punished, he might possibly stop interrupting the lesson as before, yet begin to rebel secretly as a kind of avoidance behavior. On the other hand, punishment carried out appropriately (see below) and leaving no room for reinforcement is thus perfectly likely to contribute to the extinction of undesirable behavior. In Michael's case, punishment would not produce desirable, constructive classroom behavior; this could be undertaken using the steps described in Section 5.7.

At this point it is helpful to take a look at Bower and Hilgard's comments (1981) on Skinner's early studies on punishment (Skinner, 1938):

> Skinner's views on punishment have undergone revision over the years. Some early studies by him (Skinner, 1938, 154) using a mild punisher (the lever slapped upward against the rat's paw when it was pressed) came to the conclusion that punishment was a relatively ineffective means to produce any permanent change in behavior. It was claimed that punishment did have a suppressive effect on behavior while it remained in force, but that when punishment was removed the former response "recovered" and was emitted nearly as much during extinction as was a nonpunished response. This interpretation that punishment is relatively ineffective in altering behavior has been widely quoted and used for various liberalizing arguments in practical applications of behavior modification. The prescription was to use only positive reinforcement since punishers were ineffectual and had only bad side-effects.
>
> But the interpretation, in retrospect, is rather odd. By this strange logic, one might also claim that positive reinforcement is ineffective, is "only temporary with no lasting effects," because the response extinguishes when reinforcement is withdrawn. Later studies and analyses of punishment by Azrin and Holz (1966) show how very effective punishment can be in suppressing appetitive behavior, how it varies in a lawful way with the parameters of punishment, and also how behavior recovers after punishment is removed and reinforcement is continued. (Bower & Hilgard, 1981, 187)

Azrin and Holz (1966), mentioned above, summarize their extensive investigations as follows:

> (1) The punishing stimulus should be arranged in such a manner that no unauthorized escape is possible. (2) The punishing stimulus should be as

intense as possible. (3) The frequency of punishment should be as high as possible. (4) The punishing stimulus should be delivered immediately after the response. (5) The punishing stimulus should not be increased gradually but introduced at maximum intensity. (6) Extended periods of punishment should be avoided, especially where low intensities of punishment are concerned, since the recovery effect may thereby occur. Where mild intensities of punishment are used, it is best to use them for only a brief period of time. (7) Great care should be taken to see that the delivery of the punishing stimulus is not differentially associated with the delivery of reinforcement. Otherwise the punishing stimulus may acquire conditioned reinforcing properties. (8) The delivery of the punishing stimulus should be made a signal or discriminative stimulus that a period of extinction is in progress. (9) The degree of motivation to emit the punished response should be reduced. (10) The frequency of positive reinforcement for the punished response should similarly be reduced. (11) An alternative response should be available which will produce the same or greater reinforcement as the punished response. For example, punishment of criminal behavior can be expected to be more effective if noncriminal behavior which will result in the same advantages as the criminal behavior is available. (12) If no alternative response is available, the subject should have access to a different situation in which he obtains the same reinforcement without being punished. (13) If it is not possible to deliver the punishing stimulus itself after a response, then an effective method of punishment is still available. A conditioned stimulus may be delivered following a response to achieve conditioned punishment. (14) A reduction of positive reinforcement may be used as punishment when the use of physical punishment is not possible for practical, legal, or moral reasons. Punishment by withdrawal of positive reinforcement may be accomplished in such situations by arranging a period of reduced reinforcement frequency (time-out) or by arranging a decrease of conditioned reinforcement (response cost). Both methods require that the subject have a high level of reinforcement to begin with; otherwise, no withdrawal of reinforcement is possible. If nonphysical punishment is to be used, it appears desirable to provide the subject with a substantial history of reinforcement in order to provide the opportunity for withdrawing the reinforcement as punishment for the undesired responses. (Azrin & Holz, 1966, 426–427)

From these statements we can see that the teacher could stop Michael's disruptive behavior only by employing extensive aversive measures. At the end of this chapter we will consider an alternative. We return to the theme of "punishment" in Chapters 7 and 8.

5.12 Learning by Observation and Imitation

Let us now look at Michael's situation from the point of view of another learning theorist, Albert Bandura. Bandura fully accepts that certain parts of our behavior can be triggered by stimuli, and that other parts are influenced by the consequences of behavior. He stresses, however, that the actions of an individual are primarily governed by the memory of earlier experiences and by cognitive processes. Thus, in contrast to radical behaviorists, he takes cognitive processes, particularly the individual's capacity for *self-control* and *self-regulation*, into consideration.

In his research project on the origins of aggressive behavior patterns in children, Bandura's attention was drawn to the importance of learning processes based on the mere observation of other individuals. This founded his theory of *observational learning* (also known as *modeling* or *imitation learning*). Bandura developed this theory further until it became an entire *socio-cognitive learning theory* (Bandura, 1977, 1986). In his later years, Bandura became increasingly preoccupied with the system of the "self," in particular "self-efficacy." In doing so he was in the process of turning away from behaviorism.

We can now investigate what effect Michael's disruptive behavior is likely to have on the rest of the class against the background of *modeling*. Whether his fellow pupils imitate him or not depends on several factors: First, he must be fully accepted by his peers, and, second, his classmates must pay close attention to his disruptive behavior. Third, the consequence of Michael's behavior – the teacher's response – must be recognized by the rest of the class as reinforcement *(vicarious reinforcement)*. Last, pupils who imitate his behavior must receive the same reinforcement as he does. If all of these four conditions are met, Michael's behavior will be imitated.

Conversely, Michael could learn cooperative, constructive classroom behavior from his classmates, provided the same conditions were met. For Bandura, the relationship between behavior and the consequences of behavior is formed through cognitive processes, not in a mechanistic way, as behaviorist theorists believe. He believed that the *expectation of the consequences of actions* causes certain behavior to be imitated.

We can also use expectations to form the basis of a new interpretation of Michael's disruptive behavior. If we consider his behavior to be a consequence of his expectations rather than merely operant behavior, it seems reasonable to assume that Michael no longer expects to perform adequately in the classroom by behaving in a normal, cooperative way. Or as Bandura would put it, Michael has a low *expectation of self-efficacy* in the subject at hand. If this is the case, the main task of teaching staff would be to help him to improve his actual competence and knowledge, for example, by giving him extra tutoring.

5.13 The Diversity of Learning Processes at Work in a Single Lesson

If we take a look back at the situation we have analyzed in this chapter, it is astonishing how many aspects of the various learning theories contribute to our understanding of the circumstances and provide suggestions as to how behavior can be modified. The theory of *operant conditioning* explains how the consequences of behavior influence its development, maintenance, or extinction. It suggests ways of encouraging Michael to develop constructive classroom behavior. We also discussed the role of emotions in learning processes from a theoretical point of view. We examined the conditions that must be met for punishment to be effective, thereby concentrating on the ideas of Bower and Hilgard (1981) rather than on Skinner's earlier findings. We then examined the more extensive theory of *sociocognitive learning*, taking modeling and its relevant cognitive processes into account to gain an understanding of further aspects of the classroom situation. In particular, this provided us with a new interpretation of Michael's troublemaking as behavior resulting from his feeling of inadequacy in completing the lessons (low expectations of self-efficacy).

There is, however, another aspect of the lesson we have ignored until now: Apart from encouraging Michael to develop desirable classroom behavior or putting a stop to his disruptions by using extinction or punishment, the teacher also has the possibility of taking him aside after the lesson and having a casual chat with him. She could tell him that she does not approve of his permanent disruptions, and that she, as he will surely have noticed, has no intention of acknowledging his unpleasant way of putting his hand up. She expects to see an immediate change in his behavior. If Michael is a reasonably bright pupil, he will immediately *understand*. In theoretical terms, he has received a kind of mild punishment, but also *feedback*; the teacher's remarks are of an *informational nature*. The mild punishment stimulus contained in her remarks works through Michael's *own interpretation of her words*, rather than mechanically. Michael is also informed of what he can do to make the teacher take notice of him in the future. Again, we see here that a *cognitive interpretation of reinforcement* (the teacher's remarks as a stimulus situation) can provide an explanation for learning processes. The teacher's remarks lead to new expectations regarding the consequences of action, as Bandura would say.

If we consider the option, discussed above, of encouraging the adoption of *alternative behavior* (a very good solution to the problem!), we can clearly see that there are at least two sides to adequate management in the classroom: (1) the *thorough preparation of material*, i.e., content (not our concern here), and (2) *management planning*. The careful preparation of teaching material provides a teacher with the security, intellectual superiority, and resources (energy and strong nerves!) needed for the second point: the organization and control of the course of the lesson, in which the teacher must continually react, give feedback, and adapt. A teacher must never forget that his or her own behavior represents a stimulus situation for the pupils and continually observe how they respond to it.

Memo

1. Operant conditioning occurs when behavior is reinforced by an event (the consequence) following it. How often a particular behavior occurs can be increased either by introducing a positive reinforcer or by removing a negative reinforcer (aversive stimulus).

2. The theory of operant conditioning was first developed by Burrhus F. Skinner (1904–1991).

3. In contrast to classical conditioning, in which an association is made between elementary behavior and new stimuli (see Chapter 1, Memo point 1), new modes of behavior are learned in operant conditioning.

4. If behavior is reinforced when a certain stimulus is present but others are not, in the future this behavior will be displayed only in response to the stimulus present at reinforcement. This stimulus is called the discriminating stimulus. It can be used to control behavior in the future.   (anything tempting)

5. Undesirable behavior can also be established through reinforcement. It may be modified by
   - extinction
   - punishment
   - reinforcement of an (incompatible) desirable alternative behavior
   - comprehension (cognitive interpretation of the consequences of behavior)
   - learning of alternative behavior from a model (observational learning, imitation)
   - changing of the expectation of self-efficacy and actual competence

6. In the method of self-control, a controlling response (e.g., breathing deeply) is learned to suppress the effect of discriminating stimuli (e.g., a pupil's disruptive behavior) on a controlled response (e.g., anger).

cumulative process
step by step (e.g. circus animals)

7. Shaping a certain behavior entails, on the one hand, differential reinforcement, i.e., reinforcing desirable behavior and completely ignoring undesirable behavior, as well as, on the other hand, encouraging the gradual formation of the desired final behavior through successive approximation. In the latter, the most elementary components of the desired final behavior are first reinforced. Then the criterion for the reinforcer is gradually moved in the direction of the desired final behavior.

8. An increase in the probability of a response's occurring is generally achieved only by coupling the response with a reinforcer many times. The speed of learning and the resistance to extinction (i.e., the number of nonreinforced responses required to extinguish the initial response) depend on whether a desired response is reinforced *every time* it appears *(continual reinforcement)* or only occasionally *(intermittent reinforcement)*.

9. Continual reinforcement produces a rapid increase in the frequency of occurrence of a response – but the response is also rapidly extinguished when reinforcement ceases. Intermittent reinforcement results in a much slower increase in the frequency of a response, but it also ensures a much higher resistance to extinction.

10. Intermittent reinforcement can be given by using an interval schedule or a ratio schedule. Interval schedule reinforcement is given for the first desired behavior to be displayed after a fixed period. Ratio schedule reinforcement is given for the first desired response to be displayed after a certain number of nonreinforced responses, according to a certain ratio (e.g., 3:1 or 40:1). Interval and ratio schedules can be fixed or variable; i.e., the time interval and the quota ratio can be set at a certain level for the entire conditioning process, or they can be varied (variable interval and variable ratio both with a given average).

11. In order to profit from the advantages of both types of reinforcement program, one can build up behavior patterns initially by using continual reinforcement, then change over to variable-ratio reinforcement, gradually increasing the average ratio, i.e., gradually reducing the frequency of reinforcement.

12. Punishment is defined as the introduction of an aversive stimulus or the removal of a positive reinforcement as a consequence of behavior. It can lead to avoidance behavior. According to Skinner, the probability that the punished response will recur is reduced only inasmuch as and as long as the punishment contingency continues to be present. There are, however, principles that can be followed to ensure that the effectiveness of punishment is upheld over long periods (Azrin & Holz, 1966). *(from Wlin)*

13. According to Bandura, behavior can also be built up by modeling (observational learning, imitation). Whether or not behavior is imitated depends on certain characteristics of the model, of the reinforcement that the model receives (vicarious reinforcement), and of the reinforcement received by the imitator.

14. Bandura believes that most behavior is not conditioned (classically or operantly), but is subject to self-regulation. Cognitive processes, particularly expectations of the consequences of behavior and expectations of self-efficacy, play an extremely important part in the explanation of behavior. The expectation of self-efficacy can be successfully increased by providing skills to improve the deficiency in competence.

(social learning)
→ modeling – key concepts

6. How Rita Unlearns to Like to Draw: On Reinforcements and Rewards

6.1 Introduction

This chapter once again deals with reinforcements and rewards, that is to say, with reinforcing stimuli and other phenomena held to be reinforcing stimuli. First, we take a look at the midterm effects of reinforcements on the development of a child's drawing ability as well as on the motivation that is inherent in the drawing activities themselves. We will concentrate on the child's "learning history," particularly on the "reinforcement history," and how they have affected the child's desire for exploration and curiosity.

This chapter sets a surprising limitation to the laws of reinforcement as previously known: There are reinforcements that do not support certain behaviors but rather quite clearly deter or inhibit them – including any and all motivation present therein. This is true, however, only for behaviors that are in themselves of great interest and are thus executed. This does not nullify the basic laws of reinforcement.

The keywords in this chapter are *reinforcements* and *rewards*, *intrinsic* and *extrinsic motivation*, the *effects of extrinsic rewards on intrinsically motivated activities*, the concept of *overjustification* of an activity, i.e., the justification of an activity from without which is in fact superfluous because there is sufficient *intrinsic* motivation available. Further, we will speak of *self-determination* (as opposed to *other-determination*) of behavior as well as of the *attractiveness, open-endedness,* and the *controllability* thereof, all of which contribute to intrinsic motivation.

6.2 Positive Circumstances and the Development of a Drawing Skill

Rita is a 7-year-old with a great talent for drawing. She has always loved drawing. Her parents have been keen on supplying her with whatever materials she needs: large sample books of wallpaper to draw on as well as all necessary pencils and colors. Rita is allowed to hang up her drawings on the walls of her room, and she enjoys doing that. Every once in a while she rearranges the drawings, but a few always remain in the same position: She likes them there! Extra drawings are gathered in a portfolio, and nothing is given away. The themes in her drawings deal with her everyday life, that of her family and her dolls.

Spontaneous Activity, Supportive Feedback, and Observing Models

It is very difficult to trace Rita's learning history and the history of her drawing talents, though a few of the intermediate steps are clear. Let us first take a look at the circumstances that were necessary to her developing her drawing ability. The following consists of interpolations of her behavior and her environment on the basis of the few biographical details known.

It is certainly true when we say that Rita's family atmosphere offered her the prerequisites to her developing drawing skills as well as her desire to draw – the instruments, the materials, sufficient space, peace and quiet, and security to take up these activities. Of course, she also needed to have experiences she could draw on for her pictures. Rita surely will have primarily employed those experiences occurring in her immediate family, but also some in her everyday life including her contacts with other children and adults. There were also models for her – people in her surroundings with great skills in drawing and crafting, in particular one of the local neighborhood children and a man living in the same apartment house.

But the presence of such models was not everything: Her parents also pointed her at an early age toward drawing, indeed toward the entire visual world in general. And when the child reacted and took the initiative, they were sensitive enough to react to their child's observations and statements.

Even before Rita began to draw on her own, a wealth of very valuable learning processes, indistinguishable to others and even to those in her immediate surroundings, had already taken place. An example: Rita discovers in a children's book a drawing she really likes and runs to her mother to show it to her. The mother's positive reaction at her child's discovery is of utmost importance. This reinforcement means the child will come to her mother again with another drawing she likes, will tell her something about it, perhaps ask a question, will be reinforced again by the mother, who in turn may tell a story herself, just listen to the child, or whatever. In any case, she will display a positive reaction. The child's spontaneous behavior, triggered by the *discriminating stimuli* of the pictures in a book, is reinforced according to Skinner's *operant conditioning paradigm* (cf. Chapter 5). A similar situation will surely have also occurred later when Rita showed her mother her first *own* drawings. In terms of developmental psychology, such interactions between child and mother correspond to what Bronfenbrenner and Ceci (1994) called *proximal processes,* i.e., *processes of regular, reliable exchange in a stable environment over a long period of time,* activating potentials of all sorts (e.g., artistic potentials) and consciously and actively maintaining and furthering them.

If we view the above as examples from the broad realm of such experiences in a child's everyday life, we recognize that it is the *sum* of the mother's individual, regular, and predictable reactions that is so decisive. The mother obviously could have reacted very differently: She could have scolded the child for removing a book from the bookshelf on her own; she could have, without further comment, made Rita return the book to the shelf; she could have simply noted her lack of time for such matters. She might even have become angry with the child for not noticing that she (the mother) has so much work to do, the cooking, the housework, and so on. The results are clear when we remind ourselves that, according to Skinner, behavior is developed or hindered on the basis of the *subsequent consequences.* The latter reactions of the mother would represent negative events that follow the child's spontaneous activity – aversive stimuli, in fact. Were the mother to repeat this behavior toward the child, she would most likely come to the mother less and less with some interesting object, a picture, an idea, a question – or at a later point in time a picture of her own. In terms of learning psychology, aversive stimuli are simply punishments that lower the probability that the respective response or activities will recur. The cognitive interpretation would be that the child anticipates the mother's reactions, presumes a particular reaction pattern, and in the light of the consequences of spontaneous activities begins to modify her own behavior: She stops telling the mother about her discoveries or even stops trying to discover things altogether.

The plenitude of positive reinforcements as well as the additional support given through technical assistance in the form of better materials and helpful comments – all in all, a sort of *verbal feedback* – create a favorable set of circumstances leading the child to draw of her own accord and without any external "pushing" required. The behavioristic explanation for this would be that the repeated, though only intermittent, reinforcement of the mother becomes linked to the act of drawing, making the activity itself (drawing) a *secondary reinforcer* that strengthens the rewarding characteristics of the entire situation (Keller, 1969, cited in Deci, 1971). This would explain, in behavioristic terms, why Rita likes to draw in spite of a lack of reinforcement from her social environment. The *cognitive* explanation for her behavior would be that the informative verbal feedback and reinforcement she receives serve as *memories* or *mental images* that allow her to *anticipate the positive reactions* of her surroundings. Drawing thus becomes an *intrinsically motivated activity* in need of no obvious external reinforcement or reward – except that stemming from the activity itself (Deci, 1971, 105).

What keep the intrinsic motivation to draw alive are the *feeling of satisfaction* and the *experience of joy* in carrying out the activity. According to Bandura (1986, 1989) the joy of drawing could also be explained as a result of the child's *self-efficacy:* Rita comes to understand that there are many important goals for her, and that she has sufficient means and skills at her disposal to reach those goals. It was not necessary that her drawing activities arose from operantly reinforced spontaneous situations; there were many other impulses available from models (siblings, neighbors, etc.) in her surroundings whom Rita could observe and eventually imitate (Bandura, 1977).

Technical ability and intrinsic motivation, though very different, worked hand in hand throughout her learning history and became to Rita what we generally call an *artistic talent*.

6.3 Specific Characteristics of the Intrinsic Motivation to Draw

There are principally three groups of characteristics that describe Rita's intrinsic motivation to draw:

1. the great *attractiveness* of this activity for her,
2. the *open-endedness* of the tasks the child begins, not determined in advance
3. the *controllability* of the activity, which in turn also depends on the other two. she decides to pick up the book.

important

The Attractiveness of the Activity

The attractiveness of drawing as an activity – or the child's interest in that activity – arises when the structure of the activity coincides with the child's abilities. While drawing the child experiences enough difficulties to make it a challenge (which Heckhausen, 1969, called "optimal fit"), yet the task at hand is also solvable, so that one's own success is assured – almost preprogrammed, in fact.

The Open-Endedness of the Activity

The second characteristic, open-endedness, implies first that the activity is not wholly determined in advance by some hard and fast rules or set order of steps (algorithms), but that it is heuristic in the sense that each new step has to be determined for the respective task. Further, one decides from one moment to another what is decisive for the progress of the activity and the improvement of one's own skills. The child also has the ability to end the activity when the time seems appropriate: She has the stop rule.

The Controllability of the Activity

Applied to drawing, the stop rule may be seen as another aspect of *controllability*. Further aspects of controllability are that the drawing child always knows that she is drawing only for her own purposes, has the sole control over the instruments, and can ask for help when she deems it necessary. In this respect the child experiences the feeling of competence or self-efficacy. The activity is thus satisfying in and of itself for a number of reasons.

Csikszentmihalyi (1978) added a number of other characteristics for such activities, for example, reduced awareness of surroundings through increased concentration on the task; the feeling of control, which may lead to a sort of transcendent "high" and a "loss of self-awareness" (1978, 213) as well as to a meshing with the activity and one's surroundings, something Csikszentmihalyi calls the "flow experience." Whether Rita experienced such enrapturement while drawing is unknown. But perhaps the reader can remember having had such experiences. They may especially be found in aesthetic surroundings, in corporal–erotic experiences, during sport activities or meditation.

All of the characteristics listed above we find more or less clearly situated in Rita's drawing activities. Now we must discover why and how Rita lost her joy of drawing in such a short period of time.

6.4 The Systematic Loss of Intrinsic Motivation

What Happened

In her first year in school Rita was known for her lively and technically excellent drawings. Her work was shown around, compared to that of others, and Rita even won a prize or two. Drawing had a special role in school in that the children were allowed to draw on their own when the lesson was done or when the teacher was correcting other classwork. The children thus tended to draw a lot. The strange thing was that Rita began liking drawing less and less, and at home, much to the consternation of her parents, she hardly ever drew at all. At first her mother tried to get her to draw, but without success, so the father offered her a prize or something special for every nice drawing she did. Still, after a few weeks Rita had no more interest in drawing at all – and no activity arose to take its place.

Research Results and Theoretical Explanations

The loss of intrinsic motivation as a result of the presence of external reinforcements or rewards has been a subject of scientific inquiry for more than 20 years now (cf. Deci, 1971; Lepper, Greene, & Nisbett, 1973; Cameron & Pierce, 1994, for an overview). For a long time the consensus was that of one experimental study: "If a person is engaged in some activity for reasons of intrinsic motivation, and if he begins to receive the external reward, money, for performing the activity, the degree to which he is intrinsically motivated to perform the activity decreases" (Deci, 1971, 108).

The Overjustification Hypothesis

Lepper et al. (1973) thought the reason for the *loss of intrinsic motivation* for a particular activity lies in the unnecessary extension of rewards to do something one already finds interesting. This only doubly motivates the activity or unnecessarily *overjustifies* it. Intrinsic motivation, according to Lepper (1981), is decreased whenever extrinsic rewards cause a change in the perception of cause, particularly when the extrinsic reward is salient and, furthermore, produces no rise in competence (after Cameron & Pierce, 1994, 370).

Deci and Ryan's Cognitive Evaluation Hypothesis

Deci and Ryan (1985) assume that intrinsic motivation has its roots in self-attribution (attribution of cause by the individual herself), based on the innate need for competence and self-determination. But the feeling of being *competent* and *self-determined* can also be influenced by external events, depending on whether these events are *informative, controlling*, or *neutral*. Positive and informative external feedback and reinforcement confirm one's abilities (like drawing) and thus do not harm intrinsic motivation. Controlling events, on the other hand, are experienced as an other-determination of some activity; they do harm self-determination and reduce intrinsic motivation. In a concrete situation, the question is thus whether the reward is *informative* or *controlling*. Here, we are dealing with a *cognitive evaluation*: Verbal rewards such as praise or positive feedback give us information about the execution of some

activity, whereas material rewards such as prizes, awards, or money have a
controlling character to them, especially when they are *expected* (expected
rewards). The latter is even more so the case when there are no qualifying
strings attached to the reward – when only participation is required and thus
even unqualified execution is rewarded.

Experiments on the effects of extrinsic reinforcement and rewards on intrinsic motivation have produced rather contradictory results. Yet they have
succeeded in directing our attention toward many different and apparently
important factors (Cameron & Pierce, 1994):

1. the *kind of reward*, be it verbal or material,
2. the *informative or controlling nature* of an external reinforcement (see
   above),
3. the way the *intrinsic motivation is comprehended* (duration of the free-will
   activity versus quality of results of the activity),
4. whether the reward was promised versus given after the fact *(reward expectancy)*,
5. whether the reward has any connection at all to an activity or a performance
   level (simple execution versus goal attainment: *reward contingency*).

Here, the difference is also made between reward and reinforcement:

> A reinforcer is an event that increases the frequency of the behavior it
> follows. A reward, however, is not defined by its effects on behavior.
> Rewards are stimuli that are assumed to be positive events, but they have
> not been shown to strengthen behavior. (Cameron & Pierce, 1994, 364)

*In this sense, many rewards are, in learning psychology terms, not necessarily
reinforcements.*

How to Explain Rita's Loss of Intrinsic Motivation

In the light of the research results discussed above, we may assume that the
verbal feedback and the reinforcements Rita received in school for her drawing talents did not damage her intrinsic motivation – on the contrary, they may
have actually increased it because of their informative nature. More likely, the
father's offer of material rewards had a negative effect on Rita's intrinsic
motivation. This may be interpreted as a case of *overjustification* (*sensu* Lepper et al., 1973): The reward was salient, it did nothing to increase Rita's
competence, and – last not least – it was simply superfluous. How extensive
such reinforcement effects actually are is a matter of debate in the literature;

in Rita's case, we would need to determine the other reasons for the decrease in her intrinsic motivation. That there indeed was such a decrease is certain, as can be seen in the reduction of both number and quality of her drawings.

Of particular importance for the loss of interest and pleasure (in this case, Rita's loss of intrinsic motivation to draw) are four factors:

1. the *decline of attractiveness*,
2. the *loss of an open-endedness* to the skill,
3. the *loss of control* and thus
4. the *recognition of the instrumentality* of the skill, that is, that the particular skill serves a purpose foreign to the activity itself, namely, to fill time, to please someone else, etc.

The Decline of Attractiveness

What made drawing so attractive to Rita was her ability to express her own experiences through this medium: spontaneously and in accordance with her capabilities and desires. This was lost when she *had to* draw something in school; no longer was she absorbed with drawing, concentrating on her expressive talents (the "flow"). Little remained of the original excitement! The loss of attractiveness is accompanied by a feeling of being "underchallenged": Skills are not employed to attain a reachable goal, and so the possibility of self-realization (the realization of further skills) is lost as well. Drawing is no longer a challenge, since the "optimal fit" (see above; Heckhausen, 1969) is now missing. Under these circumstances it is not surprising that Rita sacrificed her love of drawing to an aversion, with all the respective verbalizations.

The Loss of Open-Endedness and Control

The same can be said about the *open-endedness* of an activity: The teacher, by using drawing as a filler (and, moreover, associated with a certain prearranged topic), ended up limiting the amount of freedom Rita enjoyed as to the content of her pictures. This procedure expressly laid out exact ways and means: Pictures were to be drawn in a certain order and with certain steps using certain materials, etc. Above all, Rita no longer enjoyed the stoprule: She was forced to begin and end her drawing when the teacher said to do so. Drawings were interrupted and taken up again at all the wrong times. This means that the *controllability* of her own activity on a temporal as well as thematic level had been lost, giving Rita the feeling of *other-determination*. As de Charms (1968) said, one suffers the shift from self-causation to external causation – like being a pawn on a chessboard. Lepper and Greene (1975) showed that even relatively small children have a good feel for whether someone is trying to manipulate them through such an activity (e.g., to get them to do some unpleasant duty).

The Instrumental Character of Drawing and Extrinsic Motivation

But the worst revelation for Rita was that she had to draw for a particular reason or purpose. Drawing was no longer something that she did of her own free will; rather, it attained a clearly *instrumental character.* As mentioned above, particularly the father's offer of a reward when things weren't going so well (however well intentioned it may have been) was a factor here. Material rewards can indeed serve as positive reinforcements, but in the case at hand they caused the activity in question (drawing) to be attributed to a goal or purpose that had nothing to do with the activity itself. This, in turn, results in the activity's being carried out only as long as the reward is offered or can be expected when a certain person is present. Rita's activity stopped being spontaneous and interesting in and of itself – and she stopped being intrinsically motivated. Here, motivation becomes *extrinsic* and lasts only as long as a reward is given. *Extrinsically motivated behavior* is behavior that clearly displays external controlling variables.

An Important Differentiation of External Reinforcements

External, material reinforcements can, under some circumstances, result in a debilitation of the behavior as soon as the instrumental character is recognized or learned. McGraw (1978) proved that external reinforcements have a negative effect only on *attractive activities and not on more negative ones,* as it were, aversive activities (such as having to learn vocabulary). The destructive effect may be found only in attractive activities that have a *heuristic* character, that is, that are not guided by set algorithms. This is clearly the case with Rita's drawing skills. The results, of course, are not surprising.

Laws of Reinforcement Still Valid

The example given in this chapter demonstrates a limitation in the laws of reinforcement studied up to now (e.g., Thorndike's law of effect). The question is, which of the laws of reinforcement *are* valid? In any case, Thorndike's general comment that reinforcement is a complicated process consisting of more than pleasure and displeasure would appear to be true (Bower & Hilgard, 1981, Chapter 2; cf. Chapter 3, this volume). Lepper and Greene (1978) show (1) that many behaviors, especially those that cannot be intrinsically motivated as well as those we met with in the previous chapters, can indeed be furthered via extrinsic reinforcements (cf. the results of McGraw, 1978, given above), and (2) that destructive reinforcements are more or less limited to cases of intrinsically motivated activities and behaviors.

This does not mean that every form of drawing lesson will necessarily destroy the natural intrinsic motivation to draw; nor that every sort of prize as a reward for excellent performance will necessarily be damaging and should thus be abolished. There are drawing lessons that can indeed set the stage for the creation or furtherance of the intrinsic motivation to draw; many a drawing teacher is painfully aware of his or her great responsibility in this respect. This chapter serves to point out events or actions that may have a negative effect.

Handing out prizes on special occasions or at the end of the school year may have a very positive effect on some children, and indeed may serve some as a sort of substitute vicarious reinforcement in the scope of modeling. Such rewards usually emphasize not the individual activity, but the overall performance and tend not to be harmful to the intrinsic motivation for the activity in question.

6.5 Reinforcements Are Effective via Their Interpretation

When seen from a learning theory perspective as stimulus situations, reinforcements are grasped and processed cognitively, much as every stimulus situation that causes some behavior is grasped or interpreted cognitively. The effect of these stimuli depends on the mode of interpretation. If, however, as in the situation described here, the person is supposed to react positively to reinforcing stimuli, then the overall circumstances must be positive: The learner must pay attention to the stimulus, and the stimulus must be strong enough to be noticed. Yet the necessary attentiveness of the learner is not dependent solely on the present state of the organism (tired? excited?), but also on the developmental level of the individual. Small children may simply not have reached an adequate level (Aebli, 1969) to recognize or interpret the reinforcement (e.g., money) as such – that might even be their saving grace. In the case at hand, it would have been possible that Rita as a teenager would have recognized the instrumental character of the reinforcement and accepted it as such in order to beef up her allowance by drawing the desired pictures. Whether or not she would have enjoyed continuing her drawing activities would then have depended on her cognitive interpretation or evaluation of both the reward and her own artistic activity.

Even in cases of reinforcements associated with a person's anticipations or expectations, the corresponding effect may not occur or may occur only to a limited extent. For example, a worker who is expecting a reinforcement for his excellent work in the form of a raise will not be properly motivated if he receives flowers and a certificate: His cognitive evaluation of the reward is negative because of the discrepancy between his expectations and reality. He will feel improperly rewarded for his good work, and his intrinsic motivation may be damaged for future endeavors. If, on the other hand, flowers, certificates, and a round of applause are the usual rewards given out in a particular company, then the expectations associated with such reinforcements will be fulfilled, thus in turn affecting the worker's job behavior. This is the case in many companies, for example, McDonald's (cf. Peters & Waterman, 1982) and in Weight Watchers.

Memo

1. Reinforcements are events that raise the probability that past behaviors will recur. Rewards are not defined by their effect on any one behavior. Although they are in principle positive events, whether they in fact reinforce a behavior is not always certain.
2. Rita's drawing talent most likely has a genetic basis to it, which, however, must be activated and furthered through regular and consistent interactions over a long period of time with important persons in a stable environment – so-called proximal processes.
3. Intrinsically motivated behaviors are behaviors that need no external reinforcement to persist; they are carried out solely because of the activity itself.
4. Extrinsically motivated behaviors are behaviors that depend on external support and rewards to persist.
5. The attractiveness, open-endedness, and controllability of drawing activities played a major role in Rita's intrinsic motivation to draw.
6. Reasons for the loss of intrinsic motivation for an activity following an external reinforcement may lie in overjustification and the person's cognitive evaluation of the reinforcement. The overjustification hypothesis says that any external reinforcement of an intrinsically motivated activity is a superfluous motivation that serves only to weaken the intrinsic motivation. The cognitive hypothesis evaluation assumes that external reinforcements of previously intrinsically motivated activities are interpreted as being controlling, thereby having a negative effect on the intrinsic motivation.
7. The effects of external reinforcements depend largely on their type (verbal or material), their content (informative or controlling), the time when they are given (in advance, thus creating an expectation foreign to the activity itself, or afterward), and direct relation to the quality of the performance.

8. Verbal reinforcements may well strengthen the intrinsic motivation if they contain informative feedback about the respective activity. Material reinforcements (prizes, money) have a negative effect on intrinsic motivation, especially when they are salient and given for attractive activities with high heuristic behavior content.

9. Rita's loss of intrinsic motivation to draw is directly related to the loss of attractiveness, open-endedness, and direct control over the activity, particularly that drawing takes on an instrumental character, that is, is used to reach a goal (e.g., filling time) foreign to the original nature of the activity.

10. Reinforcing stimuli are effective only according to their interpretation by the learning individual. This may result in a reinforcement's having no effect if it does not correspond to the expectations of the learner.

(Deci + Ryan)

7. Waiting and Doing Without: Learning to Control One's Own Impulses and Behavior

In Cooperation with Joachim Hermann

7.1 Introduction

In this chapter we turn to the learning of a skill that plays an immense role both in an individual's life and in social life in general: the ability to do without something or at least to wait until the proper time has come (for all concerned) for its fulfillment.

This chapter may be seen as a sort of review of learning theory. Some themes will be treated more systematically, particularly punishment and learning by observation, i.e., modeling. But the most important theme of this chapter is learning or constructing plans or thought systems that allow one to control one's own impulses and behavior. In the previous chapters we have seen that certain behaviors can be learned with the help of external reinforcement; nevertheless, we expect of others (including children) that *their* behavior be determined from within – without any external help or control. The following case of "Ronald" shows just how difficult this can be. The various behavioristic and cognitive psychological aspects of learning present in this case will be discussed at some length.

Besides the most salient features of learning theory gathered from previous chapters, the following keywords will play a major role in this section: *withdrawal of positive reinforcement as punishment, the model effect of punishment, physical and psychological means of disciplining, plans for controlling impulses and behavior, cognitive structures regulating action* (action-regulating thought systems), *modifying stimulus situations, learning alternative behavior, delaying rewards, verbal self-control of behavior, reinforcing one's own activity, goal- and reward-oriented plans, correlations between specific behaviors of children and their parents* – the latter with particular respect to the ability to control one's impulses and behavior. Thus, the following pages contain a number of thoughts leading beyond what we have studied up to now.

Chapter 7 is typical of this book inasmuch as it attempts to demonstrate the extraordinary complexity of everyday learning situations and just how carefully the circumstances must be created to induce fruitful learning processes, which in turn work together to promote the development of the individual.

7.2 Action Outcomes and Their Reinforcing Effect

A young mother is at the supermarket. It is terribly hot. She's pulling her three-year-old son Ronald, who listlessly hangs on to the shopping cart, through the aisles. When she comes to the soft drinks section, he suddenly says, "I'm thirsty!" The mother acts as if she didn't hear and continues to put other goods in the cart. "I want something to drink," the boy says again, "I'm thirsty!" The mother takes a small box of orange juice from the shelf and puts it into the cart. "I want some orange juice. I'm thirsty!" he whines. The mother pulls the cart on toward the meat and cold cuts section, where she has to wait in line. "I want something to drink, now: I want some orange juice!" the boy cries, now somewhat louder than before. "Not now!" his mother answers, causing the boy to prove his thirst with loud cries and stomping: "Orange juice, I want orange juice!" Some of the other shoppers turn to observe the little boy. The mother shakes him: "Shut up, just shut up." That brings forth even louder cries and stammering only the mother can understand. Now, unsure of herself because of the looks of the other shoppers, she jams the straw into the juice box and gives it to the boy, who finally settles into drinking it.

Such a situation takes its course sometimes less, sometimes more dramatically than the one described. But the result is clear: The mother stopped the whining successfully by giving the boy something to drink. The boy can satisfy his need, and his mother is glad to end the unfriendly glances of the other people.

Let us analyze the event from a Skinnerian point of view, i.e., without considering the feelings and the cognitive processes going on internally in all those involved. Ronald is activated (a process that would be termed "motivation" within other theories) by the drinks on the shelves, and later by the box of orange juice in the cart. Such juice cartons have always been *stimuli* that preceded the satisfaction of needs; they are, therefore, *discriminative stimuli*. The fact that the mother does not focus her attention on Ronald's demand does not lead to a reduction, but rather an intensification of his activity – something that can often be observed at the beginning of an extinction phase. The mother puts the juice box into the cart without any consequences for Ronald; she shakes him when he starts screaming and stomping, both behaviors being *operant behaviors*. Her shaking him can be understood as an *aversive stimulus* – as a punishment. It is, however, more probable that the shaking will become

an *unconditioned stimulus* for a strong *emotional response* that is now accompanied by uncontrollable screaming: The mother has triggered a sort of reflex
(a *respondent behavior* in Skinner's terms). She then gives Ronald the juice,
and both his screaming and the staring of the other people wane. Both effects
are *negative reinforcers* for the mother which enhance the probability that at
some point in the near future she will once again give Ronald some juice.
Other behaviors by the mother (pulling Ronald away from the soft-drink
shelves or shaking him), on the other hand, were not reinforced, but rather
punished, by the increasing intensity of Ronald's behavior. This, in turn, may
have prompted her emotional arousal of equal strength. For Ronald drinking
the juice is both a *positive reinforcement* of his demands and a *negative reinforcement* because his emotional arousal decreases during drinking. Again,
this is the phenomenon of *mutually effective conditioning processes in social
interactions* (cf. Chapter 5, where Michael and the teacher also act mutually
in their social interactions): Ronald's inadequate demanding behavior is reinforced by the mother's giving him the juice, and there is a high probability
that the mother will give him juice again because she knows she can stop his
inadequate demands by doing so.

Other theories would stress different aspects in this situation. Dollard and
Miller (1950) would interpret Ronald's intensifying demands in the sense that
hindering him from attaining his goal – to have a drink – would lead to frustration accompanied by anger, an emotional state that has motivational effects
and may lead to aggression. Ronald's stomping might be explained in terms
of the so-called frustration–aggression hypothesis. Still other aggressive reactions would be possible in this situation, e.g., verbal aggression like "I hate
you!" Other theories would focus on the role of cognitive processes, particularly on expectations.

The same situation can be analyzed under very different aspects, whereby
the various theories are not necessarily contradictory, but try to explain different aspects. In the following section, however, we shall present the behavioristic learning view before giving a cognitive interpretation of the crucial processes in learning how to control one's own impulses and behavior.

7.3 How Mothers Can Control Learning – Alternative Possibilities

Yet not *all* mothers react as detailed above. The example given serves to point
out as well some *alternative patterns of behavior*, particularly the power of
extinction and *punishment*. For the child it is important to find ways to enable
him to *learn to wait* and to help him to come to terms with *frustration*; put

more broadly, to help the child to control his own behavior, including his own needs and subsequent impulses. Up to now we have observed how a child's *undesirable behavior* is reinforced through a mother's (apparently) successful actions. Yet the child has not learned to wait for the desired object and thus to control his own behavior.

Extinction

The mother did not respond to the child's first mentions of thirst. If Ronald cannot have something to drink, his behavior will not be reinforced: a case of extinction. After a short period of intensifying demands, they would probably eventually fade away. Yet, one might expect the complete extinction of the demanding behavior only if several visits at the supermarket were unsuccessful for Ronald. In our case the mother interrupts the extinction process during the phase of Ronald's intensifying demands by plucking a box of orange juice from the shelf and putting it into the cart. This *discriminative stimulus* now controls Ronald's demanding behavior because it has become permanently present, making an extinction no longer possible. The mother should have continued her walk through the shop to prevent this *stimulus control* from becoming active.

The child's own behavior control would not have come into effect, however, because the child himself would not have been its activator; nevertheless, the situation would have lost its impact. Here, we see the first solution for behavioral control based on Skinner's theory: The child learns by means of reinforcement to introduce a change in the stimulus situation by just passing the drink shelves and walking on.

Punishment

Why did the *physical punishment*, the shaking and the scolding of the child, fail to achieve success? No doubt, scolding is a rather strong aversive stimulus that would usually lead Ronald to stop his undesired behavior and lead to an avoiding behavior. But unfortunately, the juice box as a discriminative stimulus for controlling his behavior was permanently visible in the cart. Moreover, Ronald was really thirsty. But why does the shaking, which is in fact a much stronger stimulus than the juice box, not interrupt Ronald's behavior? Our assumption is that shaking was so strong an aversive stimulus that it triggered an unconditioned reflex, namely, a very strong emotional response. Ronald's screaming is, in this case, not an operant response, but rather part of a respondent behavior (reflex response). In such situations, the constant view of the juice box (or any other particular feature of the situation) could – in terms of classical conditioning – become a conditioned release for the emotional response which in turn raises the probability for later avoiding behaviors. We do not know whether or not Ronald has built up a conditioned emotional response; this would become evident only during future visits at the supermarket. Thus, it cannot be excluded that the mother's harsh *physical punishment* would have been successful, and that it would not have been necessary to give Ronald the juice box.

Let us speculate what the nature of a punishment, or a *threat of punishment*, would be that would have to be administered before the demands intensify and before the discriminative stimulus exerts behavioral control over Ronald. (We'll skip here the idea that the mother could have reinforced an alternative behavior of Ronald's by saying, "If you keep quiet I'll take you to the playground afterward.")

Since physical punishment would clearly not have been appropriate, there remains only the *threat of withdrawal of affection* or of *privileges* or the threat of *isolation*: "Either you stop right now or I won't tell you a story tonight!" Or: "Stop right now or you'll have to wait alone at the entrance for me!" Obviously, there are many other ways of uttering such threats.

Both methods of threatening punishments could cause anxiety in the child and a subsequent termination of his demands. For Skinner such threats of punishment are *aversive stimuli* that trigger anxiety and *avoiding behavior*. But let us look at the cognitive processes: The child interprets the mother's utterances, and the *expectation of the consequences* causes anxiety. On the one hand, Ronald stands to lose a special privilege (his mother's love and affection); on the other hand, he would be left alone in a crowd of shoppers. And the *knowledge* that the mother will indeed carry out the threatened punishment would substantially raise the level of anxiety.

Such threats of punishment, uttered at an early point in time, may in fact be able to direct the child's behavior to a certain extent. The child's fear of losing his mother's love or of being isolated may induce the child to control his behavior. Thus, a verbal threat of punishment (an aversive reaction by the mother) *inhibits* the child's reaction, which in turn is part of a larger set of behaviors that develop as described in our example if unchecked.

If one intends to employ punishment to inhibit reactions, it is better (as many studies have shown: Walters & Demkoff, 1963; Bandura & Walters, 1963, 162 f.) to use it early rather than late in the situation. In the case at hand, this would mean answering the first or second call for something to drink –

the undesirable demand to be inhibited – with the threat of withdrawal of affection. This stimulus situation, which would then occur every time the child wants something to drink, would be coupled with an anxious reaction and lead not to the undesired behavior, but to *waiting*. The reinforcement in this case is clearly a *negative* one: The child's ceasing all further whining and begging means there is *no* association with anxiety; that is, an *adverse situation* (standing at the entrance alone) does not occur. That is *negative reinforcement* in its purest sense. Such reinforcement may suppress or repress the undesired behavior during the ensuing waiting period.

Punishment as described above is an *aversive stimulus* of the mother. But this stimulus can be applied in various ways, with much or little aversion, with massive threats and aggression (reflected in one's facial expression, gesticulation, and voice patterns), or from a *positive stance* with *genuine affection*, in the sense of "That's not very nice of you!" Or a clear (and firm) *explanation* follows about the possible consequences of such behavior. This type of punishment, a *psychological* and not a *material* measure, can often be carried out with relatively little effort, as the child quickly becomes attuned even to *very faint stimuli* emanating from the mother telling him that he should not count on the mother's giving in to his demands. Here, it is said, children have an "antenna" for such messages and can "feel" whether or not they will be successful (the same is true of interactions between adults, of course). Such an "antenna" allows the perception of *discriminant stimuli* the mother emits, be it consciously or, more often, unconsciously (cf. the section in Chapter 5 on operant conditioning as well as Holland & Skinner, 1961). Thus, this "antenna" is not a particularly special gift of a few children, but rather a function of the respective person(s) responsible for bringing up the child: The person initiates the – for him or her – positive reactions in the child, which in turn influence his or her own behavior, including the type of discriminant stimuli the person emits. (Of course, these perceptions of even the faintest stimulus situations may have been learned *implicitly*, as already mentioned in Section 3.5.)

In Skinner's view all these variations of aversive stimuli are at the same time discriminative stimuli indicating that *no reinforcement* will follow, meaning the demanding behavior will be extinguished in one situation but will be reinforced in another: *differential reinforcement*.

But our example contains a further possible method of punishment, of a more positive nature: The boy whines and cries, and the mother does not try to stop him – but she puts the orange juice back on the shelf before leaving the store. Another way to prevent a new crying fit would be to buy the juice but not to give it to the boy later: the *material withdrawal of a positive reinforcement*, making the boy's crying in vain. The positive reinforcement is withdrawn, no doubt a strong frustration for Ronald! The effect is not easy to predict, probably an aggressive response by the child.

Yet, and this cannot be emphasized enough, the *context* of the disciplinary measure plays a major role. Here, too, there are a number of possible alternatives: First, the mother could start home and *explain* to the child calmly and casually just why the child will now *not* be getting the juice (delineating the contingency): She did not like his behavior and thought it rather naughty and will save the juice for another day when they can enjoy drinking it together – when the boy has done something *good*. Second, the mother could reproach the child: "Don't think you can whine and cry in front of all those people and get a reward for it." The third, and very sarcastic, possibility would be for the mother to drink the juice herself in front of the child. *And this does happen!*

The various methods of *withholding a positive reinforcement* have a variety of effects that are hard to predict since they are determined by the child's *early socialization and learning patterns* or, in Skinner's terms, by his reinforcement history.

The Model Effect of Punishment

One should note that a *model effect* can occur in the *way* the mother (the socializing agent) provides the punishment (Bandura, 1977, 1986); not only are such undesirable behaviors as whining and crying inhibited in the future, but at the same time behaviors such as affective attention, explaining, aggressivity, rebuking, etc., can be *learned* by imitation. Although the mother is probably not aware of her modeling effect, it may in fact be more important with regard to learning to control the child's own impulses and behaviors than the mother's conscious measures to suppress the screaming.

The punishments treated up to now belonged to the category of *psychological disciplinary measures*. These can be compared to the other type of punishment, *physical punishment*. The mother could in fact have given the boy a spanking or slapped him. The effects of physical punishment are varied and complex and are determined by the *context*, the *manner*, and finally the *extent* of such measures. In the situation at hand, but also in the long run, the mother could have made the child wait: By means of the *unconditioned reflex* (see above), this time induced by physical punishment, the characteristics of both the situation and the maternal behavior would have been classically conditioned. Even a *stimulus generalization* could occur such that the learned inhibition of an undesired behavior in this situation would be transferred to similar social situations. From expectation theory one would suppose that the child would anticipate the disagreeable consequences of his behavior and would behave himself appropriately.

Two major problems, however, surround the use of physical punishment (the same is valid for extremely aggressive scolding): From the above it becomes clear that the punishment must always be more severe or intensive than the behavior meant to be eradicated (cf. Azrin & Holz, 1966; Chapter 5). Yet this has its downside: The more compulsive the measures taken to force a child to obey, the less effective they will be. Such "obedience" does not last long when the punisher is not (or no longer) around (cf. Sears et al., 1953; Rosenhan, 1969; Lepper, 1973). Skinner says that punishments generally do not lead to the *extinction*, but merely to the *suppression* of a behavior as long as the punishment contingency is present. Yet, with reference to Bower and Hilgard (1981), we have critically taken up a position in regard to this point and stressed the effectiveness of punishments (cf. Chapter 5, Section 5.11, as well as Azrin & Holz, 1966).

Second, as mentioned above in connection with the withdrawal of positive reinforcement, we must reckon with *secondary* learning effects. Physical punishment or aggressive verbal rebuke can result in *model effects* in that they signify the *only* ways available – without exception – to control or regulate behavior. They are then eventually deemed the *best* methods at one's disposal to control or correct the behavior of others in *all* interactions. The child may not (yet) be able to employ these methods toward the mother, but he will certainly try them on his little sister or brother. Studies have shown that children whose mothers primarily or exclusively use corporal or verbal aggression to discipline their offspring use these same means with their playmates to guarantee and secure influence. Very prominent in these children is that they are then not open to, or even resist, other means, such as *positive reinforcement, explanations*, or *logical argumentation*, displayed by other important persons in their life (grandparents, teachers, or even playmates).

Thus, there are considerable detriments to the employment of physical punishment because of the secondary learning effects ensuing from the model effect of such disciplinary measures. What is missing are other *models of alternative, nonaggressive* means of dealing with undesirable behaviors in a social context; in other words, in situations in which one has to live with frustration.

With physical or verbal punishment, the following is also of importance: If the child were to get a spanking or a slap because of his fit at the meat counter, this negative experience would, for him, become connected with *a specific*, namely, the *last stimulus configuration*, which is in effect only the final one in a long series of stimuli and their corresponding responses. This was certainly not the mother's goal – in regard to the whole situation. As mentioned above, if a punishment is to be of any use at all, it must occur at an early point in the behavior sequence to prevent extreme reactions like the one described. Thus, the *time of punishment* plays a major role (cf. Johnston, 1972).

Even if a punishment contributes to an enduring removal of an undesired behavior, we must not forget that a desired behavior still has to replace the undesired one (see also Chapters 4 and 5).

7.4 Learning Plans to Control Impulses and Behavior

Components of Efficient Impulse and Behavior Control

1. Ronald had to be taught to *inhibit an undesirable behavior* produced by an environmental stimulus. His discovery of the juice boxes raised his need to drink and provoked his first statement: "I'm thirsty!" Thus, the first component of self-control of one's own impulses and behavior would be the ability to inhibit such reactions.

2. Ronald must, therefore, learn *not to do certain things*, something that is easier to realize if some other behavior takes the place of the undesirable behavior – an alternative behavior (to satisfying his needs) that has some connection to shopping. Among other things, this means that he has to learn that there are courses or sequences of actions consisting of a series of steps and goals, and that shopping is such an action sequence. In other words, the trip through the many aisles, having to wait occasionally, sometimes being served, sometimes taking things directly from the shelf, paying, and – finally – leaving the supermarket: all of these belong to the experience of going shopping.

    The simplest way of providing an alternative behavior is to change the stimulus situation. It would be to Ronald's advantage if he were to learn to change the stimulus situation *on his own*, for example, by going away from the shelves with the juice boxes, to avoid the stimulus completely. Such an alternative behavior is, in Skinner's terms, a *controlling response* (see Section 5.9).

3. Further, Ronald must learn to delay the satisfaction of a wish or need until later. It may be helpful to seek out a goal to pinpoint a more or less certain time when the reward is attained. However, one must take care that the

child does not develop goal representations that become anchored in his fantasy. Above all, the child must learn that *it is worth it* to wait patiently for something, and that the rewards, the enjoyment, as well as the pleasure of the mother and one's own pleasure, are then greater and give one the feeling of having accomplished something.

4. Finally, one should not forget to mention preventive measures that can facilitate the construction of plans to control impulses and behavior.

Ronald's learning to wait in the example given above is an example of the *learning of structured plans* that guarantee the control over a course of an *action sequence with a set goal.* If we include the goals of *all* persons involved (and they need not be the same for the mother and her child: She wants to shop in an orderly fashion, he wants to go home), we then speak of plans for the *action system "shopping."*

Looking Ahead

Let us take a look at what is to come: In Chapters 13 and 14 we will study such a system from the vantage point of memory psychology. A number of designations are possible: *encompassing cognitive structures, plans for action sequences* or *scripts,* i.e., the long-term schematic storage of conceptual information on more or less stereotypical situations, events, or occurrences in everyday life. Social knowledge is stored in this form as well, for example, as an organized and coherent series of events that can be anticipated in a particular situation (from the stimuli present); from this one draws one's expectations and extrapolations about what may or will occur in one's social environment. A script of this kind is then *recalled* (here, the "shopping" script) and employed to *guide* or *regulate* one's behavior (cf. Schank & Abelson, 1975; Abelson, 1976).

7.5 Crucial Areas in Learning Plans to Control One's Impulses and Behavior

In the following we discuss the four learning areas mentioned above in more detail.

1. *Suppressing Undesirable Behavior and Impulses – Learning to Do Without!*

Verbal Behavior Regulation

A number of studies (e.g., Mischel & Patterson, 1978) show that children can effectively deflect distractions from a task if they have a plan telling them how to act. Under the influence of a seductive stimulus (e.g., a small machine that starts running), children say to themselves (aloud), "No, now there's no time for that!" In our example in the supermarket with the undesirable desire for something to drink, Ronald would have had to say, "No, now's not the time for drinking – now we are shopping." This would have put a stop to the temptation.

Of course, we still have to discover just *how* one comes to learn such a plan for self-instruction. It is certainly not to be taken for granted that every child has such a plan and is able to use it.

The Model Effect of the Mother

Such plans are rarely spontaneous occurrences, but rather are the effect of *modeling processes.* Above, in connection with physical punishment, we saw that the mother has a model effect as an agent of disciplinary measures or, more generally, of *socialization.* Of course, such a model can have a very *positive effect* on the skill of learning to suppress undesirable wishes and acts; the mother must merely *demonstrate* the behavior to be learned: "Oh, I would really like to have some orange juice now! But I say to myself: *No, now's not the time to drink; now I'm shopping.* But I'm really looking forward to when we are finished with shopping!"

In the situation at hand, when the child said, "I'm thirsty," the mother could have reacted by saying, "Me, too. But I say to myself: *Now's not the time for drinking; now I am shopping!*" This would have made her the perfect model for Ronald, and at the same time she would have anticipated an incentive by setting a goal [see Section 7.5 (3)].

How to Reinforce One's Own Behavior Control

Ronald's learning of plans to suppress undesirable behavior will always be reinforced by the mother (operantly) whenever he displays even the smallest signs of trying to do without (Skinner's "shaping of behavior"), that is, of suppressing improper impulses and undesirable behavior. To this end she employs social reinforcers along with affective attention by saying that she's very pleased at how well he can carry out a certain behavior.

A short digression on the theory of learning: What we are discussing here is how one *establishes plans for self-control*, that is, the construction of thought systems or, as the experts say, of *cognitive structures* that guide behavior. It is interesting to note that very elementary phenomena well known from learning theory (e.g., operant reinforcement) appear in the context of these complex learning processes. Even if *cognitive learning* is a complex matter, elementary learning processes turn out to be integral constituents at lower levels of the entire construction process. In other words, cognitive learning processes known from everyday life do not rule out the elementary learning processes put forth by the behavioristic learning theorists.

2. *Focusing on the Main Activity: Trouble-Free Shopping According to a Plan*

The *first* skill Ronald needs for learning self-control is learning to inhibit impulses or behavior or to do without completely. Above we have seen that this is easier to accomplish if alternative reactions can take the place of the undesirable ones. In our example, this would mean all behaviors that serve to *shorten the necessary waiting periods*. This is true not only when shopping, but also in all other more or less stereotypical situations or ritualized occasions (ceremonies, church services, etc.). Of course, it is also important in the many unexpected situations experienced, such as when the mother is called to the telephone while playing with the child, who then has to wait for her to return.

Modeling

The mother shows Ronald how to wait (in the sense of learning by observation or by imitation; Bandura, 1977). First, she develops a plan for shopping that also contains activities to fill the waiting periods. She talks to herself out loud and gives the child simultaneously a running account of the coming stations or goals: "Now we go to the milk section, the vegetable section, the meat section." Or she relates exactly what they have to buy, how much remains to be bought at any one moment, before reaching the cashier. These are measures designed to direct the child's attention to the sequence of actions involved in shopping. Though they do not offer alternative reactions or activities to bridge the time gaps, they do prepare the ground. Together such actions form a shopping *plan*, and the mother demonstrates both the planning and the execution stages. Further, she hints at the role Ronald can play in this plan.

The child can predict and then experience more or less accurately how shopping occurs; he can also determine relatively well just how far it has progressed. The mother is his model especially in waiting situations, and it's the *way she* tackles the chore of waiting, e.g., at the meat counter or at the cashier's, that determines the model effect. Her patience or her impatience and irritability are transferred to the child and his behavior, respectively.

Waiting at the cashier's, by the way, is a situation that has been expertly mastered by crafty businesspeople: They present the customer with a broad spectrum of stimuli (especially sweets) as discriminative stimuli that become behavior controlling and cause alternative reactions – completely improper shopping behavior. An alternative in such situations is to occupy the child, e.g., by having him or her help load or unload the shopping cart and bags.

In this section we are reflecting on how to *focus* on the main activity. From earlier comments on unlearning undesirable behavior we know that *new stimuli* cause *new reactions*. In our example situation this means, quite simply, that the old stimulus causing a need in Ronald (the juice box) has to be removed and a new situation created. Ronald can learn from his mother's example how to create such a situation, viz. by moving on and turning one's attention to the other shelves. Of course, a verbal explanation by the mother would help, for example, "Whenever I see something I'd really like, I just keep on going." Below we take a look once again at methods of verbal behavior control.

The Child's Activity – Stimulations for Cognitive Learning

Since the child probably cannot retain all the steps his mother explained to him from her shopping plan and thus cannot judge when the longed-for end at the cashier's will come, he will ask again and again, "How much longer?" The mother can act preventively here by putting Ronald to work and not letting him sit by idly: "Today you can get the milk, and the butter, and the cheese." These are true *behavior alternatives* to waiting, which can be directly reinforced during the plan's unfolding. Helping load and unload the shopping cart or bags has the same purpose.

Further, the mother can involve Ronald more directly in the shopping plan (i.e., in the *semantic* context of the shopping plan). What used to be the rule in the small shops of yesteryear, namely, that the shopper calls out the wares taken from the shelves, is implemented here. She asks Ronald: "Do you know what this vegetable (fruit) is called?" Thus, he learns the names of items at an early age, elaborating in the true sense of the word on his knowledge of fruits, vegetables, and noodles! Of course, one could object that few mothers have the time for such games – shopping is stressful enough. The readers should make their own cost/benefit analysis! Later Ronald can take the items directly from the shelf *on his own*, a grand opportunity to reinforce his own activity.

Further, the mother can draw a larger context for the goods: "Let's see, we need flour, because we want to bake a cake. And what else do we need for that?" And one can explain early on things that Ronald does not necessarily fully understand: "I always buy the large package of orange juice since it's cheaper than buying four small ones." Here, Ronald gets to know the larger *semantic network "shopping*," even if he doesn't yet understand or remember everything. He becomes active, makes mental connections, notes what is "missing" and may even have a request the mother can fulfill. These are all cognitive prerequisites for Ronald's developing his own activity.

Verbal Self-Control

Since the child cannot take all wares from the shelves and cannot load or unload all items from the shopping cart, waiting periods will necessarily occur, creating an opportunity to use verbal statements for behavioral regulation. Such words focus directly on the activity or situation at hand: "I can help!" or "I can wait!" or "One thing after another!" The first two comments are of a general nature and refer to the child, whereas the third comment has the goal of behavior regulation.

It is obvious that the mother's model effect in verbal behavior regulation and control is very important. We should mention again, however, that the mother, by offering attention, affection, and social comparisons ("Look at that little girl over there helping her mother; how good you are at that, both of you"), consciously reinforces all new skills learned, in this case verbal statements.

Mischel and Patterson (1978) showed that plans for focusing on the task at hand are less effective than those employed to *resist a temptation*. Such studies, however, concern relatively boring activities such as copying squares filled with characters. Here, on the other hand, we are dealing with activities that actually help the mother and thus have a direct value. For this reason, it is reasonable to assume that the role of the action plans and their implicit semantic networks (knowledge structures) as behavior-control mechanisms for shopping is very large indeed.

3. *The Role of Incentives and Rewards – Goals and Goal Images*

Setting a Goal and (Once Again) the Mother as Model

Our story could have taken a very different turn: The mother could have recognized Ronald's thirst early on. She then becomes angry with herself for forgetting to give him something to drink at home and for not preparing him for the fact that shopping makes you thirsty! Thus, she develops a goal, both for herself and for Ronald: "When we're done shopping, we'll get some juice from the shelf. Please help me not to forget it! Then we can drink it when we've paid for everything."

This statement includes an *incentive* and creates a goal for a behavior sequence without creating a permanent stimulus that would cause the need for something to drink. The incentive becomes a definitive one, not only for the child, but also *for the mother*, who becomes the *model* for behavior control, viz. for *waiting for the delayed reward*. Such a procedure raises the child's chances really to learn what he is striving for, namely, to regulate and control his own behavior as well as to inhibit undesired responses on the way to the goal [for details, see Sections 7.5 (1, 2)].

From studies like that of Mischel and Patterson (1978) we know that *goal- or reward-oriented plans* have the greatest effect when they direct the child's attention toward the *positive consequences* of some action. The mother clearly did this through her statements to the child. Simultaneously, she also showed how the child can direct his behavior *verbally* toward the goal: "At the end, when we have gotten everything, then we can."

Reinforcing the Desirable Behavior: A Cognitive Interpretation

After they have paid for the groceries, together they receive the reward for waiting (or for the successful shopping tour, one could also say): Now they can have something to drink. That was the deal. The mother inserts the reward into the global context by showing her pleasure that Ronald has completed the task so well, helped her, and waited patiently to quench his thirst. She also tells him that she assumes this behavior in such a big boy and he has not disappointed her. It's worthwhile to wait, for the reward then tastes twice as good.

Experimental Findings

It is difficult to examine, empirically or experimentally, the learning of self-control in its broad complexity. On the one hand, there have been studies of children's ability to *delay* deserved rewards for good performances, i.e., to choose a later, larger reward instead of an immediate, smaller one. Here, *waiting for a reward* represented the control of one's own behavior (Mischel & Staub, 1965; Mischel & Underwood, 1974).

On the other hand, scientists have observed children to see whether they do forbidden things once left alone in a laboratory room (e.g., touching something, cheating): in other words, whether or not they can *resist temptation*.

A number of studies on the delaying of rewards have proved that learning self-control is one of the primary *sociocognitive* skills of great long-term importance which also allow generalization: The ability to renounce or voluntarily to delay immediate reward correlates with *reduced aggression*, with *increased social responsibility*, and even with *higher performance* expectations for oneself. Also, the parents of such children who have an increased ability to delay rewards tend to attach explanations to their disciplinary measures, above all concerning the *possible consequences of undesirable behavior*. They also *regularly reinforce* the desirable behaviors of their children and take their role as *model* very seriously. This shows that the process of learning self-control is one of learning more complex behavior plans.

4. Preventive Measures

Before going shopping the next time, the mother, as mentioned above, will try to satisfy the child's thirst at home. She could, of course, point out to him that the reward for helping her shop is already in the refrigerator. But it need not always be something to drink or eat: It could be a story or a game that is promised. It is important that the *character of the delayed reward* to be gained be clearly formulated. Thus, the mother's contribution is to control the child's reactions during the waiting period, for example, by providing alternative stimuli herself (diverting the child's attention), by removing or modifying existing stimuli that could cause disruptive reactions, or by reinforcing desired reactions.

Much as the mother can check on her child's needs (thirst, hunger, stool) before leaving home, she can also preventively control certain *expectations* in advance: "Today we'll probably have to stand in line a long time since we're starting out so late." With this she points out the difficult situation coming, sets up an expectation and *reduces the discrepancy between what is expected and what is actually experienced.* As well, the mother can anticipate the desirable actions of the child during shopping: "I'd be so happy if you'd get the milk and all the other things from the milk section for me today and put them in the cart." In addition, she can express her *personal expectation* of the child by making clear that she is counting on his help.

7.6 Behavior Control as Part of Comprehensive Plans of Behavior

A Brief Preliminary Summary

Of major importance is that the child assume the goals set by the mother (based on her explanations) and slowly become able to recognize such goals, to accept them (not always very easy), to set them herself or himself – and to judge whether or not they have been reached. With this the child begins to control his or her behavior independently.

At the beginning at least, success in setting up plans to control impulses and behavior depends on whether or not they have been adequately prepared, be it at home or while under way: that is, whether they have been explained *clearly* and *extensively enough* in a way fitting the child's understanding. The child can probably retain simple plans of how to encounter verbally any distractive or tempting stimuli, whereas the mother must occasionally repeat more complex plans of several steps to help the child remember them.

Action Plans as the Overall Framework

The preventive measures mentioned provide a *structure* for the coming events. This in turn prepares one mentally for the shopping environment in a favorable way. The child is spared major *discrepancies between expectation and reality* which might lead to resistance. The entire course of action, the roles the two persons involved (mother and child) play, are integrated into the process. If we take the other variables into account – the supermarket workers, the other customers, and perhaps the (incomplete) range of goods, which means they will have to go to another store – we see that in this situation the child learns to control his or her own behavior, to do what is desirable at the proper moment, and to stop doing undesirable things; that this is not simply a series or a chain of mere responses provoked one after the other by the foregoing stimulus. Rather, the child has learned a whole system of plans or an overall plan (after Miller, Galanter, & Pribram, 1960).

Such an *action-regulating cognitive system* includes the interpretations of stimulus situations in the respective context, expectations (i.e., mental images of fixed points in a behavior sequence such as reaching the cashier as a joint goal of both mother and child), interpretations of the reinforcements (including *understanding* why they cannot always occur immediately), as well as a broad network of relations among the individual elements of this system. Identical responses in different courses of behavior (e.g., verbal statements to oneself) can gradually be generalized, i.e., cognitively linked to very different stimulus situations, such as various shopping surroundings. Thus, they are caused not only by identical situations or the respective discriminative stimuli. Because of its high flexibility, including exchangeable elements of actions, such a plan or a cognitive system is more than a sequence of responses or a habit (in Guthrie's sense; cf. also Lashley, 1951).

Learning plans to control impulses or behavior means building up or (later) expanding action-regulating cognitive systems. When the child becomes capable of *metacognition*, i.e., becomes able to reflect on and judge his own thoughts and actions and to compare his behavior with socially acceptable values, he will *attribute successes* properly and develop a sense of self-esteem for his own capability to control his impulses and behavior.

Memo

1. Besides the display of aversive stimuli resulting from undesired behavior, a punishment can consist of the withdrawal or withholding of positive reinforcements.
2. Learning to control one's impulses and behavior means (1) inhibiting undesirable impulses (needs) and actions, (2) initiating alternative behaviors, and (3) delaying rewards.
3. The inhibition of impulses and actions can be achieved through verbal self-instruction. This skill is learned through modeling (the mother as model).
4. Alternative behaviors can be initiated by changing the stimulus situation; one learns them more readily if they are part of the main activity (in our case, shopping).
5. Delaying rewards is directly related to the verbal articulation of a behavior goal implying the positive consequences for the child (for suffering the delay). Such behavior goals are the most important components of plans for regulating and controlling behavior.
6. To learn and subsequently apply behavior-controlling plans the child must (1) cognitively grasp the situation at hand and the mother's goals in her dealing with the situation, (2) observe the mother's reactions. (3) The mother has to reinforce all attempts by the child at controlling his or her own actions within this situation.
7. Studies have shown that there are clear correlations between the ability to delay rewards and reduced aggression, higher social responsibility, and enhanced performance demands made on oneself.

8. There is also a high correlation between the ability of children to delay rewards (as a form of behavior control) and the following rearing methods of their parents: their disciplinary techniques, which typically include explanations of the possible consequences of undesirable behavior; their regular reinforcement of the desirable behaviors of their children; and their conscientious performance of their role as model.

9. Preventive measures provide a prestructuring effect: They ease the learning of behavior-regulating plans and can reduce possible discrepancies between expectations in regard to the situation and reality.

10. Constructing plans for impulse and behavior regulation is a sociocognitive learning process. (The cognitive processes are often considered to belong to the "higher" learning processes.) On the level of the elementary behavior organization of everyday learning situations we find elementary learning processes, e.g., operant conditioning. From this it is clear that a cognitive learning theory need not rule out the phenomena embraced by behavioristic learning theory.

8. Learning Prosocial Behavior: Sociocognitive Processes and the Acquisition of a Social Value System

8.1 Introduction

In the last chapter we looked at the ability of individuals to control their own behavior; in this chapter, we are more interested in the social interaction of human beings – or more precisely: in their *prosocial behavior,* that is, their behavior to the benefit of others. Here, too, we need an *action-regulating cognitive system* as well as a *social value system.* In the following we study the role of the emotional involvement of persons who trigger and maintain the respective learning processes. The learning of social value systems is a life-long process; below we take a look only at its beginnings.

Further key concepts in this chapter derive from the thought systems and behaviors to be learned: *the learning of expectations, the construction of expectation systems, understanding the social situation, inhibiting aggressive behaviors, punishment through exclusion, orienting responses to the emotions of others, learning empathy* in connection with *"affective explanations,"* and, once again, learning by observation and vicarious reinforcement: *learning from a model.*

8.2 A New Aspect of Punishment: Time-Out

Some small children, all between the ages of 2 and 4 years, are playing in the sandbox at a playground. Their mothers are sitting at some distance talking with one another. The children have yet to acquire much experience in cooperative activities; each is busy building his or her own towers or making sand pies. Now and then there is a little spat among the children, but the mothers take no notice thereof. Once, however, something apparently more serious happens: Though surely not without reason (of which we have no further knowledge), Peter bites Mary in the arm and leaves the clear imprint of his baby teeth in her flesh. Mary's mother comforts her and rubs her arm; Peter's mother takes her son aside. "You can't go on playing like that, Peter; you hurt Mary and made her cry. It's not nice of you to bite her like that." After these words she puts Peter with a few toys at a distance behind the benches where the mothers are sitting. "You'll have to play here for the rest of the day. If you play with the others tomorrow more nicely, you can return to them. Mommy wants you to be a good boy when you're playing in the sandbox." The mother has punished Peter by removing him and excluding him from the others' play. This is a particular type of punishment called "time-out" (Johnston, 1972).

The situation described above is, of course, somewhat simplified and thus idealized. The mood around the sandbox is not always so rosy, but rather tense, making it difficult for some mothers to react with such adeptness. Still, let us take a look at the most important learning processes active in this situation.

8.3 The Importance of "Affective Explanations"

The episode described is not an example of prosocial behavior; quite the contrary, it describes Peter's aggressive behavior, and yet it allows us to recognize clearly some of the mother's reactions – and to interpret these reactions in learning terms. The mother punishes Peter's aggressive behavior by *excluding* or *isolating* the child (time-out). Furthermore, the mother emphasizes her actions through *clear and insistent explanations.*

Imagine the situation in a more extended framework. *Prosocial behavior* (often also called "altruistic behavior") means *helping, comforting, saving, relieving, sharing, standing up for, protecting.* A study by Zahn-Waxler, Radke-Yarrow, and King (1979) produced a number of interesting insights into the relationship between maternal child-raising patterns and the prosocial behavior of the mothers' children.

Researchers were amazed to find that they could observe prosocial behavior even among very small children (ca. 20 months). One might have expected that children can first demonstrate helping behavior only when they are in the position to recognize the needs of the other person, that is, when the helper is able, to a certain degree, to take the role of that person and "walk in his shoes." Such *role-taking abilities* appear, as developmental studies have shown, only much later, during the grade-school years (cf. Flavell et al., 1968).

The children Zahn-Waxler et al. (1979) studied may be demonstrating an early form or *preform of prosocial behavior.* The important thing to us is to understand the circumstances necessary for learning such forms of helping, comforting, etc., behavior. In about one-third of all cases in which the approximately 2-year-old children caused others to experience negative feelings driving them to cry or scream, there followed spontaneous gestures of restitution such as the offering of toys, consolation, help, or enlistment of another person to help – all of which are classic forms of *prosocial behavior.* Yet the children did differ greatly in the *extent* of their offers of help. This inspired the researchers to consider the connections between the children's behavior and the child-raising behavior above all of their mothers. This was easy enough to do: The mothers participated in the study, and their upbringing patterns were observed. The mothers' *affective explanations* correlated most with prosocial behavior, for example, the mother's explanation in the previous tale: "You hurt Mary and made her cry. It's not nice of you to bite her like that." In other cases, the affective explanation might imply forbidding something coupled with an explanation, or withdrawing or withholding a positive reinforcement (one method of withdrawing love; see also Chapter 7). Another possibility lies in the expression of a certain amount of understanding (though not of the unconditional type) for the child's act, with a simultaneous expression of a clear and generally valid ban on some behavior: "I can see that you're very angry with Mary, but that does not justify biting her. That hurts!" There was no correlation between *neutral statements*, that is, *explanations without affective emphasis* (playing down the emotions of both the perpetrator and the victim) – for example, "Monica is crying because you shoved her" – and the learning of prosocial behavior. (More precisely: There was no correlation between this behavior by the mother and the behavior of the child.) A clear connection, on the other hand, was proved for a low level of prosocial behavior in the child and a mother's expression of complete but otherwise unexplained orders, "Stop it!" "Don't do that!" etc. – especially when coupled with physical punishment.

Thus, we can indeed observe some prosocial behavior among 2-year-olds, especially in children whose mothers present not only intellectual (cognitive) explanations, but also emotional involvement in understanding of both the victim's feelings and the anger or pain of the other person. They clearly show the child the limits of acceptance and demand respectful (later, socially responsible) behavior from their children (cf. Maccoby, 1980, 346 f.). One way to learn prosocial behavior is likely the early correction of aggressive behavior. In other words, if a parent can stop aggressive behavior with the help of positive learning conditions and offer other, nonaggressive alternatives, the aggressive behavior is replaced by its opposite – prosocial behavior.

8.4 Learning to Empathize

But what exactly is imparted to the child through ideal parental behavior (in the sense mentioned above), and what exactly does the child learn? First, there are the reinforcement mechanisms mentioned in previous chapters, which in this case do not reinforce aggressive behavior, but rather weaken it and clearly inhibit it. Isolating the child removes the child's privilege to be with other children: time-out. Of course, we are dealing here only with the final links in the behavioral chain that are touched on by maternal reinforcement/punishment; it is impossible to know whether the right stimulus situation (Mary again takes away Peter's sand pail or smashes one of his sand pies) might not once again trigger undesirable aggressive behavior.

A mother's emotional involvement apparently has a great effect even on 2-year-olds, in two ways: (1) Peter comes to understand clearly that Mary is experiencing pain, that she has some inner feeling not necessarily obvious from without, that the marks his teeth have left behind in her arm are the direct source of her pain. Peter learns about the *existence of pain* and learns that pain is associated with a *feeling*. (2) But the mother's reaction also demonstrates that we are not dealing with something peripheral, but rather with *something very important* and *valuable* to her. Thus, Peter is forced to deal with something that cannot be directly observed – with the *feelings of others*. This focusing is a particular type of *orienting response*, though it is also more than that (at least when repeatedly experienced): It is the *vicarious* experience of the feelings of another human being, expressed in crying, for example. This is what we call *empathy*: the involuntary, at times very intense experience of the emotional state of another person (see e.g., Hoffman, 1976). What we don't know is how much empathy in children is in fact partially the result of role-taking behavior. It is certainly important that small children understand that the presence of other children is something more than just a "spatial event" (which may at times lead to unpleasantness); that they experience each other as acting and reacting beings; that they become aware that other people have feelings. It is important, first, that Peter himself learn to experience the emotions of the other child, and, second, that the situation teach him that the emotions of another person have both a source (his own active participation) and consequences: His mother judges his behavior as not nice and has different ideas and expectations of him. Mentioning the affective results of Peter's behavior implies, implicitly or explicitly, that there are alternative, nonaggressive behaviors, including restitution (at the proper moment) and proper interaction with others in critical situations. (Here, we will not further consider the fact that Peter, too, has feelings, namely, anger. His mother can show that she understands his feelings while still reprimanding his behavior and pointing out the affective consequences of his behavior in the other child.)

8.5 Building up Expectations and Value Systems in Social Contexts

The learning process that a mother who gives *affective explanations* initializes is one of learning to *understand the social situation*, of lending meaning leading to the construction of a cognitive system of mental images and expectations, which in turn correspond to the mother's own values in social interactions. Although this cognitive system is a very rudimentary one in such a small child, it nevertheless forms the basis for a broad and encompassing system. A mother's neutral explanations cannot spawn such *expectations*, and least of all through unexplained demands ("Stop that right now!"), as is well known to all from daily life.

The establishment of such *expectation systems*, which in turn may later lead to action-regulating cognitions, represents the very elementary genesis of more complex sociocognitive learning. Remember that the development of such a system, assumed by the child or not, does not stop here; rather, because we are dealing with just one facet of the mother's value system, there are the behavioral consequences of the mother to be reckoned with: She reinforces according to her own value system, and Peter learns that his mother's behavior, which serves as a reinforcement (both positive and negative) for him, is directly connected to his rudimentary cognitions ("I shouldn't bite because that hurts others" and "Even if I'm mad at her, I shouldn't bite her").

8.6 An Alternative Explanation

For the sake of completeness, I should mention that there is another way of interpreting both the origin of empathy as well as subsequent prosocial behavior which makes no use of cognitive elements, leaning solely on conditioning mechanisms. The readers can decide on their own the merits of this method.

Empathy arises from a primitive form: Small children who see other small children fall and hear them cry will also start to cry. This sort of empathy may be explained via the classical conditioning paradigm: A small child has cried many times during his or her life, at various junctures, for various reasons. The common element to all of these events, however, is that there was always a feeling of discomfort present, a feeling of misery, of pain or something similar. Crying, be it one's own or that of another, can easily create feelings of discontent (or something similar) – even memories of earlier, similar events can have this effect. Thus, if a child hears another child crying and tries to put an end to this crying (by talking to the other child, helping the child get up, etc.), the child will feel good since he or she has just stopped this negative crying by his or her own actions (an example of negative reinforcement, cf. Chapter 5). It is in the child's own best interest to try to stop the other child's crying, giving rise to prosocial (altruistic) behavior.

According to Aronfreed's (1969) studies there are two prerequisites to prosocial behavior: First, the second-graders he studied who were to show prosocial behavior had to experience discontent or pain at the same time as their partners; and second, the partners had to emit *clear signals* they were experiencing *pain* (or some other emotion). Simply *knowing* that someone was not very well off did not elicit prosocial behavior. Whenever the mothers of those children who exhibited early prosocial behavior gave affective explanations, they turned the perhaps relatively weak emotional expressions of the children into more potent signals; or they led their own children to recognize even subtle emotional forms of signals that demanded empathy – the *vicarious experience of the feelings* of another person. According to this interpretation, the stimulus was now present which was able to elicit the empathy reaction and the respective behavior in the child. This makes the alternative explanation, supposedly based on conditioning mechanisms, a highly cognitive one; by addressing the affective part of behavior ("it's not nice of you"), a cognitive system which contains ideas and expectations that can control behavior is established.

8.7 Observational Learning

The facial expression interpreted as pain may indeed serve as a stimulus for some action that ends up changing the emotional situation. But what reaction is meant to be triggered? And where does the child learn what reaction is appropriate? Prosocial behavior in all its various forms probably does not occur solely because of some signal (in the sense given above), that is, from the ability to empathize; nor is it based only on some elementary cognitive system: Empathy and expectations may foster helping or supportive behavior, but they do not in themselves define the action fitting or necessary to the respective situation. Here, it is the behavioral patterns obtained through *observation* and *imitation* (Bandura, 1977, 1986) that slowly add to the repertoire of prosocial behaviors available to a child. Clear stimuli for exhibiting empathy or helping behavior on the basis of associative connections do not suffice; rather, complex systems of action-regulating cognitions must be present. This may be seen in the horrific and plentiful examples of people who, despite the extreme stimuli of someone being brutally beaten by another, do not interfere and help (so-called bystander effect). (One can, of course, argue that the strong associated emotions inhibiting immediate action have been conditioned.) Intimate knowledge and a broad understanding of the reactions of close persons as well as a sure interpretation of (facial or gestural) stimuli based on what they say and do (in other words, a well-established system of cognitions of one's immediate social surroundings): all these foster empathy and produce prosocial behavior. And the more shared identity is present, the greater prosocial behavior becomes, in which case it might be more appropriate to say that empathy merges into altruistic behavior (Krebs, 1975).

Empirical Findings

The studies of Yarrow, Scott, and Waxler (1973) have shown that it is possible to teach children prosocial behavior through observational learning. The authors observed firsthand the situation in a kindergarten chosen for the study. They removed those children already spontaneously exhibiting prosocial behavior and initiated the study with the remaining children. In individual training sessions each child was shown two successive series of similar scenes in which a human being, or sometimes an animal, was shown experiencing an unfortunate or painful situation. The experimenter took the role of the model from whom the children were to learn prosocial behavior. He began as follows: "Oh, Grandma, now the whole sewing box has fallen on the floor and you can't get to it because of your bad back. I'll help you gather everything up and put it back into the box. There, see, I put everything on the corner of the table. Now it'll soon be all right."

The experimenter expressly mentions the uncomfortable situation for the person(s) or animal(s) in the scene and thus emphasizes their *emotional state*, showing his own empathy both in word and in deed. But he also emphasizes the emotional value of the outcome: his own joy at seeing the situation take a positive turn for the unfortunate person in question.

The four phases of observational learning become clear (cf. Bandura & Walters, 1963; see especially Bandura 1977, 23): (1) The model (here, the experimenter) moves the child's *attention* toward his own words and actions during the negative and difficult situation for the grandmother. The affective *valence* of the situation is verbally emphasized. (2) One may assume that the child *codes* the most important elements of the scene (the action sequence) and (3) *reproduces* the behaviors, initially by imagining them, and can recount the most important parts of the conversation. (4) Finally, through the emphasis on the positive outcome of the story (the grandmother is now joyous at having received assistance), the child experiences the *vicarious reinforcement* that the grandmother is now happy, as is the experimenter, who (as model) is pleased at the way the story ends.

Following this observation phase, a second similar scene (in pictures) is presented in which the child participates. At the end of this second scene, the experimenter again becomes active: He emphasizes how happy the grand-mother is about being helped out of the unfortunate situation. The indirect reinforcement for the child is that he now knows that he has helped someone; there is no direct reward. If the child does not react prosocially in this dual-phase training period (by helping, comforting, etc.), the experimenter pro-ceeds to the second round of training without negative comments on the be-havior of the child.

The Conditions for Observational Learning

The most important question was whether and how prosocial behavior learned through modeling can be transferred to everyday life and made active there. It turned out that only when the training was relevant to real-life situations and when the child had a good relationship with the trainer (who had met the children two weeks previously) did prosocial behavior emerge. This confirms the results of the study of mothers' child-raising style mentioned above, that there must be a close and affective relationship between the two agents. Inter-estingly, the training sessions showed, if the child identified with the trainer, that what he *did* was more important than what he *said*. The *identification* of the child *with the model* included a number of commonalities: similar actions and verbalizations as well as a comparable planning structure. The establish-ment of such identification implies the construction of a system of cognitions that control and regulate subsequent actions. That "deeds speak louder than words" may have to do with the easier controllability or combinability with the overall system and the higher level of emotional valence.

A child's learning of prosocial behavior is not rooted in conditioning pro-cesses, but rather in the establishment and extension of a whole system of action-regulating cognitions, including the social value systems of the most important persons in that child's life.

Memo

1. A further form of punishment (e.g., of aggressive behavior) is exclusion, so-called time-out, the withdrawal of the privilege of being with others (withdrawal of a positive reinforcement).
2. The emotional commitment of one's most important persons (significant others) to the establishment of prosocial behavior, particularly in the form of affective explanations, has the following consequences: (1) emotions are directly created in the child, but the emotions of others are also recognized by the child, allowing the learning of empathy; (2) it shows that the important person (e.g., the mother) sees an inherent value in changing the emotional situation of the other person involved, and that one's own reaction to that value has its consequences (such as happiness with or punishment of behavior); (3) the explanations parents give, especially affective explanations as opposed to orders, help the child to understand the situation and thus establish a network of sociocognitive structures (construction of a social value system). The educating person can signal to the (aggressive) child a certain understanding of his emotions (anger) without approving of his behavior and its emotional consequences for others.
3. Empathy is the vicarious experience of the emotions of others. It is a prerequisite for prosocial behavior. Sometimes the ability of role-taking is also mentioned as being necessary. Prosocial behaviors are acquired through observational learning
4. Observational learning comprises four partial processes: (1) One's attention is concentrated on the model and – particularly in our example – on the emotional meaning of the situation and its social value (attentional processes); (2) the observed actions of the model are coded (retention processes); (3) the observed actions are reproduced internally (reproduction processes); (4) the learning individual receives a vicarious reward based on the outcome of the observed action (motivational processes).

9. Stop Test Anxiety!
More than Just Desensitization
In Cooperation with Joachim Hermann

9.1 Introduction

In this chapter we are concerned with the unlearning of test anxiety. To overcome this specific fear, the behaviorist theory of learning suggests using Guthrie's *toleration method* (see also Chapters 4 and 5) or Wolpe's *systematic desensitization* (1958); these will be examined more closely in Section 9.4 below. We will treat the same theme from the point of view of cognitive psychology in terms of "coping with anxiety," which concentrates on an *imbalance* the anxious individual perceives between his *interpretation of the demands of the test* and his *appraisal of his own potential*. First, we discuss the complex nature of test anxiety and how it is learned, and finally we look at the various possibilities of unlearning this fear.

The main terms used in this chapter will be *components of test anxiety, relaxation training, counterconditioning, desensitization, active inhibition of a conditioned response, antagonistic relaxation response, coping with anxiety, anticipatory phase and confrontational phase, controllability of the examination situation, expectations, antecedent determinants, adequate and inadequate coping strategies, verbal self-instruction, task-irrelevant cognitions (disturbing factors),* and *metacognitive competence.*

9.2 The Phenomenon of "Test Anxiety"

Test anxiety is the *feeling* that arises when someone before or during a test situation experiences a *discrepancy* or an *imbalance* between the demands he feels being made upon him and his assessment of own abilities and behavioral alternatives. Further, one is aware that one is not able to cope with this imbalance in a satisfactory way. The anxiety is not necessarily perceptible to others. In most cases, the sufferer first experiences it as action uncertainty before a test situation and as *stress* during the test itself.

The Components of Test Anxiety

The Behavioral and Cognitive Components

The action uncertainties mentioned above are quite easily recognizable: A student anxious about a forthcoming exam does not exhibit fully coherent actions. He stops work and starts doing something completely different, for example, drinking a cup of coffee or talking with his girlfriend on the phone. His notes are carelessly prepared; quotes taken from literature are unstructured.

He is exhibiting a clear disturbance in the cognitive control of his activities; he himself notices a marked *lack of concentration*. He allows himself to become distracted not only by stimuli around him, but also by his own thoughts. Ergo, his study plan suffers. Even if he has made a plan setting himself goals over a longer period of time, he does not stick to it. If the plan concerned the learning of subject matter in preparation for an exam, the learning process as a whole will have been inadequate. The subject matter is not divided up into suitable sections; rather, the sections are too large or do not correspond adequately with the material to be learned. This makes it difficult for him to code the information properly – to remember keywords, for example, or to be on the lookout for examples or analogies – i.e., to establish elaborate, complex associations between new and known facts, or to code certain contents as visual images (see also Chapters 13 and 14).

Particularly disturbing factors among the cognitive components are thoughts, fantasies, or daydreams revolving around the *anticipation of failure*, in which the possible consequences of failing are dwelled on continually.

The Emotional Component: Anxiety

The experience of one's own action insecurity and especially the (true or untrue) anticipation of the inadequacy or futility of any efforts and measures taken to improve the situation provokes a state of general *excitation* in the student, which may evolve into *worry*, considered a preliminary stage of test anxiety. Whether the individual student is merely worried or is already beginning to experience true fear depends largely upon the success of the measures taken to relieve the pressure – learning activities, getting help on the subject matter of the exam, etc. Here, the timing is important: Measures taken long before the exam date are generally perceived to be far more effective than the same activities effected only shortly before the exam.

The intensity of test anxiety, which we discuss later in more detail, is also related to the physical reactions accompanying it. This leads us to the next point.

The Physiological Component

Even people who do not suffer from test anxiety are conscious of a certain *restlessness* surrounding the time and place where an exam is to be held. This is a completely common physiological reaction. Test anxiety, however, goes along with more marked physiological symptoms. The most obvious ones – at least for the person experiencing them – are changes in pulse rate and galvanic skin responses (sweaty palms), though indigestion, muscular-tension headache or backache, and especially sleep disorders may also occur. Neuro-physiological reactions connected with memory activity and attention focusing go more or less unnoticed, as they are uncontrollable and not much is known about them.

Many of these physiological reactions can be triggered by simple stimuli and have been learned through *classical conditioning*, as we saw in the example of the small child in Chapter 1. Yet, it is clear from what we have observed so far that most reactions connected with test anxiety are not triggered directly by *specific stimulus conditions*, but rather by the the complex *processing* and *interpretation* of these conditions, i.e., through one's attempts to cope with anxiety.

Factors Determining the Intensity of Test Anxiety

Generally, there is a greater risk of an exam's becoming stressful the higher the standards of achievement demanded by it. Of course, this is only the case if the examination candidate accepts these standards and personally identifies with the goals set. It is important to note that the intensity of test anxiety is not determined by the *objective* standards of achievement required, but rather by the candidate's own interpretation thereof. This in turn is influenced by present learning characteristics and possibly by some personality characteristics.

The greater the *discrepancy* or *imbalance* between an individual's interpretation of the demands and the assessment of his own coping potential (behavioral, cognitive, and emotional), the greater the probability of an increase in test anxiety.

Here, the perception of how *controllable* or *manageable* the demands are is crucial. The more *knowledge* and *skills* the candidate has at his disposal, the easier it will be for him to control the demands. He is more capable of assessing both where the *gaps* in his knowledge lie and which primary *cognitive and behavioral measures* can be taken to fill these gaps. *Familiarity with the situational conditions*, including the *social context* of the exam, may also be decisive. Any clear *difference in competence or status* between examination candidate and examiner could increase the uncontrollability of the exam situation in a *socially interactive* sense. The less the candidate knows about the examiner and thus how he is likely to examine, the more stressful the situation becomes.

Finally, we must consider that every exam situation appears relatively uncontrollable when there is *insufficient preparation time*, whereas ample preparation time always imparts a feeling of freedom and controllability. Time is not meant as a constant, physical value here; rather, it can be interpreted only in terms of how the examinee perceives it and puts it to use.

The assessment of the *consequences of failure* also clearly influences the degree of intensity of test anxiety. The consequences may be *material*, *social*, or *individual* in kind. Questions such as "What will it cost me if I lose a semester in my studies?" "How will it change my relationship with my future parents-in-law?" or "What will my fellow students think of me?" may serve as some examples. Most importantly, the consequences may be experienced as a *threat* to the examinee's own *self-esteem*, resulting in feelings of anxiety.

9.3 Learning Processes Leading to Test Anxiety

Behavioristic Interpretations Are Insufficient

Any stimulus related to examination failure at school or in previous exams as well as any one of a multitude of generalized stimuli can function as a conditioned stimulus triggering anxiety, provided the corresponding response has not been extinguished by subsequent exam experiences of a positive nature. *External (physical) stimuli* are less significant; important are *internal stimuli*, sometimes extensive cognitions, such as *memories, knowledge, fantasies, anticipation, expectations, and appraisals* related to the exam situation and the consequences of failure. Bandura's (1977) sociocognitive theory of learning deals with this fact at length in terms of *antecedent determinants*. In other words, early (unpleasant) experiences relating to examinations do not cause a (classically conditioned) stimulus–response effect; rather, they cause one to learn highly differentiated *expectations* (Bandura, 1977, 55f.; see also Chapter 11). Therefore, the radical behavioristic point of view, which does not take internal stimuli (cognitions) into consideration, is too limited.

How would the radical behaviorist explain the fact that an exam *success-fully* passed despite intense anxiety does not generally cause a subsequent reduction in test anxiety – as logically ought to be the case? Test anxiety has probably been built up over many test experiences in school and is therefore lodged extremely deep: It would take more than one success to extinguish it. That is a satisfactory explanation for why *one* positive exam experience does not lead to an extinction of the response of anxiety to conditioned stimuli. The argument remains, however, that test anxiety essentially arises through mediating cognitive processes and is not triggered by *external conditioned stimuli*.

If we want to pinpoint the anxiety triggers, we must look for them in complex interpretational and evaluational patterns. In this chapter we will examine *desensitization* as one *method of unlearning anxiety* and discuss *specific stimulus conditions* and learned *response tendencies*, customarily found in behavioristic anxiety therapy. We will, however, also be stressing the fact that more is at stake here – anxiety must be dealt with more comprehensively. *Coping with anxiety* will be the keyword from the point of view of cognitive theories. (This continues what was discussed on the subject of desensitization in Chapter 5, Section 5.8.)

The experience of personal inadequacy that results from examination failure, the accompanying emotional stress, the loss or at least impairment of self-esteem, and the possible damage to social prestige are such *complex* (unpleasant) consequences associated with the subject of exams that we are forced to include cognitive explanations in order to understand the underlying learning processes. An explanation is even more difficult if the individual suffers from test anxiety without ever having actually failed an exam. This is also discussed below.

Learning from a Model and the Assessment of One's Own Competence

It is not necessary to have personally experienced test failure to suffer from test anxiety. In principle it suffices to imagine a fellow student failing, put oneself into his shoes, and imagine how he must be feeling (empathy). This sort of imagination can usually be traced to *modeling*: The individual has known other students who have failed examinations and has *observed* their behavior (including emotions, remarks made concerning possible consequences, etc.) before or after taking the exam.

But why does one student focus his attention on a fellow student who is about to take an exam? The model is currently in the situation the observer will soon be experiencing. In other words, the model has a *functional* value, providing both individuals are on a fairly similar level as far as competence, attitude toward studies, and so on, are concerned. Of course, the model also has an *affective valence*; the observer is not indifferent to his fate – perhaps they are even friends. As examinations are salient events in the academic year, those about to take them stand out as quite *obvious models*. Thus, the observer has a fairly large interest in observing the model, combined with a sort of social commitment to accompany the other person down one of life's paths.

So much attention is paid, in fact, to the observations that they become intensively *assimilated*. In the terms of *sociocognitive learning* (Bandura, 1977, 22f.), they are *symbolically coded* (in visual images and in words – people do converse with one another!). They become *cognitively organized* and are thus more effectively stored, and by remembering particular experiences one has observed (agitation, failure, and related behavior) one keeps them "alive" and *symbolically reproduces them*. The vicarious reinforcement of behavior patterns learned in this way probably stems from the important shared experience and the identification with the other person, leading to a commitment to try to help the other person in his precarious situation. In this way the student develops certain *expectations* relating to the situation and the demands of his own exam, along with all the usual symptoms of test anxiety.

As we saw in Chapter 8, the processes of attention, retention (storing), reproduction, and motivation or reinforcement are all very significant partial processes in *learning from a model* (see also Bandura 1977, 23).

Two concepts are particularly important to Bandura's explanation of behavior: *reinforcement* and *expectations*. Bandura, too, thinks that reinforcement processes are important, though he tends to emphasize *vicarious reinforcement* (in observational learning) and *self-reinforcement* as being just as significant as external reinforcement. However, Bandura does not consider the connection between behavior and the consequences of behavior to be a mechanical one, as behavioristic theorists would have it. Rather, he claims that this connection is mediated by cognitive processes: One's perception of the consequences of behavior leads to expectations concerning the outcome of an action. It is, therefore, the expectations that are learned. Whether learned behavior is activated depends not only on the stimulus situation and the expected consequences of the action *(expected result of action)*, but also very much on whether a person feels capable of carrying out the action. This is the so-called self-efficacy expectation. For many years Bandura studied self-efficacy (Bandura 1982, 1986) – for him it is a vital factor in the explanation of behavior. There is a close relationship between self-efficacy expectation and efficient action. The most important source of the expectation of self-efficacy is personal achievement.

Thus, the cognitive components of test anxiety can be unfavorable expectations of performance outcomes, for example, the expectation – for whatever reasons – that an examination in a particular subject will be "difficult," but especially a low expectation of self-efficacy. The latter has the following effects:

- doubts and fears, often an inadequate utilization of one's abilities and resources, which programs failure in the sense of self-fulfilling prophecies (Merton, 1948; also Rosenthal & Jacobson 1968);
- avoidance behavior according to one's assessment of self-efficacy;
- reduced effort in the face of difficult tasks and less persistence, and lack of motivation when the discrepancy between task difficulty and expectation of self-efficacy is high;
- reduced activities to plan one's actions and to modify the environment;
- greater dependence on external reinforcement and reduced self-reinforcement.

According to Bandura, therefore, test anxiety is learned on the one hand through modeling and on the other through a generalized low expectation of self-efficacy. (The case of Michael and his difficulties in the German lesson provides us with a similar example of this phenomenon; see Chapter 5.) In the following section we investigate possibilities of counteracting these effects. (Chapter 11 discusses the related phenomenon of learned helplessness.)

9.4 Reducing Test Anxiety through Counterconditioning and Desensitization

If we assume that specific stimuli trigger test anxiety of a particular type and intensity, i.e., that there are conditioned stimuli that produce anxiety as a conditioned response, then it must be possible to use methods drawn from the theory of conditioning to reduce this anxiety. But let us go further than the radical behavioristic theory suggests and assume that mental images and expectations may also function as conditioned stimuli.

The Search for the Triggering Stimulus Situations

What are the actual stimuli that trigger test anxiety in the examination candidate? Is it the entry on the calendar? Is it the leaflet bearing the official announcement of the exam or the books whose contents have to be learned? Is it the seminar room or the lecture hall where the exam is to be held? Is it the professor responsible for setting the exam, or the assistants who will be correcting the papers? Is it the fellow students asking "How're you doing?" Or is it the fact that, say, 30 of 70 (43%) of all candidates failed the last time? Or is it something completely different?

Obviously, the ballpoint pen used during a written exam is a weak stimulus for triggering test anxiety, though as an initially neutral stimulus it might become a conditioned stimulus (CS) for the anxiety response. At the moment, in any case, it serves to trigger the response of writing and not anxiety. It's a different matter altogether with the seminar room where the exam is to be written, with those ugly, gray-plastic-topped tables – not to mention the professor who decides which questions are to be asked.

As we can see, different stimuli have completely different degrees of potency or valence in triggering the responses of test anxiety. Anyone who tends to suffer from test anxiety should first determine which stimulus situations might be *his personal triggers*. The next step is to list these potential triggers according to their strength, from weakest to strongest. This look at the stimuli helps the student to get to know better his *own responses*. But what are his actual reactions? Does he begin to ponder – to imagine – how he or his parents will react if he fails? Does he start sweating? Does he run away from his desk? Does he start drinking coffee whenever he thinks of the exam? Or alcohol? Or does he light up a cigarette? Does he start listening to music? Is he tense? Does he realize when he is tense and when he is relaxed? It is useful to be familiar with one's whole range of reactions and to be aware of how diverse they can be. This helps in recognizing one's own *response tendencies*.

If a person recognizes phenomena of test anxiety in himself, then we are definitely dealing with an undesired response (or a number of undesired responses) to certain trigger stimuli. One could try to *avoid the stimuli*, but this would prove difficult, as they are encountered everywhere or are constantly present within oneself, i.e., in the form of *mental images* or *expectations*. You cannot evade them – on the contrary, the more you try, the more potent they become. The other possibility would be to try to *change the responses*. Since these always occur when the corresponding stimuli are present, as the association between them has been learned through one's own experience or observation, the only chance would be either to *anticipate* the anxiety responses and replace them with other responses or to *reinterpret* the potential anxiety triggers and thus produce other, more favorable responses. Let's have a look at the first possibility!

Counterconditioning and Systematic Desensitization

At home, the student could *imagine* his way into the various stimulus situations that cause him to feel anxious. Of course, this will not be easy: It's no fun to force yourself to feel fear. Nevertheless, it is possible, through continual repetition of an imagined stimulus situation, to *weaken* the response via the process of *exhaustion*. (We were introduced to this method in Chapter 4, Section 4.5.)

It would, of course, be better if the anxiety-triggering stimulus situation were to come to be newly associated with another, a *nonanxious* response. This is actually possible in a roundabout way. First, it calls for learning a new skill – that of deep *relaxation*, muscle relaxation in particular.

There are many relaxation techniques that can be used, ranging from deep breathing in a comfortable sitting position to autogenic training or transcendental meditation. The aim of relaxation training, whatever the method, is to condition muscle relaxation to become a response to a particular (conditioned) stimulus, to a keyword from everyday speech, or a so-called mantra (an accepted effective formula, originally from Indian meditation) such as "Peace," "Take it easy," or "Shumanom." This is a completely new learning process that must be undertaken independently of the test-anxiety problem.

Once the skill has been learned, a process that may last some time (at least several days), the student is ready for *counterconditioning*, whereby a new response is conditioned to inhibit an old response: The response of relaxation (the so-called antagonistic relaxation response) is to take the place of the anxiety response. To achieve this, the conditioned stimulus that triggers relaxation, i.e., the keyword, is brought into association with the imagination of the weakest anxiety-inducing stimulus, for example, the folder the student will take with him to the exam. The well-practiced relaxation response inhibits the response of fear – it is a stronger response and will thus become coupled with the anxiety-triggering stimulus, the folder. Through the conditioned state of muscle relaxation, which now replaces the anxiety response, the anxiety will be driven out, as it were; i.e., the anxiety is extinguished as a conditioned response (CR). Here, we recognize the active inhibition of an earlier conditioned response. *This is the deciding factor in the process of extinction.* (We referred to this Pavlovian interpretation of extinction as the inhibition of responses in Chapter 2, Section 2.4.)

Whoever tries to reduce test anxiety in this way will have to repeat the procedure many times before the anxiety reaction to the weakest stimulus finally gives way to the learned relaxation response. A student must practice the technique on many different occasions and give himself reinforcement every time it works, for example, by saying, "Hey, it's really going well!" When he has reached the stage at which the weakest of the possible stimuli produces relaxation without the anxiety reaction breaking through at all, he can continue to the next step by taking the next strongest stimulus from his list, coupling it with the relaxation-inducing keyword, and continuing with the counterconditioning process. His goal is to come gradually closer and closer to the exam situation in his imagination by working through the succession of increasingly potent stimuli while remaining relaxed at each stage. In other words, the idea is that if the progression is taken slowly enough, the anxiety responses (or phobic responses, as they are also called) can be extinguished one by one throughout the original sequence of anxiety-inducing stimuli. The result: The individual never again experiences the alarming anxiety responses (cf. Bower & Hilgard, 1981, 80).

Deciding on the order of precedence of weakest to strongest anxiety-triggering stimuli may prove to be a difficult task, since the variance between the stimuli that cause anxiety is in fact *not* of a gradual nature (like musical notes); rather, they actually differ from one another *in nature*. The step from *material* stimuli (the folder) to *personal* stimuli (the examiner) may prove to be a particularly large one, or the transition from *imagined* to *actual* stimuli may represent a huge stumbling block in the whole procedure. The success of the method depends on whether steps of a suitable size for the individual concerned can be found. Thus, the subject must from the beginning pay particular care and attention to the *sequencing of the relevant stimuli.*

This progressive technique is known as *systematic desensitization,* and it was developed by Wolpe as early as the late 1950s. As we have seen, it consists of *counterconditioning* with a *selection of stimuli continually progressing in strength* – here, relative to the triggering of anxiety.

The toleration method, which we looked at in Chapters 4 and 5, basically refers to the same technique: Stimuli of gradually increasing intensity are prevented from triggering an undesired response. The difference is that desensitization calls for the learning of an explicit antagonistic reaction, whereas with the toleration method this happens only implicitly and not systematically.

Not only in his imagination will the student be confronted with the increasingly potent stimuli; he will meet them face to face in daily life. It is, therefore, also advisable to bring the real stimuli into association with the relaxation response. This means going into the examination room, for example, and actually trying to relax by using the verbally conditioned stimulus ("Peace!" or whatever), though obviously only after successful completion of the relaxation training! This causes the room to become coupled as a stimulus configuration with the relaxation response. Here again, verbal *self-reinforcement* ("It's going really well!") should be used to support one's success achieved in the examination room, etc.

9.5 More than Desensitization – Coping with Anxiety: Cognitive Aspects

As stated in the introduction, test anxiety stems from a discrepancy or an imbalance perceived between the demands of an exam and the assessment of one's own potential. It arises when a person realizes that his own attempts to cope with this imbalance are unsuccessful. The goal is to learn how to get this imbalance "under control."

We can put it another way: Test anxiety arises when an exam situation seems *uncontrollable* to the candidate. Coping thus implies learning how to make the exam situation – and all that leads up to it – controllable.

Coping with test anxiety consists of two separate phases, each characterized by specific requirements: the *preparatory* or *anticipatory phase* and the *confrontational phase*, i.e., the phase during which the exam actually takes place (Krohne, 1985; also Krohne, 1975, 1981; Prystav, 1985; Lazarus, 1966; Spielberger & Sarason, 1978).

Learning Processes in the Preparatory Phase (Anticipatory Phase)

Assessing the Degree of Difficulty of an Examination

Coping with examination anxiety is primarily and most closely a matter of knowing exactly what is expected of the candidate in the exam. It is of great advantage, then, if one can determine – not directly before the exam but with ample time in advance – exactly what information needs to be learned in preparation for it. In this way the examinee actively controls the exam situation as far as its material contents are concerned. Of course, this is not enough: He must analyze the material closely enough to recognize where his own personal *comprehension difficulties* lie, i.e., where he is likely to encounter problems. But he can assess these adequately only if he has the ability to observe or review his own learning or knowledge-acquisition process objectively, by regularly reviewing his knowledge. He must not only be able to divide the subject matter into realistic portions, successfully code it (in examples, analogies, visual images, etc.), and then store it, but also to *retrieve from memory* as required, i.e., reconstruct contents (e.g., write down parts in a so-called free recall and evaluate their accuracy). In this way, he prepares useful retrieval paths.

This *process of retrieval or reconstruction* of learned information places high demands on a person not only in stress situations, such as during a test; it is above and beyond any particular situation in itself something that deserves much more attention than is normally given it. Practicing the conscious and voluntary retrieval of acquired knowledge is probably the most reliable way of systematically preventing the dreaded situation of "going blank" during an exam and not being able to remember things one is sure one knows.

Coming to terms with the subject matter of the exam puts the student in the position to estimate how much time he has or wishes to allocate for learning. Preparation for an exam can rarely extend to all areas of subject matter with the same thoroughness; one's learning capacity, interest, and limited time would not allow for this. A thorough analysis of the subject matter will help the student to get to know where his weak points lie, which areas he has merely learned by heart without really understanding the subject matter, and thus where he is likely to encounter reconstruction or memory problems.

Social Aspects of Learning and Examination Behavior

Many students learn best on their own, although this need not be the case. There are many advantages to be gained from setting up a social learning network (see Dansereau, 1988; Brown & Palincsar, 1989; Sharan, 1990; Steiner, 1997, pp. 97f.), which gives participants the opportunity to learn effective strategies and approaches from various models (namely, the fellow students), to test each other on the subject matter, to give and take feedback, and, of course, to keep learning motivation high!

There are a number of other socially relevant processes involved in assessing the difficulty of an exam situation which we have not yet mentioned, for example, interaction with the examiner. The student should make an effort to get to know him, to find out how he phrases his questions, and, more generally, to learn how he himself behaves in an examination situation.

The procedures outlined here imply various learning processes that we cannot discuss here in detail. In most cases they are processes of *knowledge acquisition* (see Chapter 13). But the *acquisition of social competence* is also important here.

Lazarus and Launier (1978) use the term *primary appraisal* to describe the process of *information acquisition* used to evaluate the degree of difficulty or stress a particular situation holds. They call its counterpart – the *appraisal of one's own action competence or potential – secondary appraisal* within the assessment of a situation as a whole. Let us take a closer look at the second term.

Assessing One's Own Action Competence

To judge one's own action competence realistically, one must be familiar with the situations (stimulus configurations) that trigger test anxiety and how they work. We introduced one possible method of coping with anxiety through the regulation of emotions in the section above on desensitization.

Other problem-oriented coping strategies can be used in the preparatory phase. Let's start off with inappropriate strategies. Gearing oneself toward *incorrect* information, such as exaggerations of the demands of the exam by others or its content at the *wrong* time, should be avoided at all costs. It is usually extremely unfavorable to procure "last-minute information" from fellow exam candidates, as it can have the effect of exposing one's own gaps in knowledge, thus increasing the perception of a discrepancy between demands and own competence at a time when practically nothing more can be done about it. This discrepancy may in turn lead to extreme test anxiety – even to panic!

Another particularly *inadequate coping strategy* (in fact a *defense mechanism* well known from psychoanalysis) lies in trivializing the importance of the exam or the consequences of possible failure.

We have already discussed adequate strategies in the section above describing how to *appraise the degree of difficulty of an examination.* Anything that leads to an increase in competence and of the controllability of the situation as well as to anticipation of better results is a good strategy. These include planning the learning process, especially *retrieval practice* (cf. also Chapters 13 and 14); practicing the reconstruction of connections; giving oneself or being given feedback on one's progress; realistically assessing one's own capabilities; and rewarding oneself for good progress – treating oneself to something of high incentive value, a visit to the cinema perhaps. Under no circumstances should the student reproach himself or try to convince himself he is incompetent because he has failed to achieve his goals or is progressing too slowly. Rather, he should review his learning techniques or quite simply increase his actual learning time, for example, by doing without leisure activities for a while (unless, as we mentioned above, they have a specific reinforcing or motivational purpose within the framework of the learning process!).

What actually has to be learned in order to achieve all this? First, *metacognitive skills* – the ability to analyze one's own thoughts and learning processes

– must be developed: in more general terms, *action-regulating cognitions*. In other words, plans of action must be formulated and the respective action put into practice. Finally, the plans have to be reviewed to see whether they were feasible and whether they were in fact carried out as planned. If not, they must be modified, and the whole procedure starts again from the beginning. This is in the Miller, Galanter, and Pribram (1960) sense of plans (cf. Chapter 3 and Chapter 7). How easy this process is for the student and how consistent the student is in carrying it out – if necessary several times – depend greatly on the importance attached to preparation and the exam itself, and how successful he feels his attempts are. Another important factor could be the support gained from a study group (social support system).

Learning Processes during the Confrontational Phase

Once carefully developed, many of the action-regulating cognitions discussed above also work in the exam situation itself (confrontation situation). However, we must take certain characteristics and requirements of this special situation into consideration.

Keeping Calm

The anxiety-triggering stimuli in an examination environment can be brought under control with the help of desensitization training. Even last remaining "twitches of excitation" can be tweaked by this method. In difficult cases, one can resort to the verbal self-instructions that created a state of inner calm during relaxation training ("Peace!"). But it is paramount to remember that a higher state of excitation than under normal circumstances is quite natural and in fact essential for high achievement.

Finally, we have the regulation of *internal anxiety triggers* and the *control of further disturbing factors* to deal with. Internal anxiety triggers include the sudden flaring up of doubts of one's abilities or anticipation of failure. Of course, anxiety can also be activated during the test situation if the examiner openly disagrees with what the student is saying (see below; also see Revenstorf, 1982).

Clever Strategies to Achieve Partial Success

Internal anxiety triggers can be deflected or weakened (at least in a written exam) by choosing an intelligent problem-solving strategy. One begins with simple tasks, thus ensuring partial success. This satisfies the immediate need for the experience of success, and the feeling of overloading or incompetence is less likely to appear. The possibility of negative self-assessment is turned around to become positive reinforcement ("It's going really well up to now!").

"Imprisoning" Task-Irrelevant Cognitions

Further disturbing factors stem from task-irrelevant cognitions such as fantasies, perseverating ideas, imaginations, or daydreams, which draw concentration away from the theme of the task, waste time, and leave one prone to anxiety triggers. Two behavior patterns can be learned and then practiced to prevent these disturbing factors and their corresponding cognitions from appearing. First, one must somehow "imprison" the disturbing cognition. The most successful way of doing this is briefly, but assertively, to turn one's attention to it, as follows: "I'm not interested in what my girlfriend thinks of me until quarter past twelve!" This serves to tie up the problem "girlfriend" (or its corresponding cognition) into a "package" and consciously to set it aside for a limited time. If this is not possible, the disturbing cognition will appear again and again. If the action is successful, however, one is able to concentrate fully on the task of the examination.

With less disturbing cognitions one can try a second behavior pattern. It starts off with either the verbalization of ideas related to the task situation or problem-solving or *verbal self-instruction* (discussed in Chapter 7) such as "Write, write, write!" and continues with the writing down of everything thought about. These methods help to steer the cognitive processes back to *task-relevant contents*. (For clinical applications of verbal self-instruction see Meichenbaum & Cameron, 1974, or Meichenbaum, 1977.)

The first method, the imprisonment of task-irrelevant cognitions, can also be applied to the disturbing interventions of an examiner during an *oral* exam. It is nothing out of the ordinary that a candidate cannot answer every single question posed during an exam; however thoroughly he has reviewed, he cannot have covered everything. Nevertheless, he is aware that he does have *a great deal of knowledge at his disposal*. So he can tie up a "package" containing the situation of "not knowing everything," just as he would with any task-irrelevant cognition (see above), and encourage himself to concentrate inwardly on matters relevant to the present task. This is a relatively safe way of preventing the occurrence of a *panic spiral* (Revenstorf, 1982, 155), in which a state of *excitation* leads to *self-devaluation*, which leads to the *anticipation of failure*, and finally even to possible *resignation*.

Looking back, we can see that the learning processes involved in *coping* with test anxiety are *constructional processes* of *thought systems* (cognitive structures). They can hardly be explained in terms of the behaviorist learning theory, counterconditioning, or desensitization.

The cognitive *learning* processes for overcoming anxiety we have discussed in this chapter can certainly be described as *higher learning processes*. They are extremely complex; i.e., they do not consist of clear, standard learning steps (algorithms) valid for all individuals. Furthermore, there is no absolute guarantee that the coping strategies learned will always be effective, resulting in their constant revision. The learning processes introduced in the following chapters will display more and more of these kinds of characteristics!

Memo   Key words in notes + underlined

1. Test anxiety arises when an individual perceives an imbalance between his interpretation of the demands of an examination and his assessment of his own capabilities (e.g., low expectation of self-efficacy). It also occurs when one's attempts to cope with this imbalance and the stress it causes are unsuccessful.

2. The intensity of test anxiety depends on the controllability of the situation (i.e., the amount of material to be learned, the examiner, time pressure, consequences of failure, especially damage to self-esteem).

3. Test anxiety is produced not only by specific stimulus situations, but also by what Bandura calls the antecedent determinants, e.g., memories or imaginations of exam situations when anxiety was present (even in others).

4. Test anxiety can be controlled by using the method of systematic desensitization, based on counterconditioning: An antagonistic response to the anxiety-inducing stimulus (relaxation) is learned and is then used to inhibit the anxiety response.

5. Methods based on cognitive psychology concentrate on coping with test anxiety. The individual learns to stabilize the imbalance between the demands of the situation and his own behavioral alternatives.

6. The coping process comprises a primary and a secondary appraisal; i.e., an analysis of the test situation and of one's own behavioral alternatives in both the anticipatory phase and the confrontational phase.

7. The learning processes in the anticipatory phase (the preparation time leading up to the exam) include an assessment of the degree of difficulty of the exam, various social aspects associated with learning and being tested, and cognitive processes related to the assimilation of the subject matter, most importantly the retrieval of knowledge.

8. The learning processes in the confrontational phase (during the exam itself) are concerned with staying relatively calm, using intelligent work methods to achieve partial success and to prevent experiences of incompetence, dealing with task-irrelevant cognitions and (sometimes linked to this) verbal self-instruction.

9. More importance should be attached to the founding of study groups that offer intensive cognitive exchange (retrieval training), social support, and strong mutual motivation within the framework of coping with test anxiety.

10. A Group Leader Learns to Cope with Stress: Cognitive Behavior Training and the Development of Action-Regulating Cognitions

10.1 Introduction

This chapter is a continuation of some of the prominent ideas presented in the preceding two chapters. Again we will deal with the development of thought systems that determine behavior. As in Chapter 8, we are primarily interested here in social interactions, though under a certain pressure. We will not dwell on the associated fears as we did in Chapter 9, but rather turn our attention toward the phenomenon of stress and how to cope with stress.

Our everyday situation will be that of the *leadership situation* of a newly promoted policeman who heads a commando group (for other police stress situations, see Ellison & Genz, 1983). However, *any* manager at *any* level in *any* company could experience a similar problem that would put him under psychological pressure for a certain period of time and require him to deal with the problem (investing additional personal resources, perhaps without success); in the end stress would result. Most of the learning processes for coping with stress will be demonstrated through a protocol from a leadership training program for policemen; the results thereof may be easily applied to other professions and work situations.

The keywords in this chapter are *stressor, levels of stress reactions, representation* or *mental model of the social or leadership situation, perspective and role-taking ability, role-playing* and *cognitive behavior training, dealing with one's own emotions* (e.g., *anger management*), *self-assertion and I-statements*, as well as *self-reinforcement*.

10.2 Stress as a Result of Subjective Interpretations

The Situation

At 7:00 a.m., before the night shift has been relieved, the day-shift group of policemen gathers in the courtyard military style in two rows. The group leader, Sergeant Jones, promoted just a few days ago to this position, is waiting to begin the morning report. He sees what the other men clearly see as well: One of his men, Corporal Smith, is standing with his hands in his pockets and letting his eyes wander about, as though not really a part of what's going on. To someone outside the group nothing special would have been noticed, but to those on the *inside*, someone was clearly about to undergo great stress.

Only an Interpreted Stimulus Becomes a Stressor

This clearly shows what our previous analyses of situations and learning processes have revealed: that stimulus situations are not *objective (physical) events* that cause a certain behavior, but rather that they become triggering stimuli through *interpretation* by the person in question. A neutral person might, if not distracted by some other characteristic of this man, see the corporal with his hands in his pockets as perhaps a somewhat sloppy member of the group. One wouldn't, in any case, perceive any signs of nonconformity in his actions. For the new group leader, however, things are quite different. Cpl. Smith makes Sgt. Jones see red – he's an antagonist bent on "getting" him. The very thing that the neutral person doesn't much notice (the hands in the pockets) is what becomes such a strong stimulus and in the end a *stressor* for Sgt. Jones.

An outsider can understand this situation only by taking a look at the leadership structure of the police station. Up until a few days ago, both Smith and Jones were corporals with the same rank, and for the most part they did the same jobs, assigned to them by their common superiors. Now one of them has been promoted to a higher level and has assumed the *leadership role* of his former superior. Smith, on the other hand, was apparently not considerd for promotion. This nonpromotion has taken on the role of an *aversive measure* – a punishment. It is at the least a cause of *frustration* affecting Smith's behavior, as we can see: He ignores the usual rules of behavior, for example, by putting his hands in his pockets and looking around as if completely uninvolved. He is exhibiting *passive resistance*.

Jones doesn't take very long to notice his colleague's behavior. The stress he is feeling is caused primarily by the fact that he doesn't know how to handle the situation. He realizes that he is being tested. To make things worse, the whole group is watching and just waiting for something to go wrong. What if Smith's behavior were to be taken up by the others? How would he ever be able to manage the situation then?

10.3 Characteristics of Stress

The above demonstrates some of the most important *characteristics of stress situations* (cf. Ulich et al., 1983; Laux, 1981; Lazarus & Launier, 1981; Ellison & Genz, 1983; Stein, 1986; Steiner, 1986). The person under stress has one goal, namely, to begin the day in an orderly fashion. And he is greatly interested in doing so *successfully*. That's his goal, his personal interest, and more still: his *ego involvement* in this matter, without which he would not be disturbed by the situation and would not feel stressed. Moreover, Jones feels directly and personally involved; that is, he feels responsible for what happens. If everything goes badly, his *well-being* will be affected – his *self-esteem* will be threatened! At the moment he feels completely inadequate and unable to master the situation.

Stress Reactions on the Emotional Level

Stress reactions on the *emotional* level have many faces: *Anger, irritation*, and *fear* characterize Jones's feelings. His anger is directed toward the corporal with his hands in his pockets; his irritation at the fact that his former partner has upset his plan; his fear as a result of his anticipation that he will be unable to cope with the present situation. He clearly sees the danger that he will make a fool of himself in front of the whole group, do something wrong or idiotic. And he must acknowledge the risk that everything may become even worse in the future, that everything may repeat itself, that *everyone* may come to act like Cpl. Smith.

   This description illustrates an *imbalance* between a *subjective interpretation of the situation and its demands*, on the one hand, and the *appraisal of his own competence* by Jones on the other.

Stress Reactions on the Physiological Level

We do not know what Sgt. Jones's physiological stress reactions are. We may, however, assume that the situation has affected his pulse, blood pressure, and galvanic skin response; that his brain waves (as might be measured by an electroencephalogram [EEG]) have increased; and that hormonal reactions (epinephrine [adrenaline!]) are also taking place.

One well-known emotion theory, that of the American psychologist William James and the Danish physiologist Carl G. Lange, proposes that it is such somatic, that is, physiological, changes that are noticed and *interpreted as emotions* relative to the situation at hand such as anger, irritation, or fear.

Stress Reactions on the Behavioral and Cognitive Level

On the behavioral level, no discernible reactions – or reactions noticeable only to very good friends – may be found. Perhaps Jones shifts his weight nervously from one foot to the other. He himself may, on the cognitive level, have the feeling of being unable to view the present situation objectively and to avoid overreacting. On the other hand, he may have the feeling of just simply having run out of ways to react and to save this difficult situation.

Stress thus arises in Jones's interaction with his environment. What he needs at the moment is *highly developed competence* in dealing with such situations. He notices this discrepancy, does much as the exam candidate of the previous chapter does between the demands made on him as group leader and his own ability to react appropriately. He feels externally controlled (Rotter, 1966), since his antagonist has put him on the spot. Certainly he feels incompetent, and he may be blaming himself and assuming his failure is the result of inadequacy (cf. Chapter 11 on the attribution of causes for failure).

The situation described above, which actually occurred as stated, shows that the new superior officer is in fact capable of getting through such a situation, even if he didn't react completely adequately on that particular day.

10.4 Learning Behavioral Alternatives in Coping with Stress

Thus, the question is, What would the sergeant have to learn to be better able to cope with this and similar stress situations in the future? When we assume a discrepancy between the demands made on someone by the environment and that person's own perception of his behavioral alternatives, there are two possible ways one may proceed: by changing oneself or by changing the situation.

Behavior Regulation through Action Delay and Verbal Self-Instruction

The physiological reactions arising during a stimulus situation interpreted as threatening can hardly be controlled (as illustrated by what happened to the jail guard in Chapter 2 and the teacher in Chapter 5). What can be modified, however, is how that stimulus is *interpreted* by the person in question. Maybe the interpretation came too quickly, too hastily, too thoughtlessly. If this is the case, the sergeant must learn to judge situations with more reserve and be less impulsive. Some sort of braking or inhibiting behavior would have to be inserted between the interpretation and the reaction. In such cases, a verbal behavior has often been recommended, such as saying to oneself "Now stay calm!" or "Easy does it!" – similar to the fervent prayers of earlier times. It's amazing how "modern" some of the "old recipes" can become: The Roman philosopher Seneca, a Stoic, considered counting to 10 to be a good method of "stress management" (cf. Schimmel, 1979; Tavris, 1984).

In fact, time *can* be gained by such methods, heading off quick and aggressive reactions. Further, quiet and smooth rather than crude words spoken to oneself (thus, no swearing) have a certain way of checking aggression and can be employed in such situations as well.

Learning to inhibit or to stop hasty reactions through *verbal self-instruction* or *self-stimulation* is based on positive experiences gained during learning experiences which have reinforced one's behavior. Such situations could, of course, be simulated in training, but by and large they are individual experiences that can be mastered by each individual. Reinforcement is obtained via mechanisms of *vicarious reinforcement* through observation or via self-reinforcement (Bandura, 1977). We'll return to this in the last section of this chapter.

Behavioral Control through Proper Representation or through a Mental Model of the Entire Social Situation

The sergeant in our example interprets the behavior of the corporal as a stimulus situation in the scope of his own representation or *"mental model"* of the social situation "boss–subordinate." We can only guess what is contained in this mental model. It most certainly contains *ideas, mental images, knowledge, opinions, views and perspectives, role assumptions,* and *role expectations* typical of a young superior; it probably also has its share of prejudices, perhaps even strong distortions in the perception of the present social situation: His social position within his peer group has greatly changed in the recent past through his promotion. In any case, under time pressure his present mental model of the situation, and thus his interpretation thereof, has led to an improper reaction: "It's about time that [expletive] Cpl. Smith obeys the rules during report times so that we can begin with our work!" This confrontation was not crowned with success: The other men looked around, exchanged glances, mumbled something, and Cpl. Smith only slowly adhered to the usual disciplined attitude.

The sergeant was not yet very happy with his role as superior officer, with all its social implications; i.e., he couldn't quite find his place and the proper social behavior in the social system he was a part of. First, he had to go through a *learning process* addressed to his mental model of social matters as well as the modification and flexible employment thereof.

Analysis of One's Own Role and Perspective: Change of Perspective and Role-Taking

It is above all important for our superior to take a critical look at his new role. Like nearly all newly promoted persons, he has the tendency to practice his new function so as to justify his promotion. He will probably want to change some things he didn't like before being promoted, though in a strongly hierarchical and traditional organization like the police (and in some private companies as well) there is not all that much latitude for change. Above all, however, he will want to gain acceptance, i.e., show that he possesses a certain measure of decision-making authority (we need not call it "power"), and that he intends to *lead* his group to the fulfillment of goals.

Some of his former colleagues in the lower ranks will be somewhat bothered by his new and strange attitudes. This new superior officer (like anyone who has been promoted) must understand that now others consider him a *stressor* and a stimulus causing annoyance (or worse) – with all the subsequent reactions that may ensue. Once he has accepted this fact, he will have the chance to understand the *reciprocity of social stimulus–response situations* or, put another way, of *complex social interactions*. His *mental model of the social system* will have to undergo a radical change. This understanding of the new circumstances is absolutely essential. The process is furthered if the person promoted takes a close look at the situation (the new hierarchical structure, the new procedures, etc.) from the vantage point of those not promoted, in this case particularly from the vantage point of Cpl. Smith (Averill, 1982; Tavris, 1982).

Establishing Action-Regulating Cognitions through One's Own Actions and Learning by Observation (Modeling)

Simulation of Different Roles to Promote Learning Processes

Imagining situations from the viewpoint of others is difficult for anyone. For this very reason it is important that various critical situations be simulated through *role-playing*, in which everyone involved has to play both his own role at the workplace and that of others. Such role-playing alone can serve to make one aware of many problems, whereas other problems – perhaps even the most important ones – remain undiscovered until observing someone else playing one's own role.

Experiences of this nature may initially be felt by some participants of such courses as producing real *stress*, perhaps even as *threats*, especially when the scenes are being recorded on videotape. But that too must (and indeed can) be learned: to play out one's own role, to endure the ordeal of looking in the mirror and of knowing that one is being watched by a small group of colleagues, to comment critically on one's own behavior, and to accept the (well-meaning) critical comments of others.

Why are experiences in such "make-believe" training situations so frightening? A simple answer might be, because we have not *learned* to deal with such situations, because we are not used to them. But there is more: there is the uncertainty about how much and in what way one will be exposed to danger or, in other words, the extent to which one's self-esteem is in peril. The participants of such training courses are not reacting pathologically when they feel threatened; rather, the initial discrepancy between their expectations and their experiences during the role-playing is simply too large, leading to emotional reactions and in part to improper defense against ensuing fears. For this reason, it is absolutely necessary to reduce this discrepancy as much as possible via *preliminary trials* of a more funlike nature or by initially carrying out the sessions without the help of a video camera. If these measures are successful, the participants will be much freer to "be themselves" and to be open to theretofore unknown phenomena.

The goal of such exercises cannot be the training of *behavior routines* for situations in which someone improperly stands around with his hands in his pockets. Thus, there must be a conscious effort not to promote recipelike reactions in certain circumstances. On the other hand, it must be made clear how little time usually is available in critical situations for considering appropriate alternatives. The goal of courses that teach participants to deal with such predicaments might thus be to instill in them a series of fitting and approximately equivalent reactions (cf. Meichenbaum & Novaco, 1978; Sarason, Johnson, Berberich, & Siegel, 1979).

A Course Protocol with Notes for the Group Leader

Sgt. Jones played his own role during one trial in the course, whereas someone else took the part of Cpl. Smith. This thus set up the original situation and allowed Sgt. Jones to deal once again with his predicament. But in order for Jones to learn to deal properly with stress, it was important that he have the opportunity to experience his own behavior from the vantage point of Cpl. Smith. An exchange of roles brought him some unexpected insights: Now in the role of Cpl. Smith, he was the one who provoked his new boss, recognizing that as the challenger he had a number of expectations toward his superior officer. A third variation, namely, repeating the scene with someone else playing Sgt. Jones, showed him as Cpl. Smith how his expectations toward his superior were being fulfilled or not, and whether or not he was "toeing the line" or becoming more and more aggressive (cf. the "spiral of anger"; see Schimmel, 1979).

The first round of role-playing was thus of an exploratory nature for the whole group: Each participant could adopt Sgt. Jones's attitude toward Cpl. Smith slightly differently. The participants were all more or less *verbally aggressive,* differing from one another only slightly. This, of course, did not yet fulfill the goal of discovering *alternative, nonaggressive forms of behavior* in stress situations. Jones had gained the important experience of being a subordinate and had, at least partially, come to know the effect of being talked down to by one's superior in aggressive tones – especially considering that that superior had previously been a colleague. It was strange to see how the same man who had become aware of his subordinates' feelings through role-playing reacted as thin-skinned and as aggressive to his own superiors. Up until his participation in the role-playing course he had not understood the *interchangeability of roles* (or *reversibility of viewpoint*) involved. Today he thinks differently: Everyone is both a subordinate and a superior.

Developmental psychology has shown us that *reversibility* in social matters, i.e., the capacity for perspective and role taking (cf. Flavell et al., 1968; Doise & Mugny, 1984), arises during early school years. If these capabilities are missing, as in our examples of police (and certainly in many other superiors as well), it is not necessarily a case of *developmental deficits* in the sense of *lack of competence*; rather, *situational* or *emotional factors* are probably impeding development of competence or its application in the situation at hand. Timely utilization of one's ability to assume roles is, however, the very thing that must be learned. Certain improper (= aggressive) and, for whatever reasons, readily available behaviors must be checked (or inhibited) and replaced by other more appropriate reactions. And this has to take place in stressful situations (e.g., emotionally explosive memories or in the presence of observers).

The variations practiced in role-playing are discussed in the group in terms of their appropriateness. Positive variations are repeated and reinforced by the group and the group trainer. The participants must above all understand that the discussions serve to expand and modify the (previously mentioned) *mental model of the entire social situation*, and thus to *build up action-regulating cognitions* in the participants – though practicing on one's own is also absolutely necessary during the course and afterward.

The Crucial Learning Processes

Especially decisive in initiating and completing the development of action-regulating cognitions in a mental model are *change in perspective* and *role-taking* (Averill, 1982; Tavris, 1982). This development comes about through the thought processes that take place when the learner has to deal with the views of another person during the same situation, and when the learner is forced to compare his own views with those of others. This is the great advantage of a group discussion over individual contemplation of some problem (there are parallels here to the *learning group* mentioned in Chapter 9, Section 9.5). Because many of the insights are not gained solely through discussions, but in active role-playing, they become more broadly and thus better coded. And this means that this knowledge, being a function of one's own learning experience and learning through observation and imitation, can be retrieved more quickly and is more appropriate for initiating proper behavior in everyday situations.

New Behavior Alternatives through Modeling

Should a participant not arrive independently at proper behavior alternatives, the experienced group trainer can suggest of better (nonaggressive) possibilities. This in fact was necessary in the course described here. One participant repeated the role of Cpl. Smith, and the trainer assumed the role of Sgt. Jones. He went over to the corporal and whispered a few orders to him, whereupon the participant looked at him with astonishment, smiled, took his hands out of his pockets, and stood up straight. What had caused this change of attitude?

During this phase, Sgt. Jones had stood aside and observed the trainer (the model); he saw how his behavior was *rewarded* through Cpl. Smith's adherence: He had *vicariously* experienced the reinforcement. Even if he didn't know exactly what the group trainer (portraying Sgt. Jones) had said to Cpl. Smith, he had indeed had the perfect experience of model learning! So what were those words addressed to Cpl. Smith? It was part of the learning experience that the participants were to contemplate what statement could have motivated the corporal to cooperate. Of course, there was not just one single solution, but rather many more or less good solutions. Each participant was requested to write down one possible version, some of which were played out and shown to be good models. Anyone not participating in the role-playing learned through the model. Because of the relatively large variety of different versions, there was little danger that the participants would learn only to implement clichéd behaviors. Replaying the video recordings also gave the participants precise feedback, through which they (especially Sgt. Jones) could make corrections to any discrepancies between their own behavior and the posited behavior. The slowly acquired behavior alternatives received an initial reinforcement in the sense of *operant conditioning* whenever proper initial reactions were supported. However, in the light of what had preceded (e.g., a growing awareness of the entire social situation), the reinforcement also covered important *cognitive aspects* (e.g., feedback) and led to an integration of the learned behavior into the overall mental model of the leadership situation under study. This turned the acquired cognitions into action-regulating and action-controlling ones. Such training, if properly carried out, is nothing more than behavior modification embedded in a *cognitive context.*

10.5 Requisite to Coping with Stress: Learning to Deal with One's Own Emotions

Once Again: Reactions on the Behavioral and Cognitive Levels

If we recall the different levels on which stress reactions take place, we may conclude (1) that reactions on the cognitive level can be influenced with the help of the extended and modified mental model of the overall social situation, and (2) that problems on the behavioral level can be solved (at least in part) by behavior modification training.

Physiological and (Particularly) Emotional Reactions

The question remains whether the stressor (here, the insubordinate corporal) also fails to cause a reaction on the emotional and physiological levels. Since emotions such as fear can be conditioned through classical methods (cf. Chapters 1 and 2), it would seem reasonable to assume that the stimulus (Cpl. Smith) would also lead to *physiological* and corresponding *emotional* reactions (cf. Chapter 5, Section 5.8, on the activation syndrome phenomenon). Proper coping with stress thus also encompasses another area in which behaviors must be learned. During behavior training like that described above only reactions appropriate to a *current* situation are learned. But coping behavior has a much broader task than that! On the one hand, Sgt. Jones's emotional reactions, which can flare up at any time through another confrontation with Cpl. Smith, were reduced or extinguished after the successful training sessions; on the other hand, because of the concrete situation Sgt. Jones faces, we are still dealing only with theoretical results: Jones has yet to exert his authority properly toward his subordinate in real life. Since having taken the training he knows how one *might* succeed in that task, but an everyday situation is of course different, and he stands to be surprised by some unknown and critical situation confronting him at any time. This *fear of surprises*, a special form of fear, together with his fear of not having the proper coping mechanisms at his disposal, remains active, at least in part. This can even make Cpl. Smith a permanent *stimulus of fear and irritation*: the red cloth and the bull.

Expressing Emotions in I-Statements as Part of Anger Management

In order to cope with such emotional reactions (or at least to temper them), one must directly confront them. Authors specializing in conflict solving or in assertiveness (esp. Gordon, 1977; cf. Bower & Bower, 1976) suggest at this juncture not to let matters progress to a confrontation with its many aggressive over- and undertones, but rather to present the emotion openly both to oneself and to one's antagonist (Holt, 1970; Alschuler & Alschuler, 1984; Biaggio, 1987). This should occur within a specific framework: It has proved positive first to describe to the other person what one observed and didn't like as a fact (in our case, the impolite treatment by the corporal). The second step is to express the emotion one experienced clearly: "It really upsets me every time you ..." or "It makes me so mad when you ..." or "I just don't like the way you ..." or "I'm disappointed that. ..."

Laying open his emotions will help Sgt. Jones let off the pressure he is feeling, and Cpl. Smith will, perhaps to the surprise of all, understand that his superior had a certain *feeling* that he too knows and can relate to. This makes the whole situation more *transparent* to all, both cognitively and emotionally speaking.

An emotion revealed in this way is difficult if not impossible to rationalize away. On the contrary, the road is now free to look for solutions to the conflict. The superior officer will thus give his subordinate or colleague the chance to change his behavior and to reestablish good relations: "Do you see a way of dealing with this in the future?" Such *nonaggressive confrontations* are called I-statements (Gordon, 1977), and they can substantially serve to defuse stressful situations or eliminate conflicts.

10.6 The Necessity of Self-Reinforcement

Being a Leader: Having the Courage to Intervene

The difficulty for most superiors lies not, as might be expected, in an inability to learn nonaggressive behaviors in order to lead their subordinates better or to express their own feelings better – although the latter *is* the source of many problems. Indeed, in some situations it is not easy to tell whether the person is angry, disgusted, offended, annoyed, sad or just fearful. A much greater difficulty would appear to lie in summoning enough *courage* to let the other person come forward of his own accord or to speak with the other person on one's own initiative soon after the incident and to confront him with an I-statement (Gordon, 1977) that would iron out differences and lead to a true change. That, in short, is the essence of *leadership*!

But many *inhibiting activities* work against this. Perhaps there's no time for such a conversation or one's calendar is already full. Sometimes, however, one's calendar is kept full (purposefully or not) just to avoid having the time for such conversations. Sometimes it is argued that there's no use in making a mountain out of a molehill – a very well-known psychological defense mechanism: playing things down. The disadvantage of this type of argument is that the molehill is no molehill, that the problem causing the conflict is very real and will continue to cause undesirable emotions. Also, the argument "That won't help anything" is only a pretense to avoid confronting the task at hand that *every superior* has: to lead his people so that both *they and he* feel well and contented. What needs to be *learned* is to have the *courage* to take such actions as superior. This is, of course, easier to do if one has learned to act like a superior in stressful situations and has learned to deal properly with one's own emotions. What stops a superior from taking such actions is usually the *fear of failure* and with it the fear of becoming unpopular with one's subordinates. To overcome this fear, one can undertake the same basic steps involved in coping with test anxiety (cf. Chapter 9, Section 9.4), though it need not go quite that far. The important thing is that it be *reinforced* that a superior has found the courage in a particular situation actually to *lead*. Reinforcement from others should be not be counted on, since most activities of this nature take place behind closed doors: What is needed is *self-reinforcement*.

The person involved needs only to think about what could be positive reinforcers – rewards – to him. Once he has set up a list of positive rewards (ranging, for example, in increasing intensity, from watching a movie on television, to opening a bottle of champagne, going to the movies, or taking in a meal at a fancy restaurant), he is in the position to reinforce himself at an opportune time following a successful activation of courage. It is obviously important that only rewards be chosen that constitute a strong incentive and are not part of one's everyday life.

Initially, what is not important is whether the intervention was successful or not, but that one had the courage to begin the intervention at all (letting the colleague come forward freely or addressing the matter directly via I-messages).

Though at the beginning such actions will mean having great energy and nerves, after a while they will become routine. This is important because there sometimes may be longer phases of high pressure, from the company or agency one works for or from personal matters (family, health, etc.), where such behavior is required.

Self-reinforcement is envisioned and consciously employed much too little!

10.7 Integrating Learned Behavior into Larger Structures

A successful exchange of thoughts (e.g., between Jones and Smith) provides on its own – prospective – reinforcement. This is a highly cognitive type of reinforcement, one that implies a complex interpretation of the new situation and of future perspectives.

We are interested here in *learning*, and that means in this situation practicing such interventions as a superior. This leads not only to *behavior changes*, but also to an *extension of the structure of the action-regulating cognitions* (of one's mental model) involved in being a superior. This integrates the self-reinforcement mentioned above into a broader scope, namely, into the same structure that guides social interactions as actions. With regard to the learning processes relevant to the development of leadership qualities, we can say the following: Behaviors are learned in the context of cognitive representations or structures that can guide action, and some of these behaviors initially appear to have been conditioned according to operant learning principles. But we should note that not every instance is an example of *spontaneous reaction*, as would be the case with operant conditioning; rather, we are dealing with cases that are *triggered by complex cognitive processes* (in part, by processes practiced in behavioral training sessions).

As to reinforcements, they too are not simply or exclusively *contingent reinforcements* given immediately after the decision to speak with the colleague. Normally, in fact, the *reinforcement is delayed*, and at the time at which it has been truly "earned" it can only be anticipated in thought. In this sense the reinforcement is a part of the same all-encompassing cognitive structure guiding one's behavior as superior – once it has been established as such. Still, it cannot be excluded that simple conditioning as well, especially operant conditioning, is active on a level of elementary behavior organization, something we pointed out earlier (cf. Chapter 7, Memo 9).

Memo

1. Stress is a temporary (transient) psychological state of overload that arises from the experience of a discrepancy (imbalance, disequilibrium) between the interpretation of demands from some ongoing situation and one's appraisal of one's own action potential, leading to increased effort (activation of additional resources). Stress arises only when important personal interests or motives are at stake.
2. Stress is not triggered by a stimulus situation per se, but rather by one's interpretation thereof. One and the same stimulus situation can lead to very different interpretations and thus responses in different individuals.
3. Stress reactions can be observed on various levels important to coping with stress: behavioral, cognitive, emotional, and physiological.
4. Coping with stress has as its goal the reestablishment of equilibrium between one's interpretation of the situational demands and one's appraisal of action possibilities.
5. Coping with leadership stress on the cognitive and behavioral levels is effected via behavior training to develop a cognitive representation (or mental model) of the social situation and to train nonaggressive behavior alternatives in stressful situations.
6. Learning to deal with one's own emotions is part of any strategy in coping with stress. This can be learned from assertiveness training, e.g., with the help of Gordon's I-statements.
7. Besides the behavioral skills learned in the scope of stress-coping courses (perspective and role-taking), initiating leadership efforts demands the courage to intervene, which can be acquired with the help of direct self-reinforcement procedures.
8. With the exception of operant conditioning on an elementary behavioral level (spontaneously demonstrated positive reactions), the learning processes involved in coping with stress are all higher learning processes. Because of intensive social interactions, which imply comparisons with the opinions of others, they lead to the development of a system of cognitions representing the leadership situation. These cognitions become action-regulating through proper training.

9. The higher learning processes mentioned above are complex, offer a plurality of different solutions, demand great scrutiny and judgment, and contain a measure of uncertainty in their results (Resnick, 1987). They are in constant need of revision (e.g., in the sense of TOTE units).

11. Learned Helplessness in a Secondary-School Pupil: Noncontingencies and Causal Attribution

11.1 Introduction

Human beings do not only learn skills and obtain knowledge; they also can learn attitudes that influence their learning, in this case, of mathematical operations. In this chapter we observe how a secondary-school pupil gains the feeling or even conviction that he is helpless when it comes to mathematics tests and will inevitably fail them. We will also study the conditions and learning processes necessary to *unlearning* such attitudes and putting confidence of success in their place.

As in the learning of higher processes examined previously, here, too, many layers become evident: In addition to the *cognitive* and *emotional* levels, we discover the *motivational* level.

At the center of this chapter lies the question of the *assumed cause of academic failure* in a particular course. We will meet with *causal attribution, complex contingencies, learned helplessness, unfavorable expectations of the controllability of a situation, motivational and cognitive deficits*, and *affective reactions*. As well we will consider the *shifting or transferring of causal attribution;* the *elimination of cognitive and motivational deficits*; the *regaining of self-efficacy*, i.e., the construction of adequate action and self-efficacy expectations; and the *reduction of emotional stress.*

The difficulty in this chapter lies in the confusing number of dimensions responsible for success or failure. Figures 6 and 7 present an overview of the situation.

11.2 The Situation

The situation is simple and unassuming: A pupil in his next to last year of secondary school gets the results of a mathematics quiz with the second-best score of the whole class. The honest praise of his classmates leaves him cold, and he replies with little enthusiasm, "Luck, all luck. The next time it'll be as always, I'm sure."

First, it is apparent that he reacts differently to his good grade than others. He fails to see his performance as a success, and he apparently *anticipates* poorer results. In a discussion of the situation he appears completely unsure of himself and cannot see any *clear links* between his actions during the math test and his present judgment thereof.

Anyone familiar with the boy's situation knows that a number of poor grades preceded this good one; his recollection of these earlier performances and the grades by his teachers has had a tremendous effect on him.

11.3 Complex Mechanisms of Reinforcement

Let us begin our discourse with the terminology of classical learning theory: Grades in school are certainly *reinforcers* – good grades reinforce *positively* – unless of course even better grades were expected, and poor grades serve as *aversive stimuli* and as such are certainly *punishments*. In the case at hand, however, the latter do not simply inhibit or dampen a certain reaction (after all, they did occur some time ago); rather, they cause much more complicated cognitive mechanisms. On the one hand, the reinforcers (grades) are *interpreted,* and it is this *interpretation* ("What does this grade mean for me?") that has the greatest effect. Later we will see that the boy attributes his success or failure to certain causes *(causal attribution).* On the other hand, in test situations we are dealing not with simple reactions that can be influenced positively or negatively or even modified in their intensity through praise or punishment (= good and bad grades). Rather, many *motivational, cognitive*, and *emotional* components are present in test situations: effort in preparation of the pupil, goal-oriented activities, learning ability, mental capabilities, fear about a particular test subject or test anxiety in general, depression over past failures. Also of importance is the person's own self-esteem. A test is thus a highly complex configuration of processes with innumerable reactions that, at best, can be reinforced in their overall complexity. But neither a single grade nor a simple learning theoretical explanation is sufficient to do this.

11.4 Complex Contingency Learning

Looking at the situation surrounding all types of tests and judgments more generally, we see that besides the actual content (e.g., solving integral functions or discussing a mathematical function) candidates learn that there is a *link* (a *contingency*) between (1) the *effort* invested in *learning* for the test as well as the activities during the test and (2) the result or judgment by the teacher. In terms of learning theory, one thus learns, besides mathematics, an *event contingency* over a midlength span of time and in a complex cognitive and social context. We already are acquainted with the fact that event contingencies can in fact serve as the basis for learning: Recall that even superstitious behavior can be learned from event contingencies (under operant conditioning) (cf. Chapter 5).

If our pupil is to be successful in learning mathematics, he will need the conviction that the complex events mentioned above are indeed related to one another; that his *learning effort*, the activities connected with the test and the results of the test (including a *judgment* in the form of a grade) are *contingent*. Such a contingency, however, implies considerably more, and more complex, semantic links on the factual and meaning level than a contingency in classical behavioristic learning theory. This must be remembered when reading the term *contingency* in the following.

11.5 How Helplessness Is Learned

But just what has the pupil actually learned (besides the math content)? Before we give an answer, we must first take a look, within the proper time scope, at the overall situation arising through the previous math examination and the respective grade: This is a prerequisite to understanding the *present* situation. We can discern a number of learning steps.

Becoming Aware of Noncontingencies and Discovering the Uncontrollability of Results

On the occasion of an earlier examination the pupil must have become clearly aware of the *noncontingency* between his activities during a math exam (including all preparations for the exam) and the respective grade achieved. In other words, he must have noticed some time ago that the results of math tests are not predictable, but rather *uncontrollable*. These experiences have sensitized him to the uncontrollability of the situation.

Causal Attribution

In the earlier situations he sought an explanation for his successes and above all for his failures; this can be seen in his statements to fellow pupils. Now,

	internal	external
unstable	diligence effort hard work	luck chance
stable	own skills talent	difficult of task

Figure 6: Simple causal attribution matrix with the dimensions internal–external and stable–unstable.

having achieved success, he attributes it to *luck*, a cause *from without* (external) that cannot be influenced and that is very *unstable* and *incalculable*. Thus, his success has an uncontrollable cause (cf. Figure 6).

This type of causal attribution of success has, as many studies have shown (Weiner, 1974; Abramson, Seligman, & Teasdale, 1978), parallels in corresponding situations of failure. In the example at hand, we do not directly learn of the attributions used but can presume them from the overall situation: Our secondary-school pupil most likely assigns himself the blame for his failures: "I'm just not good in math." Thus, he seeks the explanation for his failures in *internal, stable* factors (Weiner, 1974). Clearly, such interpretations of the reasons for failure can have severe consequences for one's overall learning patterns.

Setting Up Negative Expectations

The pupil's reasoning – his causal attributions – that his failure was due to insufficient talent leads to the *expectation* that future results will turn out to be the same, namely, uncontrollable (see also Chapter 9, Section 9.3): Talent is a relatively *stable* factor that cannot be greatly or quickly influenced. From this emerges a feeling of *helplessness* in math test situations. Here, we might speak of a *specific helplessness* restricted to the field of mathematics. But above all, the helplessness is of a completely *personal* and *individual* nature: The boy sees that others are quite capable of getting good grades, and that there is a *contingency* between their test behavior and the results of their tests (including the resulting grades). This causes him to *compare* himself with others, and that, as we shall see below, affects his perception of self-efficacy (Bandura, 1982, 1986) as well as his feelings of *self-esteem*. This is solely the result of his comparing himself to persons who are in fact similar to him and important to him.

The Consequences of Expectations: Learned Helplessness and Its Symptoms

Learned helplessness is characterized by *four aspects:*

1. *Motivational Deficits:* These we find in the pupil's statements: "The next time it'll be the same old story again." Obviously, he is not contemplating doing anything to change the situation. Motivational deficits are characterized by the fact that they do not *precipitate timely reactions or measures to modify the situation.* In our case, this does not come as a surprise: The boy has *learned* that whatever he does is useless, uncontrollable. In other words, he has lost his *motivation* to put an effort into learning or even focus his entire *attention on the subject.* This can be seen in his statement about the "same old story." "Who cares?" is often heard from such persons caught in situations of helplessness, though one cannot be sure that such a statement is not already the attempt to work through the failure by (falsely) playing it down.

2. *Cognitive Deficits:* It is very difficult for someone who has learned that his reactions (here, activities during a math exam) have no effect on the results to *relearn* that at least some activities in fact *do* have an effect and lead to desired results. Possible positive effects are simply *ignored.* In experimental situations (Hiroto & Seligman, 1975) it was found that cognitive deficits also have an effect on so-called cognitive control mechanisms, e.g., rehearsal for the retention of information, categorization, or drawing of conclusions. In this sense we see how easy it is to *generalize* helplessness to other areas.

3. *Affective Reactions, Particularly the Feeling of Depression:* Someone experiencing the uncontrollability of the results of own activities does not remain neutral. First, he feels *insecurity*, which, however, quickly turns into a clear feeling of depression. Should a success nevertheless emerge, such as in our example of the pupil and his math exam, then the person is unable to experience joy at the situation. Noncontingencies with a positive result (that is, unexpected and equally uncontrollable positive results) do not lead to depression; yet they still lead to insecurity and unfortunately do not dispense with helplessness, causing strong *motivational* and *cognitive deficits.*

4. *Damage to Feelings of Self-Esteem.* When, in cases of *personal* and *individual* helplessness, the subject has learned to attribute the causes of his failures to talent (internal and stable), he knows that *others are better off.* He compares himself to them and judges himself on that basis: He estimates his worth lower than others would. This is the consequence of *per-*

sonally and *individually* experienced helplessness. This reduction of self-esteem and with it the danger of damaging one's feeling of self-esteem are absent when the helplessness is of a more general nature, i.e., if *all* pupils were to fail the math test and experience the uncontrollability of the situation.

From our initial search for behaviors typical of this situation we can conclude that our pupil has learned to perceive better than others the uncontrollability of the results of his own efforts. Above all, he has learned to ascribe his failures (and even unexpected successes!) to negative causes and to set up negative expectations as to future efforts.

11.6 How to *Unlearn* Learned Helplessness

The behavior we have designated *helplessness* corresponds in many respects to what we know as *depression*. It is worth considering whether helplessness can be *unlearned* or at least how one could help the pupil in our example.

Shifting the Causal Attribution for Failure to External, Unstable, and Specific Factors

As we have already seen, the symptoms of helplessness arise from the negative *expectations* of uncontrollable events; the source of these expectations lies in the attributions of the cause of success and, especially, failure. Thus, unlearning means *modifying causal attributions.*

If we were able to influence positively the noncontingency expectation, we could treat the symptoms of helplessness. For example, we could lessen the danger of jeopardizing the self-esteem or perhaps even *raise* the self-esteem. To this end, the expected uncontrollability would have to be turned into controllability. An event becomes controllable when the causative factors are not hard and fast for all time: when they are not stable. If we could make clear to the boy that his failure does *not* have to do with any lack of mathematical *ability* (stable and internal attribution), but rather with his *insufficient or inadequate preparations* for the subject (unstable and internal attribution), he might experience the result as a controllable one (if other parameters were amenable). Thus, he would have to *learn* to attribute the causes of his failure differently than in the past.

Earlier, however, we pointed out that another symptom of helplessness – cognitive deficits – is manifest in the fact that subjects have difficulty believ-

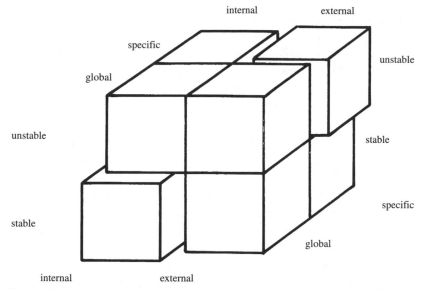

Figure 7: Extended model of causal attribution based on Abramson, Seligman, and Teasdale (1978). The attribution dimensions are internal–external, stable–unstable, and global–specific. The dimension containing the two poles general–personal/individual is not contained in this model. A student confident of his own success will attribute his successes as shown by the cube at the bottom left-hand front corner; failures will be attributed as shown by the cube at the upper right-hand rear corner. Our pupil, however, attributes in exactly the opposite directions: The recent success according to the cube at the upper right-hand rear corner, the failure according to that at the bottom left-hand front corner. To extract the boy from his learned helplessness, one would have to shift his attributions of failure toward those of the more confident student: external, unstable, specific. It should be noted that this model cannot contain all possible attributions. It cannot, for example, explain the successes of a religious person acting in accordance with Max Weber's Protestant Ethic or Gregor's credo "Omnia ad maiorem Dei gloriam."

ing that their efforts will actually lead to better results. Thus, changing only the causal attribution does not suffice to induce an unlearning of helplessness! More on this later.

As to feelings of self-esteem, the situation described for our pupil is probably better than other possible situations: His helplessness is at least limited to mathematics and is therefore *specific*, not *global* in nature. Comparisons with the performance of others turn out to be less extreme than in cases in which failure could be attributed to an overall lack of intelligence (internal, stable, and global!). From this we may conclude that the expectation of failure is highest when the causes lie in *internal, stable, and global factors* (cf. Figure 7). And such expectations depend on how important a particular examination is felt to be. To unlearn helplessness we must thus strive for an *external, unstable, and specific attribution*. Further, the importance of the event must be properly estimated.

Here, our pupil displays a specific attribution of his helplessness (solely in mathematics), so that there is a good chance that he can learn to focus on his successes in other areas. It is therefore important that he not attribute positive results in these other areas to external and unstable, but to internal and highly stable causes, i.e., his own abilities leading to these results. In any case, this must be considered as an adjunctive measure in the entire process of unlearning helplessness.

Shifting the causal attribution of failure from a lack of mathematical talent to the absence of proper preparation is only *one* way to make the move from stable to unstable attribution of failure. It is also possible (though not in our example) that another stable type of attribution is present, an *external* one: the teacher giving the exam. If failures are attributed to the teaching or the testing methods of a particular teacher (too difficult, too tricky), then we are dealing with an *external, stable, and possibly global* (valid for *all* tests) attribution. The resultant helplessness would then be a *general* and not a personal or individual one equally valid for all (or most) of the pupils in the class. The result would be motivational and cognitive deficits. The emotional strain, however, would be considerably weaker, and there would be no danger of decline in self-esteem since comparisons with fellow pupils would turn up no differences.

A further possibility of *external* attribution lies in judging the *difficulty of the exam* (the problems to be solved) as the reason for failure: an *external, stable, specific* causal attribution (cf. Figure 7). The question is *why* the tasks are too difficult. And the only answer can be, because the gap between the pupil's knowledge and the demands made on him by the tasks is still too large. The goal would then be to close this gap – to *reduce the cognitive deficits.* A causal attribution (for a failure) of the *task difficulty* would then be an *un*stable one since task difficulty could be changed according to the effort invested in the pupil's preparatory work.

Reducing Cognitive and Motivational Deficits

Above we said that shifting the cause for failure from the *abilities and skills* (stable) to the *effort* (unstable) is the first step necessary to unlearning helplessness: "I've got to work at it!" We also noted, however, that such a shift alone is not sufficient. Rather, the *cognitive deficits* must also be neutralized. The pupil must learn the missing skills with the goal of obtaining an *interim success* that will prove to him that one's own activities do in fact have an influence on the outcome. This is the decisive step toward *correcting expec-*

tations of uncontrollability or failure so necessary to any healing process. Further, such interim successes help someone suffering from helplessness with distorted attributions of failure (internal, stable, global) to gain a less distorted view of his own situation.

In terms of Bandura's sociocognitive learning theory (Bandura, 1977, 1986), we can say that a pupil's successive attainment of intermediate goals contributes to his construction of adequate action outcome as well as self-efficacy expectations: He recognizes that there are, indeed, goals he can reach (Bandura & Schunk, 1981), and he believes anew that he has the abilities and skills necessary to reach them (Bandura, 1989, 1991). If the discrepancy between the task requirements and the self-efficacy expectations is very big, however, a whole series of specific abilities that we know from the action-regulation literature (e.g., Kuhl & Kraska, 1989) is compulsory: In the case of very hard tasks, the student has to concentrate on the problems and *not allow diverting activities* (which would lead to *avoiding behavior*), but instead to enhance his persistence by shortening the learning steps and by tenaciously continuing the learning process only after having ensured that the intermediate goal is being reached, i.e., that he has attained a high level of understanding. In case of strong resistance by a learning problem, he would have to look for learning alternatives and avoid in any case lamenting the difficulties at hand. In other words, he would have to behave in an *action-oriented* manner (Kuhl, 1984, 1985). Such measures are of a motivational or volitional nature and refer to the regulation of the learning activities; they are, all in all, an indispensable foundation for reducing cognitive deficits as is required by our pupil (cf. again Chapter 9, Section 9.3).

Yet it is not always easy to acquire new skills in school. One prerequisite would be a detailed analysis of errors made on the examination tasks and a corresponding analysis of the learning processes. But there are only limited possibilities in this respect. On the one hand, it is often heard, the class time is not sufficient for the teacher to attend to the individual problems of all pupils; on the other hand, when the results are handed out, the exam is often already two weeks past, and it is difficult to reconstruct exactly where the class was in the curriculum at that particular time. For the pupil it is almost impossible to determine a *causal link* between cognitive learning (including all *efforts*) and the solution to mathematical problems in the test, i.e., the retrieval of the respective processes. This situation is widespread and from a learning psychological point of view shows the absolutely scandalous state of affairs in school classroom instruction. Analyses of errors and learning processes are virtually impossible in such cases. In addition, because of the widespread teaching method in which the instruction is simply continued without giving individual *feedback* to the pupils, it is clear, if not inevitable, that there will be *cumulative learning deficits* that both teachers and pupils do not register. What they note, of course, with great surprise or consternation, is that the results become poorer.

Despite all problems present in the classroom situation, our pupil must try to attain interim successes and thus a *confidence in the controllability* of test results by more intensive learning efforts. One form of the above-mentioned *analysis of learning processes* by the pupil, however, is indispensable; apparently there is a discrepancy between the *subjective interpretation of learning* or *understanding* of mathematical operations and the "objective judgment" of such operations by the teacher. Only after one has grasped the nature of the tasks at hand (and this is true not only for mathematics, but also for every subject in school in which a network of operations or conceptual knowledge, of facts and connections, is to be learned) can one learn just where the "root" of failure lies. What leads to success: *efforts? skills? chance? difficulty of the tasks presented* (cf. Figures 6 and 7; see also Meyer & Hallermann, 1974; Meyer, 1984; Weiner, 1974, 1985)?

In other words, only by first learning to *judge the difference* between the teacher's and one's own performance standards can the pupil truly deduce the actual *controllability of the situation*: The contingency of events becomes clear. Such insights into the processes of learning and (in mathematics particularly) understanding are accompanied by the *rectification of motivational deficits*. The experience of interim successes makes it easier to launch other measures, for example, commencing immediately with intensive learning efforts. But also the *cognitive deficits* are reduced: The gradual understanding of mathematical operations mobilizes cognitive control processes (see above) that are of great importance to overall learning.

The Role of Social Interactions in the Reduction of Cognitive Deficits

The best thing for our pupil would be to reduce any deficits in his understanding of mathematics by cooperating with other pupils in his class. Such cooperation allows comparison of one's own approaches with those of others and helps solidify processes of mathematical thought structures necessary to pass exams. (In Chapters 9 and 10 we discovered a parallel to this type of cooperation to establish cognitive structures.)

Of course, it would also be advantageous for the pupil to interact with the teacher, who could give concrete tips as to what else the pupil should concentrate on. Perhaps the teacher would even then discover the true problems pupils have, and that in turn would surely have an effect on his own teaching.

Reducing the Emotional Stress (Depression)

The emotional stress in the learned helplessness situation is a product of the perception of the uncontrollability of events. Yet one should also note that a multitude of uncontrollable events occur in life without provoking any emotional stress. Stress in the sense of learned helplessness arises, first, when one experiences personal–individual helplessness (not present in global helplessness) and, second, when the result is very important or desirable or when the occurrence of a negative event is greatly feared. (This reveals a parallel to the development of stress discussed in Chapter 10, Memo 1.) Only by shifting the attribution of cause to unstable factors and by acquiring the missing skills does the situation become, at least in part, controllable once again. This, in turn, enhances the probability that the emotional stress (depression, disappointment, ctc.) will find relief.

Further, it is important, as noted above, that the pupil become aware of the nonglobality of his failures. And we noted that the importance of the upcoming event (exam) influences the intensity of both the expectation of failure and the resulting emotional stress. These insights lead us to propose the following, further possibility of diminishing helplessness: The pupil must be convinced that progress in school matters is not dependent on the results of a *single* examination. In other words, he must spread out his efforts over the entire year and thus circumvent any "critical" situation from the very beginning.

Other Factors

The above obviously does not cover *all* learning steps or learning sequences necessary to unlearning helplessness. That would be possible only if we were to take into consideration the individual characteristics of the pupil in question, for example, his *style of attribution* or his ability to cope with stress. We have chosen to depict the *overall conditions* according to the theory of cognitive learning; these form the basis for *unlearning helplessness* and *(re)learning the controllability of events* (cf. Abramson et al., 1978; Alloy & Abramson, 1979; Seligman et al., 1984; Nolen-Hoeksma, Girgus & Seligman, 1986).

Memo

1. Helplessness arises from the experience of the noncontingency of one's own efforts and the interpretation thereof, and from a subsequent sensitivity to the overall uncontrollability of events through one's own efforts. One presumes certain causes for the failures experienced in such situations; that presumption leads to negative expectations with respect to future demands.
2. The symptoms of learned helplessness are as follows: (1) motivational deficits, (2) cognitive deficits, (3) affective reactions (e.g., depression), and (4) threat of or loss of self-esteem.
3. We attribute causes to any successes and failures experienced. These causes are situated in the dimensions internal/external, stable/unstable, specific/global, and personal–individual/general (see Figure 7).
4. The characteristic causal attribution for failure with learned helplessness is internal, stable, and global: "I'm completely untalented. It's not worth the effort. Nothing I do succeeds, not just in math."
5. Learned helplessness can be corrected by shifting the causal attribution toward the other poles of the dimensions (at least unstable and specific) and by systematically reducing cognitive deficits.
6. The shift in causal attribution for failures must be as follows: "The problem does not lie in my abilities; I can achieve much by my own efforts [not stable, but unstable]; I'm pretty good in other fields [not global, but specific]." Or sometimes external: "I had a real bad day!"
7. For reducing cognitive deficits even in small steps, adequate motivational as well as volitional measures are necessary, above all measures of one's own action control. In case of discrepancies between task requirements and self-efficacy expectations, the pupil has to strive for the construction of action outcome and self-efficacy expectations. He must not allow avoiding behaviors to reign (e.g., doing something totally irrelevant to the learning task); rather he must reach individual short goals by taking easily accomplished small learning steps – in the case of resistance from a learning task, behaving in an action-oriented manner, i.e., trying out alternative learning procedures and not lamenting the obvious difficulties.
8. In social interactions and cooperation with others lie important chances to reduce cognitive deficits; they stimulate and further the development of mathematical thought structures by revealing as well as dealing with the approaches of others (see also Chapter 9, Memo 9).

12. Learning to Juggle: The Acquisition of a "Juggling Grammar"

12.1 Introduction

This chapter shows that learning motor skills, viz. a sequence of periodic movements, is not a matter of setting up a series of motor stimulus–response units to form a motor behavior chain (cf. similar thoughts presented in Chapter 3), but rather the construction of *systems* of motor activities and *schedules* for their regulation. These in turn are subject to more dynamic forms of unit construction and thus more elaborate forms of behavioral organization. The learning process is characterized by *progressive changes in the type and size of the behavior units* as well as by *their integration into the overall course of the sequence to be learned*. The result is an *automatization* of *ever more encompassing movement segments*.

The most important keywords of this chapter will be, besides the terms *movement segment, movement sequence, schedule,* and *automatization,* mentioned above; *representation of the movement sequence*; the *control of movement through rhythms*; the *formation of behavior and regulatory units*; *error feedback;* and the *systematic elimination of errors (debugging)*. With respect to practicing juggling, we will speak of *generalized motor programs, blocked* versus *randomized practicing,* as well as different *forms of feedback* about errors or the achieved state of learning.

12.2 Five Phases, Twelve Individual Movements – but What Are the Important Behavior Units?

Nearly everyone has stood in awe of the circus or street juggler who, despite great concentration, seems completely at ease juggling three, five, or more balls, or rings, or whatever, tossing them in the air and catching them again and again – all the while talking and telling jokes. How, we ask ourselves, can

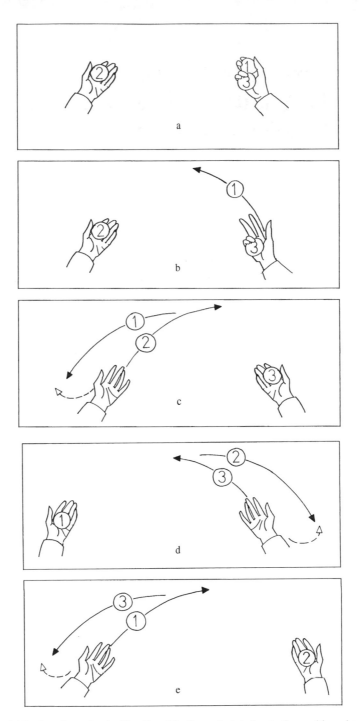

Figure 8: The five phases (a–e) of juggling. The figure depicts the starting position where ball 3 is already in the right hand.

a "normal human being" learn how to do something like that? Well, it is possible!

Learning to juggle means learning a sequence of movements that recur in a certain period; that is, the starting point returns after a certain time, the ball coming back to where it was first launched – the whole procedure beginning anew (something much different from trying to solve the nail puzzle in Chapter 3).

We shall be interested here particularly in studying how *one period* of this movement sequence is learned. What is the *basic unit* of this procedure? What *movement segments* are relevant? And how can they be combined to form a whole *sequence*?

The Course of Movements

Juggling with three balls is done in the *five phases* depicted in Figure 8 (cf. also Norman, 1976, 207 f.). In juggling literature this is referred to as the "three-ball cascade," meaning the balls form a somewhat lopsided numeral 8 in the course of their journey. (We will not refer to any other juggling figures here.) The juggler starts with two balls in the right hand and one ball in the left hand (Figure 8a). Ball 1, the upper of the two in the right hand, is now thrown over to the left hand (Figure 8b). The juggler must keep in mind that the altitude of the ball (or the thrust it is given) determines the time it is in the air and thus the time one has to prepare and execute the next step. When ball 1 is on its descent, the left hand throws its ball (ball 2) on a similar, though not identical trajectory to the right hand and thus becomes free to catch ball 1, which is about to land (Figure 8c). In the meantime, ball 2 has passed its zenith on its way to the right hand, giving the right hand time to send off ball 3, and, during its flight toward the left hand, to catch ball 2 (Figure 8d). Ball 1 has to be sent to the right hand again before ball 3 reaches the left hand, so that it is free to catch ball 3 (Figure 8e).

The Order of Throwing and Catching and the Problem of Unit Formation

We can depict the course of *one* period of juggling with three balls somewhat more formally by using a table. Anyone who wants to study this situation more closely and has no balls available can simulate juggling by using three paper balls (cut-out circles) with 1, 2, and 3 written on them. The "juggling" then takes place on the tabletop!

1. Throw right ball 1 (TR1)
2. Ball 3 is in the right hand from the beginning. This is a special case. During actual juggling, of course, it would not be there, but would arrive from the left hand and be caught with the right. This special situation is called, "catch right ball 3" (CR3).
3. Throw left ball 2 (TL2).
4. Catch left ball 1 (CL1).
5. Throw right ball 3 (TR3).
6. Catch right ball 2 (CR2).
7. Throw left ball 1 (TL1).
8. Catch left ball 3 (CL3).
9. Throw right ball 2 (TR2).
10. Catch right ball 1 (CR1).
11. Throw left ball 3 (TL3).
12. Catch left ball 2 (CL2).
13. = 1. TR1

Thus begins the second period with CR3 – this time with a true catch.

Here are the individual movements in shorthand notation:

    TR1 CR3 TL2 CL1 TR3 CR2 TL1 CL3 TR2 CR1 TL3 CL2

Even a theoretical study of the situation throws up the question as to whether individual movements may be combined to form larger blocks of movements within *one* single period. It is clear that each hand has to carry out alternately *two* activities – catch, throw, catch, throw, etc. – a total of three times each period. Thus, each hand alternately has the role of thrower and catcher. Do throwing and catching then form a larger unit for each hand since they occur spatially and temporally in close proximity? If this interpretation is correct, the next row, representing a single period, depicts unit building (pattern no. 1):

    TR1 CR3   TL2 CL1   TR3 CR2   TL1 CL3   TR2 CR1   TL3 CL2

But one might also ask, Don't in fact the throws of the one hand and the catches of the other belong together as logical *and* spatial units, connected by the trajectory of the respective ball? If this is the case, we would depict the units as follows (pattern no. 2):

    TR1 CL1   TL2 CR2   TR3 CL3   TL1 CR1   TR2 CL2   TL3 CR3

It should be noted that throwing ball 2 (for example) from the left to the right side is not directly followed by catching the same ball; rather, a *different* catch occurs in between, that of ball 3, which was already in the air when ball 2 was thrown. Thus, pattern no. 2 is only a theoretical case.

It could, however, be conceivable that two other movements, one of each hand, might form a unit, for example, throwing ball 1 with the right hand and throwing ball 2 with the left hand and the respective catches: first ball 3 with the right hand, then ball 1 with the left hand. That would result in the following sequence (pattern no. 3):

TR1 TL2   CR3 CL1   TR3 TL1   CR2 CL3   TR2 TL3   CR1 CL2

But at the moment at which, say, the right hand catches ball 2 (in the middle of the period) the left hand must release ball 1 a split second later in order to be free to catch ball 3! This leads us to combine the following movements to units (pattern no. 4):

TR1   CR3 TL2   CL1 TR3   CR2 TL1   CL3 TR2   CR1 TL3   CL2

Yet even larger units are possible, for example, "packets" of actions of the right *and* the left hand, until the right hand again throws a ball (pattern no. 5a):

TR1 CR3 TL2 CL1   TR3 CR2 TL1 CL3   TR2 CR1 TL3 CL2

Or "packets" beginning with the left hand (pattern no. 5b):

TR1 CR3   TL2 CL1 TR3 CR2   TL1 CL3 TR2 CR1   TL3 CL2

Finally, an even larger unit, which at first glance may seem somewhat absurd, is possible: The whole period is divided into two parts according to the rhythm "right–left–right" – "left–right–left." But it is not absurd at all! In swimming the crawl, for example, there is the same rhythm, whereby one turns the head for air first to the right after three strokes and, after another three strokes, to the left. Why shouldn't such units also be present in juggling? This would look like the following (pattern no. 6):

TR1 CR3 TL2 CL1 TR3 CR2   TL1 CL3 TR2 CR1 TL3 CL2

How behavior, and thus how control and regulation, units are established will concern us later on in this chapter.

12.3 Discrepancies between Representation and Course of Movements

Anyone familiar with the order of the movements depicted in Figure 8 has gained a preliminary *representation* of one juggling period. That this representation does not suffice to constitute the ability to juggle becomes immediately clear: The balls tend to hit each other; i.e., the trajectories cross at the wrong time. The *spatial and temporal precision of movement* leaves much to be desired.

One might try guiding the balls as long as possible with the hands and keeping the elevation low; that would surely raise the precision, but would also mean the juggler would have to work very quickly since flight time is also reduced by this method. Elevation and time are not linearly correlated: If the juggler wants to gain time to carry out the actions, he must throw the balls *higher,* since the time a ball is in the air is proportional to the square root of the height of the throw. If the juggler thus increases the height, he gains time to make corrections in his catching, but his overall precision is lower, since even small errors in the angle of throwing cause large changes in the trajectory, which in turn means correcting hand motions to catch the balls properly. A beginner has no choice but to work on *mastering regular throws*. This goal implies that the relatively broad scope of possible movements must be reduced to the proper amount of stable patterns of movement so that the muscles involved can tense and relax in an orderly fashion. Learning to make the throws with the necessary regularity is easier if the balls are not caught and thrown with the fingertips but with the *palms* of the hand. This ensures fewer irregularities.

If the balls continue to collide in midair, one will eventually conclude that the trajectories of the balls have to be skewed slightly so the balls can pass each other, and that the timing of the throw has to be such that they do not come into contact with each other.

This modifies the rather vague representation of the sequence of movements present at the outset. Sometimes the desire to improve one's performance has the effect that the balls are thrown ever farther from one's body, making short steps forward necessary. To combat this problem, Austin (1974), an expert in the field, suggests the drastic method of training directly in front of a wall.

Anyone who wants to learn to juggle must thus first learn a few very important *partial movements* (cf. Figure 9), for example, throwing a ball and catching it with the same hand; doing the same with two balls; throwing a ball from one hand to another – in both directions. It is important not only that the

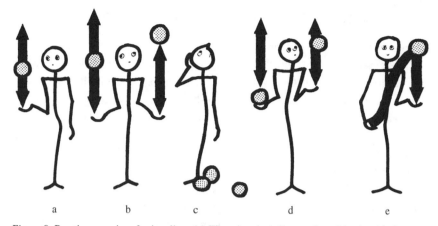

Figure 9: Practice exercises for juggling. (a) Throwing the ball up and catching it with the same hand. (b) Throwing two balls up the in air and catching them with two hands. (c) What goes up must come down! (d) Alternately throwing two balls up in the air and catching them. Don't rush! (e) Throwing the ball from the right to the left hand and vice versa. Keep it smooth!

throws be even and regular with both hands, but also that any irregularities in the coordination of the two hands be smoothed out.

Yet these partial movements do not yet form the *movement units* of juggling: The motor movements of throwing the balls from left to right, and vice versa (Figure 9e), are those of real juggling, but the temporal sequence – the *synchronization* – is not. In juggling, when one hand catches, the other cannot be catching at the same time, but must be throwing the ball to be free to catch the next one coming. These temporally delayed steps are not (yet) present in the preliminary exercises noted above. More on them later.

If one is able to make the throws from the right to the left hand more even, then catching the balls will also become easier: The first exercise contains the slight movement of the hand from the throw to the catch position (Figure 8c–e). We haven't mentioned such almost imperceptible movements up to now, but they are paramount for the formation of movement units and thus for the success of the overall movement, if difficulties are to be prevented at the joints between throwing and catching (tardy or spatially imprecise movements). These subtle movements serve as modifiers of the main movements mentioned above (TR1 CR3, etc.) on a low level of movement patterns, and together with them they form very fine movement segments that are integrated into the overall movement. A final note on evenness in juggling: Even experts reveal a certain unevenness in their movements that requires tiny but steady corrections.

12.4 Monitoring the Sequences of Movements through Rhythms

A more intensive study of learning to juggle requires one to bring the individual movement segments practiced into their correct order. Thus, one must learn to toss one ball at the right time and not have to follow its flight path completely through, but to see it to its zenith and then leave it to one's *peripheral field of vision*. Beek and Turvey (1992) showed that only very little visual information from the vertex of the trajectory is necessary to trigger the order to throw the next ball. The question is how to achieve the regularity of the balls reaching that point. This is not done through spatiovisual control; rather, the entire sequence is primarily controlled through timing, based on a certain *rhythm* one has to learn. This rhythm provides the learning juggler with an ever more exact time pattern for tossing the next ball.

A rhythm can in fact be practiced quite easily (Figure 10). It is *verbally* controlled by saying to oneself (initially out loud), "Throw, throw! Catch, catch!" while throwing the one ball from the right hand to the left hand, and the other ball from the left hand to the right hand, by catching both balls in sequence ("Catch, catch!") and then starting over again, "Throw, throw!" This ensures that the rhythm becomes routine. Changes in the elevation of the tosses help regulate the timing.

This method, however, applies only to the initial learning phase, which is soon followed by a modification. The more the flight of the balls becomes regular, the more successful this phase is felt to be. Taking the second ball in the right hand (but not yet throwing it) is another step toward success; this step does not change the act of *practicing the rhythm*.

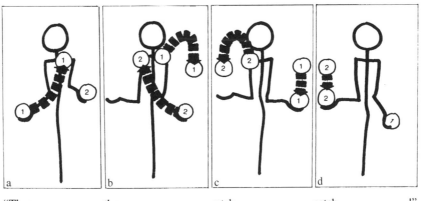

"Throw ...., throw ...., catch ...., catch ....!"

Figure 10: Four intermediate stages in the exercise "throw – throw – catch – catch." Each panel shows what happens to the two balls during a certain period of time.

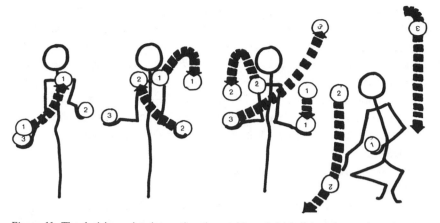

Figure 11: The decisive point: integrating the catching of the ball into the previous throwing movement. In these four scenes (cf. Figure 10) the beginning juggler has yet to completely integrate the movements. He begins with two balls in the right hand (left). In the next sequence, the movements on the left correspond to those of the previous exercise (cf. Figure 10b), except that ball 3 is still in the right hand. The third picture shows the decisive moment: Ball 2 is coming in, and ball 3 takes off at "Now" – though with too much force; ball 2 is missed, and ball 3 falls to the ground (last picture).

But as soon as the third ball is to be thrown, there is a major new action to be learned (Figure 11). First, the right hand throws its first ball as before to the left hand, keeping the second ball in its place. Then, however, this ball too *must* be thrown to make a place for the ball incoming from the left hand. This is the moment when most beginners get very nervous and speed up. One can temper this by giving oneself the verbal order "Throw (right), throw (left), catch (left), now!" This "Now!" does not follow the previous rhythm but squeezes itself in directly after the first "Catch!" With "Now!" and the throwing of the respective ball the juggler crosses an important threshold: The right hand is once again empty and thus ready to catch the next incoming ball. Should this not succeed at first, don't despair; the important thing is that the ball really leave the hand at "Now!" All of a sudden the right hand catches the incoming ball once, twice, and thereafter everytime. Then the routine starts again: "Throw, throw, catch, now!"

In contrast to the first lesson described above ("Throw, throw, catch, catch"), now both hands have to throw the balls quickly, since for every ball in the hand there is one coming in as well. The additional order introduced into the rhythm ("Now!") usually suffices to trigger this action. The beginner, however, must take care that the "Now!" order does not lead to throws that are too strong (cf. Figure 11, third picture from the left). The throw following the "Now!" order must also be as regular as the ones already practiced.

Initially, the practice run ends after *one* round with two balls in the left hand, since this hand has not received the "Now!" order, or the hand has "ignored" the order by not throwing the ball before the next one arrives. The first time this action *is* successful, the juggler is usually so astonished that he forgets to throw the ball from the right hand. Too much is happening all at once! But it doesn't take long and the motions are correctly repeated two and three times in a row. To be sure, the balls may still occasionally go somewhere they weren't supposed to go, but the key experience of actually juggling is overwhelming! A major step in the learning process on the path toward the complete integration of the action sequence has occurred (more on this below in Section 12.8).

The rhythm, which in the end consists only of "Now! ... now!" is a *plan* for monitoring the movements and plays a major (and helpful) role in the temporal integration of individual movement segments. We may assume that the rhythmic regulation of juggling is the dominant one, at least as long as the juggler uses three elements, and that visual control is limited to a very short part of the overall course of action (see above). With increasing skill, the visual control becomes less and less important – some jugglers, in fact, can juggle for some time in complete darkness.

12.5 Error Feedback and the Testing of Hypotheses during the Construction of Movement Sequences

Errors, such as two balls colliding in midair, are immediately seen as such and interpreted: "I've got to train some more so that my tosses become more regular." Or "I've got to gct my timing down!" Sometimes, however, the result is simply chaos: Two balls can't be caught because they have too much impetus and fall to the ground. The beginning juggler now begins to *establish hypotheses* about possible causes. Maybe the timing of the throw from the left to the right hand was wrong; an alternative is tried – *the hypothesis is tested.* *Knowledge of the result* of this trial is important for evaluating the hypothesis. Making progress lies in reducing the difference between result and hypothesis, i.e., minimizing the difference between factual and theoretical values (cf. the *cybernetic hypothesis* of Miller, Galanter, & Pribram [1960], as well my comments in Chapter 3). In other words, one does not just associate some stimulus with a new response, be it a proprioceptive stimulus (emerging from one's own muscular system) or a visual one; rather, one compares a *movement segment and its temporal regulation* with a hypothesis and checks it for its appropriateness in a larger motor context. The juggler's answer may be very

simple: "No, that's not the way." There's no more to say at the moment because the beginning juggler has yet to discover what the error is and which of
the many measures to correct it is indeed the proper one. Sometimes the
hypothesis can be expressed more exactly: "Throw the ball only when the
incoming ball is at its zenith." As we have already seen, this action can be
accompanied by verbal control, by giving oneself the respective "orders" derived from the hypothesis. But sometimes one only has a *feeling* about how
to solve the problem – perhaps through a different movement that cannot be
followed up or described completely, being perceived only in the peripheral
visual field. In such cases the most important thing can turn out to be the
learned rhythm. This *feeling* may also be the expression of having learned
some things *implicitly*, i.e., unconsciously, which nevertheless had a clear
influence on a later learning success (cf. Reber, 1993; cf. as well Chapter 3,
Section 3.5).

The process of learning is closely related to *recognizing errors* and to *correcting* them (Minsky & Papert, 1972; see below). Of course, the feedback
from a completed movement segment ("No, that's not the way") is also response-produced, but the following movement segment is not (as Guthrie or
Watson assumed) activated as a response to a proprioceptive stimulus and an
existing habit (a reinforced association), but is associated because of the error
that has been discovered (cf. Adams, 1984). The impact of *error feedback* lies
in *differentially exacting corrections* in one's movements, depending on the
quantitative and qualitative extent of the error.

It is difficult to avoid all mistakes while juggling. The reason is that there
are many different variables to watch out for simultaneously: positions, speed,
and force as well as the elevation and timing of the ball tosses. Research has
shown that the so-called resting ratio, i.e., the fraction of time between two
throws of the same hand and the time the respective ball is held *in the hand*,
is of major consequence. Beginners tend to have longer resting ratios than
experts, leaving them less time for any corrections.

12.6 The Construction of Plans for Movement Courses

As we have seen above, one can assume that the most important movements
are triggered by a temporally defined rhythm. Thus, on a high organizational
level this temporal pattern determines the plan for the movement course. A
juggler who has mastered this pattern with its corresponding movements possesses the basic structure of the plan.

Coding and Further Hierarchical Organization

In addition to verbal codings (our "orders"), which may also include explanations and tips from more experienced jugglers, the initial learning phase also produces some codings of a visuospatial nature: the space required to carry out certain movement segments and the explicit positions of hands and arms. A learner can code some of this information by observing a model (Bandura, 1977). From these verbal and visuospatial codings the juggler knows whether his movements and the trajectories of his balls are more or less correct. And he is in the position to make corrections to his actions, should the factual values not correspond with the (coded) theoretical ones.

Many important parts of the entire sequence are coded without our knowing exactly *how*. By this I mean a number of fine-motor movements, for the most part in the early learning phase: moving the hand back and forth during irregular throws, or making a quick correction of the hand or arm position when a ball has been thrown too late. It is certainly possible that *proprioceptive stimuli* (*sensu* Watson's behavioristic learning theory) trigger some responses on an elementary, principally physiological level of behavioral organization; these responses in turn assume the role of connecting movement elements. Together with a sense of touch they might be responsible for some very expert jugglers' being able to juggle in the dark.

That there even can be corrections to movement sequences proves, on the one hand, that the movements involved are coded and retrievable and, on the other hand, that the movement sequence is constantly accompanied by visual and other perceptual processes through the principle of *feedback loops*. The organism waits for the feedback or is at least ready to react to these messages – how else can we explain the extreme speed with which corrections to movements are carried out? All of this points toward a *hierarchical organization* of the entire sequence of movements via rhythm routines, which for their part are fine-tuned through further feedback subroutines.

According to the behavioristic *chaining hypothesis, any* response-produced stimulus can trigger the next response in the motor chain. According to Watson (1919) and others, the *proprioceptive stimuli,* i.e., those triggered through one's own movements, are the most important of all. This type of stimulus has the advantage that the organism "carries it around" with it all the time. Thus, the proprioceptive stimuli (again according to the behavioristic theory) could regulate segments of a larger movement pattern. From the preceding statements on the formation of units we know that the individually practiced movement segments are temporally organized in a specific manner. The movement of throwing with the right hand, even if it produces a proprioceptive stimulus, does not trigger the appropriate follow-up response; rather, the necessary response must take place somewhere else – in the *left* hand ("Throw!"). And this response is controlled by the rhythm. This is why we prefer the interpretation of the sequence based on *temporal–rhythmic control* to the behavioristic chaining hypothesis. We agree with Lashley (1951) that even the most elementary physiological movements of juggling (the *response-produced stimuli* and the responses triggered by them) are hierarchically structured and controlled. Yet we cannot say anything about them in the case at hand since we have no access to the neurophysiological control.

The schedule necessary to learning to juggle is a cognitive representation that corresponds to the *plan* proposed by Miller, Galanter, and Pribram (1960). It organizes the movement sequence not according to the basics of associative chaining, but according to a hierarchical structure.

12.7 The Systematic Elimination of Errors

Minsky and Papert (1972) wrote some time ago that juggling is learned by a constant and systematic elimination of one's own mistakes. They viewed human behavior as analogous to computer behavior and thus called this *debugging*; i.e., the capacity and method for getting rid of the bugs in one's own behavior and avoiding such problems in the future.

They held three things to be of utmost importance to juggling:
1. First, one must know the basic conceptual memory schemata. This corresponds to learning the descriptions given at the beginning of this chapter (cf. Figure 8). Besides pretraining, the tabletop method described for simulating the motions can help here.
2. Then, one must learn to put these memory schemata into practice, in the correct order and in the correct way. One reaches the mastery level by commanding the movements required and their correct temporal order.
3. Finally, according to these authors, there is a fine-tuning of the movements, the acquisition of a fluency in the entire procedure – more intensive practice.

Thereafter, it is important that external stimuli that have nothing to do with the juggling act be *ignored*: Juggling demands great concentration and the constant availability of all resources. Repetition (practice) makes for smooth movements, especially the *transitions* between different movements such as throwing and catching. Over time, external events (e.g., observers) are no longer distracting and movements become more regular, making it easier to coordinate all aspects with less overall effort (less attention and less control). Confidence and pleasure in one's own skills increase.

12.8 From Mastering of a Task to Automatization

Anyone who juggles a lot soon notices that he can carry out the motions "in his sleep": The movement sequence becomes *automatic* (*automaticity level* versus *mastery level*). How does this happen? We recall that during the initial phase the juggler said: "Throw, throw! Catch, catch!" Then the difficulty was added that the ball remaining in the one hand had to be thrown with the order "Now!" in order to catch the incoming ball. In this phase the order was "Now!" In the course of further successful practice the following happened: The order came to encompass ever more segments of movements to be carried out. Thus, although the order ("Now!") referred only to throwing the ball, the catching action that immediately follows *became part of the throwing sequence*. The new short order "Now – now – now!" took the place of the earlier, more complicated one and included the catching as well (Figure 12). The verbal input triggers broader behaviors: the *new* units (TR3(CR2)) and (TL1(CL3)) – pattern no. 1 in Section 12.2, but written in a different way to show that the catching has been integrated directly into the throwing and no longer needs to be emphasized or controlled expressly. These new elements, called *chunks*, can now be retrieved directly. By integrating the partial movement of "catching" into the larger overall movement "throwing–catching," triggered by the order "Now!" this part of the movement has been *automatized*. Automatization thus means triggering larger segments of movements without having to retrieve the partial segments individually.

In the pretraining phase, the juggler prepared and practiced the partial throwing segments ("Throw, throw!"; TR1 TL2), as yet *without integrating catching segments* (cf. every second unit of pattern no. 3). Now emphasis lies

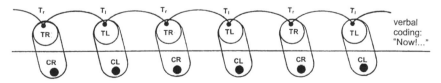

Figure 12: Depiction of automatization. The throwing motions are supported verbally by the order "Now." Slowly, the act of catching is integrated into the act of throwing; it is carried out together with the throwing motion and thus need not be triggered by a conscious order, i.e., it takes place "automatically."

on throwing and the respective orders: A throw from the right hand precedes that of the left hand. If both new throws (TR3(CR2)) and (TL1(CL3)), which now integrate the respective catching movements (i.e., the segment throw–catch has been automatized), are combined, we get a new, ever broader unit (or chunk) ((TR3(CR2))(TL1(CL3))); this corresponds to the now complete pattern no. 5a shown above. More concretely, at the moment when the right hand begins with the juggling, the left already "knows" what it has to do because its activities are synchronized with those of the right hand – they function automatically in accordance with the right hand. Here, automatization has gone a step further to include an ever larger unit of movement made up of segments that earlier were retrieved individually – without the juggler's having to address each individual part verbally. The juggler now must control only a select few points of his activity to guarantee the entire course of action (cf. Schneider & Shiffrin, 1977; Anderson, 1987). The pattern

$$(((TR < > (CR < >))(TL < > (CL < >)))$$

has now become the basic element or building block for juggling with three balls. Only the numbers of the balls (designated by the spaces < >) that pass through the juggler's hands are different. A *juggling period* with three balls consists of three of these basic forms in a row, followed by another of the same kind. This chapter puts the entire period (or several repetitions of entire periods) at the center of discussion because only an entire period (or periods) gives us enough time to study the *meaning of rhythm* for learning to juggle. The basic element mentioned above gives only a first approach to how the rhythm works.

The juggler only has to repeat such units time and time again until he has completely mastered the "schedule" and, perhaps following some own idea, starts to introduce variations to the schema, such as throwing a ball under one leg or behind the back. This may make the units unequally long, since the balls have a longer path to travel, but the feedback loops give enough information to let the juggler know what partial movements of the basic form have to be modified (slowed down temporally or lengthened spatially) in order to compensate. Unequal periods are the result, and normal ones alternate with longer, more interesting ones! This, in turn, leads to *higher-level rhythms.*

It is characteristic of automatization that the larger sequences of movement can be controlled as single units and not as a series of individual segments. This is what makes or breaks the expert: the ability to juggle in all sorts of bodily positions without great additional efforts at conscious control – both parallel to the body and at a right angle, with rings or balls or almost any other object. For all of these, the major points of the schedule (the *generalized motor program*, discussed below) remain the same, though arm and hand motions must be adapted on the elementary levels of the hierarchical organization of movement.

The expert juggler has at his disposal large movement units and their respective rhythms, which he can unfold at will, i.e., adapt and vary. But if he wanted to introduce new elements into the overall scheme, for example, by adding two balls and juggling with a total of five balls, he would have to count on more than 10 times the learning time. The best thing is to start off by buying three balls and first becoming an expert there. (Information about purchasing juggling equipment may be obtained at http://www.hal.com/services/juggle.)

We may conclude that building up units on a higher level is dependent on various factors: the level of one's ability (novice versus expert), in particular the degree of automatization that has occurred, and of course the individual differences in motor skills.

12.9 New Studies on Practicing Motor Skills

Minsky and Papert (1972) pointed out that juggling skills can be brought to a mastery level only by intensive *practice* (cf. Section 12.7). In the field of *motor learning* there are some newer studies available that do not concretely concern juggling, but nevertheless are valid for that activity. They concern, on the one hand, the *type of external feedback* and, on the other hand, the question of *optimal order of training or practice.*

Less Feedback Can Increase Learning Effects in the Long Run

Even if a beginner were in the position to notice that he is making a particular mistake, it would often be advantageous in the beginning if a practiced juggler would give him tips (feedback) on his style. Recent studies (Schmidt, 1988, 1991a,b; Schmidt, Lange & Young, 1990) have shown that *less direct knowledge of results*, for example, instead of after every period, after every tenth period, did not lower the number of mistakes in that practice session, but that later on, when training was resumed *without feedback by an expert* (in a retention test), the number of mistakes was dramatically lower and a learning effect was present. This contradicts current ideas about how motor skills are learned, but can be explained quite plausibly:

According to the *guidance hypothesis* of Salmoni, Schmidt, and Walter (1984), feedback can certainly help lead a learner to a goal, as information that offers a correction for subsequent training trials. Yet such feedback can also have negative effects, by *interfering with* or even *blocking* the learner's own spontaneous *error interpretations*. Too much feedback can have a negative effect on one's own *internal error-detection and processing mechanisms*. Too much feedback could also lead to *permanent corrections of the movement sequence* and effectively prevent a *stable representation of this sequence* from arising. A reduction of feedback or a summary feedback, say, after 10 periods, on the other hand, does not have these drawbacks, as it does not hinder the learner's own activity.

On Practicing Different Content and Optimal Order of Practice

Research into motor learning (e.g., Winstein & Schmidt, 1990) presumes that the learning of movements does not consist of learning individual segments, but rather whole *classes of movements*, i.e., movements with common characteristics, above all *timing* and the use of *relative forces*. These researchers assume that the movements in these movement classes are regulated by *generalized motor programs*. For juggling this program would control the basic movements (on the basis of rhythm), while allowing the length of certain sequences and amount of energy invested in them to vary within the individual sequences or periods. This would mean that the same program could control higher tosses involving larger and heavier balls or even rings. But the generalized motor program has first to be learned and practiced – and newer research suggests that this act can be optimized. Instead of practicing a *single type* of juggling, e.g., a cascade with three balls, over a long period with many repetitions in blocks (blocked practice), one would be better off alternating the content after every few repetitions and practicing a different type, e.g., with heavier balls, with a higher toss, with a different figure from the cascade, or with rings. The order in which two different styles or materials are alternated is systematically modified *(randomized order)*. The research on these types of order and their effects speaks of the paradigm of *context interference* (cf. Magill & Hall, 1990; Wulf, 1992a, b), since randomized order introduces a new context, i.e., new material or styles, between two phases of the same content. This change in the order of practice (randomized practice) has the result that the increases in the training effects of an individual style may be minimal or even missing on that day, but that quite prominent effects are to be found *at a later point in time* (e.g., the next day).

There are three reasons for this more middle-term learning advantage with randomized practice:

1. The representations of the movements in memory are more differentiated and more elaborate than under block conditions (elaboration hypothesis: Shea & Morgan, 1979).

2. With randomized practicing, the representations in memory, i.e., the movement plan of a particular practice form, must be *reconstructed* each time, since another form of practice has been inserted, so that each is better learned (reconstruction hypothesis: Lee & Magill, 1983).

3. Randomized practice is effectively a *reduction of feedback*, since each practice phase is followed by another phase with different content – and this reduction, as mentioned above, is positive for the long-term learning of movements.

12.10 A Final Plea for a "Juggling Grammar"

The creation of an ever more perfect rhythm appears to be of great importance to the retrieval of movement segments and their integration into a consistent flow of movement. Of course, other information – nonverbal, visuospatial, proprioceptive, and tactile information – may also play a role, and something may exist along the lines of internal "cognitive maps" or spatial movement sketches for representing the movement sequence. But for the schedule and its instantiation it is the *rhythmic impact* that decisively determines the *temporal control of the movements* – they are not the result of motor chaining. The *representation* of the sequence implies a *hierarchy* (Lashley, 1951), which sees to it that the patterns found in juggling are *prepared, neurally triggered, carried out, and concluded* with the proper (holistic) rhythm and in the right order – providing as well continual *feedback* on these processes and the success thereof. Similar to the situation surrounding natural language production with its syntactic flexibility, in which one word does not simply follow or produce another (note here Lashley's famous sentence spoken in 1951, "The mill-wright on my right thinks it right that some conventional rite should symbolize the right of every man to write as he pleases"), but rather in which hierarchically ordered plans ensure that the order of words is correct. In the world of juggling, in turn, it is the "juggling grammar" that leads to the retrieval of the movement segments such that the desired pattern ensues. Only a hierarchically well-organized "grammar" gives the juggler the ability to introduce jokes into the routine (similar to the introduction of adjectives or subordinate clauses in natural language) and especially to correct slightly deviating or incorrect movements so that no one in the audience notices. We can see that juggling is not simply a chaining of movement segments, in that after a mistake the juggler cannot begin anew at every point along the track of the rhythm; this would be the case if *every* reaction as one link in the chain were triggered by the previous link. In fact, the juggler must begin a new rhythm from a "joint" of two *larger units*, much as when we misspeak we have to begin the sentence or linguistic phrase again from the beginning.

Memo

1. When learning to juggle one must learn individual movement segments by intensive repetition, finally reaching the level of high regularity.
2. The temporally correct order of movement segments is learned by mastering a clear rhythm supported by verbal regulation.
3. The breakthrough comes when the catching movement immediately following the throwing movement becomes part of an independent movement of its own, the throw–catch–movement, triggered by verbal control ("Now!").
4. Small movement segments are combined to make larger movement segments. This so-called chunking is one aspect of the automatization of juggling actions. Automatization occurs through advanced integration of partial movements into larger chunks, eventually resulting in a whole sequence (a period).
5. Automatization is characterized by the fact that behavior units become ever more encompassing and are triggered by a shortened verbal control impetus. Less and less attention and verbal control are required.
6. The organization and sequence plan for juggling, the so-called juggling grammar, can be compared to grammar in natural language inasmuch as movements do not serve as triggers for the following movements (nor does one word lead to the next). Thus, there is no chaining present in the sense of behavioristic learning theory; rather, juggling grammar (like language grammar) is hierarchically organized, something Lashley postulated in 1951 to be true for serial behavior patterns in general. Put differently, the "schedule" every juggler has to set up is a cognitive representation corresponding to a *plan* in the sense of Miller, Galanter, and Pribram (1960). This representation organizes the sequence of movement not according to the laws of associative motor chaining, but according to the rules of hierarchical structure.
7. The hierarchical control of juggling movements is supported by the fact that after a mistake in the routine the plan cannot be continued at just any point along the line, but that there are joints between the larger movement segments (corresponding to the linguistic "joints" between phrases in the sentence structure) at which the juggler must pick up the rhythm. Also, the timing necessary to control, for example, the catching of the right hand and the subsequent throwing of the left hand cannot be explained on the basis of the behavioristic motor chaining paradigm. Rather we are dealing here with hierarchical movement control: The proprioceptive stimuli of the right hand do not trigger the responses of the left.
8. Practicing a particular form of juggling (e.g., the cascade with three balls) can be optimized: by reducing the frequency of external feedback of a trainer or by introducing some variety through other forms or material. This does not lead to short-term, but rather to long-term successes.

9. Reducing external feedback means the learning juggler strives on his own to obtain error information (knowledge of results) and integrates that information into the next trial, leading to longer lasting representations of the movements to be learned.
10. The employment of randomized as opposed to blocked practice sequences leads, in the long run, to better success in learning motor movements. The insertion of varying content into the movements to be learned means they become coded (represented) in a more elaborate way, and it forces the representations of the movement sequences to be reconstructed anew every time they are carried out (at least at the beginning). These two reasons correspond, in short, to the elaboration and reconstruction hypotheses.

13. Learning from an Illustrated Text: The Construction of Mental Models

13.1 Introduction

This is the longest chapter of the book – and for a good reason: It deals with perhaps the most important and most demanding type of learning in our hemisphere – knowledge acquisition from text. Learning textual content presupposes *understanding* textual content. But also, what has been understood must be *stored* such that it can be *retrieved* and *used* at any time.

Thus, we shall first investigate the idea of *understanding*. Four theoretical concepts are treated: (1) The *process* of understanding is described as the analysis of a text through a previous synthesis of expectations; (2) understanding is viewed as the *integration of new information* into the structures of prior knowledge, in other words, the *assimilation* of textual information to existing conceptual schemata; (3) further, understanding is seen by some as the *addition of semantic units,* so-called *propositions*; and (4) it is seen by others as the *integration of semantic units* of different kinds (propositions, mental images) into a holistic "building," a so-called *mental model.*

Learning from text always begins with the *activation of prior knowledge* with which new textual information is integrated. This integration, in turn, leads to changes in the prior knowledge, that is, to the construction of new knowledge structures or knowledge representations. This integration requires both *elaborative* and *reductive processes:* The first are processes that merge the new with the old; the second, processes that reduce the amount of linguistic information to an amount capable of being stored. Some of this information can be culled from illustrations (pictures, graphics); like text, they too must be understood and integrated into the mental model "under construction." Newly established knowledge structures must also be consolidated and prepared for retrieval. All of this is the stuff of learning from text.

This chapter is best read in several sittings. It contains a number of new terms the reader will come to understand. In connection with *understanding*, we will meet terms such as *schema* or *proposition as semantic units, concepts, arguments, and relations*; further, with respect to the cognitive processes, *analysis-by-synthesis; data-driven or concept-driven processes; summing up of proposition and argument overlap; integration of propositions into (holistic) mental models; elaborative, integrative, reductive, and metacognitive processes; flow of meaning* when reading a text; and the *macrostructure* thereof. In connection with the storage and retrieval as well as the "reading" of illustrations in a text, we shall be confronted with such concepts as the *activation of conceptual and graphical schemata; procedural knowledge; semantic coding; setting up of retrieval paths; representation, organization, interpretation,* and *transformation function of illustrations and graphics*; as well as the *necessity of making graphics "dynamic."*

13.2 A Basic Economics Text as Example (Including the Learning Goal)

In the following, we will use, as our illustration of learning from text, a *written text*. The example we have chosen for this chapter – the European Common Market's surplus butter problem (the "butter mountain") and its ramifications (taken from a well-known introduction to national economics by Frey, 1981) – may not be of major interest to readers concerned with psychological or pedagogical themes, but that is in fact our intention: The reader should experience above all what it means to learn something from a text; the reader should try to observe his own behavior while trying to learn the information given in the text.

The text given below is an excerpt from chapter 2 of *The Law of Supply and Demand* (Frey, 1981, 24–43). Two figures appearing there are also reproduced (Figures 13 and 14). One passage has been eliminated because it is irrelevant to our purposes.

> *Price Fixing:* Supply and demand meet head-on with each other in the market. Imagine an Italian market where buyers and sellers still strike deals with each other. The sellers first demand a high price and are intent on selling a large number of items at that price. The buyers, on the other hand, do not want to buy as much as the sellers might wish at that price and quote a very low price. The sellers open the second round by lowering the price somewhat. Then, the buyers are ready to buy more, and interested customers begin to appear, though no sales are completed: The sellers' desires do not yet correspond to those of the buyers. The sellers' original prices would have led to an excess supply of the respective wares, the lower prices desired by the buyers would have led to excess demand. The dealing must continue for so long until the amount available for sale equals the amount willing to be bought. The resulting price

– the *market price* or *equilibrium price* – means the wares indeed change hands from seller to buyer. . . .

Minimum Price for Butter: In nearly all countries of the world the law of supply and demand is disturbed in the realm of agriculture by governmental intervention tactics. To ensure that farmers receive a higher income, the state sets a minimum price for butter. This minimum price, which must not be undercut, is of course higher than the market or equilibrium price. A supply/demand schema (Fig. [13]) demonstrates the negative side-effect of such methods: excess supply (BC). The farmers want to sell considerably more butter (OE = AC) at the reigning intervention price (OA) than the public is willing to buy (OF = AB). The result is the now famous "butter mountains" that plague nearly all countries. In the long term, such a situation is not tenable – what to do with all that butter? Further measures have to be enacted, in particular the following three, which are usually also mixed:

(1) The government buys up the excess supply (BC) at the minimum price and destroys it or resells it at dumping prices on other, underdeveloped markets, usually in other countries. Dumping prices here are prices that lie below the production costs or own purchasing prices. The taxpayer foots the bill, that is, the difference between the price paid the farmers or cheese factories (in Fig. [13]: OECA) and the proceeds from sales to the population (OFBA). (The only exception is when the excess goods are destroyed at no further cost.)

(2) The government demands a reduction in quantity from the agricultural producers, who are allowed to produce only as much as the population is willing to buy at the intervention price (AB). This measure is not practical in its most extreme form: As Figure [13] shows, it reduces agricultural income tremendously, especially compared to solution number (1) above (OFBA instead of OECA). However, with strong demand independent of price, the proceeds of the farmers are still higher than those achieved with the market solution (ONGM).

(3) The government pays price subsidies, meaning there are two prices for butter: One is an intervention price (OA), which lies above the equilibrium price (OM) and is valid only for the farmers; the other lies below the market price (OH) and is valid for consumers. The latter price is set such that the amount of butter produced can actually be sold (AC = HD). The difference between production income (OECA) and consumer price (OEDH) is paid for by the taxpayers (HDCA). (Frey, 1981, 32–38)

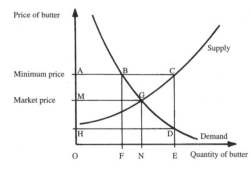

Figure 13: Minimum price for butter as a governmental intervention and as a disruption of the interaction between supply and demand (from Frey, 1981, 36).

This text shall form the basis of the following discussion. The middle part will serve as our example for learning to understand text information; later we will see what the first part tells us about learning from text in a stricter sense as well as how to "read" a graph (Figure 14). Finally, we look more closely at the last section along with the respective figure (Figure 13) to study the storage and retrieval of text information. Let us begin with the learning goal!

Learning Goals

What do we mean by "learning from text," particularly from this very factual text? What *content* do readers learn and in what *form* do they learn it? What do readers really want to *know* after having read something?

In our case, the learning goal is defined as follows: The learner should explain to a friend the problem of "excess butter production and governmental intervention procedures" on the basis of what he has learned from the text passage given above; he should employ the pertinent termini and use no other supplemental means.

There are, of course, any number of *other* goals one could define (also for oneself):

– to write an *abstract* or summary of the text;
– to determine the *most important statements* of the text;
– to determine the *most important terms* used (e.g., intervention price) and *explain* or *define* them on the basis of the text;
– to *answer questions* posed by someone else in order to prepare for an exam on the subject of "price fixing";
– to understand the principles of governmental interventions and the consequences thereof and to transfer these principles to other excess productions, or to other governmental control measures;
– to *demonstrate* the situation through use of graphics;

- to *copyedit* the text for typographical mistakes;
- to *memorize* the contents of the passage word for word.

The last goal listed will likely be a rare one, though it is relevant in the case of a poem. Sometimes rote learning can also be a final alternative, if the reader has in fact *failed to understand* the text and yet must, for whatever reason, repeat the content.

13.3 Understanding Text

There are a number of recent theoretical approaches dealing with the question of how text is *understood*, how knowledge is *extracted* from text, and how such knowledge is *represented in memory*. The following deals with the respective considerations of four such theorists.

Kintsch and others (Van Dijk & Kintsch, 1983; Kintsch, 1992, 1994) pointed out that understanding text is not an "all-or-nothing" process; rather, there are *different levels of understanding*. We shall meet with several examples thereof in the following. Further, we should already note that our differentiating between understanding and learning in this chapter is a difficult matter, both from a theoretical and from an empirical vantage point (cf. Kintsch, 1994; Steiner, 1997).

Understanding Text as "Analysis-by-Synthesis"

Some time ago Neisser (1967) stated that *every* piece of information we process – and thus also text information we want to understand – is *analyzed through a continual process of synthesis*. That may sound somewhat paradoxical at first, but it is not difficult to understand: From the moment the learner starts reading he *synthesizes* (constructs) internally the information he will probably be confronted with in the text; i.e., the reader creates *expectations* in regard to what he is reading. If the text is written in the reader's mother tongue, this is not problematic: He already knows what the individual letters look like and what forms to expect. Such *expectations* represent the initial *synthesis* of the print. With the help of the product of this synthesis (it is apparently something along the line of inner, imagined script or type models) the reader analyzes the printed text and gives himself continual feedback about the success of his synthesis, that is, whether his (inner) expectations have indeed been fulfilled. In an adult, this process takes place so quickly that these thoughts rarely reach the conscious level. For cognitive psychology, these processes are not easy to come by. Neisser made the attempt at just that in his *analysis-by-synthesis model* published in 1967.

Of course, the situation described above concerning the synthesis of letter forms and printed words marks only the most elementary level of processing. A reader equally builds up expectations concerning the *order of words* and thus the sentence structure. This is easy enough since he naturally understands the *syntax* of his mother tongue and is well acquainted with the grammatic regularities contained in the sentence "The dealing must continue for so long . . . " The native reader knows that an *until* will eventually follow a *for so long*, or that an *either* will produce an *or*. Obviously, even simpler grammatic rules (and their respective exceptions) belong to the reader's prior knowledge, which offers him a multitude of clues about what may be expected in the syntax of the text. These processes of *syntactic synthesis*, too, occur almost completely automatically: They have in fact been *overlearned* to the point that a reader would stop to think only if a grammatical form did not correspond to expectations, that is, if there were places in the text where the analysis-by-synthesis of the expectations did not "work out."

At this point, the third level of analysis-by-synthesis becomes evident: the semantic level. Readers not only synthesize their expectations of visual patterns to construct letters, words, and grammatically correct sentences, but also await a *meaning* of the text in front of them. This starts with the attempt to delimit the topic of the text; the title alone already reduces the variety of syntheses. Once readers have recognized that they are dealing with an economics text concerning agricultural pricing, they have limited the number of "synthesis paths" still open to learning and understanding the information offered. The text does *not* deal with variable currency rates, it does *not* touch on the export problems of tool and die makers, it has *nothing* to do with inflation. It is dedicated to a specific theme that the reader can synthesize in advance and employ for the analysis of the text.

Schema-Theoretical Explanations of Text Understanding

More recent authors (Rumelhart & Ortony, 1976; Rumelhart, 1980) have called the *units of prior knowledge* activated upon reading schemata or *cognitive schemata*. With this vocabulary, these authors return to a term that was introduced by Bartlett (1932) in his experiments on memory and that played a major role in Piaget's developmental studies (Piaget, 1936, 1947). (To be fair, however, the term *schema* is older, e.g., in Selz [1913] or even going back to Kant [1781].)

Schemata – or "scripts" when talking about relatively stereotypical courses of action (cf. Schank, 1980) – form the basic *building blocks* of the understanding process for many situations or goals as well as, more generally, for all cognitive construction processes (inferences, problem solving, retention or application of information). To understand this idea better, think of a schema as a *generic structure of knowledge*, that is, the schema possesses a certain specificity of genus or type and thus a certain *generality* assigned to it by the respective person over time. Thus, an individual "has" a schema of "tennis" or "democracy" or a script for "going to a restaurant" (a so-called restaurant script). We mentioned above the stereotypical nature of schemata; in this connection, however, it is more important to note that a cognitive schema represents an *organizational unit* of our knowledge – a *structured holistic entity* describing the components, characteristics, and relations present in any particular situation in the real world (Rumelhart & Ortony, 1976; Graesser, 1981).

If we assume that the knowledge of any one human being is available in semantic networks, then we can say that schemata are *active semantic networks* or *network components*. They are the units of knowledge that are activated for use, i.e., recalled to consciousness.

Readers working through the economics text above will activate any number of schemata based on the printed letters: Known letters are identified (*identification* of schema), and the words formed therewith are recognized (also an identification, albeit on a higher level). But all of these schemata are active on only a relatively primitive level, being controlled, as it were, by the data presented (printed text). Thus, authors such as Lindsay and Norman (1972) call these schemata "data-driven," and with regard to the activated processes in schema construction they refer to "bottom-up processes" triggered by the physical data (the printed letters) because they lead to a meaning from bottom to top.

Yet understanding a text is not solely a "bottom-up" process; on the contrary, many schemata are activated on the *semantic level* (e.g., while reading a headline or a subheading): They work "top-down," are "concept-driven," and correspond to what we previously called the expectation on a semantic level. Schemata of this sort guide the *search* for information in the text and contribute to resolving unclear meanings, an ambiguous sentence structure or an unknown specific word. Sometimes a reader *misreads* a part of the text by improperly using "top-down" schemata as expectations, that is, as search aids for further text information. On the whole, processing text for the purpose of understanding its content must be seen as an activity that proceeds in alternating interactive cycles of bottom-up (from the printed text) and top-down (from the meaning of the text and from one's prior knowledge) processes.

A reader rarely becomes conscious of this process, except in special situations. For example, if the text consists of a handwritten note of life-and-death content on a wet piece of paper that must be deciphered in candlelight during a raging snowstorm – here we see, quite dramatically, the interaction of bottom-up and top-down processes to work out those schemata that allow the text to be interpreted properly (or, at least, optimally for the respective situation). Because of the assumed semantic context (conceptual, meaningful schemata: top-down), the barely decipherable letters are *interpreted* (handwritten visual patterns as information carriers at the lowest level: bottom-up) in the syntactically and semantically most likely form.

All in all, the *schema constellation* activated here (with schemata on all three levels: visual patterns, sentence structure [syntax], and meaning) corresponds to the inner *representation of knowledge* one has built up over time – something we will later on call a *mental model*. Of course, under the very difficult circumstances described, but also in normal reading situations, there will be many interactions between the various schemata activated on the different levels; any reading or understanding problems cropping up, for example, about the meaning of a particular word or the structure of a particular sentence, can be solved only by using feedback loops. (The same is true, by the way, also for the model introduced above of "analysis-by-synthesis" and the respective processes taking place on the three levels described.)

A very important mental activity emerges from the assumption that schemata have a *tendency toward completeness;* that is, a schema activated on a high level of meaning *activates* the *search* for the specific missing piece of information in the text that would fill up the characteristic "slots" every schema necessarily has. If this information cannot be found in the text, the reader is usually able to complete the schema by drawing *inferences* based on prior knowledge – thus guaranteeing the completeness of his representation of knowledge.

Let us now turn to the middle part of our text. We recognize that the introductory sentence "In nearly all countries of the world" activates various cognitive schemata, such as "agriculture," "supply and demand," "governmental intervention," and "countries." The latter may even lead to the assumption that the text contains examples of such states and that the respective names may be found somewhere in the text. But since this is not the case, the reader may choose to ignore this and read on, or the reader may make the *inference* that neighboring countries with large agricultural production (though not Iceland, for example) are meant. The schema "governmental intervention," on the other hand, probably creates expectations that are less clear as far as the minimum price for butter and the butter mountain are concerned. There are many unknowns, and the reader develops an expectation of (and surely also a certain *curiosity* about) finding answers in the text to fill in the slots in his schema of "governmental intervention." These answers then in fact do emerge in the third part of the text.

If we look more closely at the entire knowledge representation that is constructed during the reading process, we see that it is constantly being checked as to whether it is congruent with prior knowledge and with the text in question, whether it is *consistent, coherent,* and *complete.* If this is the case, the text is somehow understood; if the result is negative, the reader becomes active and *seeks out* information in the text in order to understand better. Or the reader *revises, differentiates,* or *extends* his present knowledge representation. In short, he begins to *learn.*

Thus, we now stand at the threshold that leads from understanding to learning. If working through a text meant only *rediscovering* or *identifying* schemata on several levels, then the reader would *understand* everything (albeit on different levels) but *learn* nothing.

Understanding Text as an Addition of Units of Meaning (Propositions)

Here we want to try to see our previous comments on understanding text information in another light and present the results of recent studies. The following refers to the middle part of the text on the "minimum price for butter."

The reader *understands* the content of the text because of his *factual prior knowledge* and his *actual dealing* with the text he is reading. As mentioned above, besides factual knowledge he needs further prior knowledge: He must have the words of the written language present in his own internal *lexicon,* and he must understand and have mastered the *syntax* of the language in question. This alone, however, does not guarantee that he will be able to extract a *meaning* from the flow of text information.

Most theories of text understanding arising in the early 1970s assumed that the meaning of a text is represented in *semantic units.* Some saw the units of prior knowledge at the forefront and conceptualized them as schemata (see above), whereas others referred to the text and chose as semantic units so-called *propositions.* The latter are *hypothetical constructs for representing meaning in sentences.* These are very similar to schemata, but lean more on relational logic and consist of *specific ideas of contents formed by language* (concepts) and a *relation* that connects these concepts with one another. An example from our text:

The meaning of the sentence "The state sets a minimum price for butter" may be expressed by the following proposition:

(1) SET (STATE, MINIMUM PRICE, BUTTER)

"State," "minimum price," and "butter" are the specific concepts or, in another terminology, the *arguments*, with "set" the *connecting relation*. Proposition (1) is thus one *semantic unit* of this text. The reader understands that something is being set, by someone, for something, and with the help of a certain means.

But the text consists of many sentences and thus many propositions, each representing a meaning (or semantic) unit. The main thing is not that the reader *understand* every semantic unit as an entity, that is, be able to integrate it coherently into his prior knowledge, but that he grasp the larger scope of the text as well. These higher levels are guaranteed in various ways: first, through the fact that whole propositions are "compressed" into a single argument that flows into a later proposition. Thus, Proposition (1) can be compressed into the argument "minimum price" by packing all the information into that one term. We can then reformulate the meaning of the proposition as follows: "The minimum price set for butter by the state." This meaning is now implicitly present in the concept (or argument) "minimum price." The following sentence in the text begins with "This minimum price. ..." The demonstrative pronoun *this* implies what is contained in the compressed argument "minimum price," namely, "the price set for butter by the state."

The third sentence of the text ("This minimum price, which must not be undercut. ..."), displayed in the form of a proposition, reveals the following:

(2) IS HIGHER THAN (MINIMUM PRICE, MARKET PRICE)

We see that in this proposition the minimum price is present as a concept or argument, representing, as it were, the entire Proposition (1).

When reading the third sentence, which again mentions the minimum price, the reader brings along all previous knowledge gained about this price. This is the very essence of the *meaning flow* (Aebli, 1978, 1981) of such a text (cf. as well Steiner, 1997).

Sometimes, however, a concept that has played a major role in giving meaning to one sentence, i.e., has served as an argument in the respective proposition, pops up again in another sentence much later in the text. It then again becomes part of the proposition in that sentence and thus links the two propositions. Such repeated arguments create connections between the arguments via *overlapping of parts of the propositions,* and one speaks of *argument overlap.* An example may be found in our text in the concept of "governmental intervention" in the first and fourth sentences.

Broader textual meanings often occur through somewhat more complicated circumstances. For example, in our text is the following sentence: "The result is the now famous 'butter mountains' that plague nearly all countries." Its meaning can be clothed in the following proposition:

(3) PLAGUE (COUNTRIES, BUTTER MOUNTAIN)

The meaning of this proposition cannot be understood completely without further details about the "butter mountain" in the text or some prior knowledge. The reader must know in advance what "butter mountain" means – the excess production or supply of butter! This excessive supply arises mentally from the *link* between two propositions whose meanings are present in the text (and, as we shall see, in the figure as well):

(4) WANT TO SELL (PRODUCERS, GREATER AMOUNT OF BUTTER PRODUCTS)

(5) WANT TO BUY (PUBLIC, AMOUNT OF BUTTER PRODUCTS)

The meanings of these two propositions are compared to one another, resulting in a certain difference – the excess supply of butter – which produces the meaning of the concept "butter mountain." Further, the two propositions have an *argument overlap* in the element "amount of butter products." The overall meaning of Proposition (3) becomes clear if Propositions (4) and (5) are implicitly included in one's considerations. That, in turn, is the meaning flow mentioned above which arises while reading or processing text information. Because the propositions present in a text form a coherent whole, one can comprehend the meaning of that entire text as a whole and sum it up in *proposition lists* (for more details and research results, see Van Dijk & Kintsch, 1983). Other connections between semantic units (propositions) are established by elements connecting sentences such as "thus," "if ... then," or "because," creating even larger semantic units.

The early, and later widely expanded, theories mentioned here propose that textual meaning thus consists of a (sometimes very complex) *addition of prop-*

ositions. This type of *additive–elementaristic* method of processing and understanding text information resembles the way a mountain climber scales a cliff: Since he is positioned very close to the rock he is trying to surmount and thus has no overview, it sometimes happens that he has to retrace his steps and start anew. This "lack of overview" becomes noticeable in the understanding of a text if we follow the model based on adding propositions: Sometimes the meaning of a passage no longer agrees with the overall text, so reading must begin anew.

The metaphor of the mountain climber to describe the imperfections of the additive–elementaristic interpretation of textual understanding shall suffice for now (for more theoretical details, see Collins, Brown, & Larkin, 1980, 385–406); let us now turn to a *holistic* interpretation of the processes of understanding text (cf. as well Schnotz, 1985; Mandl & Schnotz, 1985; Kintsch, 1988, 1994).

Text Understanding as the Construction of a Holistic Mental Model

Characteristic of someone intent on learning something from the economics text is that he, reading the title "Minimum Price for Butter," *activates* parts of his prior knowledge and tries to "draw a picture" of the subject the text is concerned with. Some theories have tried to use this idea of a picture by speaking of "scenarios" that the reader builds up during text processing (Sanford & Garrod, 1981). Collins, Brown, and Larkin (1980), who among others are very critical of the above-mentioned theory of additive interpretation of text understanding, posited that an inner *mental model* is formed on the basis of the text to be processed, and that this model represents the meaning of the entire text and contains the knowledge that is present in that text and that the reader assumes and represents. The term *model* means in this context that the *structural* and *functional* elements are represented as a model within the reader *analog* to the real situation – in our case analog to the true economic facts of the situation. For this reason, Kintsch (1988, 1992, 1994) speaks of a *situation model*. We will use this term and the more general term *mental model* synonymously in the following.

Such a *mental model* contains, besides verbal semantic units (the propositions), other information, for example, visuospatial *images* that in fact correspond or, in current cognitive terms, are analog to the circumstances of the true situation; i.e., they represent spatial and temporal relations. (This is important to our understanding of illustrations, discussed below.) Propositional representations do not have this characteristic of analog representation; rather, they describe reality in their own way, in a sort of *unitary language* (Pylyshyn, 1973, speaks of *interlingua*) that corresponds to the nonanalog "digital" format of the proposition. Thus, we can conclude for the moment that knowledge representations of various formats, namely, both propositional and analog ones, are present in a mental model.

Understanding our economics text thus occurs in the following order: The text just read is elaborated on the basis of existing and at least partially activated prior knowledge; i.e., it is expanded and formatted such that the propositions fit the structure of the prior knowledge. More and more of these propositions – the *text base* – are gradually integrated into the activated prior knowledge (one obviously can't integrate everything immediately!). It is Kintsch's argument that through these processes of elaborating and integrating text information into prior knowledge the reader builds up his *situation model* – or, more generally put, his *mental model* – of the content of the text in question. But understanding text content is not an all-or-nothing process; on the contrary, there are many different levels of understanding. First, there is the surface level – the words and their syntactic relations; second, the level of the text base, which encompasses the meanings of the individual sentences of the text; third, with the help of the mental model, there is a "deep" level of integrated understanding of the text information.

Semantic elements of the text to be read serve as retrieval cues for prior knowledge: The reader uses the text read to activate ever more prior knowledge (if available!), and, vice versa, schemata may be activated from prior knowledge that serve to search for information in the text to complete the respective schemata. Voss, Fincher-Kiefer, Greene, and Post (1986) and other researchers have pointed out the great importance of prior knowledge to understanding and learning from text.

In the light of the above, the following would appear to be plausible: The more semantic units one possesses in one's prior knowledge structure, the easier it is to elaborate and integrate the information flowing from the text. But prior knowledge also allows the reader to "read between the lines," as it were – to find meaning and content not explicitly present in the text. This important activity is called *drawing inferences* from text information.

The process of elaborating and integrating the text base into prior knowledge may be influenced by the way the text is presented. By means of appropriate *headings* and *signalings* (introductory sentences of a paragraph) the *macrostructure of the text* can facilitate the organizing processes in mental model construction. Or small gaps in the text content can lead to an increased activation of information processing (or information search processes), thus allowing better development of the mental model. There are, however, some limitations to the elaboration and integration processes in mental models due to the limited capacity of human working memory. Kintsch (1994) assumes that these constructive processes are cyclical, with about one sentence being processed per cycle. In contrast to the additive model of text understanding, the mental model forms an entity that gives the reader direct and relatively broad access to the information: The information can be integrated at different places in the model and thus must not adhere to the strictly linear order of additive processing.

The *analog* character of mental models implies, for example, that spatiovisual information or descriptions in the text are present in the reader's imagination (cf. Johnson-Laird, 1980, 1983, who sees visual images as a *special variant of mental models*). This probably became clear to anyone reading the text given above with the description of the Italian marketplace (see Section 13.2).

13.4 On Learning from Text

Up to now we have concentrated on *understanding* a text and noted that the process of understanding text takes place on several different levels. The question now is, How does *learning* from text differ from *understanding* text? Succinctly put, *understanding* is the proper integration of new information into existing knowledge structures, effected through the construction of a mental model (or a situation model). *Learning*, on the other hand, goes beyond the proper integration of knowledge to change significantly the structure of prior knowledge. Learning modifies, differentiates, compresses, or expands prior knowledge – it *changes knowledge representations*, thus modifying existing mental models.

Someone not well versed in economic matters might admit that understanding the text about the minimum price of butter caused some problems, as some of the terms (schemata) or the background of the figure (Figure 13) were unclear. With respect to those cases in which the text does cause problems, it is correct to say that the readers were not able to activate the subschemata (those forming the substrate for higher schemata) in their prior knowledge necessary for the processing of the text information, in this case, for developing the higher schemata "supply" and "demand" or the schema signaling the economic *connection* between the two terms and thus the schema "supply and demand" and the schema "market/equilibrium price."

The author of the economics text was aware of these difficulties and added to the section "Price Fixing" a figure (Figure 14c), which can help to illustrate the cognitive schema "supply and demand." We return to this matter below in Section 13.5. But first we want to take a look, from a schema-theoretical point of view, at the question of the extent to which learning (knowledge acquisition) goes beyond understanding.

Learning as a Modification of Mental Models: Accommodation, Differentiation, Restructuring, and Recombination of Schemata

The construction of the mental model "butter mountain and governmental intervention" encompasses *more* extensive processes than just understanding: The schemata that had previously made up the "scaffolding" of the model must be *adapted* to the latest information stemming from the text. Piaget called this the *accommodation* of schemata. But the schemata may have to be *extended* somewhat, or even a *differentiation* or a *restructuring* is due. That is *one* form of *learning* (cf. Rumelhart & Norman, 1976) – the *modification of existing schemata*. Another, no less important form of learning during the construction of a mental model is the *recombination of schemata* to higher-order ones, to more encompassing and yet simultaneously more coherent knowledge or semantic units (a sort of "superschema"); this is of great importance to the storage and later recall of knowledge.

Let us turn again to the first section of the text on price fixing and view it once again in the light of this type of learning!

> *Price Fixing:* Supply and demand meet head-on with each other in the market. Imagine an Italian market where buyers and sellers still strike deals with each other. The sellers first demand a high price and are intent on selling a large number of items at that price. The buyers, on the other hand, do not want to buy as much as the sellers might wish at that price and quote a very low price. The sellers open the second round by lowering the price somewhat. Then, the buyers are ready to buy more, and interested customers begin to appear, though no sales are completed: The sellers' desires do not yet correspond to those of the buyers. The sellers' original prices would have led to an excess supply of the respective wares, the lower prices desired by the buyers would have led to excess demand. The dealing must continue for so long until the amount available for sale equals the amount willing to be bought. The resulting price – the *market price* or *equilibrium price* – means the wares indeed change hands from seller to buyer. ... (Frey, 1981, 32)

We can assume here that the reader will have to develop new knowledge on the subject of "price fixing" in order to understand the following texts.

The first sentence may, and surely the second sentence will in any case, trigger the construction of a situation model or a mental model, particularly if the experience described (an Italian market) is available to the reader. First, the reader activates the existing schemata of the concrete situation in the market and thus implicitly the knowledge elements "buying" and "selling." These in turn are connected to the schemata "wares" and "price" as well as (and this is what is important to an understanding of the text) "supply" and "demand." If we assume that a sale has not taken place but only an offer, then we can present the meaning of one passage of the mental model under construction in the following proposition:

(6) TO SUPPLY (SUPPLIER, DEMANDER, AMOUNT, PRICE)

In more colloquial terms, a seller (supplier) offers a buyer (demander) a certain amount of wares at a certain price.

Here, something is being offered, and if we "condense" Proposition (6) into the activity of supplying (TO SUPPLY), then we have what we would normally call a supply (or an "offer") (cf. Aebli, 1978, 1981; on the process of condensing, see also Steiner, 1997). If we focus on the buyer and *his* activity of *"demanding,"* a corresponding proposition can also be condensed into this demanding, giving rise to the concept of "demand." The terms *supply* and *demand* can thus be described as the results of the process of turning verbs (representing activities of the persons involved) into nouns. One could call this linguistic process the "nounification" of verbs. The activities of these persons are the respective relations (or *predicates*) of the respective propositions or the relations of the respective activated schemata.

According to Rumelhart (1980; Rumelhart & Ortony, 1976) schemata can be represented like propositions. At the center is a *relation*, in our case TO SUPPLY, which has a number of slots just waiting to be filled: for example, by an *actor*, who offers something; by a *receiver*, who needs something; by *objects* (wares); and by other instrumental, temporal or local pieces (see also the case grammar of Fillmore, 1968). If we now connect both schemata (the supplying and the demanding) by sentence connectives, we get the economically important schema *supply and demand* – a *new schema*, signaling that new knowledge has been constructed, i.e., *learned*.

The question may arise, Is cognitive learning really such a complicated process? Much of what has been described here in great detail does in fact proceed in reality quickly and easily. Our goal here was to show how schemata relevant to the learning of text are developed from prior knowledge activated in a provisional mental model. We have seen that the text passage "Minimum Price for Butter" can be understood only in the presence of a certain quantity of conceptual knowledge. Both schemata (or concepts) "supply" and "demand" must also be understood in their relationship to the other schemata "price" and "amount of wares." This is done first through the concrete connection with those actors who offer or want something. The wishes and goals of the buyers and sellers flow into our understanding, and without them it is not possible to understand how they meet. The respective proposition can be formulated as follows:

(7) TO MEET (SUPPLIER, DEMANDER, PRICE)

If the meaning of this would be condensed into "to meet," the result (again, after a "nounification") would be a *meeting point*, in the form of a price equal to the term "market or equilibrium price." Here, one again sees that the meaning contained in Proposition (7) runs parallel to a *specific linguistic transformation* (for which we coined the term "nounification"; again, see Aebli, 1978, 1981). Such transformations apparently take place in our thinking and learning completely on their own.

　　If we look back at what has been said in this section, we see that completely new schemata have been constructed which are immediately put to use in the mental model for processing the ongoing text "Minimum Price for Butter." It should be noted that the previous results show that Piaget's terminology for the construction of conceptual connections does not suffice: With Piaget we can say, *Understanding* is the *assimilation* of text information through existing schemata, inasmuch as there is no resistance to assimilation. *Learning*, on the other hand, is a reaction to resistance to assimilation and the *accommodation* of existing schemata. With this it becomes clear, however, that learning is more than simple accommodation of schemata – it is the coordination and the completely new construction of schemata within a mental model.

13.5　How to Read a Figure and Integrate It into the Mental Model

With respect to the figure (Figure 14c) which the author of the text has attached to the section on price fixing, a question of great relevance to learning psychology arises: What influence does it have on the construction of the mental model of "price fixing"? The figure has three possible effects: (1) on

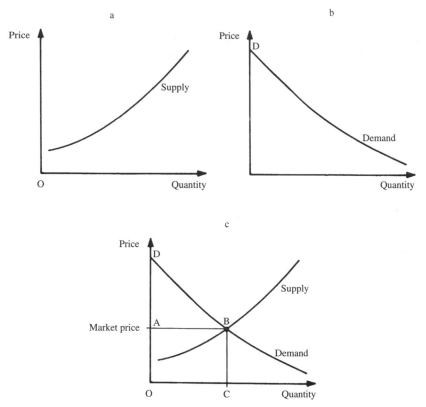

Figure 14: Supply and demand. (a) Supply curve. (b) Demand curve. (c) Interaction between supply and demand: attainment of market or equilibrium price (Frey, 1981, 33).

the text base, i.e., the reader (re)discovers statements from the text in the figure – the structures of the text and the figure can mutually be mapped onto each other; (2) the figure affects the reader's prior knowledge, its components serving as retrieval cues for activating respective knowledge schemata; (3) the figure can affect the construction of the mental model, i.e., the elaboration and integration of the text information into the reader's prior knowledge, by helping to connect the meanings of the individual sentences of the text (or the respective propositions) via the spatial relations shown in the figure. This allows one to grasp even larger connections and integrate them into the mental model.

One can derive a number of things from the figure by analyzing it in a concept-driven way, inasmuch as the necessary *conceptual schemata* and the specific *graphic schemata* are available in one's *knowledge structure*. For the latter, for example, we need the *global* schema for "reading" (= handling) a coordinate system with abscissa and ordinate as well as *local schemata* to process the information contained in the curves. In the figures shown here we are dealing with depictions that have no similarity to our perception of economic reality. This has the disadvantage that we cannot take recourse to everyday perceptual schemata in order to understand and integrate what is being shown. The abscissa (*x* axis) and the ordinate (*y* axis) depict the amount of wares and price, respectively. The relationship between amount and price is shown (for the sake of clarity) in two separate parts, one from the vantage point of the sellers (Fig. 14a) and one from the vantage point of the buyers (Fig. 14b). Figure 14a shows the curve for the supply side. It is important that the *single different points* on this curve can be focused on *individually* (information extraction of the first order, according to Wainer, 1992) and *compared to one another* (information extraction of the second order), and that the relationship between the individual points can be described. For example: If we look at the upper right-hand end of the *supply curve*, we see that this end point corresponds to a high price on the ordinate and a large amount on the abscissa (information extraction of the first order). This visuospatial *double* relationship corresponds to the sentence in the text "The sellers first demand a high price and are intent on selling a large number of items at that price." Thus, the figure has a *representation function* of illustrating something (Levin, 1981; Levin & Mayer, 1993), something we would of course expect of figures. The effect of a figure with respect to the learning process lies in the reader's being able to check whether the elements read about are also present there. This provides a sort of feedback for one's own understanding of both the text and the figure. In the present case, the figure has the function of "double-stitching" knowledge; i.e., it repeats what has been learned by serving as a redundant source of information (Ballstaedt, Molitor, & Mandl, 1987). But, as we see below, the figure can also play an even greater role in the retention and retrieval of information.

Yet, the interpretation of Figure 14a is not yet complete. What does the point at the *other* end of the supply curve mean (again information extraction of the first order)? A point in the lower left-hand corner would mean that the sellers are not willing to offer or to sell anything at such a low price. Only a proper explanation of the most important points along this curve, e.g., the two end points and one point in the middle, suffices to prove one has in fact understood the whole curve (information extraction of the second order). Only then do text and figure reach the point of being structurally matched – or as Bruner (1966) says, the same structural element can be illustrated both *iconically* and *symbolically* (linguistically) (cf. Chapters 3 and 16).

The same procedure may also be used for the demand curve. In the upper left-hand corner, where the curve begins (Figure 14b), the high price on the ordinate corresponds to an amount of zero on the abscissa: Potential customers will buy no products at this price! The right end point of the curve, on the other hand, shows that they would be willing to buy a large amount at this very low price. We can associate the verbal statements made for both curves to certain points along the respective curves.

Now let us combine the two curves (Figure 14c), as the author has done in his textbook. First we look at the supply curve: The sellers are willing to offer a large amount of wares at a high price (approximately at the level of the S in SUPPLY). If we look directly left of that point we hit the demand curve at a certain point. There are two corresponding points to this point: one on the ordinate and one on the abscissa, showing the price and the amount of wares, respectively – all of which corresponds to the statement in the text "The buyers, on the other hand, do not want to buy as much as the sellers might wish at that price and quote a very low price." This *comparison* of the two curves is what Wainer (1992) calls information extraction of the third order. It implies moving one's gaze from a point on the supply curve to the corresponding point on the demand curve, and from there looking to the left to see the price and below to read the amount. This is what Piaget, though in a developmental context, called the *recentering* or *decentering* in the construction of knowledge. He considered this the basis of the process of connecting – which for him was central to all structural development.

Anyone who has had some experience with figures or diagrams will find *decentering* easy enough, though beginners will be dependent on hints in the text on how to process the figure, or on tutors to help them out. In other words, "reading" a figure requires either *self- or other-regulated perceptual activity*.

A look at the lower points of the curves tells us even more about the relationships between supply and demand, or, rather, about the wishes and goals of the sellers and buyers at any one point. If we read the demand curve from left to right (perceptual activity!), we discover that the end point corresponds to the statement in the text "The buyers ... quote a very low price." The decentering toward the lower left-hand corner of the supply curve demonstrates the goal of the sellers, who refuse to sell any of their wares at such a low price. At the low price level put forth by the buyers, the lower left-hand corner of the supply curve corresponds practically to zero wares to be sold. This is not said explicitly in the text, but can be read from the figure: an example of how the visual or figural can go *beyond the written*.

Whenever we process or "read" the figure in this dynamic way, we notice its *organization function* (Levin, 1981; Levin & Mayer, 1993): The figure creates relationships almost immediately (when we move our eyes), and it organizes important facts that could not be organized in that manner in a text. This, in short, might show how the elaborating processes work during the development of a mental model.

But we should not forget the main thing here: The goal of the author of the textbook is to explain to the reader the economically important term *market or equilibrium price*. Our (learning psychology) goal, on the other hand, is to see how the mental model of the respective economic term comes to be established. The latter goal may be somewhat more difficult to reach, but it will provide us with important insights into what the microprocesses active during the development of a mental model actually look like.

In a real-life market situation, sellers definitely *want to sell*. That's why they "open the second round by lowering the price somewhat." Taking a look at the supply curve somewhere between the upper end point and the point designated by "B," we can discover the point at which the price was lowered. Let us now decenter horizontally toward the left: From the corresponding point on the demand curve we can risk the following statement about the willingness of the buyers to buy: The price can be related to a certain amount of wares the buyers are apparently willing to buy (value on the abscissa somewhere between 0 and C), though this amount is by far not the amount that should be related to the respective point just mentioned on the supply curve (at the lower price). This *difference* in the amounts envisioned by the sellers and the buyers, which can be gauged (though not precisely) along the abscissa, is what the text described as *excess supply*. This is a case of the *interpretation function* of figures (Levin, 1981; Levin & Mayer, 1993): One can interpret and understand an element through spatial means, in this case excess supply. (Now that we've discovered this possibility, we can enter the proper value into the figure – it is the line between points B and C in Figure 13.)

Because of a structural mapping process from the figure, the concept of *excess supply* is presented in the mental model in an *analog* manner: that is, the "visible" spatial relationships, such as the increase or decrease of the supply, remain intact. Retrieving this information in the mental model is not done exclusively through descriptions (and propositions containing the respective content); rather, it is done *directly* via the analog representation of the model, as it were "metrically." Here again, the figure goes beyond the text in its ability to present information graphically, giving the learner direct access to the conceptual information. Other terms may similarly be presented in an analog format, for example, *excess demand*. This makes clear that buyers, if they want more wares, must be willing to pay more for them (decentering to the supply curve). And if the sellers want to sell more, they have to modify their prices to meet demand. But how far must they go? The answer can only be a complicated one – which is easier to demonstrate graphically. Again, we see the *organization function* of a figure. The meeting point of the two sides, their interests and willingness to compromise, lies at the cutting point of the two curves: at point B, which comprises this fact *and* represents the "market or equilibrium price." In order to understand this concept, one must understand the entire mechanism of bargaining between supply and demand price and amount. This will more likely be the case if the reader has made *comparisons* including *decenterings*, that is, has used the *organization function* of the figure properly and is able to translate such figural knowledge into words.

The perceptual activities described above, present only *implicitly* in our text, are paramount to understanding a text and may have to be triggered by a tutor or teacher. Thus, figures, as integral analog parts of any mental model to be established, are fruitful only if their inherent "reading processes" – the specific perceptual activities carried out for the purpose of linking conceptual knowledge elements – can be fully established. These activities are important parts of the so-called graphical schemata, for example, the schemata "understanding a two-dimensional coordinate system" and "interpreting curves in a coordinate system" (see above). The *procedural components* of the respective schemata activate very specific *procedural knowledge*. Anyone lacking this knowledge, that is, lacking this procedural *prior know*ledge, can – despite the very concrete text – only *view* the figure but never really *see* it or *comprehend* it. The figure in effect will always remain a *puzzle*. In other words, neither the organization nor the interpretation function of the figure will ever become clear. (This, however, is generally true for all functions of figures and graphs; cf. among others Levin, 1981; Levin & Mayer, 1993; Schnotz & Kulhavy, 1994.)

The above has demonstrated the most important prerequisites of something that is "graphic," "illustrative," or "visualized." Clearly, not everything placed in our line of vision truly becomes insightful or comprehensible. A figure represents a number of associations between various elements (Bruner's "iconic representation"), which, however, are by nature completely static. Only the learner, of his own accord or through an external impetus, can turn them into something *dynamic* (via the above-mentioned decenterings), by bringing the elements into such close temporal and spatial range that the associations become clear and understandable. Such *specific perceptual activities* are requisite both to *seeing* the connections that have been visualized (cf. Chapter 16) and to *restructuring one's field of perception*, as the Gestalt psychologists postulate for problem solving and for *insightful learning* (cf. Chapter 18).

"Dynamizations" in figures or illustrations become even more clear when their subject is physical objects, organizational or production processes, chemical processes, and the like. In these situations dynamizations become, as De Kleer and Brown (1983) call it, *mental simulations* or, more precisely, *qualitative simulations* (e.g., movements of a machine or a sequence in a flowchart; cf. Steiner, 1997). It is often indispensable that, for example, a technical diagram clearly display which parts are moving parts and which parts are static or fixed, and whether the movements of the moving parts are displacements or rotations around a single point or an axis.

13.6 Specific Processes in Knowledge Acquisition from Text

Besides *learning* from text, up to now we have particularly emphasized *understanding* text. There is a good reason for this: Many researchers, in particular Kintsch (1988, 1992, 1994), interpret existing empirical research as proving that a solid understanding is an important prerequisite to *retaining* the information and *acquiring* knowledge. Learning from text, we have postulated, is knowledge acquisition. In the following we turn our attention once again to the processes that further *knowledge acquisition* and *knowledge retention*. These processes can be divided into three groups (cf. Ballstaedt, Mandl, Schnotz, & Tergan, 1981; Resnick, 1985; Mandl & Friedrich, 1986): *(1) elaborative, (2) reductive, (3) metacognitive. Coding processes,* particularly *semantic coding,* and *retrieval processes* may also be found among these three kinds of processes.

Elaborative Processes

As we have already seen, elements of prior knowledge are activated during understanding of text (schemata or "scripts," i.e., the building blocks of cognitive constructions) and in turn interact with text information during reading. This combination of *prior knowledge* (of cognitive structures already present in the learner) and *new material* in a text often takes place quite consciously, and the processes active at that moment are called *elaborative processes.* That is to say, the text information is *elaborated* by being joined with the properly fitting elements from prior knowledge, which expands (elaborates) that information in one way or another.

Such elaborations are in part *indispensable*, in part *complementary*. A textbook often presumes a certain level of knowledge the reader has to supply in order to understand the text. This type of elaboration combines the "old" with the "new," and it is plausible to say that knowledge acquisition is more successful the more intensive and varied the elaborations (i.e., the connections with prior knowledge) are. Kintsch (1994) even goes one step further when he speaks of *text reproduction* and *usable learning* from text: Applicable knowledge can be derived from a text only if considerable prior knowledge has been activated, and only if text information gained in this manner becomes highly integrated into existing knowledge (cf. McNamara, Kintsch, Butler-Songer, & Kintsch, 1993). As far back as 1968 Ausubel noted that successful learning requires *anchoring* the newly learned material in existing knowledge, and that *advance organizers* can be helpful in this process.

The effectiveness of intensive and varied elaborations most likely lies in the availability of partial knowledge structures that help one to recall *or reconstruct* the knowledge elements. In other words, these partial knowledge structures play the role of *retrieval cues*.

The consequence for efficient learning is that *as much prior knowledge as possible* must be available at the beginning of a learning attempt – and kept available throughout the operation – so that intensive elaborative processes can take place. Ballstaedt, Mandl, Schnotz, and Tergan (1981) suggest to this end the application of the following three actions (which we will later apply to our example text):

1. *Preparatory questions:* What do you know about price fixing? about supply and demand? about excess butter production? about the position of government in questions of agricultural production? Such systematic questioning, which serves to prepare the ground for important conceptual terminology, is also suggested by Diekhoff, Brown, and Dansereau (1982).

The introductions to each of the chapters in this book have been written with this goal of activating prior knowledge, though not through the use of questions, but rather through short descriptions of the vocabulary and concepts from learning psychology which will occur in the respective text. A similar effect may be obtained by reading the "memos" at the end of each chapter *in advance*, even if one does not understand everything.

2. Another way of activating prior knowledge for elaborative purposes lies in presenting information that raises the reader's *curiosity* by suggesting something amazing or astonishing, that is, by creating *discrepancies* between previous knowledge and the expectations arising from such infor-

mation, e.g., headlines ("A Learned Heart Attack?"). Such actions are well known in didactic literature as ways of motivating learning (see, e.g., Copei, 1950; Wagenschein, Banholzer, & Thiel, 1973; Neber, 1973; Brunnhuber & Czinczoll, 1974). Asking questions and provoking cognitive dissonances (contradictions, inconsistencies, etc.) probably activate prior knowledge on the conceptual level, that is, on a high level of information processing.

These first two types of elaborative processes mean that the reader can build up schemata of prior knowledge and thus expectations; as we have already learned, this structure corresponds to the synthesis process found in Neisser's (1967) model of text understanding via analysis-by-synthesis.

3. The third possibility, namely, that of *generating visual images,* takes place on a lower, more subtle level of information processing; it affects the "microprocesses" of coding, decoding, and recoding information. The "power" of visual images for learning individual verbal elements or word pairs has been studied rather extensively (cf. Paivio, 1971, 1986, 1991; Bower, 1972). One can discover it as well in the context of much more complex verbal information, such as during problem solving (Steiner, 1980; Kosslyn, 1980), and it is present in the elaboration of text. It would appear, however, that mostly "virgin" learners – children and adolescents – can profit from it. The reason for this may lie in the fact that adults have great difficulties changing their elementary cognitive processes (or microprocesses, like those active during imaging).

Reductive Processes

Activating prior knowledge by elaboration increases the overall amount of information, which can overload working memory. The texts in textbooks alone are full of information to be learned. Working through information, even elaborated information, happens in "packets." Indeed, because of the limited capacity of working memory, it *has* to happen that way (cf. Chapters 14 and 19). The human information-processing system apparently tries, and indeed is able, to *reduce* or *condense* large amounts of information, though these processes do demand considerable constructive efforts of the person doing the learning.

Clearly, the amount of information contained in a textbook has to be reduced greatly to allow storage. In our comments on *understanding* throughout this chapter we have noted that complex, meaning-giving structures (linked

schemata) are condensed, then carried along and presupposed as simple elements during one's dealings with a text (elements in the meaning flow). Whenever necessary, such elements can be *(re)unfolded* so that their content becomes available as it was during acquisition: as detailed text information. For
the condensing of connected semantic elements (or of parts of semantic networks) Aebli (1978, 1981) used the term *objectification*, meaning that the
broad structure, seen from one particular vantage point, can be made a "smaller" piece of information (a "chunk") or an "object" for further semantic connections. This greatly relieves working memory, since the "chunk" of information is now moved to long-term memory with a verbal tag on it (e.g.,
"supply" in our example above). It is thus stored in and is retrievable from
long-term memory (Steiner, 1997).

Reduction of information in texts is normally done directly via *reductive
processes*. The simplest form is the *elimination* of content not relevant to the
reader's goals. Eliminating information is a sort of negative measure, the opposite of *searching, identifying, and acquiring* information considered important to one's goals.

Other reductive processes are cognitively more demanding and require
complex *controlling activities,* such as *subsumation* under a higher-level term
or *paraphrasing* with the help of a limited number of words (a constructive
process in and of itself). *Summarizing* of text in short abstracts has to be
planned carefully and demands a *sensitivity to what is important* in a text,
which can normally be decided only on the basis of the learner's prior knowledge and individual goals.

This is a major problem for adults striving to learn something, as can be
seen when they use text markers or underlining to emphasize (and thus reduce)
information in a text. Often they highlight so much of the text that no true
reduction is achieved for efficient learning. Condensing large semantic units
to very few words or even one single keyword is something that must be
learned and practiced.

The research literature contains many examples of studies of rules for reducing information; we do not go into them further here but recommend the
treatment by Van Dijk (1980) or Brown and Day (1983).

Storage and Retrieval

The elaborative processes mentioned above are relevant again when dealing
with the storage of such condensed information. They help to integrate the
new pieces of (condensed and reduced) information into prior knowledge.

Even if this succeeds immediately, the learning process is not yet over, since we cannot be sure that the elements that have been understood and stored can in fact be *retrieved*. For example, if the learner is preparing for an exam (cf. Chapter 9) or wants to learn something for use sooner or later in his profession, he must first check to see how much he has retained and can *recall freely* (i.e., without resorting to cues).

We should not forget one thing at this juncture: Higher learning processes like those of learning from text rely on *repetition*. Only very few readers and learners are able to store and recall at will all important contents after one read-through. Thus, it is possible that for later recall conceptual contents must be trained by purely mechanical means.

In the case of our economics text, the most important terms such as *intervention price, excess supply, reduction of production, price subsidies, consumer price*, and *producer turnover*, could be written on one side of a card, the definition thereof on the back of the same card, and both used to learn the term. The strict meaning of the word is not learned, but rather a text describing it is. This method of learning presumes, of course, a certain amount of understanding of the learner! This is the case, for example, if the theme "the butter mountain and governmental intervention measures" is the topic of a lecture. (We will return to the topic of efficient learning by the card method in Chapter 14.)

With respect to our learning goal it would also be possible to reduce what is to be learned to a small number of *short* and *pregnant* sentences that constitute the quintessence and can be repeated literally or nearly so, for example:

1. The butter mountain represents the excess supply of butter arising from the government's maintaining an intervention or minimum price that the consumer does not want to pay.
2. The intervention price is set in order to secure a minimum income for the producer, the farmer.
3. The government buys up the excess production (butter mountain) and then sells or destroys it. Disadvantage: The taxpayer has to pay for the state's purchasing of excess supply.
4. The government demands a reduction in production. Disadvantage: Farmers' income sinks – a contradiction to point 2.
5. The government pays price subsidies. Disadvantage: The taxpayer must foot the bill for the difference between the producer's and the buyer's turnover.

One could also memorize the figure (Figure 13) as an *analog model*, though keeping the conceptual background one has learned in mind. First, the concepts given above would have to be pointed to in the figure; second, the elements of the figure would have to be named and, if necessary, explained. The latter might be called explicit *retrieval practice*. The task chosen by the learner would thus be "Name the following paths and areas of the figure (Figure 13) and explain their origin!"

OM	OE	ONGM
OA	AC	OFBA
BC		OEAC
OH		OEDH

The elements in the figure could also serve as cues for further reconstruction processes through which the learner could prove his knowledge in a (real or simulated) test situation. Using the figure in this way would correspond to Levin's fourth function, the *transformation function* (Levin, 1981; Levin & Mayer, 1993). The learner would, as it were, "follow" his inner picture of the figure and continually express his thoughts by formulating the corresponding statements.

A further way of retaining text information by reducing the amount of information lies somewhere between that of pregnant sentences and use of a figure, namely, "mapping" (also called "mind-mapping"): the spatiofigural presentation of knowledge elements and associations between these elements in a special kind of graphical network. Some learners use box diagrams or some other form of spatial learning strategies (see e.g., Holley & Dansereau, 1984; Pflugradt, 1985). The structure of such diagrams can have either a network or a treelike structure. The most important thing, on the one hand, is that the concepts that form the nodes of the network or the tree have clearly named relationships with one another. Concretely speaking, the relations "follows . . . ," "is one of . . . ," or "results in . . . " are depicted through the use of arrows or lines in the sense of *named associations* (Norman & Rumelhart, 1975). On the other hand, there is some evidence that it is important that the learner introduce a sufficient amount of his individual prior knowledge into the mapping procedure; otherwise, the connections between old and new do not adequately bond, making retrieval or reconstruction difficult.

One thing should not be forgotten with both the reductive and the elaborative methods mentioned above: These are high-quality techniques that demand from the learner both an *overall willingness* and *motivation to better one's own learning strategies* as well as extreme *self-discipline* (high demands on self-instruction) during the acquisition of the respective technique. Adult learners usually conclude that their learning strategies are sufficiently good and trustworthy and need little revision. For this reason, they are, and quite understandably so, not willing to put great effort into optimizing their learning skills. In fact, one must recall the long learning history of nearly all adults, which has formed them and their cognitive mechanisms used to process, store, and retrieve information, making any change whatsoever a complex and difficult matter (high *resistance to change*; cf. Pflugradt, 1985).

Metacognitive Processes

Anyone who has used elaborative or reductive processes, be it sporadically or systematically, to learn from text has had the experience of dealing more or less consciously with his or her own learning capabilities. The thought processes that focus on learning, thinking, acquisition of knowledge, and problem-solving skills are *metacognitive processes* – a third kind of process that has a more or less direct influence on learning from text. If the learning process is to be improved in the sense of "learning to learn," most authors agree that it does not suffice simply to learn strategies; rather, one must be aware of the processes that control and regulate these strategies (cf. among others Fischer & Mandl, 1983; Weinert & Kluwe, 1983). According to Flavell (1978), who was concerned particularly with the development of metacognitive knowledge in children, we are dealing here with (1) *knowledge about oneself* (so-called person variables, e.g., what one knows, what one feels capable of doing, what are one's strengths and weaknesses in learning); (2) knowledge about tasks, i.e., knowledge about which tasks are easy or difficult (*task variables*); and (3) knowledge about the cognitive strategies to be employed (see the analysis of elaborative and reductive processes). The metacognitive processes that serve to facilitate learning and raise efficiency can now in practice be directed toward the different variables mentioned. In contrast to Flavell (1978), Brown (1978) considered the *executive processes* of one's own cognitive activities to be considerably stronger. In her opinion learning skills should be developed by teaching not only strategies for coping with concrete learning tasks, but especially *control and regulation mechanisms* that provide *planning, temporal structuring*, and, globally seen, *coordinating*. A number of studies (Brown, Palincsar, & Armbruster, 1984; cf. also Mandl, Stein, & Trabasso, 1984) have shown that metacognitive modeling processes can be trained and applied. But it has also been shown that it is difficult for adults to revise or reorganize their long beaten paths of learning to any great extent.

Memo

On Text Understanding

1. Learning from text presumes an understanding of the respective text information.
2. Generally speaking, understanding means integrating new information from the text coherently (i.e., without contradictions) into existing prior knowledge structures.
3. Depending on the theoretical background, understanding is thought of in various ways – as analysis-by-synthesis processes (Neisser, 1967) or as based on activated schemata of prior knowledge to which new information is assimilated; as an addition of textual propositions (i.e., the semantic units in a text); or as the integration of semantic units in a holistic mental model.
4. Propositions are hypothetical constructs of semantic units which represent the meaning of sentences. Depending on the model of so-called predicate logic, they consist of a relation and at least one, but normally several, conceptual elements (arguments). The relation connects the arguments.
5. Larger semantic contexts – the flow of meaning in text understanding – arise through argument overlap or through the condensing of whole propositions into new arguments (elements) that are subsumed into propositions that later appear in the text.
6. The meaning of whole text passages can be depicted in proposition lists, which form the so-called text base (Kintsch, 1988, 1994).
7. Schemata too are hypothetical constructs for semantic units. They represent parts of existing knowledge structures. According to Rumelhart (1980), schemata are activated parts of a semantic network.
8. According to the schema theory, schemata are organizational units or building blocks for understanding inasmuch as prior knowledge is activated in the form of schemata and new knowledge is assimilated into these schemata. The text is understood only as long as this is possible without resistance to assimilation.

On Learning from Text

9. Learning from text means more than understanding a text: It also contains the adaptation of the schemata to the details of the text information (accommodation of schemata for overcoming resistance to assimilation), and it contains the linking of existing schemata to schemata of a higher order as well as the construction of completely new schemata. These are the processes that make up the construction of mental models. Text understanding and learning from text are greatly dependent on both the level of prior knowledge available and the learner's individual goals.
10. Learning from text can be supported by illustrations or figures. Illustrations also represent information that must be understood and integrated into the mental model. Illustrations can further understanding of the text information, they can function as triggers for activating prior knowledge, and they can support the process of establishing mental models via their four functions (see below).

On Processing Illustrations (Figures)

11. Illustrations (e.g., figures) can have four functions: (1) in their representation function they present text elements in a visuospatial manner (repetitive effect); (2) their organization function allows relationships to be established (sometimes through decentering); (3) their interpretation function allows the expression of things that are difficult if not impossible to express verbally (e.g., difficult concepts or connections); (4) their transformation function allows recoding for storage purposes.
12. Reading a figure presupposes the availability of conceptual schemata as well as typical graphical schemata (with respective procedural knowledge). Because of their essentially static nature, a "dynamization" is necessary to understanding and learning from figures. This is done by the concerted use of perceptual activities (decentering).
13. A figure can serve as the basis for reconstructing the mental model "The butter mountain and governmental intervention." The single elements thereof serve as retrieval cues.
14. Mental models are broad knowledge structures that contain information in propositional and analog formats.

On Specific Storage and Retrieval

15. Acquiring knowledge from text demands elaborative processes, i.e., processes that help to combine new information with existing knowledge. Examples are questions and considerations that structure a text in advance (e.g., based on the title), specific phrases or gaps in the text that raise the reader's curiosity, as well as generation of visual images before and during reading.
16. The mass of information must be reduced during learning. This is best done through reductive processes: condensing, eliminating, selecting (important) content. The relative importance of some piece of information results from one's prior knowledge and the goal of the learning process.
17. The storage and retrieval of information can be practiced in many different ways: through mechanical mapping and storing of pertinent concepts and their definitions (and vice versa); through learning of pregnant sentences; through the association (of a one-to-one mapping type) of concepts and the respective elements of a figure.
18. The metacognitive processes active during learning from text focus on one's own learning: learning capabilities (person variable), use of one's own learning strategies (process variable, e.g., with respect to strategies of storage and retrieval), and properties of the material to be learned (material or task variable).

14. Learning Vocabulary: Self-Regulated, Adaptive Learning

14.1 Introduction

For most people, learning vocabulary is an unpleasant matter – perhaps because they go about it in a purely *mechanical* way, concentrating solely on the words themselves without stopping to think about the *meaning* behind them. Yet, the more one takes the learning of a foreign language into one's own hands and the more one pays attention to the meaning and sense of the words, the more efficient, interesting, and meaningful the task becomes. Rather than memorizing isolated pairs of words, a network of meanings (a semantic network) is built up, into which vocabulary can be integrated and recalled at will through *well-established retrieval paths*.

In many areas of life, various forms of rote learning *(repetition learning)* are indispensable. Using vocabulary learning as an example, this chapter demonstrates their implications within the field of learning psychology.

Important terms used in this chapter are the development of an *adaptive self-learning system (adaptive learning)* or *self-directed learning with assessment of own learning progress (success history)*, which implies a certain individualization of the learning process; *paired-associate learning, generation of mental images, construction of cribs, cued recall,* and *free recall; repetition,* in particular *strict self-testing in the form of expanded retrieval practice, systematic learning, selective learning, semantic elaboration, self-discipline,* and *self-reinforcement;* and *construction of semantic networks* such as *linguistic and semantic clustering* of the verbal material to be learned (including the development of so-called word families). We will also be looking at how the vocabulary of a foreign language gradually becomes detached from one's native language and becomes organized within a *foreign language semantic network,* accessible through specific internal cues, thus losing all links to the equivalent words in the native tongue.

Foreign language vocabulary is not just a topic at school; indeed, some of us are forced to extend the process throughout our entire lives, so that we can keep up to date and read newspapers, professional journals, or important authors in their original tongue. This makes it worth taking a closer look at the learning processes involved.

Of course, we must remember that learning the vocabulary of a foreign language is not the same thing as learning a foreign language as such, although it doubtlessly constitutes an important part of it.

14.2 What Is to Be Learned?

A Typical Textbook

As an example, we will take the following words and phrases typically found in a French "learning dictionary" at an American high school level (Lübke, 1975, 3–4):

Subject: Lumière électrique – electric light

la lampe	the lamp	la < > de poche
le bouton (électrique)	the switch	tourner le < > /appuyer sur le < >
allumer	to switch on	< > la lampe/ < > le feu/ < > une bougie (candle)
éteindre	to switch off	< > la lampe/ < > le feu/ < > la lumière
une ampoule	a bulb	l' < > fonctionne/changer une < >
éclairer	to light	< > la lampe < > la chambre
la prise de courant	the socket	brancher une lampe sur la < >
le fil électrique	the cable	
le courant (électrique)	the (electric) current	le < > alternatif/un < > de 110 volts
l'électricité (f.)	electricity	une machine qui marche à l' < >
électrique	electric	le circuit < >
l'énergie	power	l' < > électrique
la centrale	the power station	la < > produit l'électricité
le barrage	the dam	un < > sur la Durance (river)
la pile	battery	des < > s pour le transistor
un électricien	an electrician	faire réparer la lampe par l' < >

Three didactic suggestions can be made for learning the vocabulary:
1. The pupil covers the French words (left column) and names the words from memory with the help of the remaining two columns.
2. The pupil covers the English translations (middle column) and names them from memory, again using the other two columns for help.
3. The pupil covers the French vocabulary in the first column and completes the phrases (right-hand column), where the sign < > appears in place of the relevant word. This is the most effective way of using this kind of "learning dictionary," especially if the phrases are spoken out loud.

14.3 Learning for Cued Recall

Paired-Associate Learning?

Using suggestion (1) above leads to learning the *foreign word*. Then *word pairs* are *associated* – a known English word is linked with a new French word that has to be learned. Research in the field of learning psychology includes a well-known paradigm of verbal learning: *paired-associate learning*; i.e., pairs of words, usually nouns such as WHALE and CIGAR (Simon, 1972), are learned by heart. During the test the researcher says one of the words, usually the first one, and the test subject has to name the second. But isn't that the same as learning vocabulary, apart from the fact that the researcher plays the part of the teacher and the test subject that of the pupil? No! In paired-associate learning, word elements (or more generally items, since they can also be pictures) with different meanings, sounds, and typefaces and, thus, different ways of being written are learned, whereas learning vocabulary concerns something quite different: Namely, two items that are usually *identical in meaning* but generally different in sound and face have to be linked together.

In the case of paired-associate learning, each of the two items has its own *conceptual* or *meaning network*, its own *semantic network* (e.g., for *whale* or *cigar*); in vocabulary learning, the two words represent two *different labels* for the same *semantic network*. Consequently, the requirements of the learning process are quite different. Some methods helpful in memorizing words in paired-associate learning cannot be applied to vocabulary learning at all. The two items, e.g., *lumière* and *light*, cannot be made into a meaningful sentence, nor can the two objects implied by the words be linked in a *visual image*. This linking of two objects to form a *compound picture* is one of the most effective mnemotechnical methods in paired-associate learning (see Paivio, 1971, 1983, 1986; Bower, 1972; Steiner, 1980), but in this simple form is worthless for learning vocabulary! Of course, we can imagine lights, *lumière*, and light, but the image acting as a cue for retrieving one of the two items offers no real help in remembering the other. In paired-associate learning, on the other hand, this works differently: Naming one item, e.g., *whale*, can act as a good retrieval cue for *cigar*, especially if, for example, the picture of a whale smoking a cigar was originally imagined while learning the word pair. In summary, this method will not help us to learn French vocabulary.

More than Associations

Generally, vocabulary pairs are associated simply by reading the words one after the other, i.e., on the basis of *spatial–temporal proximity* or *contiguity*. However, we can assume that other characteristics are also at work, giving additional help in differentiating the words and linking them together. For example, *lumière* and *light* both begin with the letter *l*, a characteristic that could help in learning the two words particularly if they are articulated clearly or spoken aloud: *l–ight* and *l–umière*. The fact that the French word begins with the same letter as the previously known English word is coded during learning. This is important, for what other factor apart from the *l* could act as a trigger stimulus for the *retrieval* of the corresponding word here? But perhaps the coding linked with the word *light* is more detailed, as follows: The French word begins with *l* and continues on with the sound *u*, not *i*! Furthermore, the man who invented cinematography was *Louis Lumière* (1864–1948)!

Or: *the lamp – la lampe*. This is, except for the terminal *e*, exactly the same word, originating from the Latin root, except that (1) it is spoken in the typical French way with a nasal tone, and (2) it has the article *la*, the feminine article. This is important to remember, as the gender of a noun has grammatical consequences, as in all Romance languages.

Cribs or Peg-Word Mnemonics

The switch – le bouton: The two words are completely different from one another, in both the way they are written and the way they sound when spoken! The same applies for *to switch on – allumer, the socket – la prise de courant, the power station – la centrale, the light bulb – une ampoule,* and many many more.

The latter example opens up a possibility that many readers are familiar with: The French word immediately reminds us of the English word *ampulla* (= ampule, a small medical glass flask), which has the same Latin origin. So the learner can use the "peg-word mnemonic method" (see Paivio, 1971, 1986; Atkinson, 1975) to make an acoustic connection: *ampoule – ampulla*. Yet we must decide whether this is really worthwhile, as the introduction of a further word is an added complication to a learning procedure in which there are already many words present; the risk of confusion is high. The important factor is *elaboration* (for *elaborative processes*, see Chapter 13), which helps to establish a connection between the new word and existing knowledge.

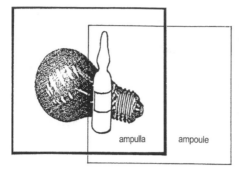

ampulla   ampoule

Figure 15: Example of the peg-word meth-od. Ampulla sounds like the French word to be learned "ampoule" (light bulb).The box on the right points up the acoustic similarity and the association of the two words. The picture of the ampulla can be interactively visualized together with that of the light bulb to form a unit (a compound picture, shown by the left-hand box). Ampulla, the key word, thus is related to both words. Recalling the word light bulb calls up the picture of the ampulla, which in turn calls up the picture of the near homophone "ampoule."

Ampulla is an element of existing knowledge and can in fact be used to estab-lish an (acoustic) relationship with the new word *ampoule*! Furthermore, as already mentioned above in connection with paired-associate learning, mental imaging could also help the learner: By *visualizing* both the *light bulb* and the *ampulla* in his imagination, he forms a compound picture in which the two objects representing both items interact with one another (see the above ex-ample of the whale smoking a cigar and Figure 15). This interactive visual image contains both glass objects, and although they will vary in appearance from learner to learner, they will always appear in a certain spatial, perhaps even instrumental or causal, relationship with each other. The light bulb will probably be somewhat larger than the ampulla, they will be different in shape, but in both cases they are shiny and made of glass. Furthermore, the learner's experience will tell him that both have to be handled with care!

This compound picture provides the learner, in a second step, with a *figural link* between the peg-word *ampulla* and the French word for light bulb. Be-cause of the link in the imagination between *light bulb* and *ampulla*, the two elements of information are joined to form *one* new element, *one* image of the two elements, *one* new unit of meaning, which is only a slightly larger burden on the memory than the single item "light bulb" *alone*.

Now let us look back at why we undertook this paired-associate learning – why two completely unrelated items have been stored together. The reason is that it provides us with a retrieval cue because of the stored image (*light bulb* recalls *ampulla*) and because of the acoustic link (the similarly written and similar sounding French word *ampoule*).

Of course, the fact that the French word sounds different from the English one, and moreover is spelled differently than it sounds, must be stored together with the English word *ampulla* (though this soon becomes a matter of course!). We will return to how specific spelling is learned in more detail later.

The cognitive learning psychologist would call this roundabout way of using the pair-association *light bulb – ampulla* an *elaboration*; in everyday language it is known as a *crib*. In the literature this procedure is sometimes also called the *peg-word method* (Atkinson, 1975; Atkinson & Raugh, 1975; Paivio, 1971). The intermediary element or the *peg word* (in this case *ampulla*) is not always nearly identical to the word concerned (*une ampoule*); often it may just sound somewhat similar, or some characteristic of its spelling recurs in the foreign word. The task of the intermediary link is to provide effective cues for the corresponding foreign word. They can be related to the word in the native tongue in different ways – as a whole concept or in another context of their meaning. Levin (1982) points out that *illustrations* can be effective as visual cribs; however, drawing illustrations for the purposes of learning vocabulary would probably be too time-consuming. A vivid visual image is just as effective for such purposes!

It has often been pointed out, and correctly so, that the crib method for learning vocabulary can work only if the individual has a good command of it and puts it to use in an imaginative way. In fact, it is of little consequence how "complicated" the construction of the cribs are; the important thing is that they make good sense to the learner (and only to the learner!); i.e., that they are compatible with available prior knowledge! The processes involved in constructing cribs are an individual matter and vary greatly from person to person.

Repetition Provides Possibilities for Elaboration

Using a strip of card 4–5 cm wide and about 15 cm long, the learner, according to the first didactic suggestion mentioned above, covers up a word from the top of the French column (leftmost column) *after* having spoken the English translation out loud (Figure 16). He can be even more resourceful: An additional indent cut into the card at the right place allows him to read *the lamp*. The solution *la lampe* is easy, so he doesn't have to think for long. Once he has repeated this word to himself, preferably out loud, he looks at the covered solution by moving the card a few millimeters downward and sees that his solution is correct. This is a well-known procedure that has already been used earlier (with the help of a computer program, e.g., Atkinson, 1972). But now the next English word, *the switch*, for which there is no similar sounding translation and no simple crib, becomes visible. Our pupil does not know the solution, so he pushes the card downward to look at the solution *le bouton* and reads it out loud, hoping that he will remember it when he repeats the proce-

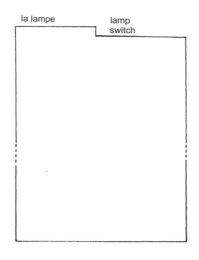

Figure 16: Repetitive learning with the help of the cover-up technique.

dure a second time. Obviously, the first time around he will not know any of the solutions, as they first have to be mentally processed, i.e., *coded and stored.*

Each time the learner repeats the procedure, the number of correct items increases, until finally only a few "difficult" ones remain. In our lesson the words *allumer, éteindre, une ampoule, le bouton, la prise de courant,* and *la pile* will probably be the ones that require the most work; perhaps four or five repetitions of the learning procedure will be required before the pupil can name them confidently.

During all this the learner will make useful observations such as the following: "To switch off" is *éteindre* in French. Another way of saying "switch off" in English is *extinguish*, and this verb is linguistically related to *éteindre*; this can be heard if we make an *x* out of the accent in the *é: exteindre.* With some imagination, one can make an acoustic link with the word *extinguish.* This is an *elaboration*, leading to a slightly different kind of crib from the one described above.

Sooner or later, orthographically difficult words have to be *written down* to trigger suitable visual and possibly motor coding. The pupil can, of course, write down *everything*; i.e., instead of saying the French words out loud he writes them down on a piece of paper or some reusable surface, correcting his solutions each time he moves his piece of card downward. Or he can wait until he feels that he knows all the words *orally* and then start writing them down. Alternatively, he may choose to write down only those words that require some kind of special attention in the way they are written. For example, they may contain accents (such as *électricité*) or their plural ending is tricky.

Anyone who learns in this careful way, not just "cramming" and getting it over with as quickly as possible, will always be able to establish some *meaningful connection* in his thoughts between a foreign word and a word he already knows – a word that sounds similar, looks similar, or has a similar meaning. *"Chômage* sounds rather like *chaumière,"* a pupil may say to himself, "we learned that word not so long ago – but careful, it is spelled differently!"

In cases such as this, *visual images* may well also take the role of elaborations, as we saw above in connection with *cribs*. In other words, these *images* form new links within the semantic network that is gradually being built up from the store of vocabulary (of course in the beginning the mesh of this network is rather loose, but this is not so important). These links can be significant for the pupil in terms of coding and storing, and for retrieving information. Any pupil who wants to practice *repetition learning* is advised to build up elaborations *systematically*, until the procedure becomes a habit.

In the case of *mix-ups* that can occur from time to time, the pairs of words that are becoming confused must be accentuated by *contrasting* them. For example, if the (incorrect) solution *écouter* is given for "to hear," a clear differentiation must be made as follows:

to hear in the sense of *being able to hear* → *entendre*

to hear in the sense of *listening* → *écouter*

This clearly shows that, as is often the case when learning vocabulary, it is not a matter of linking simple pairs of words, but rather a *whole group* of words with the same or slightly different meanings have to be linked with a single word in the foreign language. Of course, this also works the other way around, although it is rare in educational material!

The above-mentioned procedure can also be applied to the third didactic suggestion given at the beginning of this chapter in connection with the learning dictionary: Rather than reading the English word and saying the French word out loud, one can quote *examples* of phrases from the right-hand column.

Symmetry and Detachment from Native-Language Cues

By starting off with the native word and quoting the corresponding French word the pupil builds up a kind of *asymmetry*. It is, therefore, important, as recommended in the second didactic suggestion, to repeat the learning proce-

dure the other way around as well, starting off with the French word, so that
a certain level of *symmetry* is attained.

The procedure we have described up until now is equivalent to the *cued
recall learning* paradigm often used in the fields of memory and *verbal learning* research work. Another type of cue can also be used to recall words that
have been learned: *visual cues*. A good educational aid would be a test in
which there is a picture related to every current learning topic; the objects,
activities, and certain properties shown in the picture would then have to be
named or labeled. The picture can also leave out certain things, so that the
pupil is required to activate his own imagination. If this is done conscientious-
ly, even better results are likely to be achieved by using this method, as it
encourages a higher level of cognitive activity than simply "reading" a given
picture. This type of word recall encourages the pupil's thinking to become
gradually detached from recall cues in the native language: After a while, the
cues contained in the picture produce a direct response in the foreign language, without mediating links from the mother tongue.

14.4 Adaptive and Self-Directed Learning: The Seven "S's"

There are at least three objectives for learning vocabulary in a foreign language: (1) It must be learned *as efficiently as possible*. This means that it must
be learned according to the *degrees of difficulty* inherent in the material. (2)
It must be learned for long-term retention. (3) The vocabulary must be built
up according to its *usefulness* and held constantly *available*. Each individual
will experience differences according to his own existing knowledge and personal learning habits, and these can be adapted to vocabulary learning. This
is known as *adaptive learning* (Atkinson, 1972), a highly self-directed and
self-controlled form of learning (Steiner, 1997).

Up to now we have concentrated on the technique of covering columns in
a textbook. This is a popular method, though its effectiveness is limited. In
some ways and for many pupils a related method, the *card method*, is considerably more efficient if used properly and thoroughly. Here, the pupil takes
neatly cut small pieces of paper or cards and writes the English word on the
front and the corresponding French word on the back. In this way he becomes
familiar with the words contained in a lesson the first time he writes them
down, *reading them out loud* at the same time. Of course, one must take great
care to write down all the vocabulary absolutely correctly, so as not to memorize incorrectly spelled words. Of the 16 words in the lesson mentioned
above, we could leave out *la lampe* and probably also *l'électricien* as "already

known" right from the beginning. The pupil does not leave learning to chance, but checks the material and sorts out the items that are completely new to him and have to be learned from scratch. Moreover, his goal is to learn 100 percent of the vocabulary thoroughly.

S_1 *for Self-Discipline*

Learning can begin once all the cards have been written. The pupil reads the word on the front of the card (if he is alone, out loud), then turns the card over and reads the French translation (ideally twice). From the second time around, the procedure requires a high degree of *self-discipline*: It is important that the card *not be turned over* until a *final formulation* of the French translation has been given *without* looking at the back of the card.

The learner should not make his memory search too easy. He should first make a concerted effort to find the best solution he can *before comparing it* with the solution on the card. If he is uncertain, he should give an imperfect answer on purpose and provide himself feedback by turning the card over. The *processing of this error feedback* is an essential part of learning.

S_2 *for Self-Reinforcement*

As we saw above, turning the card over provides us with feedback on the correctness and completeness of our own solution. If the *correct translation* or the *right phrase* was given, *reinforcement* – "Good!" or "Well done!" – can also be given before moving the card to the back of the pile and carrying on. If the solution given was wrong or incomplete, the English and French words should be repeated out loud once or, even better, twice. The pupil should then carry on *without criticizing himself* for not having known the correct answer. *Self-reinforcement* serves to strengthen the correct responses and extinguish or correct the incorrect ones, in the latter case by the pupil not blaming himself, on the one hand, and by his taking suitable measures to correct the error on the other.

S_3 *for Spontaneous Semantic Elaboration*

The attentive learner will quickly realize that he is not simply learning to link pairs of items together, but rather undertaking *spontaneous* semantic elaborations for almost all pairs, making it easier to recall them. Often, this will lead to cribs, as described above.

S₄ *for Selectivity*

After repeating the process a few times, the pupil will feel confident of one or more items and will systematically leave these out, selecting the more difficult items for further learning. A particularly effective variation is to include *two or even three* cards for a difficult word in the set, so that it appears more often (at irregular intervals) than the others. It is also advisable to code words that are difficult to spell additionally in a visual (and motor) way by writing them down. Here, it is clear that the learner has *adaptive* possibilities for accommodating personal progress and adapting to the demands of the material or own learning experience. In other words, the pupil develops an *adaptive self-learning system*. In this way the learning process becomes highly individual or, as it is also called in the literature, "idiosyncratic." The cards with the most difficult words (sometimes collected systematically over a series of lessons) can be studied on the bus, in the waiting room at the dentist's office, or in other places until all the words become known. This kind of systematic learning is not possible using a textbook alone.

S₅ *for Sequencing*

After repeating the process several times, some pupils will notice that they instinctively know which word comes after a particular item: An association between sequential items in a set of cards has been developed. This kind of association is not favorable to the use of the words (i.e., their application or transfer), and it is advisable to introduce a method not possible in textbook learning (and which in fact leads to such inadequate learning processes) but is typical of *systematic learning*: The cards are mixed so that the individual words follow one another in *variable sequence*. A systematic variation in the sequence of the cards means that each individual item is learned *independently of its predecessor*, thus preventing any sequential or successive effect that can cause dependence on preceding items. If the cards are mixed again and again while the vocabulary is being learned, the words will become independent of one another in everyday use. However, an important point must be made here: Semantically or linguistically related words, i.e., synonyms or antonyms, words with the same root, or verbs with their corresponding nouns should be kept together and learned as meaningful groups. We will come back to this point at the end of the chapter. For now, let us note that it is advisable to write an adjective and its corresponding antonym or a verb and its noun on the same card and learn them together.

S$_6$ *for Symmetry*

The card method also *allows symmetrical* learning, i.e., from one's native language into the foreign language and vice versa. This kind of learning is always advisable, even though we know that in school we are usually tested only in *one* direction! But should we have to speak the language in a normal situation, i.e., in a foreign country, we must be in a position to *produce* and to *receive* the foreign language: That is, we need to be able to recall in both directions.

S$_7$ *for Self-Testing in the Form of Strict Retrieval Practice*

It's happened to all of us at one time or another: We work really hard to learn something by heart, but by the next morning half the information is simply gone. Here, we are dealing with medium- to long-term learning success, i.e., retention over a longer period. As Bjork (1988) showed in his experiments, *strict repeated retrieval practice with ever longer time intervals (expanded retrieval practice)* is an effective way of promoting successful retention. The individual learns the vocabulary, then tests himself the same day again using the cards, but without looking at the solutions on the reverse sides. In this way he knows exactly what he has already forgotten and what he needs to work on to achieve his ultimate goal. This is the prerequisite for closing knowledge gaps. The next retrieval practice is done the following day or evening, and a third time in the same way about a week later. This systematically extends the retention intervals. Each time the process is repeated, existing knowledge is *reinforced*, and the knowledge gaps become ever smaller until they're eventually closed and the vocabulary becomes a part of one's permanent knowledge bank.

If the intervals are allowed to become too long, however, existing knowledge is impaired or no longer available, and retrieval practice is of no help anymore. Of course, the important question is, What are the *optimal intervals* at which much of the information learned is still accessible? These intervals can only be set individually on the basis of empirical learning procedures, although they do vary in length, depending on the contents of the material to be learned. Thus, if vocabulary is to become long-term intellectual property, a strict, expanded retrieval practice as described by Bjork (1988) is an essential mnemonic technique.

If the card method is used according to the seven "*S*'s," i.e., focusing primarily on the more difficult vocabulary, it will be well worth the time and trouble taken. The advantages of the procedure are that it is *systematic, indi-*

vidual, and *adaptable*; those qualities produce a considerable increase in learning efficiency.

Other kinds of information can also be memorized using this method of adaptive and self-regulated learning, for example, the *terms* and *definitions* outlined in Chapter 13; nomenclatures and their meanings, such as those encountered in trade school when learning to distinguish different kinds of substances; the color codes in electronics (on resistors, etc.) and what they mean; or the various commands on a computer and their functions (although the last example is best learned by actually *doing* it). The important thing is that all this information must be *understood* in its context or in its function: The pupil should not memorize items that make no sense to him and should *never get into the habit of learning meaningless information!*

14.5 Internalizing the Retrieval Cues

The extent to which words and whole phrases (see the right-hand column in our example of a lesson at the beginning of the chapter) are *freely* available is one way of measuring the degree of existing language skill or vocabulary knowledge. It is essential that the retrieval process be practiced explicitly in *free recall*: How many of the examples in this lesson (phrases) can I quote *freely*, without being cued by the English word first or a card? How many of the words can I remember and write down if I imagine a particular scene in my mind? The learning process must include these steps, so that the retrieval mechanisms become detached from the cues given by the book, the card, or the teacher and attuned to internal cues, for example, those contained in one's imagination. Only too often does the pupil close the book or put the set of cards aside after learning without truly making sure that he can recall the vocabulary *freely* from memory *without the help of the corresponding cues*. Here too we find further opportunities for improving one's learning processes!

Many of the arguments used up to now are based on the recent results of experiments on coding and recall in memory psychology. Other findings from the field of *semantic memory research* can be put to use for learning a foreign language; we will return to this in Section 14.7.

14.6 How Much Information Can Be Learned in One Go? Some Rather Unsatisfactory Answers

In memory experiments, the upper limit for learning a list of words has been found to lie at around 20 words, assuming the introduction of 1 new word per second. This figure should not mislead us as far as vocabulary learning is concerned, as it is typical for *experiments* in which researchers are interested in avoiding so-called ceiling effects, i.e., when they do not want *all* test subjects to attain maximum results in the shortest possible time.

In experiments concerned specifically with vocabulary learning, Atkinson and Raugh (1975), for example, had participants learn 40 different Russian words within a typical experimental procedure: The test subjects first heard the Russian words three times over headphones and were then asked to type the English (i.e., native-language) translations into the computer.

Vocabulary learning in school under nonexperimental conditions is quite a different matter. There, the learning process is individual, and the words are not simply taken from random lists that clearly will be forgotten again as soon as the memory test is over – at least we hope that the pupil will not adopt this attitude! Also, *all* words must be learned and not (for whatever experimental reason) only some of them. The aims are a *100 percent mastery level* and then *long-term recall* of all words.

Traditional memory research in the early 1970s produced a great many interesting results on the conditions required for storing and recalling information, and on capacity limits (time and quantity) in the processing of all different kinds of material (verbal, pictorial, etc.). Unfortunately, however, there is to this day still no reliable study that can give us detailed information on the number of vocabulary units that can be learned in one go. The following observations are based on rather broad extrapolations from experimental research, or more or less plausible speculations.

Let us start off with Miller's (1956) magical number of 7 ± 2. This is an experimentally determined measurement for the *number of information units (chunks)* an individual can retain in short-term memory. Since we can assume that some of the vocabulary to be learned is very simple (*la lampe – the lamp*), we could interpret 7 ± 2 generously and say that it would be reasonable to attempt to learn nine difficult words at a time. This means that the same number of vocabulary units or vocabulary pairs (the *pair* is the *information unit* here) could be learned at one time. This implies that lessons containing considerably more items would have to be divided up.

Yet, Miller's magical number is a measurement for information units that must be stored in the memory for a short time, such as the digits of a telephone number. If we take a closer look, we realize that this is not applicable to vocabulary learning. A telephone number can usually be forgotten as soon as it has been used, whereas the words have to be recalled. Nevertheless, Miller's number might be relevant for the memory processes at work while the words are being transferred to a more permanent storage place via constant repetition.

Learning vocabulary, carried out carefully and with sufficient motivation, implies the storage of elements in short-term memory and *inner (silent) repetition* or *rehearsal*, as well as the *elaborations* described above. These are necessary for transferring the words from short-term to long-term storage. Here, more recent research on the *working memory* (e.g., Baddeley, 1986, 1990, 1992; Baddeley & Hitch, 1974, 1994; Baddeley & Liberman, 1977) can provide some assistance. On the basis of complex studies (often with so-called dual tasks, in which two activities have to be carried out simultaneously), the researchers claim that, in addition to *short-term storage*, there is a "place" in memory where elaboration is undertaken. The latter is, at least partly, based on information being retrieved from long-term storage (the learner's existing prior knowledge) and then linked with newly introduced information in a unique way (see also Ericsson & Kintsch, 1995). We assume today that this takes place in the *working memory*, where there is room both to store and to process information. So the question of how many items can be learned at one time or how big the "parcels" (chunks) are which contain learning information will depend on how easy elaboration for a word is, how much space or processing capacity it takes up in the working memory, and how much room must be kept available for the simultaneous short-term storage of information. One must also take into consideration the differences between individual learners' prior knowledge and the memory capacity they require for elaboration, as well as how complex and new the information is. All in all, in the light of present knowledge, the best solution is for each pupil to experiment and find out the optimal number of new words he can *personally* learn at one time. (We will return to this in Chapter 19!)

14.7 Long-Term Retention Using Systematic Semantic Elaboration

We have discussed the very useful method of self-testing in the form of expanded retrieval practice (Bjork, 1988). But other ideas can also be helpful, for example, that wherever possible *all information for long-term storage must be integrated into existing knowledge structures*. In other words, many explicit relationships (elaborations) between old and new knowledge structures must be established. The integration of new material with prior knowledge takes place within the framework of the reconstruction or adaptation of semantic networks, which can be considerably enhanced by the structure of the learning material used (see also Chapter 13 on the development of *mental models*, Chapter 15 on *numerical networks*, and Chapter 17 on *cognitive maps*).

The selection of *compound themes* for each lesson in a textbook is a very useful teaching aid, as it marks out a *curricular* and *conceptual framework* around which a network of meanings can be built up. This method is didactically simple but effective, and many textbook authors would profit by using it! A complete scene that can be imaged visually forms the basic content of this framework, though *explicitly* created associations are often missing, especially those of a grammatical, semantic, and specifically linguistic kind (e.g., those based on the *etymology of a word*).

The examples given in the third column of the learning dictionary at the beginning of the chapter are an elementary form of this kind of development of associations: Newly learned nouns are combined with verbs to make simple sentences (or at least *phrases*, in a linguistic sense), or verbs are combined with an object to form even larger linguistic units.

Of course, there are other ways of learning words with the intention of building up a semantic network: for example, when a word such as *passer* is used to build up a whole family of words based on its origin (see Figure 17; *passer*).

It is certainly advisable to build up *word families* in the foreign language, since it allows one to develop a feeling for the language as a whole. We are concerned here with learning not only single elements of vocabulary, but rather whole groups of linguistically related words. Therefore, our goal is not simply to learn by heart in response to *verbal cues (cued recall procedure)*; rather, we must check how well we have mastered a whole family of foreign-

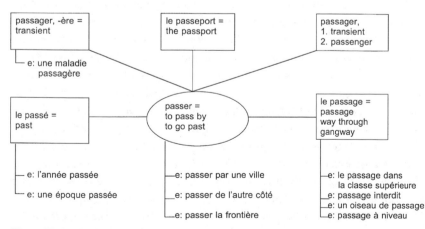

Figure 17: Graph of the French word family "passer"; e = example.

language words with their English translations in *free recall*. This task becomes quite demanding if we then try to recall whole phrases incorporating
the words, especially when, as in our case (third column), no explicit English
translation has ever been given for these phrases.

Whenever any information of a conceptual, semantic nature is learned, free
recall implies that the pupil not only concentrates his efforts on coding and
storing information, but also concentrates on practicing the *retrieval* and *use*
of that information. Free recall forces him to reproduce the coded and stored
information actively and to *practice* the retrieval mechanisms (see also Chapters 9 and 13). This is also the basic idea behind Bjork's (1988) expanded
retrieval practice.

But let us return to the words shown in Figure 17. How do they become
intellectual property? The answer: Each member of a word family has to be
learned individually! The *generation of visual images,* described above in
vocabulary learning for "free recall," can again be useful here, though in this
case the method is probably relatively limited in its effectiveness: Although
le passage, le passeport, and *le passager* could quite easily be imagined in a
single scene, the two adjective forms *passager* and *passagère* and likewise *le
passé* could prove rather more difficult.

Of course, the card method might also be employed successfully. Alternatively, or additionally, it would also be useful to take the empty diagram and
practice filling in the missing words again and again, or simply to create a new
diagram containing existing knowledge (a kind of *mapping*; see Chapter 13).
In this way the learning process takes on an additional, albeit rather arbitrary,
spatial aspect that helps in coding and retrieving the word family.

Taking more recent theories on cognitive construction into consideration
(construction of concepts, e.g., in a teacher's explanations, see Chapter 13 and
Aebli, 1978, 1980, 1981; Steiner, 1997), we must assume that nouns derived
from verbs play an extremely large role in understanding the meanings of texts
during the learning process. For example, someone first describes a situation
in which two cars *collide*. In the next sentence, "this collision" is spoken of.
The verb *to collide* has been made into the noun *collision*, which now contains
all the information previously mentioned by the speaker in a condensed form.
(Thus, when learning a foreign language, one should work toward such linguistic transformations as those shown in Figure 17.) From an early level of
language proficiency onward it is advisable to learn the nouns derived from
verbs along with the verbs themselves: *passer – le passage; chanter – le chant,
la chanson; marcher – la marche (le marché* should be learned in contrast to
la marche); courir – la course, etc.

For a teacher of a foreign language, it is perfectly feasible to begin with word families in the *native language*, as these are already stored as existing knowledge in coherent linguistic and semantic networks. Of course, learning the respective equivalents in the foreign language amounts to a process of *cued recall*, but – and this is the important factor – the cues are already available in a structure that is easy to remember. This simply means that the *retrieval paths* activating the corresponding foreign words are kept available. These are linked together semantically, but not necessarily linguistically. To give an example: *rentrer* (to go home) and *partir* (to leave) are closely related to one another *semantically*, though *linguistically* they lie far apart.

Another method of developing retrieval paths and activating them when they are needed is shown in Figure 18. Here, *meaning connections* are systematically established and used as the basis for a cue structure (a network of paths) for retrieval when it is time to learn them (see Figure 18, *causes des accidents*).

When we learn vocabulary in this way, we are using the strategy of grouping or *clustering*. As the above example shows, *semantic categories* can be selected for this clustering. But as we saw above as well, *clusters* can also be formed according to phonetic, graphic, or linguistic criteria (Bower, 1970). The advantage of learning based on a grouping according to *meaning* is that it implies the development of a *retrieval plan,* which provides *semantic cues* and also signals empty slots where the elements in the foreign language belong. These in turn can be called up while working one's way through an elaborated semantic network. However, when placing them in the given space

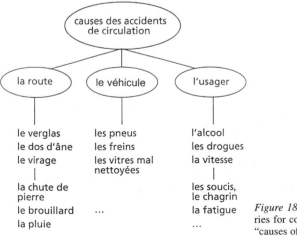

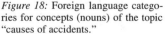

Figure 18: Foreign language categories for concepts (nouns) of the topic "causes of accidents."

in the diagram, the learner is obliged to learn the foreign words themselves (how they sound, how they are spelled), and not only their meaning. In other words, we code such important characteristics as the article (gender), pronunciation, and orthography simultaneously within the semantic network.

Finally, we must mention a further type of learning which, as discussed above, implies both a close semantic relationship and linguistic remoteness: the learning of *synonyms*. A fluent grasp of a foreign language is partly due to the availability of synonyms or other closely related words. For this reason, it is desirable to acquire as many synonyms for as many nouns, verbs, and adjectives as possible in the foreign language. Antonyms (opposites such as black–white or give–take) should not be forgotten here. Antonyms have "related" semantic networks: The elements of meaning are often the same, but the relationships, e.g., the direction of action, are opposites (to take off–to land, to buy–to sell, ascent–descent, question–answer, etc.).

However, this situation does not give us a clear idea of how to code such pairs (synonyms and antonyms) acoustically or visually. The first step would certainly be to associate both words in the foreign language with their translations in one's native language. These would then be used as cues for recalling the two items in the foreign language (be they synonyms or antonyms). Later, once the stock of words in the foreign language becomes more detached from that in the native language, one of the foreign language items will directly activate the other. The learning process then begins to move *within* the semantic networks of the foreign language and thus far outgrows the learning of more or less isolated vocabulary pairs.

Memo

1. The term *paired-associate learning* or *paired association* describes the connection of two items (usually nouns, less often illustrations). In a memory test (cued recall test), the test subject is given the first item and asked to name the other. One can facilitate the associative connection by making a sentence containing both items or by creating a visual image of the two objects the items represent interacting with one another in a compound picture (e.g., a whale smoking a cigar).
2. Although learning vocabulary is also concerned with linking word items in pairs, it cannot be explained by the paradigm of paired associations, since the two items concerned are from identical semantic networks rather than from different ones. (One can say that English and French vocabulary simply assign different labels to the same semantic network, e.g., for light bulb.) Learning vocabulary is based on diverse visual, acoustic, or motor coding, according to the sound of the word item or how it is written.
3. If there are no obvious acoustic or spelling similarities to link up, these can be created by introducing peg-words. In the peg-word method, i.e., using cribs as

mnemonics, a link is established (the peg-word) that sounds similar to the foreign word. The objects representing the peg-word and the foreign-language word *(ampulla/light bulb)* are associated with one another in a single visual image. When the word in the native language is named, the pupil remembers the generated picture in the imagination, which also features the peg-word *(ampulla)*. This in turn recalls the similar-sounding word in the foreign language *(ampoule)*.

4. All learning procedures that somehow extend the items to be learned (through similarities in sound or spelling, with the help of cribs, and so on) are known as elaborations. They link the elements to be learned, but also link those items with elements of prior knowledge.

5. Repetition learning is indispensable. It can be used for the purpose of reinforced coding, but also for the construction of elaborations. In the latter case, rote learning can be transformed into the higher learning process of semantic network building, by concentrating on the meaning of the items being dealt with.

6. Learning by heart (e.g., using the card method), when carried out systematically, optimizes its efficiency. The seven "*S*'s" stand for the key concepts of Self-discipline, Self-reinforcement, Spontaneous semantic elaboration, Selectivity, Sequencing, Symmetry, and Self-testing in the form of strict retrieval practice.

7. Successful medium- to long-term learning depends on practiced retrieval that is carried out several times, whereby the interval between each retrieval practice becomes increasingly longer (expanded retrieval practice).

8. In addition to long-term retention of vocabulary, a scheme that follows the principle of the "*S*'s" serves to further adaptive, self-regulated, and self-controlled learning, which takes the different degrees of difficulty of the items to be learned and individual learning progress into account. The learner receives ample opportunity to use individual learning procedures but nevertheless carries the responsibility for his own success or failure.

9. The optimal number of words that can be learned at one time can be determined only on an individual basis. It depends on prior knowledge, available learning strategies (e.g., the development of cribs), individual performance (rate and density of learning), but also on the complexity of the material to be learned.

10. When learning vocabulary, one creates two related networks, one in the native language and one in the foreign language. If effectively learned, the vocabulary from one language can be called up from the network of the other. However, the aim of learning a foreign language is in the end the ability to recall vocabulary using only the cues and the corresponding connections within the foreign language network.

11. The development of networks takes place via processes of systematically linguistically or semantically connecting the items to be learned or by linguistic and semantic elaboration (word families). The cues used can later be effective as retrieval aids in recalling the items. They also make a considerable contribution to the ability to apply the vocabulary learned in an appropriate way.

15. Learning to Count: Constructing Numeric Networks. Piaget's Genetic Epistemology Approach – and Beyond

15.1 Introduction

This chapter shows how a very specific semantic network, namely a *numeric network*, is constructed to deal with all arithmetic operations. We choose this domain because numbers are simpler to grasp and more direct ("transparent") to us than, say, everyday concepts (e.g., inflation).

From Piaget's *genetic epistemology* we shall adopt the idea of the *relevance of action* in regard to arithmetic operations, the *system character* of structures to be established – the numeric network – as well as his *didactically* interesting concept *mise en relation* – which simply means "putting together" or "putting into a certain relation."

The following terms will also be of particular importance: *differentiating* between *mise en relation* and *lecture des données* (which means "focusing on what is given"), *coherent systems of action, coherent numeric networks, arithmetic reference point, iteration of natural numbers*, the operations of *halving* and *doubling, operative thinking*, grasping of the *direction of changes of numeric sizes*, the *plurality of solution paths, automatization*, the *autonomy of the learner*, as well as *self-control and self-reinforcement*.

Counting consists of much more than simply associating two numbers to each other via operational signs to get the desired result; it also means *constructing, extending*, and *exploring numeric networks* – which in turn demand a very high level of learning and thought processes. Piaget's collaborator Pierre Gréco said it quite eloquently: "L'arithmétique n'est pas la logique du pauvre" (Gréco, 1963, 100; see also Steiner, 1973, 54) – arithmetic is not the logic of the dumb.

15.2 9 × 8 = 72, or Maybe 74

Let's take a look at a school classroom: The second-grade children today are learning their 8's. To this end, the teacher has decided to take the "sweet" road to success, using small square cookies, 8 of which fit exactly into a prepared box. The first, and of course the second, box contains 8 pieces each, so together there are 16, i.e., 2 × 8 = 16. The third box contains 8 more (= 24 total). Just to be sure, the children count again before writing "24" in the third row on a card: "24," they all say and think, 3 × 8 = 24. They then put together the three boxes on the table in front of them to form a single block and put the corresponding number (8, 16, 24, ...) beside each one (Figure 19).

Upon reaching 80 in this manner, they are able to recite the entire row of numbers. Individual children say the numbers aloud, and the others write them both on the blackboard and in their booklets. By this time nearly all children have learned at least half of the row of numbers, up to 5 × 8 or even 6 × 8, by whispering the corresponding calculations. The teacher thinks it important that the children practice counting by using the boxes: Repeatedly, a child would take a box, put it on the table, and recite "1 × 8 = 8, 2 × 8 = 16, ... " until all 10 boxes were in place. The boxes were not stacked, but rather arranged in a row, to prevent any confusion. At this point the children received a coloring page depicting the 10 boxes of 8 cookies each: The first 8 were colored dark brown, the next 8 light brown, to differentiate them clearly. The teacher had brought along specially for this purpose new light-brown colored pencils, which delighted the children since the pencils could be used for other things as well. The respective calculations were also written with these colors.

The last 5 minutes of class was devoted to, as they say, playful reinforcement. The children chanted in chorus, "1 × 8 = 8, 2 × 8 = 16, 3 × 8 = 24, 4 × 8 = 32," etc., up to "10 × 8 = 80." Then, the teacher turned up the heat, erasing from the blackboard a result ("24") and leaving only the calculation ("3 × 8"). The children now began anew in chorus: "1 × 8 = 8, 2 × 8 = 16, 3 × 8 = 24, 4 × 8 = 32." "Well, you've all learned that very well," the teacher said and

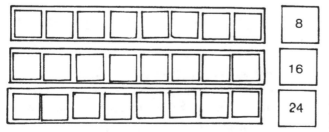

Figure 19: The rows of cookie boxes for learning one's 8's.

removed two further results (40 and 72). The recitation starts over: "1 × 8 = 8, 2 × 8 = 16 ... " But at 9 × 8 both the intensity and the certainty of the chorus subsided. Some stopped speaking altogether, some decided 9 × 8 equaled 74, others pulled through and said 72! At this point the bell rang for recess, though the greater reward was that every child received a cookie, regardless of whether he or she had said 74, 72, or nothing at all. During recess, the children played a different game, so that there was no interference from any other source of mathematical reasoning with this, the final calculation of the hour, of 9 × 8. The children left the room clearly under the impression of either knowing, not knowing, or simply presuming the correct answer. The reader will remember that this corresponds quite well to Guthrie's interpretation of reinforcement and its effect (cf. Chapter 4, particularly Memo 4).

15.3 The Teacher's Didactic Reasoning: Associative Links as a Basis for Learning to Count

Didactically, the teacher is assuming that every multiplication row can be seen as a *series of numbers or calculations* that effectively is the *repeated addition* of a set number (in this case the number 8). Reducing multiplication to repeated addition is certainly *one way* to look at the matter – and it is sufficient for use in most daily multiplication tasks. The exception would be situations in which a Cartesian product is being sought, e.g., "How many handshakes are possible between 5 Swiss and 8 American diplomats?"

In order to impart the structure of multiplication to the children, the teacher relies on a number of things: (1) the attractiveness of the material; (2) the clear order of the 8 elements in each box; (3) the countability of these elements; (4) the perceptually clear results obtained by counting, which can be written down and put next to the respective box; (5) the procedure that the children recite the calculations both aloud and inwardly in order to impress them upon their minds; and (6) the repeated praise (reinforcement) of the children's obtaining the correct results.

Three of these points derive from classical (behavioristic) learning theory: first, the attractiveness of the material, which serves as an *incentive* for participation (perhaps the children even recognized the role of the cookies as motivation since they received, say, cherries when they learned their "2's"); second, *repetition* as a mechanism of learning; third, the presence of proper *reinforcement*. This would refute Thorndike's reservations about learning *solely through repetition* (cf. Chapter 3).

The teacher's latent assumption that the children will eventually learn their 8's by simply repeating the exercise enough times, however, should be questioned. One might object that it is important both *what* and *how* things are repeated; that point (2) above – the *clear figural order* of the elements and the results being shown at every repetition – is decisive; and that such results are not just memory codes similar to those used by some people to store keyboard configurations on a computer, but rather are the product of a *process of counting*, repeatable at any time, starting with 1 × 8. But we must remember, on the other hand, that, according to the teacher's own conviction, we are dealing with a *multimedia presentation* of these calculations; i.e., the results are presented both *spatially* (in order) and *visually* (as numbers) as well as in the form of *auditory codes* (verbal "imprinting"). If necessary, one could also add a *motor coding*, by coloring the packages and writing down the calculations on paper. Thus far only the teacher's assumptions.

Learning multiplication tables clearly involves a number of different coding processes (visual, auditory, articulatory, possibly motor). But which mechanism within one of these processes is responsible for actually *producing* the result of 32 for the calculation 4 × 8 or 56 for 7 × 8? Here, it becomes clear that the relationship of the results to the calculations does not depend on the type of coding, but on the type of underlying processes by the so-called central executive.

The teacher, in slowly building up the rows of 8, *associates* the first two numbers (e.g., 7 and 8 in 7 × 8) with the result (= 56), and anyone who does not retain this association and fails to recall it at the next instance is effectively poor in mathematics; someone who properly retains the association and can retrieve it at will is considered good in mathematics.

15.4 Associative Links Do Not Suffice

But such an association does not suffice. This becomes clear, first, when the child spontaneously fails to come up with the right result and reels off the entire row from the beginning, in hopes of stumbling upon the answer in the process. Such rows of multiplication then effectively become a chain of stimuli and responses, one leading to the next, so that anything in between can be obtained only (or at least preferably) by going through the entire sequence.

Second, the association alone is insufficient because the child, after proclaiming the solution, eagerly (or perhaps nervously) awaits the reaction of the teacher or other students whether in fact it is "right" or "wrong." The child, however, does not expect information on *why* the result might be right or wrong.

Third, and most important, the simple association of a pair of numbers with another number actually detours a child's *understanding* from what the numbers and the operation signs connecting them actually mean. This can be seen (at the latest) when a second-grade child trying to solve the calculation 7×8 asks, "Is that multiplication or addition?" Here, it becomes clear that every number and every operation sign in the calculation "$7 \times 8 = 56$" *stand for* something or *symbolize* something, i.e., *represent* something. This in fact is what the child *should* be resorting to.

15.5 Arithmetic Operations and Their Action Base

All arithmetic operations are rooted in actions; learning these operations thus involves having a grasp of the action(s) in question. We must therefore be sure that the second-grade pupil learning multiplication tables thoroughly understands the *action nature of multiplication* and is able to compare it with that of, say, addition. In contrast to the plus sign (+) in addition, the times sign (×) or center dot (•) in multiplication means that the first number (the *multiplicator*) has a completely different function from the second number (the *multiplicand*): The first symbolizes an *operator* (a *mechanism*, as it were) and represents the number of actions to be carried out – do this 7 times or whatever (get or bring something, etc.), whereas the second number represents a *state* – how many there are of a particular thing being acted on. Understanding this difference between these two roles in multiplication is the primary prerequisite to differentiating between $7 + 8$ and 7×8. But it is also, as we will see later on, important when drawing conclusions from the calculation of 7×8 to 8×8 or even to 8×7!

Understanding the action nature of multiplication thus means actually *doing* (or at least *imagining doing*) what one later depicts in the form of numbers.

15.6 The System Character of Arithmetic Operations

Research in the field of developmental psychology, above all that emerging from Piaget's Genevan school (cf. Steiner, 1973), pointed not only to the *action basis* of a number of fields of knowledge (number concept, spatial and logical conceptions, for example), but also to the *system character* thereof. In other words, learning *arithmetic operations* (the subject of this chapter) is not solely based on action, but also implies the construction of coherent *action systems*, and later *arithmetic thought systems.*

Before returning to our multiplication tables, let us first touch once again – in an extension of the themes discussed in Chapters 13 and 14 – on the subject of how conceptual structures or semantic networks are constructed. Further, we will look at a few *elementary operations* that in part represent, from a learning psychology point of view, the prerequisites for dealing with multiplication tables in general.

Conceptual Systems or Semantic Networks

The numbers we are considering are in fact *concepts* (cf. Piaget & Szeminska, 1965), albeit concepts of a special sort compared to other concepts such as "supply" or "demand" or "inflation," to name but a few. As far as the *learning* of concepts (e.g., "inflation") is concerned, modern *semantic memory theory* shows us how one comes to understand concepts as elements of the knowledge structure. Concepts represent parts of more comprehensive knowledge systems – parts of *semantic networks*. Concepts such as "inflation" contain other, more basic concepts as *building blocks* or *elements*, which in turn are connected to each other by various relations. Thus, for example, the term *inflation* contains the concepts "money," "goods," "services" – but also such higher concepts as "circulation of money and goods." As a whole they constitute the concept of "inflation." Concepts can be connected with other concepts at any level, resulting in new concepts arising at *higher levels*; for example, "money policy" results from combining "inflation" with other concepts such as "federal bank intervention."

Conceptual elements are connected through *named associations*, that is, through special relations such as "belongs to" or "is part of" or some other transitive verb like "to have," "to contain," "to need," or "to hit" (cf. Chapter 13).

Two things are important here: (1) Concepts within a semantic network can be *unfolded,* much as the term *inflation* can be turned into the expression "Inflation occurs when too much money is in circulation compared to the amount of goods and services available, thus reducing the value of a money unit." (2) Any part of a network consisting of several conceptual elements and their relations to each other can be *condensed* (cf. Chapter 13) and continue to be used as a new, as it were, compact conceptual element that in turn can enter into new relations with other conceptual elements. *Conceptual learning* is thus (a) the process of *connecting* elements to form new networks, (b) the process of *condensing* (or chunking) these network elements to form new elements or "objects" of the thinking process (Aebli, 1978, 1981), (c) the ordering or *structuring* of such newly connected and "chunked" elements (Steiner, 1997).

The diversity of the elements present in any one semantic network is, like the number of relations between them, in principle infinite. The main characteristic of conceptual learning processes is their *constructive* nature. This is where cognitive learning theory meets developmental theory and Piaget's genetic epistemology (Steiner, 1997).

Numeric Networks

As mentioned above, numbers are *concepts* as well. They are infinite in *number*, though limited in *variety* (natural, whole, rational, irrational, imaginary, as well as a few other types). The number of relations possible between numbers is also limited or at least rather monotonic compared to the infinitely many (and interesting) relations found in other, nonnumeric (= verbal) systems. We should expect, then, that numeric systems, being of such a "simple" nature, would in fact be easier to understand or more transparent than colloquial semantic networks containing our world knowledge.

Numbers, being conceptual elements, are *connected* with each other through arithmetic operations, giving rise to *new elements*. Yet, they may also be *unfolded*, revealing their *constitutional elements* with all respective relations. For example, the number 8 can be unfolded to show its many elements and relations as follows:

8 is 1 more than 7	$8 = 7 + 1$
8 is 1 less than 9	$8 = 9 - 1$
8 is half of 16	$8 = 16/2$ or $8 = 1/2 \times 16$ (half of 16)
8 is twice 4	$8 = 2 \times 4$ (double 4)
8 is one-third of 24	$8 = 24/3$ or $8 = 1/3 \times 24$

And on higher levels:

8 is the square root of 64	$8 = \sqrt{64}$
8 is the cube root of 512	$8 = \sqrt[3]{512}$
8 is 2 to the 3rd power	$8 = 2^3$
8 is the log 10 of 100,000,000	

Of course, potentially the number of such statements is infinite. If we wanted to visualize this situation, all statements would meet in the one network point of "8," resulting in a picture somewhat like that of a conceptual network propounded by the semantic memory theory (cf. among others Aebli, 1978, 1981; Norman & Rumelhart, 1975). This wealth of statements connecting the number 8 to many other numbers in fact shows us the *meaning of the number 8*. One also sees that the list can be extended even further. Also, the numeric network, like all conceptual networks, contains *hidden* or *tacit information* that can be extracted from what is known under certain circumstances. For example, *if* 8 is 1 less than 9 and 9 is 1 less than 10, *then* 8 is 2 less than 10. Learning to count thus means learning to *construct numeric networks* and to move *freely within them*. Here, we have reached the level of *basic cognitive learning*.

15.7 The Construction of Coherent Numeric Networks

Didactically Fruitful Concepts

Piaget's constructive theory of development (e.g., 1947; cf. Steiner, 1973; Flavell, 1963, 1985) contains a number of ideas I consider to be extremely fruitful when discussing how we learn to count. A numeric network can be seen as a *compound* (or *holistic*) *structure* in Piaget's sense (he called it a *structure d'ensemble*), though the theoretical congruence between his *compound structure* and the *semantic network* I am proposing here is not perfect. The concept of networks is much wider and better suited than Piaget's concept of *structure d'ensemble* for explaining *open processes* such as counting (Steiner, 1994; Steiner & Stoecklin, 1997).

A second concept of Piaget's, however, is even more important, what he called *mise en relation*, i.e., putting something in relation to something else. Two or more elements are connected or *linked* to each other. Piaget differentiates this process from the simple act of "reading off the facts" (*lecture des données*). Learning to count involves establishing numeric connections, i.e., linking numeric elements through the use of relations that were originally actions.

The Iteration of Natural Numbers

The most basic relations taught in primary-school mathematics are those involving the addition/subtraction of 1, which implicitly contain the *iteration* of the ascending and descending rows of natural numbers: 8 is 1 more than 7, 7 is 1 more than 6, etc. Iteration and the respective implicit relations are not determined solely by the counting process; rather, iteration implies a certain *reversibility*: If 8 is 1 less than 9, then 9 is 1 more than 8.

Doubling and Halving

Iteration allows us to explore natural numbers and whole numbers in *small* steps. It introduces us to the additive and subtractive aspects of counting. The relations "half" and "double" or the operations of halving and doubling have their place somewhere in between addition and subtraction, on the one hand, and multiplication and division, on the other. With these relations we enter the realm of numbers in larger steps than ±1 iterations; we experience the *repetitive addition* or *removal* of equal parts larger than 1, and thus prepare the way for multiplication. Halving and doubling also imply a *reversibility*: If 8 is double 4, 4 is half of 8! Doubling one number (or doubling a number of objects) means first choosing a particular number (of objects) and adding the same amount (at first on a one-to-one basis) and then focusing not on the first or second single set, but on the whole. This whole is *double* what was present at the beginning. The prerequisites for learning such an operation are the *number concept* (i.e., having reached *number invariance,* Piaget & Szeminska, 1941), *one-to-one matching*, and an understanding of the *part–whole relationship*.

Basic Constructive Processes

Iteration and the operations of halving and doubling form the basic operations for entering and commanding the elementary space of natural numbers. But how do we construct such a numeric network, whose structure and the control thereof constitute learning how to count? The answer: By diligently building upon prior knowledge. *Known facts are related to unknown or forgotten facts.* If, for example, the equation 3 + 3 = 6 is already known (for whatever reason, perhaps in the sense "3 doubled is 6"), this knowledge can be introduced to solve the unknown 3 + 4 = ?. This is, of course, a *very elementary example*, but remember: learning to count begins with just such elementary examples. The learning process goes through the following steps:

Step 1: The learning child recognizes that 3 + 4 is *not the same* as 3 + 3. The result of 3 + 4 *must* be different from 3 + 3! For every child, and particularly for the mentally retarded child, this step is a major and meaningful one on the path toward constructing a *coherent numeric network* (Steiner, 1983).

Step 2: In this step, the child recognizes that 3 + 4 must be *more* than 3 + 3, since 4 is more than 3. This, too, is a banal but extremely important step toward understanding the *direction of change in the numeric size* of an arithmetic result. Such knowledge is relatively easy to gain with the use of the color sticks of Georges Cuisenaire, as we will see further below.

Step 3: Here, the child recognizes by *how much* 3 + 4 exceeds 3 + 3, namely, by exactly 1. This reveals the iteration insight in the series of natural numbers mentioned above.

Similarly, we can solve the equation 5 + 6 = ? or 5 + 4 = ? by using the knowledge gained with the Cuisenaire material mentioned, namely, by solving and using the equation 5 + 5 = 10. *Doubling the first natural numbers* (2 × 1, 2, 3, ..., or 1 + 1 = 2, 2 + 2 = 4, 3 + 3 = 6, ..., up to 10 + 10 = 20) as well as the *ability to iterate the natural numbers* by ±1 certainly form the initial foundation for the construction of a numeric network.

Let us now look more closely at a few processes of learning to count using elementary examples – many of which will turn up again when dealing with multiplication. For example, how can we put Piaget's differentiation between *mise en relation* and *lecture des données* to use in learning psychology? Researchers from developmental psychology have clearly shown what this differentiation means for *conceptual development* (cf. Piaget & Szeminska, 1965, one of many sources). But here we are interested in the differentiation with respect to *learning to count in school.*

Many teaching systems for learning to count require special materials or at least suggest the use of chips or color sticks (Figure 20). There is, however, a reasonable danger that children who use such materials will not really learn to establish *relationships* between the numbers or the statements made about such numbers, but rather simply *read off* the length of a certain combination of sticks or the state of a row of chips (Piaget's *lecture des données*). The materials used or the configuration visually presented more or less invites (or at least suggests to) the learner to do so. This grave danger emanating from such illustrative material is not well known to many teachers, and there is still much cognitive learning research that could be done on this subject (e.g., Nesher, 1989). Work with disabled children has shown that *less* or only very

Figure 20: Different types of materials for learning to count: chips or color sticks (Cuisenaire material), using as an example the addition of 5 + 3.

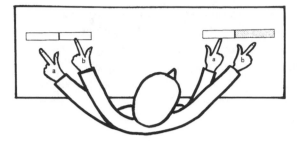

Figure 21: How a *mise en relation* functions: The two configurations are put relatively far apart on the table. By pointing with the fingers of the right and left hand, the user marks relationships, for example, (a) what is the same and (b) what is not the same. One can then deduce by iteration why and by how much they are not the same – and finally, based on these thoughts, the final result can be determined. This system allows us to set up relationships in steps, but they cannot simply be "read off," i. e., *lecture des données* is impossible.

deliberate use of materials such as the color sticks of Georges Cuisenaire actually leads to more insight into elementary mathematical operations (Steiner, 1972). (In Chapter 13 we studied the use of illustrative materials, and in Chapters 16 and 18 we shall return to this subject.)

Children's "reading off" the answer (in this case, the *numeric* answers) is what hinders them in making progress in building up numeric structures (networks). Reading off the answer *does not lead to new relations* between the elements (= numbers), and thus no new parts of numeric networks arise. Teachers should prepare teaching situations very carefully so that their students can establish true relationships, even if these are very simple ones (in fact, they are simple only for adults). Any teacher who truly wants to instill an understanding of numeric networks especially has the duty of preventing *strategies of reading off* (including counting off of elements, particularly using the fingers). The easiest method (and a minimum requirement) is to *separate* the configurations, for example, the color sticks or other elements, spatially from one another (cf. Figure 21) so that the student is forced to compare configurations and under the weight of intensive information processing to associate hitherto unlinked elements. When this is the case, "reading off" (Piaget's *lecture des données*) is no longer possible.

15.8 Cognitive Construction and the Individual Autonomy of the Learner

Constructing a numeric network does not primarily mean finding the right answer to some mathematical question, but rather determining the relationships between or among numbers, or, as in this case to *neighboring* equations (i.e., "neighboring" mathematical statements). Thus, for the student the task is not primarily to *know* what $5 + 6$ is, but to know what $5 + 6$ and $5 + 5$ *have in common*. If one already knows that $5 + 5 = 10$, it is possible to determine completely unknown results correctly. Or if the pupil wants to determine the correctness of $5 + 6 = 11$, he can *compare* this calculation to $5 + 5 = 10$. The *arithmetic reference point* "$5 + 5 = 10$" (within the numeric network) can also be associated with $6 + 5$, $4 + 5$, $5 + 4$, or even $4 + 6$, the latter being an example of *compensation*: 4 is 1 less than 5, but 6 is 1 more than 5, so that $4 + 6$ must be the same as $5 + 5$! Taking the cue from a doubling of 5 (i.e., $5 + 5 = 10$) or from a halving of 10 ($10 - 5 = 5$), one can link $10 - 6 = ?$ with $10 - 5 = 5$ or with $10 - 4$ or $11 - 5$ or $9 - 5$. All of these statements can be oriented toward $10 - 5 = 5$ as their *arithmetic reference point* (reference node in the network). The task, however, is always the same: to connect one calculation (the solution of which is either unknown or needs to be checked) with some other, known calculation.

Step 1: "If $10 - 5 = 5$ (arithmetic reference point) and if I am to calculate what $10 - 6$ is, then I know it's *not the same amount*."

Step 2: "$10 - 6$ must be *less than* $10 - 5$ because I am subtracting *more*." This is basically the verbalization of the most important step. The relevant facet of this step is the learner's insight into the *direction of change* of the result.

Step 3: "Thus, it is not 5, but 1 less than 5, that is 4. $10 - 6 = 4$." This is the pupil's conclusion. He has crossed his numeric network for a short, albeit important stretch.

Such counting behavior leads to a pupil's *autonomy*; i.e., he frees himself of *external judgments* (e.g., whether some calculation is correct or not) and becomes independent of *external reinforcement*. His own control over the correctness of his calculations gives him the power to *reinforce himself*. If the term weren't so worn one could indeed speak of "emancipation"! Seen systematically, building up numeric networks is one way of erecting a *system of self-reinforcements* – which is clearly of great importance to the further development of both a student's cognitive skills and his or her motivation.

As previously mentioned, the mathematical considerations given above are all based on an *action premise*. The child must have practically experienced that the result is actually more when he adds a relatively greater sum to an existing amount. The child must have also experienced that this is *not* the case with subtraction – that there is less left over in the end if he or she takes away a relatively greater sum. What is learned through such "live" experiences (and indeed can only be learned in that manner) is the *direction of change* some result undergoes when known and unknown amounts are compared. Then, before even figuring out a single sum, the child is able to say: "It must be more (than before)." This is pure *operative thinking*, based on action and embedded in an ever *more encompassing system*! It also forms the centerpiece in the application of Piaget's epistemology (Steiner, 1994).

15.9 Constructing an Elementary Multiplication Network

Having considered these basic thoughts on the processes involved in *constructing numeric networks* and in elementary arithmetic operations, we can now return to our multiplication tables.

Even in the field of multiplication there are some "basics" that every second-grade pupil can refer to while learning to count; here, too, we find the elementary operations of *iteration, doubling,* and *halving*. Iteration, however, can go either forward or backward by the size of the multiplier. In the 8's there are steps of ±8. If someone takes the equation $5 \times 8 = 40$ as an *arithmetic reference point in a numeric network*, he or she can associate this statement with the equation 6×8 and find or check the proper result of 48 through the iterative step of $40 + 8$, reinforcing himself or herself in the end: "Now that's right!"

A pupil acquainted with doubling (the repeated addition of the same number) can do many calculations of the 8 rows within the numeric network with the help of the doubling operation (also called the *doubling algorithm*). Say the starting point is $2 \times 8 = 16$. If we double the amount, that is 4×8, the result has to be twice the last result: 32. From $2 \times 8 = 16$, we can iteratively $(+ 8)$ reach $3 \times 8 = 24$. And if we double this amount (i.e., 6×8) we get twice the result: 48. With the inverse operation (halving) the same is true: $10 \times 8 = 80$, and half as much times 8, namely, 5×8, results in half the result: 40!

Here, too, it is important to establish *relationships between arithmetic statements* (calculations or elements thereof). Thus, in this early constructional stage we are not interested in the pupil quickly associating results with numbers and operational signs; rather, the pupil should consciously learn first to establish relationships and finally to *verbalize* them.

Obviously, teaching materials can play a major role in this process. The motto, however, remains: *mise en relation* and not *lecture des données*. Relating one thing to another, as we have already seen in the elementary examples of addition, always comprises the act of comparing. We need double the amount of cookie boxes! From those network nodes (e.g., $2 \times 8 = 16$) that are known the next – the unknown – node can be determined via doubling (Figure 22).

If the cookies are not counted off one at a time, a *reading off* of the result is nearly excluded. It is important for children that they not concentrate on that one and only correct configuration of 4 × 8; rather, it is preferable that they choose different *alternative* setups so that they understand that not the configuration, but solely the *relationship* to the equation 2 × 8 = 16 is decisive (Figure 23).

The basic difference between the construction of numeric networks and the teacher's method described at the beginning of this chapter lies in the *systematic character* of learning. Instead of many more or less isolated and at best linear associations we have *multiple linking* of mathematical statements (propositions). Further, emphasis is shifted from the multitude of visual, auditory, and perhaps motor codings to *semantic codings*, i.e., the supply and storage of arithmetic–numeric associations, which will be of great help later for easily navigating the paths of the numeric–arithmetic network.

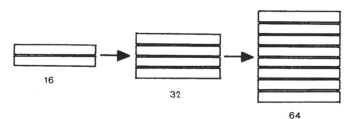

Figure 22: Doubling as part of an elementary multiplication network.

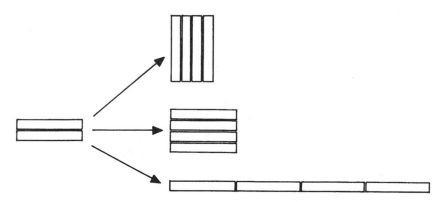

Figure 23: Different configurations for ensuring the construction of *mise en relation* situations in multiplication.

As mentioned above, this method of learning to count allows the pupil to take up *control paths*, to check 9 × 8 by calculating 10 × 8 minus 8 or 8 × 8 plus 8. If the numeric network is *coherent,* the pupil will gain security in the sense of being independent of the opinions of others and having the capability of self-reinforcement. These effects of well-planned learning are of paramount importance. This type of learning can be considered a form of a *learning-to-learn strategy*, which can be taught even in grade school – and in my opinion *must* be taught there!

The Construction of Numeric Networks and the Automatization of the Paths through These Networks

Good counters differ from poor counters in that the former have established *complete and coherent numeric networks.* (In Chapter 16 we shall speak of having as *complete a database* as possible.) Good counters, as Ericsson (1985) said, have a better *mnemonic system.* Also, they differ from poor counters in being able to find their way through the system *more easily* and *more quickly.* They know exactly what retrieval cues are relevant for what piece of knowledge, since they themselves coded them semantically while learning, i.e., by establishing a series of interconnected associations in their network. To put it differently, they have given more *weight* to their numeric activities than their arithmetically poor comrades.

Building and extending numeric networks form the prerequisites for what our teacher in fact was striving for: automatizing the retrieval of proper multiplication results. One can easily recognize where poorer pupils need help: First, one must see to it that the proper retrieval paths in the numeric network are established, i.e., that there are sufficient connections between what is already known and what is not (or insufficiently) known yet. Now we have landed at the general level of *mastery* (cf. Chapter 12). In poorer pupils one must check whether the "easier" levels of 8's have been learned; these levels subsequently serve as *arithmetic reference points* (nodes in the numeric network) for later calculations (1 × 8, 2 × 8, 10 × 8, 5 × 8; cf. Figure 24). Then, the associations between the "easy" and the "hard" calculations must be checked: from 10 × 8 to 9 × 8, from 5 × 8 to 6 × 8 and to 4 × 8. This method also reveals why the 7's in multiplication are relatively difficult for most people: They demand the *longest retrieval path* in the numeric network, i.e., either (1) via 10 × 8 to 9 × 8 and 8 × 8 and from there to 7 × 8 or (2) from 3 × 8 to 6 × 8 and from there to 7 × 8, or (3) via 5 × 8 to 6 × 8 to 7 × 8, or (4) from 4 × 8 to 8 × 8 and finally to 7 × 8.

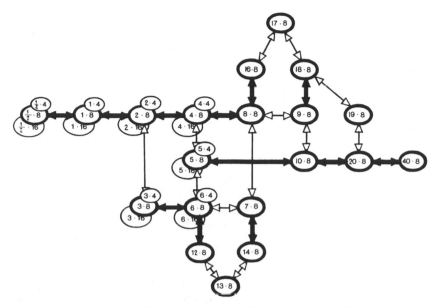

Figure 24: An arrow diagram that shows part of a multiplication network of 8's. Note the many different relations. Doublings are denoted by thick arrows, iterative (neighbor) relations by thin arrows. Obviously, not all possible relations can be shown in such a diagram. The left-hand part demonstrates the relations to the 4's and 16's rows by using upper and lower levels. The relation arrows for these rows are not shown.

Against the background of our knowledge about the semantic representation of multiplication in a numeric network, *automatizing* multiplication tables primarily means finding and describing the *shortest path* in the network (and only occasionally needing to take a longer path). Automatizing also means traveling the paths throughout the network *more quickly* since one has traveled them *more often* and thus is well acquainted with them. Repeated practice with direct reinforcement may play a role in this learning and automatization process, *albeit only when the level of mastery has already been reached.* Interestingly, studies have shown that "big" calculations have longer retrieval paths than smaller ones; for example, 8 × 16 takes longer than 3 × 16: The general speed of calculation is subject to a number of system-immanent limitations.

The learning success of the individual child during the automatization phase should be seen, on the one hand, as a function of the frequency with which the pupil "wanders" about his or her numeric-arithmetic network and, on the other hand, as a function of the quality of that network, the "synoptic" view arising from that quality, and the amount of retrieval cues that are available at all times.

Practicing and Reinforcement

A teacher who wants to practice something with the entire class must assume a high level of self-discipline among the pupils – that *each and every pupil* will be doing the counting and not just the one called on. Even a teacher who wants to keep the learning *tempo* high will be wise to wait until all pupils have raised their hands before calling on one. And when one pupil says the solution out loud, all of the other pupils should be practicing self-reinforcement for having known or having recalled the correct answer. Yet this reinforcement should also be formalized in some manner (e.g., as a mark or a star on a piece of paper), whereby it is important that this type of reinforcement always remains self-reinforcement, and that no pupil is later *forced* to reveal the result reached. A more economical – and perhaps more efficient – method of practicing in the automatization phase is in small groups or matched pairs; this ensures the greatest probability of correctly solving a large number of calculations. Of course, such small groups must "function" well, and the positive reinforcements must be regular, swift, and given only for correct results. This is something that must be practiced on its own. But it is worth it, since there is always a need for *practicing team situations* in the classroom. For very good team results (or excellent individual results achieved in a team environment) one can give extra reinforcements, something Skinner recommends in his thoughts on programmed teaching (cf. Bower & Hilgard, 1981).

Is Building Up Numerical Networks Really Economical and Useful?

A comparison of the complicated structure of a numeric network construction with the way adults usually retrieve and use their multiplication tables automatically leads to the question whether it is economical (and, indeed, whether it is useful at all) to think of counting as a construction of numeric networks. Isn't the most important thing the ability to recall the proper result quickly?

First, we should remember that two years later knowledge of multiplication tables will be demanded of the children in written form. At that stage multiplication tables become processes on a relatively low level that serve as *subroutines* within the overall scope of written operations and have to be activated very quickly; indeed, the main thing at this juncture is their *correct and swift retrieval*. One could go even further and ask whether, in the light of modern electronic calculators, knowledge of multiplication tables has any meaning whatsoever.

The answer to this question as well as the question of whether learning to count in the above-mentioned manner is economical and meaningful is to point out the fact that in the construction of numeric–arithmetic networks the main emphasis is on *establishment of relations between numbers or arithmetic statements*, and that when establishing these associations the most important thing is to recognize the *directions of change of numeric sizes*, i.e., to grasp the *operative basics* at work. All of these processes and the knowledge associated with them are of fundamental importance because they (re)appear in nearly all later areas of mathematics in one form or another, for example, in written exercises or in learning of fractions in the later years of grade or middle school (Steiner & Stoecklin, 1997). Further, the processes involved in constructing numeric–arithmetic networks establish skills such as *self-control* or *self-reinforcement* that enable pupils to free themselves generally of external control – all of which are highly desirable in pedagogical terms (see my statement on the "emancipation" of the learner).

Besides the motivational aspect, there is the cognitive aspect, which refers to the processes of *working through* numeric–arithmetic networks (Aebli, 1983) versus rote learning tasks or individual, isolated statements. Note that we are dealing here more and more with the learning of *thinking and problem-solving skills*, which can be seen in an analog form on somewhat higher levels of arithmetic (and later mathematical–algebraic) thinking. Working through numeric networks enables a fourth- or fifth-grader to make *predictions* about complex counting operations. For example, by knowing that $4704 \div 48 = 98$ (having used a calculator), the child can determine that $4705 \div 48$ is equal to $98 +$ a remainder of 1 or that $4703 \div 48$ is not quite equal to 98, namely, 97 with a remainder of ... ? Or the child can determine how big is the dividend that when divided by 48 equals 99 or 100 (cf. Fricke, 1970). Such calculations represent the treading of one or more paths in a numeric network; they show the learner that anything that has to do with such arithmetic (and later algebraic) problems can be *thought through*, and that for every problem of this type there are one or more paths leading toward its solution (cf. the above example of 7×8, which has four different paths toward the same solution). Being aware of the *plurality of paths,* and above all how to use them, is the best way to refute a young learner's desperate cry in the face of such tasks: "I can't do that." In other words, a well-practiced plurality of solutions counteracts on all levels the oft-observed *inability* to find *any* solution to a mathematical problem. At the same time, this knowledge and this ability represent *metacognitive skills* on a higher level than that of simple counting operations and defuse the question of the economy in constructing numeric networks. The efficiency of a process is not to be disregarded, but here we are concerned more with other aspects of cognitive learning and with motivational phenomena that emerge from those aspects.

One may presume that the ability to travel down many different paths to solve a single arithmetic problem (however elementary it may be) is a form of *creativity*. Furthering such skills in pupils does, however, make great demands of a teacher. The most important thing during the phase in which the numeric network is being constructed in the pupil is that the teacher concentrate on the *processes* involved and not on the *results* achieved (process-oriented teaching goals; "understanding" as a teaching goal; cf. Aeschbacher, 1986) – and that, if necessary, lessons be *structured individually* to correspond to the progression in these processes.

Memo

1. Numeric networks are special cases of semantic (conceptual) networks in which the meaning of numbers and arithmetic operations is represented. The meaning of any particular number is determined by its node in a numeric network and can be expressed by an infinite amount of operations linked with that node.
2. Learning to count is more than the associative linking of numbers, operation signs, and results; it means constructing, expanding, and traversing numeric networks.
3. The construction of numeric networks is the result of a multitude of connecting processes between numeric elements (numbers) via arithmetic relations.
4. Elementary arithmetic relations are expressed through the ±1 iteration of natural numbers, through the basic mathematical operations, and through operations such as halving and doubling.
5. As a higher learning process, learning to count implies providing numbers and operations with a meaning. This, in turn, implies connecting processes that are also heuristic (creative) and not just algorithmic, and that in many cases reveal a plurality of solution paths.
6. From Piaget's genetic epistemology we used the following to demonstrate the construction of elementary numeric networks: (1) the action orientation of all arithmetic operations; (2) the systematic character of all arithmetic operations; (3) the didactically very relevant concept of *mise en relation* (linking).
7. Didactically speaking, one must clearly differentiate between *mise en relation* and *lecture des données*.
8. The construction of numeric networks, if properly done with a process orientation, leads to operative thinking, i.e., to the ability to embark on several different solution paths as well as to employ self-control and self-reinforcement.
9. Operative thinking has its genesis in the successful completion of factually realized arithmetic operations; it is internalized, reversible arithmetic action. The internalization of one's original actions occurs through imaging and the verbalization of those imaging processes. The basic knowledge deriving from arithmetic actions or their internalizations reflects, on the one hand, the numeric results obtained and, on the other hand, their changes, in particular the direction of their changes when operations are compared with one another: equal, unequal, more, less. Such elementary knowledge retains its high value even in more complex areas of mathematics such as learning fractions.
10. Good counters differ from poor counters (1) in the quality of the coherence of their numeric network; (2) in their ability to make available relevant retrieval cues,

i.e., numeric reference points within the network; and (3) in their ability to recall quickly arithmetic relations culled or deduced from navigating their numeric network.

11. This quick recall (retrieval) forms the basis for automatized counting. It arises from the increased availability of broad areas in the network as well as their numeric elements and relations. It is also a product of the fact that one has become well acquainted with the network by traversing it often and by having discovered the shortest paths to success.

16. Visual Learning in Geometry? The Conceptual and Figural Components of Learning

16.1 Introduction

Recent literature on geometrical thinking mostly centers around geometrical proof argumentation and the development of tutorial systems for dealing with geometrical problems (to name just one typical example, Koedinger & Anderson, 1990). In this chapter, our aim is a quite different one: We will be carrying out an extensive *phenomenological analysis* of the visual and nonvisual learning processes connected with a *geometrical construction task,* particularly the *genesis* of the processes involved in solving the problem.

At first sight, the geometrical construction problem we will be concentrating on in this chapter may seem to consist of *visual elements* alone: points, lines (straight lines and curves), and angles (Figure 26). As we will see, however, a great deal of *conceptual* knowledge is required for the perception, understanding and application of these visual components. The first step in learning to solve a geometrical problem, for example, the construction of a triangle, is the setting up of a *database,* as complete as possible, i.e., an elaborate (and expandable) *knowledge representation* of its elements, both given and inferred, as well as the relationships that exist between them. Using this database, we can then establish questions and *hypotheses* concerning the data to be determined, that is to say, carry out a *means–ends analysis.* Subsequently, we can try to solve the problem, whereby important steps in the solution can be "seen" (envisioned) out of anticipations (expectations, imagination). It is important to note, however, that this "seeing" (we also speak of "insight"!) is possible only in the light of sufficient background knowledge. In other words, it depends on *activated conceptual schemata including their figural components.*

Keywords in this chapter will be *database, inference processes, schemata as activated parts of semantic and figural networks,* the *naming of elements and recognition of their dual functions,* the *"seeing" of spatial elements and*

238

relations, means–ends analyses, conceptual and procedural knowledge, as well as *the anticipation of conceptual and figural components.*

16.2 The Pictorial–Figural or "Iconic" Moment

A Look at Earlier Theories

There are countless examples of a problem's becoming easier to solve when it is presented in a *visual* way. Wertheimer (1945), in his book about *productive* thinking, used some examples to show how *insight* can suddenly be acquired through the *restructuring* of the *given perceptual conditions* (see also Chapter 18 and Duncker, 1935).

Also well known is, J.S. Bruner's (1966) approach of "iconic representation": that the pictorial presentation of facts in diagrams in order to achieve a

```
    Amsterdam  —  Berlin
    Berlin     —  Köln
    Köln       —  Basel
    Amsterdam  —  Köln
    Basel      —  Köln
    Köln       —  Wien
    Berlin     —  Amsterdam
a   Amsterdam  —  Wien
```

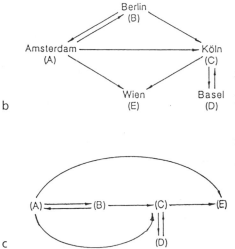

Figure 25: The difference between a symbolic and an iconic representation of information. The question at hand is: Determine the best flight connection between Basel and Berlin, i.e., the connection having the least amount of transfers. (a) The symbolic representation of flights in the form of a list of bilateral connections demands that the reader work through the information sequentially, i.e., systematically search through the connections to find the best one. (b and c) Two forms of iconic representation that allow a (nearly) simultaneous grasp of information and thus a quicker solution. The solution: There is no connection from Basel to Berlin!

simultaneous grasp of their structure is in some cases more useful than a "symbolic," i.e., verbal, representation thereof. (For Bruner, the term *representation* defined internal representation in the sense of memory coding as well as the external form of presenting a situation or problem.) One of his best-known examples deals with flight connections between various cities. The task of finding a suitable connection between two cities not linked by a direct flight is fairly complex if only a list of the connections between certain cities is available (Figure 25a). But if the towns and the flight connections are represented in an arrow diagram (Figure 25b, c), i.e., in Bruner's terminology in an *iconic* rather than a *symbolic representation*, the solution is obvious almost at first glance (Bruner, 1966; see also Steiner, 1973, 211).

16.3 Similarities among Geometrical, Numerical, and Conceptual Construction Processes

Geometrical representations are the results of constructions that have been made using compasses and a ruler: That is to say, they are the *result of actions*. The pictorial–figural configurations therefore *relate to an action*, much as do arithmetic operations (see Chapter 15). As in arithmetic operations, *elements* of the geometrical–spatial operations are connected by specific (spatial) *relations* to form a *system*. This *connection process* is common to the construction of *conceptual* (Chapters 13–14), *numerical* (Chapter 15), and *geometrical* networks; it is typical both for conceptual constructions and for arithmetical and geometrical operations.

16.4 Constructing the Database

Let us first look at the *semantic–conceptual* component and the significance of given geometrical facts. We should bear in mind that these will begin to interact with *figural components* as soon as spatial aspects are introduced.

The problem solver has as basic knowledge the *cognitive schema triangle* (see Norman & Rumelhart, 1975; Rumelhart & Ortony, 1976; Rumelhart, 1980). The more thoroughly this schema has been covered by the geometry teacher, the better developed it will be. This means that the problem solver can start off from *given* dimensions (corners, sides, angles, etc.) and conventions (e.g., "capital letters designate the corners of a triangle"), whereas other defining facts can be *made explicit* and their positions *inferred*. These deductive or *inference processes* do not occur automatically; rather, the student must *learn* the skill specifically until it becomes a *systematically applied thinking habit.*

Geometry lessons in the 8th, 9th, or 10th grade at school usually cover various aspects of the triangle (the construction of triangles, congruity theorems, various types of proof, etc.). Let us take the following problem situation: "Given are side **a**, angle γ and ρ, the radius of the inscribed circle. Construct the whole triangle including the inscribed circle!"

If only side **a** were given, the figure would be completely undefined (apart from **a**) – we would indeed have very little information available at all. Still one could draw up various triangles; the pupil could call upon *much additional information* from prior knowledge, i.e., from his *cognitive schema* "triangle" – elements, relations with symbols and their corresponding figural components. (See Figure 26.) For example, he knows that corners **B** and **C** lie at either end of **a**. The relation that associates **a** with **B** and **C** is called "lies between," that is to say, "**a** lies between **B** and **C**." Therefore, it is already clear where sides **b** and **c** will be, using the relation "opposite," i.e., "**b** lies opposite **B**." The pupil also knows that the intersection point of **b** and **c** (whose position is not exactly known) will be corner **A**. Angles β and γ will lie at **B** or **C**, and further angle specifications will depend on angle α. If the quantities of β and γ were known (even without the length of **a** being given), α could also be determined (the sum of the angles!).

The given side **a** of the triangle implies still more, for example, it implies M_a, the midpoint of **a**, from which the central perpendicular m_a leads off. This could be significant for the construction of the *circumcircle*.

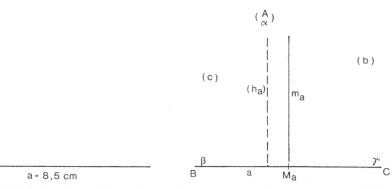

Figure 26: It is given that **a** = 8.5 cm. Of course, in fact we know much more, though not explicitly. If we activate the schema "triangle" as well as some more conventional knowledge at our disposal about triangles and use it on **a**, then we discover a great amount of information: the corners and the position of the respective angles, with M_a as the midpoint of **a** and the central perpendicular m_a. Further, we know that somewhere perpendicular to **a** lies the height h_a on **a**. We also know the approximate position of sides **b** and **c** and the corner **A** with its respective angle α.

Finally, it is also known that the height (h_a) of this completely undefined triangle leads *perpendicularly* from **a** or the extension of **a**, and that it runs through **A**, the opposite corner of the triangle (Figure 26). At the moment, all these details appear to be irrelevant, but as *elements* they activate knowledge about *certain relations between* these elements. The sum of the angles (180°) mentioned above is an example of this. On the other hand, if these apparently irrelevant details refer to *relations*, they activate *knowledge relating to the corresponding components or elements*. For example the relationship "is opposite to" activates knowledge relating a side and a corner with the same symbol (e.g., **a** and **A**). Conceptual knowledge is always activated parallel to the figural part of the schema.

In this way, the *pictorially depicted side* **a** *of the triangle* implies a whole range of information, sometimes in common language (*symbolic* in the terminology of Bruner, 1964, 1966), and sometimes in the form of an *artificial language* (e.g., the designations for corners, angles, sides, etc.). However, we can also represent the same information in a pictorial–figural way (*iconic*, as Bruner would say), some of it at first only approximately, as much of the information needed to construct the triangle is still missing.

The knowledge activated from the starting point of the given side **a** constitutes the *database,* which is then extended when information concerning the angle γ and the radius of the inscribed circle ρ becomes available.

In the last decades, cognitive psychology has concerned itself more and more with the differences between *novices* and *experts* in the way they tackle characteristic thought processes or problem-solving procedures (see Newell & Simon, 1972; Chase & Simon, 1973; Koedinger & Anderson, 1990; see also Chapters 12 and 19). The difficulty novices (be they poor students or beginners) experience when faced with a task such as this one arises mostly because of the *limitation* or *inadequacy of their database*. It has less to do with limited processing abilities found with the use of problem-solving heuristics (Glaser, 1984). The most important tool for successfully solving the task is a *complete database*, in other words, the *activation* or *instantiation* of as many schemata as possible, starting out from the given elements.

For the learning process we are concerned with here, it is important that one consciously practice the activation of a complete set of *conceptual data* for triangles. The other important thing is the ability to imagine the elements that are *not* present (the *figural data*: triangle constituents such as the location of corner **A**). This allows the pupil to go beyond the semantic–conceptual components and turn his attention to the figural components of the task. Because of the spatial relations that are part of the activated schemata, he is able

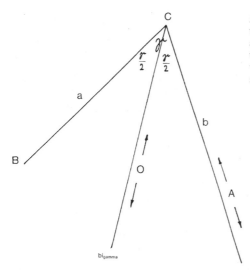

Figure 27: Here we can presume a lot after having taken a and γ into account: γ/2 and the respective bisector bi$_γ$; the direction of side **b** with the position of **A** somewhere on **b** as well as the position of **O** somewhere on bi$_γ$.

to put elements into their correct spatial position in his imagination (or at least into a position that would be possible) (cf. Figure 27). He can also externalize his imagined picture by making a sketch thereof, to keep his memory capacity free for other processes involved in solving the problem. In this way, he has at his disposal a *provisional* (i.e., freely extendible) database, with which he can continue working.

Building up a database, including the inferences suitable to obtain data not explicitly given, is a process of working forward within the problem-solving process as a whole. It helps the problem solver to recognize the missing conceptual and figural elements and relations that are vital for solving the problem. The *definition* of these missing components is a constant task that continues throughout the whole problem-solving procedure.

16.5 Means–Ends Analyses: Continual Definition of the Missing Elements

At this juncture we should mention that there is indeed more than one way of solving the set problem. In the following, we pursue just one possibility, following a student's problem-solving protocol. We realize that it is not the most elegant nor the quickest possible solution, but as the title of this chapter clearly indicates, this is not our main concern.

It is obvious where corners **B** and **C** are, so we can deduce the *position* of γ. The size of the angle γ is given; now we also know its *location*. What is more, side **a** forms one foot of angle γ, so **b** must form the other. Unfortunately, the length of **b** is unknown. If it were given, the triangle construction would already be clearly defined. At this point we recognize that it is possible to establish certain *if . . . then relations*: If the length of **b** were known, then . . . , or to ask, What must I know in order to determine the length of **b**? Which knowledge would help me out? What else could I look for to help me? Up until now we can say the following: We are looking for the length of **b**, or, it would be good to know the length of **b**. But how can I find it out?

If I knew where **A** was, the end of **b** and at the same time the third corner of the triangle, then I would know the length of **b**. But how can I find out the position of **A**? It is the intersection point of **b** and **c**, but unfortunately **c** is also unknown. So I'm also looking for **c**! What can help me to define **c**? Now we can profit from *specific knowledge* taken from the database or the information contained in the *schema* "triangle" (as an *active semantic network component*) that has to be called up individually: **c** *is not only a side of the triangle; it also forms a foot of angle* β. So if I knew β, I could construct **c**. Therefore, I am looking for β.

In this way we have defined an important intermediate goal. The *goal analysis* (= the ends analysis) we have undertaken up to now (see Duncker, 1935) allows us to solve the problem *backward,* starting from the interim goal (*working backward,* Wickelgren, 1974). At this point the information search starting out from the given elements **a** and γ has been *exhausted* (for a summary see Figure 28).

Let us not forget that we still have one more given element at our disposal, namely ρ! The ρ is a clearly defined given size factor, being the radius of a circle that lies completely within the confines of the triangle. We can visually imagine this circle, but as yet we cannot exactly locate it – the triangle it lies within does not yet exist.

However, ρ is more than just a defined visually given length of no immediate use; ρ is a *concept* for which pupils not long ago learned the schema "radius of the inscribed circle" or on a larger scale "inscribed circle." This schema encompasses *conceptual elements* and *relations*, as is the case for *any* conceptual network construction. Many of the relations are implied in *manual constructions,* i.e., in *spatial operations* using ruler, compasses, and pencil and in pictorial representations. Now it is time for the pupil to reactivate the schema "inscribed circle," with both its conceptual and its constructive (spatial–figural) elements. In the same way as with the schema "triangle," he must go through the entire schema and retrieve all the information it contains and the information that has not yet been made explicit (the elements and the relations connecting them), thereby *considerably enlarging the database*: Like any circle, the inscribed circle has a *center*. This is an obvious piece of information, but one that as yet has not been made explicit. What do we know *explicitly* about the location of this center? Only that it is the point where the

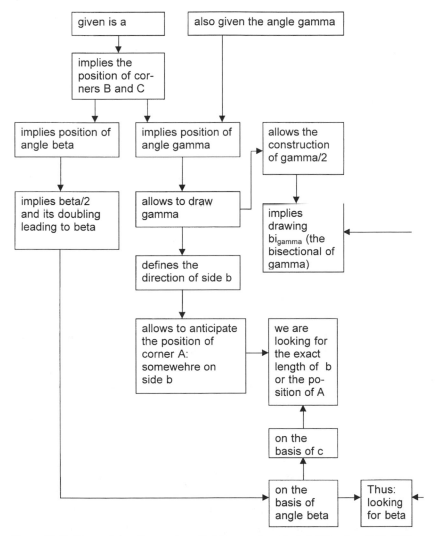

Figure 28: Problem-solving diagram (part 1): Means–ends analysis (cf. Duncker 1935, 1974; on working backward, see Wickelgren, 1974). Because of **a** and γ, further parts can be determined. This allows us to try and determine missing parts, i.e., β and **c** (our goal!). But how can we find or construct these parts? Anyone working through this problem can reach this stage by working with the parts at hand. But the arrows coming from the right hint that further information is necessary, namely, information that can be determined only on the basis of a further element (ρ).

(given!) radius ρ starts off – at least we know that! Because it is an inscribed circle, we know that its center lies at the intersection point **O** of the (three) *bisectors* of the angles of our triangle (see Figure 27, where this can partly be seen). But this triangle, and therefore these bisectors, do not yet exist. Yet, just *two* of the bisectors would be enough to determine **O** – but, unfortunately, we don't even have two! What we do have is *one* of the angles, γ, and if we *bisect* it, we will have two times γ/2, and more importantly, the bisector bi$_\gamma$. To do this, one must recall *procedural knowledge*, i.e., the information that tells us, first, that an angle can be bisected with compasses and, second, how this is done. One thing is certain: **O** lies somewhere along bi$_\gamma$. But where? Which further element or which relationship within the schema "inscribed circle" is needed to determine **O** on bi$_\gamma$?

The schema "inscribed circle" has yet to be thoroughly checked for any implicit information it might contain. The *center, radius*, and *general position of the inscribed circle* have been taken into consideration, but not the circle itself, i.e., its *circumference*. What do we know about it? We know that its length can be calculated using the formula $2\pi\rho$, but this doesn't tell us anything about its position and its relationship with the triangle! This in fact is *irrelevant* information. What is the relationship of the inscribed circle to the triangle? Here, we must put spatial relationships into the background for a moment while we concentrate on semantic relations.

It becomes evident that we must have *complete knowledge* – as *extensive a database as possible* – if we are to make progress in our chain of thoughts. The inscribed circle touches each side of the triangle at one point, at which point the side of the triangle is *not solely the side of a triangle*, but also a *tangent of the inscribed circle*. The steps that result from the previous considerations are presented in a kind of flow chart in Figure 29 and described in the following text; the corresponding geometrical constructions are shown in Figure 30.

16.6 Dual Meanings and Dual Functions of Figural Elements

If we look back at our considerations up to now, we notice that in two cases *a single element had two meanings*: Side **c** of the triangle was both a side and a foot of angle β. If we knew this angle (we said at the time), we could use this one foot to determine the third corner **A** of the triangle.

The second double meaning refers as well to the side of a triangle, which becomes a *tangent* at the point where it touches the inscribed circle (of course, this applies to any side of the triangle). In our example only side **a** was given, so only **a** is under consideration as the tangent of the inscribed circle.

Let us now turn our attention to a third schema, that of "tangent." Here, the pupil again has to call up *conceptual knowledge*, that is, to activate (or instantiate) a schema with all its conceptual and figural components: The tangent touches the circle at one point, and the radius that joins this point with the center of the circle stands perpendicular (at a right angle!) to the tangent.

In the meantime we have gathered so much information from the three schemata "triangle," "inscribed circle," and "tangent" that we must begin to decide which information can be transferred into the spatial representation of our geometry problem. Since we know the actual size of ρ, it could be placed *somewhere* at right angles to **a** and then moved until its *end*, which lies within the triangle, exactly meets the bisector of the angle γ, since we know that the radius of the inscribed circle ρ (at point **O**) lies on bi_γ. All points that lie equidistant from a given straight line form the *parallel* to this straight line, at the same corresponding distance (here: ρ). If this theorem (i.e., the schema

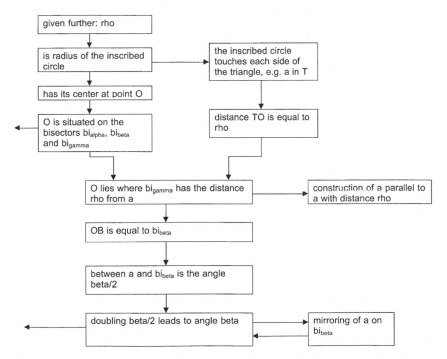

Figure 29: Part 2 of the problem-solving diagram in the preceding figure. Here, ρ is used as an additional piece of information, leading to an answer to the question put in Figure 27 after having reached the goal because of β and **c**.

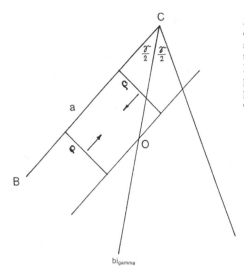

Figure 30: The construction of the center **O** of the inscribed circle by positioning ρ somewhere perpendicular to **a**. One sees that ρ can be moved such that it touches bi$_\gamma$. It is, of course, more elegant to construct a parallel to **a** at a distance ρ. The intersection point of this parallel with bi$_\gamma$ is **O**, the center of the inscribed circle.

"parallel") is known, a more elegant construction can then be used to find out the position of **O** on bi$_\gamma$ than the one described above: One constructs a parallel to **a** using distance ρ, which would intersect bi$_\gamma$ (this assumes that the *procedural knowledge* needed for the construction using compasses and ruler is available). The intersection point is point **O**, which, once determined in this way, will lead to the next step of the construction: By joining **B** with **O**, we can determine bi$_\beta$, since the straight lines leading from the corners of the triangle to **O** are the *bisectors* of the angles of the triangle, and at the same time they form the *feet* of the halved angles! Thus, β/2 is now known. By mirroring **a** onto bi$_\beta$, we can determine β as well as **c** (with its one foot) – another dual function! Up until now, the values of both β and **c** were *missing*, and now they can help us to find out corner **A** and side **b** and, finally, to construct the entire triangle. Eureka!

Procedural Knowledge Again

To construct the intersection point *T* of the inscribed circle (Figure 31) and side **a** completely accurately and without using a set square (for drawing the right angle), we would need further *conceptual* and *procedural* knowledge, which can be taken from the schema "Thalesian circle." Using this, we can construct a right-angular triangle over **BO**: **T** lies at the point where the Thalesian circle cuts side **a**, and at **T** a right angle is formed in the triangle **BTO**. In this way, one can also draw the inscribed circle perfectly, starting out from **O**.

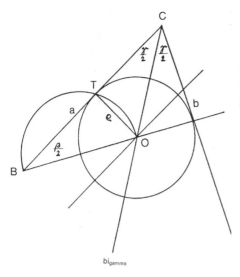

Figure 31: Construction of the Thalesian circle above **BO** and the inscribed circle. In order to mark the radius of the inscribed circle using only a compass, a ruler, and a pencil, we must mark a Thalesian circle above **BO**. At point **T** the side **a** becomes the tangent of the inscribed circle; at that point radius ρ lies at a right angle to **a**.

16.7 "Seeing" Figural Components and Spatial Relations

Let us now turn our attention to the *main issue* of this chapter, i.e., the problem of "seeing" certain determining data for the construction of the triangle and the spatial relations that are vital for solving the task. Gestalt psychologists use one of their most important terms to describe it: *insight* (see also Chapter 18). Therefore, in my opinion (and in contrast to the considerations of Koedinger & Anderson, 1990, on the application of "diagram configurations"), it is extremely important to take a closer look at this "seeing" and its *genesis* by studying certain critical situations that arise in the course of the problem-solving process shown above.

"Seeing" as a Part of Conceptual Knowledge: Concept-Driven "Seeing"

What *conditions* are necessary for "seeing" the exact position of **O**, the center of the inscribed circle? (The quotation marks with the word *seeing* indicate that **O** must be "seen" before it can be drawn and *truly* perceived as a visual stimulus.)

First of all, there is the *conceptual, nonvisual knowledge* that **O**, being the center of the inscribed circle, is determined by the bisectors of the angles, and that in the task at hand only the bisector of γ can actually be drawn. This leads to the *expectation*, already mentioned, that **O** lies somewhere on bi_γ. This *expectation* in turn leads to the anticipation of **O**, formed in a more or less vivid mental image, which helps us to project **O** onto bi$_\gamma$. In this way, a kind of "blending" of perception and imaging takes place (see Chase's [1973] *hybrid images*): We can see bi$_\gamma$, we can "see" **O**! In the same way, in a continuation of this process, we can sketch **O** in its approximate position (using paper and pencil), but only if the pupil knows the conditions the inscribed circle must fulfill; this knowledge is activated through the instantiation of the schema "inscribed circle." In the case at hand, the ability to "see" the position of **O** depends on knowing that the inscribed circle touches side **a** at a certain point (**T**), and that this point lies at the given distance ρ from **O**. However, since the exact position of **O** is unknown, we can only say that it is one of the innumerable points that lie at a distance ρ from **a**.

This knowledge thus consists of three parts: The first is related to the anticipated point on **a**, the second to the point on bi$_\gamma$, and the third to the distance between the two: ρ. At least this allows one roughly to "see" the position of **O** and possibly to make a provisional sketch, from which the actual construction can be made with the help of the parallel lines lying at a distance of ρ from **a** (Figure 30).

Thus, "seeing" results here from *knowing*, which for its part makes anticipation possible. Anticipations become active as the *mental images* of spatially arranged elements. "Seeing" initially takes place *internally* and is then, as it were, *projected outward* into the configuration and the construction. Or, to use the terminology of recent cognitive psychology, "seeing" is guided by knowledge, i.e., conceptual meanings, hence by a relatively high level of conceptual information processing. Many authors speak of *concept-driven* processes that influence lower processing levels (in this case, the interpretation of the figural components actually given and the relations between them). In the literature (e.g., Lindsay & Norman, 1972; Norman & Rumelhart, 1975), these kinds of concept-driven guided processes are also described as *"top-down" processes* (see also Chapter 13).

"Seeing" from Perceived Data (Figural Components): Data-Driven "Seeing"

However, the procedure can also work the other way around, i.e., starting "from the bottom," in which case "seeing" does not take place conceptually, but rather results from the *visually perceived* data given such as sides, bisectors of angles, or other configurations. If, as a result of quick decentering, **O** and **B** are perceived at more or less the same time, the association between these two points and their significance will be understood. (This is the *orga-*

nization function of a graphic representation, as stressed by Levin, 1981; see Chapter 13, Section 13.5.) The connection **BO** that is "seen" before it is drawn in on the diagram is a line that will be extremely important for the continuation of the problem-solving process: When it is "seen," not only can it be drawn in, it can also be interpreted as being a *second bisector of an angle*. (In this way the diagram receives an *interpretation function*; cf. Levin, 1981.) The interpretation of these straight lines, however, depends on their being spontaneously (or fairly quickly) named and labeled: bi$_\beta$.

Just as the points **B** and **O**, being data in the configuration, trigger the "seeing" of the angle bisector bi$_\beta$, the angle $\beta/2$ can be the starting point of the "seeing" of the complete angle β as the problem-solving process continues. It forms, in turn, the starting point from which an anticipated doubling of **a** onto bi$_\beta$ by mirroring, which can be clearly "seen" in advance, takes place (Figure 32). We have no detailed knowledge whether a side glance at bi$_\gamma$ and $\gamma/2$ can act as a stimulus or even be a prerequisite for these data-driven (or, as they are also called, "bottom-up") processes.

The designation $\beta/2$ (or "half beta"), by analogy with $\gamma/2$ (or "half gamma"), may also cause the intersection point of **a** and **c** at **B** to be focused on, interpreted, and ultimately "seen" not only as a mere intersection point of two straight lines, but also as an *angle*. In this case, however, we would be dealing with a concept-driven process, as the implicitly activated concept "angle" would be responsible for having triggered the "seeing."

It is interesting to consider why the figural structure of the angle β at **B** is not necessarily ("automatically") recognized as being an angle (and having the function of an angle). There are several possible explanations for this. One

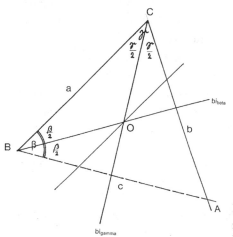

Figure 32: This figure depicts the moment when the doubling of $\beta/2$ must occur by mirroring **a** onto bi$_\beta$ – which determines β as well as **c** and in the end the entire triangle.

of them is that normally only *complete* angles of a triangle are considered to be important, and not *halved angles*. Consequently, the expectation of *complete* angles receives a higher level of priority. Halved angles may not necessarily be recognized as such, and the next logical step of doubling them does not automatically follow. The method of setting priorities implied here often takes place unconsciously in the classroom; no one anticipates its consequences, and it can lead the pupil to *fail* to "see" certain elements or associations and remain "blind" to them!

We may conclude that nonvisual knowledge and visual representations of given facts in geometry interact with one another in a complex way. In other words, an interaction of *top-down* and *bottom-up* processes is necessary in order to "see" the figural components and spatially relevant associations.

16.8 Necessary Learning Processes

What must a pupil actually *learn* to enable him to solve such problems? At least the following five points are relevant:

1. *Activation of Schemata and Continual Expansion of the Database*

To solve geometric construction problems such as the one we are concerned with here, a pupil must have a certain amount of *prior knowledge* at his disposal; as we have seen, the pupil must already know a number of conceptual schemata. These are activated according to the "cues" present in the problem, for example, "triangle," "bisector of an angle," "inscribed circle," "tangent," "Thalesian circle," and "parallel lines," along with all the figural components contained in each schema as well as the *procedural* knowledge for any constructions that have to be made using compasses and ruler.

In order to *infer* missing parts or elements not explicitly given, the pupil must be capable of activating the cognitive schemata *as completely as possible*. In other words, he must always be able to name elements that are not explicitly given (by knowing that they in fact *exist*) and to localize these elements. The task will be easier if he can "think along the data" of a triangle and add to his representation in this way. He must practice mentally imaging one or several elements that are not explicitly given as *figural elements* or even as *figural parts of a network*. The result is an optimally updated database that the pupil continually extends during the course of solving the problem. This kind of *exhaustive activation* of the relevant conceptual and figural parts of schemata according to the respective stage of the problem-solving procedure can be interpreted as "working forward" (*sensu* Koedinger & Anderson, 1990). A good pupil accomplishes this in a spontaneous, natural way, and it is characteristic of his growing expertise. Once pupils have mastered this skill, they have resources at their disposal enabling them to take further steps in the problem-solving process, implying "working backward," depending on how far they have come in solving the problem.

2. *Means–Ends Analyses: Establishing Questions and Hypotheses in Relation to the Required Data*

By inferring and naming the elements that were not explicitly given, the problem solver recognizes the elements he still needs to help him solve the problem. He can then work systematically forward or backward, *deducing* questions about the required data, *setting up hypotheses* (if I had . . . , then . . .) and initiating the *individual steps* of the problem-solving procedure (see again Figures 28 and 29).

To tie this to the previous section, we can say that the problem-solving procedure is greatly impeded if elements are *not named* or are *incorrectly labeled*. For example, if $\beta/2$ ("half beta") is not labeled, the important step of constructing β, then **c**, and ultimately **A** will more than likely not take place! The same thing applies for elements that *fail to be localized* (e.g., if the pupil does not know where the radius ρ of the inscribed circle should be placed in the diagram).

3. *Learning to Recognize Dual Functions*

As we have seen, it often happens that a figural element has a *dual meaning* or a *dual function* (and can thus be labeled in two different ways) rather than just *one* meaning or *one* function. This is not simply a coincidence, but rather a typical characteristic of this type of task. For example, the sides of a triangle always also form the feet of an angle, and the bisectors of an angle are also always the feet of halved angles. The following sequence of the learning process described above will remind us of this: We can label bi_β in analogy with $\gamma/2$, which was established by halving γ, following on from bi_γ. bi_β is not only an angle bisector, but also the *foot of an angle,* typically the foot of *half* of the same angle that it actually bisects. Knowing that halved angles can be doubled to produce the whole angle (in this case β) – provided the construction method using compasses has been learned – is not visual–figural knowledge but *procedural knowledge*. This procedural knowledge becomes visual, however, as soon as it is externalized (by drawing it!). The first step here, of course, is the *nonvisual, conceptual recognition of the dual function* of the constructed foot of the angle β: It represents the foot of β as well as being side **c** of the triangle, which was one of the missing pieces of information we were looking for. At the point where side **c** intersects **b** (for this purpose the constructed foot of the angle must be drawn in long enough), the corner **A** of the triangle is formed. Our original thoughts on how to solve the task already anticipated that **A** would lie somewhere along **b**, and we sketched this as ← **A** →. (See Figures 27 and 32.)

The keyword *dual function* often refers to an element fulfilling *two conditions*. For example, **O** must lie along bi_γ – and *at the same time* it must lie at a distance of ρ from **a**.

To learn to solve geometrical tasks of the type at hand, it will be absolutely necessary to check the respective elements for dual functions (i.e., components of the triangle as well as other relevant elements that emerge during the course of the construction); one must be constantly aware of these and adequately label them. Ideally, one can continually vary the configurations slightly, to avoid the effects of pure repetition (see point 5 in this section). This also develops the pupil's ability to focus on any given meaning or function with ease and fluency.

4. *Learning to "See" Figural Elements and Spatial Relations*

Learning to "see" figural elements and spatial relations requires a high degree of elaboration of the geometrical–semantic network (a skill that must be carefully built up during lessons). This ensures that the necessary conceptual knowledge is always *available*. Further, one must maintain this knowledge at a high level of activation; i.e., it must be easily *accessible*. Accessibility in turn means that respective figural components of schemata or network parts can be activated (by practicing the visualization of figural components) and correctly labeled verbally.

The pupil may often have to establish a spatial relation between certain perceived elements (i.e., given parts) and other elements through *decentering* (this was discussed in Chapter 13 with regard to "reading" the diagrams in Figures 13 and 14). Such decentering can be practiced by systematically naming and labeling figural elements. In other cases, the "seeing" emerges from conceptual knowledge and leads to anticipation in the form of mental images. *Practicing* such *visualization* (which corresponds to a large extent to what Koedinger & Anderson, 1990, describe as "diagram parsing") is very important for the process of learning how to solve such problems.

5. *Learning to Avoid "Absolute" Configurations*

Just as the pupil must learn not only to expect whole angles in a triangle, but also to be on the lookout for half angles (i.e., by taking the term *bisector of an angle* seriously), he must also learn to make constructions with *varying spatial orientations*. Of course, there are some useful rules available, such as always labeling geometrical forms in the same direction, as well as standard ways of completing a construction, making compass and ruler easier to handle. But a pupil can easily get into the habit of memorizing "standard positions" for pictorial configurations that are not really justifiable. The inflexibility this causes can get him into difficulties if he is suddenly presented with tasks in which the spatial orientation is completely different. Therefore, the pupil must learn a flexible way of dealing with spatial tasks, so that the steps of labeling the figural components, establishing which information is implicit and which is as yet unknown, can proceed under variable spatial conditions without causing many problems. All the facts and relations remaining unchanged when spatial orientation is changed are the *invariables,* which the pupil must be able to recognize as such. These are inferred in the five points outlined above.

Memo

1. Iconic representations (*sensu* Bruner) provide simultaneous access to information to be processed, often making a problem easier to solve. Symbolic representations, on the other hand, are less easy to survey and demand sequential processing, which can make a problem more difficult to solve.
2. Geometrical, numerical and conceptual construction processes are similar processes in that they link elements together by means of specific relations.
3. The main prerequisite for solving geometrical problems of this kind is the possession of an elaborate database. This consists of a complete set of all activated schemata that relate to the task at hand, including their conceptual and figural components. The quality of the database, i.e., the adequacy of its contents and the degree of its elaboration (for working forward), constitutes the main difference between a good problem solver (an expert) and a poor one (a novice).
4. Schemata are active, semantic parts of networks.
5. The individual steps involved in solving the problem stem from the definition of intermediate goals, which are established by carrying out a progressive analysis of means and requirements.
6. The process of "seeing" figural elements or spatial relations not contained in the original task is achieved by using an interaction of concept-driven and data-driven processes (top-down and bottom-up processes, respectively).
7. Concept-driven processes derive from specific conceptual knowledge, leading to anticipating and imaging missing elements and relations (figural components) and finally to seeing them "in the mind's eye."

8. Data-driven processes usually lead to the "seeing" of spatial relations among the data focused upon (figural components) through a process of decentering.
9. The degree to which learning processes are *visual–figural* depends on the pupil's ability to "see" geometrical elements and relations with the help of concept-driven or data-driven processes, both of which are based on activated schemata.

17. A Taxi Driver's Geographical Knowledge of a Town: The Construction of "Cognitive Maps"

17.1 Introduction

This chapter is concerned with how specific structures – so-called cognitive maps – are constructed. These contain *conceptual* and *spatial* knowledge about our immediate or broader environment, and they guide our behavior within that environment – *planning* or *carrying out changes in local positions, anticipating the location of certain places*, and *estimating distances and times*.

Important terms used in this chapter will be *cognitive maps, landmark knowledge, route knowledge* and *survey knowledge; spatial relations: spatial inclusions, metric and proximity relationships; analog and propositional representations; hierarchical integration; spatial frames of reference; the activation of action plans; condensing and unfolding of conceptual–spatial information.*

17.2 Environmental Learning, Place Learning, Learning to Get Around in Town

Though we rarely think about it, when we are trying to find our way around in a new environment, we are faced with a task similar to that of a beginning taxi driver. Some authors call it *environmental learning*; others, *place learning*. In a more general sense we can use the term *spatial cognition*, i.e., acquisition of knowledge about the immediate or broader spatial environment and subsequent use of this knowledge.

Normally, we do not need the same in-depth knowledge of a town as we might expect of a good taxi driver. However, when we are in a *strange* town, we want to be able to find our way around without getting lost too often. If we move to a new part of town or start a new job, we also have to find our way around in the new district. "Finding one's way" means being familiar with the streets in the neighborhood; knowing where the shops, the bus stops, the parking spaces and so on are situated. It also means knowing roughly how long it would take to get to one of these points from our starting point, and which direction to set off in to get there.

We have to get to know not only relatively *large-space environments*, but also more *confined* ones: a department store in which the wares have been rearranged, the new Macy's or Tower Records, a do-it-yourself or garden center, an office block, a new apartment (watch how small children often lose their way in a new apartment and have to shout for help). On an even smaller level, our new kitchen or our own workroom after we've rearranged the furniture!

But let's stay with the taxi driver for the moment. He has to learn the geography of a town in such a way as to be able to transport passengers as quickly and safely as possible to and from any point within the given area (Pailhous, 1970; Bahrick, 1983). We want to find out how he does this.

We may assume the taxi driver knows that he will be better at his job, he will derive more pleasure from it, and his customers will be more satisfied if he knows his way around *perfectly*. So he has a *motivation* for learning the geography of the town; he will make a conscious effort to acquire all the knowledge he needs to this end. Here, he differs from the rest of us, who get to know new places more *incidentally*. We hardly notice how the new area we live or work in gradually becomes more and more familiar to us.

17.3 Cognitive Maps as a Topic in Psychology

Basically, learning the geography of a town means building up a *mental map* or, as it is called in modern psychology, a *cognitive map*. The map can be consulted at all times to help us to determine places, directions, or distances – it guides our behavior within the spatial environment. The learning process or the way of learning we will be discussing is called *cognitive mapping*. The product of this learning process is the cognitive map (CM), which we understand to be a specific cognitive structure, a well-organized internal representation of a part of an individual's spatial environment.

Early Research

Spatial learning or *place learning* or *construction of CMs* has a long tradition in learning psychology, even though the specific processes involved in this kind of learning were not investigated in detail until a few years ago. Work was done on spatial learning during the first decades of this century (Galton,

1872; Claparède, 1903; Gulliver, 1908; especially Trowbridge, 1913). However, Tolman (1948) was the first to introduce and systematically explain the phenomenon of CMs to the field of learning psychology. "Cognitive Maps in Rats and Men" was the title of his article, which became a milestone in the history of recent psychology. Twenty years before, Lashley (1929) had already observed how rats, passing through a maze to reach food, learned to push aside the cover near the starting point, climb out, and run straight across the maze to the food. From such observations Tolman concluded that rats actually develop fairly extensive "maps," containing *more* than the stimulus–response associations they learn by being sent through a labyrinth several times. Tolman, Ritchie, and Kalish (1946) proved the existence of such spatial representations *(cognitive maps)* in animals with the help of a specific experimental procedure. They trained their rats (Figure 33a) to start off from point *A*, run to *B*, and over an open surface (table), through corridor *C*, then to points *D*, *E*, and *F*, and finally to point *G*. The section from *G* to *F* was illuminated by the lamp *H*. Once they had been trained to do this, the route was completely changed around (Figure 33b). The starting position remained exactly the same, but the path leading through corridor *C* was obstructed. In its place, 12 long and 6 short passageways were constructed, radiating from the table in all directions from 90° to the left to 90° to the right of the original corridor *C*, which led to the food. The animals initially ran off in the way they had learned, but when they realized that they could not proceed through *C*, they returned to the free area. They proceeded by exploring the first section of each passage,

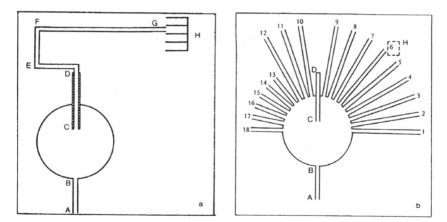

Figure 33: Two experimental setups with rats. Changing from the experimental setting a to b led to the discovery of cognitive maps. (a) The learning situation of the rat for determining where food was to be found (after Tolman, Ritchie, & Kalish, 1946, 16). (b) The new situation for the rat (ibid., 17).

then selected one which they followed through to the end. Over a third of all rats (18) chose passageway 6, i.e., the one that led them to the nearest point where the food had been situated during training. The second largest group (9) took passageway 1, which led them in the same direction as the illuminated pathway from F to G during training. The remaining animals (49%) selected one or another of the remaining 10 passageways, showing no preference for any. During training the rats had evidently not only built up a strip map and a definite pathway leading to the food, but a much more comprehensive map containing the information that the food was to be found in a certain direction within the experimental area (cf. Tolman 1948, 204)!

Tolman's experiment, however, did not show *what* kind of representation a "cognitive map" actually is. Tolman did not specify how it is constructed, nor what it consists of, nor how it is put to use. Rather, he used the term, in a somewhat strange way, to interpret psychoanalytical terms such as regression, fixation, or aggression displacement (see Tolman, 1948, 205–208). Nevertheless, his idea that complex cognitive processes in the form of "maplike" representations *intervene* between stimulus configurations and responses was adopted and expanded upon in many ways (Menzel, 1973, 1978, with chimpanzees; Kozlowski & Bryant, 1977, with humans).

The construction of CMs is quite different from stimulus–response learning. Using the example of the taxi driver's task, we will now take a closer look at how this kind of learning works. One thing should be clear right from the beginning – it is a complex learning process, containing various sub- or microprocesses that are dependent on one another.

17.4 The Outcome "Cognitive Map"

If we consider the desired result, i.e., as complete and clear a CM of the town as possible, we will see that three relevant contents must be learned:

1. Information that tells us *what* is contained in the map (some authors such as Downs & Stea, 1973, 1977, refer to this as "whatness")
2. Information specifying the *position* of all the elements making up the CM ("whereness")
3. Information about *how* the individual positions can be reached

Spatial and Nonspatial Knowledge

This broad classification already points toward the fact that the CM to be constructed will contain not only spatial knowledge, but also a great deal of knowledge of a *nonspatial, nondimensional* nature (Thorndyke, 1981). The majority of this nonspatial knowledge consists of names associated with corresponding meanings – the names of places, public facilities, and of course a great many street names. The taxi driver must learn all these names and be able to recognize them. For example, he must know that New York contains a Madison Square Garden, Penn Station, and South Beach on Staten Island, but no Capitol, Smithsonian Museum, or Superdome. Stuyvesant Street, Washington Square, and Duke Ellington Boulevard exist, but there is no Abraham Lincoln Avenue or Louis Armstrong Boulevard. A customer will often give a specific place as his destination, for example, the Bellevue Hospital Center, the Blue Note Jazz Club, or the Penta Hotel, so that the driver must know where these are, without necessarily associating them with street names. Obviously, *whereness* knowledge is required as far as these places are concerned, and presumably relatively elaborate knowledge of another kind (emotional, value-oriented knowledge) is also involved. We will return to this point later. It can be said that places of this kind are the elements or *basic units* of a CM. Other elements that are more difficult to describe, such as certain *sections* of streets or crossroads, junctions and turn-offs, may also be present. Particularly noticeable prominent buildings (high-rises, bridges), or natural landmarks (cliffs, trees, waterfalls), or objects with a symbolic value (emergency unit, historical monuments) are also elements of a CM, even whole districts or parts of a town (e.g., Manhattan and Queens, separated by the East River).

Lynch (1960), in an attempt to pinpoint the elements that make up a CM, made distinctions among the following: landmarks, paths or routes, nodes, edges, and districts. This taxonomy of the elements of a map relates more to the given geographical or *topological* factors than to the psychological processes involved in the construction and use of CMs. If we take the latter aspect into consideration, whole areas or districts can represent elements of a CM, or even a letter box or a flowerpot at the corner of a street. Evidently, the elements are governed by a scale: The whole Empire State Building can be an element, or just its impressive entrance. From this example it is clear that even *nonspatial* or *nondimensional* knowledge can be organized according to semantic or conceptual criteria (see e.g., Aebli, 1978, 1981). Learning the geography of a town literally demands a *hierarchical organization* of elements (see also Hirtle & Jonides, 1985). First of all, the town can be divided up into its basic areas – Manhattan, the Bronx, Queens and Brooklyn, then outlying districts such as Staten Island, Middlesex, Westchester, Nassau, and others. Within Manhattan, a distinction can be made between the West and the East

Side, or the areas within it can be divided in a specific order, for example, from south to north – Whitehall, Lower Broadway, Lower East Side, Soho, the Bowery, Greenwich Village, Chelsea and so on. Finally, the streets can be added to each of these areas, taking the main arterial roads first as basic points for the side streets.

In practice, however, a town is not likely to be structured in such an orderly, logical way, because its structure is not governed only by criteria of a factual, geographical nature. Of course, the elements of a CM do have a geographical position, but apart from their position and names they have other properties that could be extremely important – perceptual characteristics, specific *functions*, or a special *attraction*. The town can be structured according to emergency situations, in which case the *function* of places where medical, technical or other help will be available is in the foreground, or it can be organized according to culinary and other pleasures.

It is highly likely that the names, perceptual characteristics, functions, and values of places are to some extent learned independently of their position *(whereness)*. It is also certain that a taxi driver's knowledge of these places increases continually, without their geographical position being subjectively affected. But this independence of *whatness* from *whereness* is relative: All places can be set in a spatial relation to one another, something fundamental to the construction of a CM. In Sweden, Gärling's research group (Gärling, Böök, & Lindenberg, 1984) made distinctions among three possible kinds of spatial relations among elements, which we will investigate in the following section.

Spatial Relations among Elements of the CM

1. *Spatial inclusions*, i.e., an embedding such as the flower pot at the corner of a specific street mentioned above, or a particular office in an official building: Spatial inclusions arise because we can use objects on different scales to form elements of our internal representations.
2. *Metric spatial relations*, i.e., information about directions and distances between any pair of places on the CM: As CMs contain many places, it will by no means be possible to store information on the direction and distance between *all* possible pairs of places. Nevertheless, it is reasonable to assume that explicit metric spatial relationships do exist between the most important objects that serve as points of reference. The latter can be important communication points, such as the railway station or a subway node, but they can also be significant perceptual features such as a partic-

ularly large high-rise, a park, or a church. Even places that are important only for certain individuals can become points of reference: the house where a friend lives, a favorite uncle's shop, and the like.

Here, the question of the correctness and reliability of CMs arises (Tversky, 1981; Gordon, Jupp, & Byrne, 1989). When we turn our attention to the construction processes of the CM, we will see that it is not feasible to expect "a total *identity* between the attributes and arrangements of the spatial environment and the attributes and arrangements of cognitive representations" (Downs & Stea, 1977, 99). A CM contains only a selection from the multitude of environmental information at hand, a selection that can differ enormously from case to case (according to contents, task, and aims). The question of the correctness of a CM must thus become one of its *appropriateness* – does it contain the exact information that allows a person to solve the problems caused by the spatial environment? The correctness of a CM can be measured by how *successfully* it can be *put to use*.

3. The third type of spatial relation in CMs are the *proximity relations*: nearness relations. Many places do not have the status of being important points of reference, but we know that they are "near" some more important place or object. The Public Library is *near* Bryant Park; the McGraw-Hill Building is *near* Times Square. Places that are associated with others in proximity relations can sometimes be organized into *ordinal spatial sequences*. As a substitute for missing metric information, the order of the sequence can help to establish what is farther away from any given point and what is nearer.

We can ask ourselves whether all the information relating to distances in a CM is of this ordinal nature, and whether it contains metric information at all. As Kosslyn (1980) and others have shown, metric information can actually be represented, although we have no highly developed vocabulary at our disposal to help us define it (see also Canter & Tagg, 1975).

17.5 The Construction of Cognitive Maps

The development of CMs includes processes of *verbal learning*, *interactive processes* with the specific spatial environment, and processes of *selection* and *integration* or *organization*.

As mentioned above, it is advisable for the beginning New York taxi driver to learn the names of the streets in the town; to know that there are streets, roads, lanes, squares, boulevards, and avenues. This is primarily nonspatial verbal learning, although it implies several possibilities for *structuring* or *elaboration,* and it does not necessarily take place completely independently of position learning. In Manhattan, it would be logical to memorize the structure of the streets and avenues according to their consecutive numbers. Other names can be semantically elaborated according to the individual's general knowledge, for example, Alexander Hamilton Square, Peter Cooper Road, or Frederick Douglass Boulevard.

To some readers, this verbal learning may appear to be a stale theoretical exercise with little practical value. Yet, this is not the case: The task is to match pairs of locales – to establish an association between a real geographical element of the spatial environment and its corresponding completely arbitrary name. Possibly, both are new – one has never seen the street nor heard its name before. If our taxi driver walks or drives through unfamiliar areas, it will be easier for him to associate names with streets if he already recognizes the names. It would be far more difficult if he had to memorize both simultaneously. Here he is in the same situation as the teacher who at the beginning of the school year has to learn the names of 40 pupils in his two new classes as quickly and easily as possible. The teacher's task will be made considerably easier if, before even meeting his pupils for the first time, he knows that there are a Toby Keller, Isabelle Taylor, Daniel Miller, and Tommy Carpenter, etc., in the first class, and that Anna Hughes, Dawn Smith, and so on, will make up the other class. In other words, he learns one half of the name–pupil pairs by heart and then links the respective image of the corresponding pupils. The aim of this kind of *paired-associate learning* is to be able to retrieve the correct name on being presented with a face or to generate the correct image of the pupil's appearance when his name is heard or read in a process of *cued recall.*

In the same way our New York taxi driver, driving through a district for the first time and reading the street names, will find it easier to make pair associations (*street* with street *name*) if he has had previous verbal knowledge at his disposal. His interactive learning processes – his experience of the spatial structure of the town – will be far more efficient.

A person wishing to become a taxi driver in London would have to explore the enormous city on a motorbike for at least a year before really knowing his way around. It is highly likely that this interactive learning process, this *learning by doing,* would be much more quick and efficient if the street names and the names of other important elements were learned beforehand, enabling the pair associations to be made more easily.

This is the ideal way of going about the task; it is not likely to be put into practice. In reality, the taxi driver learns the names of places gradually by hearing or seeing them again and again. To optimize the learning procedure, however, he could at least use the time he spends waiting in traffic jams to learn some of the street names by heart, perhaps studying the city map at the same time!

Learning Landmarks

Exploring a town on a slow vehicle (or on foot) is important. It allows the opportunity and time required for *coding* the eye-catching or functionally important elements. Above, we focused on the *names* of the elements, i.e., streets, etc.; now, it is the elements themselves that will concern us. It is obviously not possible for our taxi driver to code *all* available information contained in a street or a plaza; rather, he will *selectively* single out the elements he can use as orientation points and ignore everything else. Selection criteria can be listed as follows:

1. *Perceptual discrimination or imageability*: i.e., The driver selects features from the spatial environment that stand out because of their size and can be seen from a distance, or that stand out against their background and are therefore easy to recognize, even when he is concentrating on the traffic. These objects are easy to picture in the imagination, and thus can be used as visual images for a street or part of a street and associated with the corresponding street name. If a street has few or no striking features, the taxi driver chooses other features that, although not immediately eye-catching, are exposed to his view for relatively long periods, for example, when he halts at traffic lights or stop signs. The *relative period of exposure* can therefore lead to the selection of certain features when learning the spatial structure of the town.
2. The second selection criterion is the *functional importance* of features. Our driver thus also codes relatively inconspicuous features because they indicate that he must behave in a certain way – the advertising billboard that prompts him to get into the correct lane, the damaged traffic lights that remind him that a particularly dangerous crossroad is coming up, etc.
3. Linked with this is the third selection criterion – the *value content* of particular places for the driver (and perhaps only for him!), for example, the small lawn on 20th Street East, where he recently received his most generous tip ever. 20th Street will, at least for a certain time, be a significant element of his *episodic memory* (see Tulving, 1972).

So the first step in the development of a CM is to select landmarks, code them into more or less vivid mental images, and associate them with a name. If a customer mentions one of these names, the driver can generate the corresponding image of the destination. When our taxi driver drives past one of the landmarks, he remembers its name, and that helps to *consolidate* his knowledge of the town. At the same time, it serves as *feedback* and *reinforcement*, indicating, for example, that when he passes this point, he is going the right way or at least in the right direction. Along with the *landmarks* the elements of a *spatial frame of reference* are being built up. Later, more and more details become incorporated into this framework, and more and more areas are linked with it. Finally (the last stage of the learning process, which we will return to later) he develops a *survey* (or an *overview*) of large areas of the town, which allow the taxi driver to draw spatial inferences relating to orientation, directions, and distances.

Learning Routes

To get to know the town, the taxi driver needs to be familiar with not only its *landmarks.* Even more important, he must learn *routes*, that is, spatial links for these points. The spatial association of places consists of the learning of production rules or the development of marching plans. Production rules consist of a series of *situation–action pairs,* as in the following example: Starting out from Fordham University, you wish to drive to the Hayden Planetarium. When you reach the corner at Roosevelt Hospital (situation) you have to turn left (action). At the roundabout at the New York Coliseum (situation) you have to get into the left lane (action) and at the southwest corner of Central Park (situation) turn off to the left (action). Just after the American Museum of Natural History (situation), you turn left (action) toward the Hayden Planetarium (new situation). The above description is very detailed, but this does not always have to be the case. It is possible to *know* a route without being able to describe it. Years ago, I had to drive from Carouge, a suburb of Geneva, to Budé, near the airport, every day. My landlord showed me the way in his car once, as I followed him in mine. From then on I found my way every day, although I knew practically no street names. However, it did become difficult when I got stuck behind the bus or a truck: The various situations with all their cues to call up the situation–action pairs were obstructed from view or difficult to recognize, hindering the retrieval of the production rules.

For an *orderly production* (Thorndyke, 1981, 140) it is vital that the situations that trigger actions (cues) be recognized correctly and promptly. A verbal reproduction of the individual pairs of a production rule is not even absolutely necessary: "I can't tell you how to get there, but I can take you there quickly," someone once told me on the street.

Constructing Survey Knowledge

Joining two or more landmarks using routes is the *first form of organizing* the spatial elements. Of course, it also entails the experience of distances and approximate directions. The question now is, How does a cognitive map allowing a more comprehensive survey emerge from this mass of increasing information on various routes? At first it will probably be sketchy, containing only a few coherent spatial relations – a net with large holes, so to speak, that gradually becomes finer, more detailed, and more precise as the learning process continues. There seems to be a stage in the development of a CM of a town when the *connection of routes* has not yet taken place and each individual route still relies on the association of production rules. The child in Figure 34 demonstrates this eloquently.

In theory we could say that the spatial network characterizing a CM develops from the *overlapping* of individual routes, for example, when different routes lead to the same destination or when two routes start off at the same

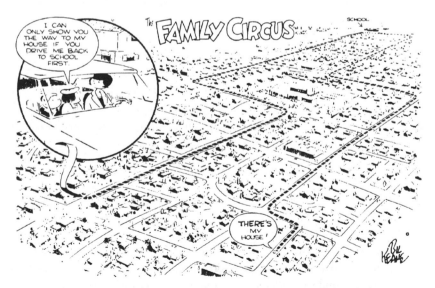

Figure 34: This figure clearly shows the consequences of the fact that the child has a command of landmarks and routes, but is not yet able to connect this knowledge to form larger units (after Downs & Stea, 1977, 14).

place, meet at some point, then continue on in different directions toward their individual destinations. Points of reference, relatively few and far between but nonetheless significant, play an important part here. If they are joined in metric spatial relations, they function as constituent parts of a *scaffoldlike frame of reference*. In New York City, as in other towns, these points of reference consist of important places that become all the more striking because of some particular eye-catching feature: Times Square with the enormous advertising facade at the corner of 42nd Street and 7th Avenue, Central Park with the Metropolitan Museum, or East River Drive with the United Nations Headquarters.

The spatial network or reference system likely develops in different ways, involving processes that sometimes take place parallel to one another – on the one hand, actually driving around taking various routes, some of which overlap one another, and, on the other hand, possibly having to study a town map.

In the first case, the taxi driver's current behavior, i.e., driving around using various routes, is linked with internal information processing through the *activation of action plans*. Action plans, or, to put it more precisely, driving plans, contain partially *coordinated route plans* linked by some obvious or simply "known" or imagined landmarks. The available representation, though still strongly based on routes, allows the taxi driver to *anticipate* the appearance of reference points directly on or close to his route. When the *expected* objects (buildings, etc.) actually appear, they act as feedback information, confirming the correctness of his representation and *reinforcing* the use of the CM he has built up so far. If his expectations are not fulfilled, he must revise his representation or correct the route taken.

Driving plans with their spatial anticipation and feedback mechanisms act as controls in the construction of CMs. By incorporating landmarks that do not lie directly on the current route, one establishes more global spatial layout systems, allowing a survey of areas that start off on a small scale and become larger and larger as the process continues.

In the second case, in which a town map is used, the driver follows the routes in his mental images, sometimes with the help of accompanying motor activities (body movements such as pretending to drive around a bend or, more likely, running a finger along the streets). The important thing here is that the driver will *selectively* choose landmarks that can be actively generated in vivid images and connect them with their corresponding symbols on the map. It is not necessary or indeed possible to recreate a perfect one-to-one mapping of the information on the town map in the CM. As we have seen, the size and scale of the elements of the CM can be changed at random. The actual map can be read this way, too, focusing on a whole area rather than individual streets, crossroads and turn-offs. The taxi driver can say: "If I keep to the left on Lafayette Street and continue on over the Brooklyn Bridge, I'll get to Brooklyn." This can mean one of two things: Either he doesn't want to go to Brooklyn, although he knows the way, or this is exactly where he does want to go. The keyword *Brooklyn* calls up a new section (partial structure) from the CM, an element on a relatively high level of the representation that can be "unfolded" into its elements (streets, single buildings, even individual house numbers) if necessary.

Actually driving or studying a town map can serve to establish integral CMs that coherently represent the *spatial environment* (large-scale environment) as a *holistic system*.

Many authors (e.g., Thorndyke, 1981) believe that CMs are *representations in long-term memory*. Yet the *construction* and reading of CMs imply processes that take place in the *working memory*, which is *limited* in its capacity. This means that a CM is not infinite in size, and sometimes it has to be activated *partially* (e.g., area by area). As discussed above, the construction of the CM also takes place part by part – first local, spatially restricted systems of reference, in which it is easy to keep track of the number of elements and relations, are built up. In order to free up capacity in the working memory, elements and relations are then *condensed* into elements on a higher level: Broadway, Park Avenue, and 14th Street, all running into Union Square, are classified together under the keyword *Union Square* or *Upper East Village* as a single higher-order element. In other words, *condensing* or *objectification processes* (Aebli, 1978, 1980, 1981) occur, corresponding exactly with the construction of concepts outlined in the modern semantic memory theory (compare with the relevant topics in Chapter 13; see also Steiner, 1997).

Are CMs Analog Representations?

A further question arises for the cognitive learning psychologist: What is the representation format of CMs? As we have seen, many elements have just the same features as nonspatial concepts and form the *nodes of a semantic network*. The information they contain can thus be represented *propositionally* (as a statement with a particular meaning). This is true of the "whatness" of the elements contained in the CM: Their name and their properties can be represented as propositions. Relations based on spatial inclusion (a mailbox on a building) and proximity relations (*A* is "near" *B*) can also be stored in this way. On the other hand, spatial metric relationships, which link certain important points of reference and represent information on directions and distances, have an *analog* format; i.e., the representation *directly* reflects the significant features contained in the environment, particularly spatial relationships (approximate angles and distances) between objects. It is quite possible that other visual and nonvisual perceptive features (colors, typical smells, the odor of a factory, etc.) are represented in a *nonpropositional* way. Considering the analog information contained in the CM, it is perfectly justifiable to use the term *map* to describe it, even though it would be wrong to think of photographic images in the minds of rats or human beings (Tolman, 1948). There is a great deal of experimental evidence suggesting the presence of *analog representations*. The main aim of this research was to prove that longer recall paths within a CM (or a visual image; see, e.g., Kosslyn, Ball, & Reiser 1978) produce slower reaction times. Thorndyke (1981) mentioned indirect proof of analog representations (i.e., figural or pictorial). He showed (Thorndyke & Stasz, 1980) that better *visual coding abilities* lead to *better map learning*. The process of building up CMs is certainly subject to significant individual differences, as it involves a great many interactive processes or "microprocesses" (Steiner, 1980, 1987), such as pair associations, semantic elaboration, and hierarchical integrative processes.

The above-mentioned authors discovered that *significant interindividual differences* can be observed in the development of CMs by studying maps (i.e., without actually driving or walking around in the area concerned), and this allows us to draw certain conclusions concerning the learning processes involved. It became evident that *good* learners were better able to *control* their *attention* while studying the map than were poor learners. They did this by concentrating on partial areas of the map and systematically learning the information contained therein, before moving on to the next section. Good learners also seemed far better able to distinguish between information they were already familiar with and did not need to learn again and information completely new to them (compare Chapter 14, the keyword *S for selectivity*). The most important factor, however, was the proficiency of good learners in *coding* the printed information. Good and bad learners were equally able to acquire the verbal information the map contained, but good learners were more skilled at *coding spatial information* by explicitly coding spatial shapes and relations. They elaborate ("it looks like ..."), they consciously *focus in pairs* ("it lies to the west of ..."), or they *integrate* complex configurations together under one category they can later use as a cue for retrieval.

17.6 Again: More than Simple Associative Learning

Looking back, we see that the construction of CMs *may* include some very simple stimulus–response associations, especially as long as it implies the development and use of production rules. We also looked at the paired-associate learning it involves in which one associates places with their names to form pairs of elements in the CM. But even simple route learning, which demands the linking of landmarks with one another, requires more than the associative connection of conceptual or spatial elements. Here, there must be meaningful relations, such as why a certain route from one point to another is so popular (because it's the way to a popular bar or nightclub) or why it is advisable to choose one route over another (because it's relatively uncongested). This shows us once again that the construction of CMs involves higher learning processes, something we have often observed in the last few chapters. Whenever *survey knowledge,* i.e., a holistic system of spatial points of reference (landmarks) or, in other words, a coherent CM, is formed, a construction process brings about new totalities of a conceptual and spatial kind which cannot be explained in terms of mere associations.

Of course, once our taxi driver has built up his CM of New York, he will have to update it continually. Special traffic conditions such as the countless one-way streets in Manhattan and the latest traffic detours will be incorporated into his representation and out-of-date information will be deleted.

Connected with *distance estimations,* he will also be able to make *time estimations.* He will make distinctions among geographical, purely spatial, and "technical" distances, so that, depending on the time of the day (rush hour, special circumstances such as demonstrations and sporting events), he may choose to go the "long way around," which is actually *quicker* as it avoids heavy traffic. He will be in a position to make a *balance of profit and loss* to the benefit of his customer (or, if he's a trickster, to his own benefit). In other words, he will learn to adapt his CM to suit current needs and circumstances.

Memo

1. The term *cognitive map* goes back to Edward C. Tolman's (1886–1959) experiments with rats (1948). In introducing this concept, he went far beyond the classical explanations for spatial environmental learning in the field of stimulus–response (behaviorist) psychology at that time.
2. Cognitive maps contain both analog and propositional representations. Analog representation reflects reality in its visuospatial structure, whereas propositional representations comprise the many semantic interpretations of reality and its parts.

Propositional representations contain conceptual and procedural, even emotional and value-related, information.

3. The construction of cognitive maps originates in landmark knowledge. Landmarks (points of reference) are then joined together to form routes or to build up route knowledge. Route knowledge is subsequently coordinated to obtain survey knowledge, initially under the influence of a process of overlapping. Often, route knowledge is also extended to obtain survey knowledge by becoming connected with landmarks or important roads or integrated within an existing scaffold like frame of spatial reference (e.g., an area between two main traffic arteries or two rivers or in a familiar part of the quarter).

4. Landmarks are chosen according to certain selection criteria and associated with corresponding names. Selection criteria consist of perceptual discriminability (high-rise), functional significance ("I have to turn off here!"), and value content (prestigious firm).

5. Spatial relationships, connecting landmarks to one another, consist of spatial inclusions (a part of . . .), metric relations (fairly accurate information pertaining to angles and distances), and proximity relations (close to . . .).

6. Route learning involves not merely the association of landmarks or of points of reference or the associative connection of the elements of landmark knowledge; rather, a meaningful relationship is established between points of reference that become integrated within a conceptual–spatial network of meaning even while routes are being learned.

7. Survey knowledge is hierarchically structured and integrated knowledge – a town is broadly divided into areas, each area containing corresponding streets, which in turn contain detailed spatial information, for example, on the sequence of house numbers.

8. Learning the geography of a town starts off (see Point 3) with the learning of individual buildings (landmarks) and series of streets (routes). Soon, however, several routes are coordinated and condensed into areas, becoming higher-order elements. These can be "unfolded" as necessary. In this way, the process involved in the construction of cognitive maps is very similar to a conceptual construction process (see Chapter 13).

9. The learning process also includes the setting and testing of hypotheses. The taxi driver anticipates landmarks (hypothesis) and uses the resulting situation to check whether his anticipation was correct (verification or falsification of the hypothesis). A verification has a reinforcing effect on the learning process; a falsification furthers the construction process according to the feedback information it contains (research).

10. Paired-associate learning, i.e., the linking of landmarks or streets with their names, is an essential part of the process and can be facilitated by first learning the names alone.

18. Playing with Matches: The Gestalt Theory, or Insightful Learning

18.1 Introduction

Before continuing, readers should first direct their attention to the problem shown in Figure 35 and observe their own behavior. This will greatly increase their understanding of the matters discussed in this chapter.

The so-called Berlin Gestalt psychologists, a group we shall hear more of in this chapter, often dealt with the difference between mechanical or rote learning and "insightful learning"; Max Wertheimer and Karl Duncker particularly emphasized the distinction. What this means and how it fits into what we have seen in the previous chapters (especially Chapter 16) are the topics of this chapter. The special language of Gestalt psychology, which is much different from the one we are accustomed to, will play a special role.

It soon becomes clear that solving the match problem of Figure 35 cannot be done through trial and error and the respective rules thereof (cf. Chapter 3). Rather, one must analyze the *structure of the problem* at hand and understand that the *organization of the operations* necessary to solve it forms a *dynamic system*. Gestalt psychologists speak of "restructuring the problem," which leads to insight and is diametrically opposed to rote learning of rules. To solve such problems, one must *organize* – and not *memorize* – the elements and operations involved (Katona, 1940).

This chapter also differs from previous ones although the phenomena under study can be described in terms of *cognitive learning psychology: building of hypotheses; deducing of rules; blind induction; insight; transferability of structure;* integration into a whole entity, i.e., into the *totality of a structure* (this is what is called *Gestalt*); *figural context, restructuring; dynamic system; "organizing" versus "memorizing."*

Figure 35: Basic form of the match task treated in this chapter: "Make four squares from five squares by moving three matches."

18.2 Trial and Error, Hypotheses and Rules, Blind Induction

Game Protocols

One evening the father had the idea of starting a family competition in solving match problems (cf. also Brooke, 1970): Whoever solved the most problems would win a prize! "Here," he said, "are five squares. Your job is to move three matches to form four squares" (Figure 35).

Let us look over the shoulder of one of the persons involved and observe how she goes about solving the problem. The individual steps involved are depicted in Figure 36a–e. The final try will lead to success and the formulation of a hypothesis.

The father introduces a second setup. All participants arrange their matches in the same way (as is shown in Figure 37a) and begin. The task is still the same as before. The first five trials result in various failures (Figure 37b–d), but eventually produce a correct solution (Figure 37e) along with a hypothesis. With this hypothesis a new trial run begins (Figure 37f); it leads, again, to failure (Figure 37g).

Analysis of the Procedure Chosen

The procedure used here corresponds to learning by trial and error. It is, however, not a completely blind attempt: When faced with her intermediate results the player formulates certain comments that serve as a sort of *feedback*. First, she notes what is doomed to failure: "Oh, if I take out the one at the bottom, it won't work" (Figure 36d). Then she states a hypothesis (Figure 36e): "Remove one at the top and two at the corner!" On the basis of this hypothesis, she attacks the problem anew (Figure 37a). Yet this, too, does not result in instant success. She tries again: There are, after all, other concerns that have yet to be tested (Figure 37b). She then tries removing from the top instead of the bottom; this fails to yield complete success, but at least she obtains a configuration corresponding to half her expectations or four squares (Figure 37c)! Now, only one match is left over! The *contingency* of her hypothesis and the resulting partial success *reinforce* the activity for further tries in accordance with the hypothesis, which has assumed the *character of a rule*. Following yet a further trial, which also fails (Figure 37d), she tries something "completely different": She sidesteps her hypothesis, without actually abandoning her previous methods, removing a match from the bottom again, albeit a different match. The subsequent *success* she achieves confirms her method

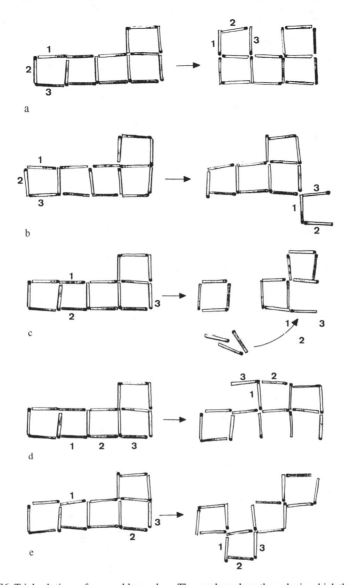

Figure 36: Trial solutions of one problem solver. The numbers show the order in which the subject moves the matches: on the left-hand side the order in which they are removed, on the right-hand side the order in which they are added. To follow the actions, use the order 1-1, 2-2, 3-3, etc. Parts a–e are a sort of protocol of what happens: (a) Three matches have indeed been moved, but, incorrectly: There are still five and not four squares left. (b) Again, three matches have been moved, but still the goal of constructing four squares has not been reached. (c) Three matches have been moved and three squares constructed, but three matches are just lying around. *All matches must be used in this task.* The subject now has the idea of putting them together as shown on the right-hand side. This results in four squares that are not contiguous. The subject now questions: "Is there really a solution at all to this?" – "But of course there is!" (d) Three matches were moved, but four squares are not obtained. "I see, taking them away at the bottom doesn't solve anything." (e) Three matches were removed and four squares are obtained. "Now I've got it. Remove one at the top and two at the corner!"

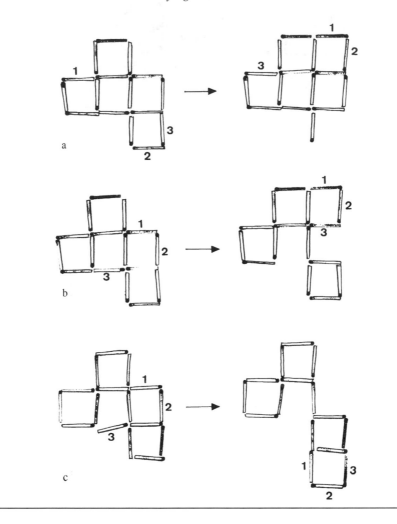

and reinforces everything she has seen or learned (Figure 37e): "It was the corner at the bottom!"

The next task, however, draws the method into question again: The previous tactics prove erroneous (Figure 37f, g). Moving the three matches this way proves to be wrong, although the procedure was reinforced by a certain *contingent* success, be it partial or complete. Our subject has effectively learned something untenable – through a series of *reinforcements*. This, by the way, is a very good illustration that the transfer of learning does not mean a transfer of identical elements (in this case, identical process or transformation steps)

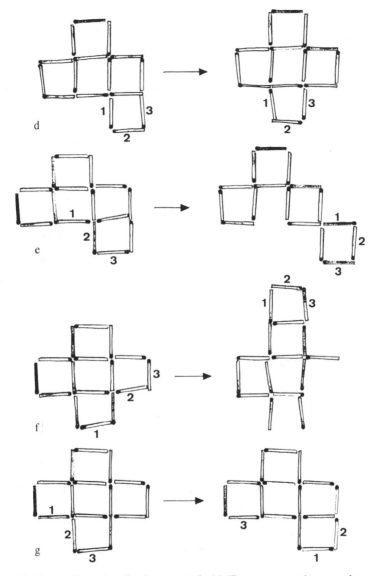

Figure 37: New configurations for the same task. (a) "Remove one at the top and two at the corner." Three matches were moved, but five squares and one superfluous match were obtained. (b) Three matches were moved, four squares are obtained, but one match is left over. "That's better! Take away at the bottom and at the corner." (c) "Oh, the same thing!" (d) Three matches were moved, but five instead of four squares are obtained. "That doesn't work! Or does it? Now for something completely different." (e) "Now I've got it. A corner one and one at the bottom." With this hypothesis, the third round begins. (f) A new task! Three matches were moved, four squares are obtained, but three open squares are left. "Well, maybe it's not corner and bottom." (g) Three matches were moved, five squares are obtained. "But I did exactly the same thing as before when it worked" (bottom and corner).

to a new situation. I say this because that was one of the original postulates of the transfer theory (cf. Detterman & Sternberg, 1993; Greeno, Smith, & Moore, 1993; Steiner, 1997).

Perhaps the proposed hypothesis was not *exact enough*. Certainly it cannot be applied *(generalized)* to all cases in which the task is to make four squares from five squares by moving three matches. One can imagine, however, that all possible cases of this nature might be solved with the help of a reinforced method that proves to solve such tasks. But that would encompass a very large number of configurations indeed (cf. Figure 38), and learning by the *trial-and-error* method would be very time-consuming.

Figure 38: A few examples of possible starting positions of the same task. In addition, turning these by 90 degrees results in completely new configurations, resulting in ever new conditions for constructing rules or hypotheses.

Even if our subject has mastered one successful method, she will have to learn a completely new method for every new constellation: Her guiding hypotheses (or the reinforced procedural rules) no longer "fit." In other words, she has learned to apply a series of actions that, on the one hand, is elicited by the new task, but that, on the other hand, for heretofore unknown reasons, does not solve it. Thus, the *transferability* of what has been learned is not guaranteed. This is the case even when only a single parameter is modified (Figure 39).

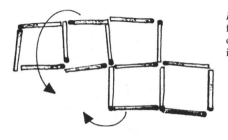

Figure 39: New task: "Make four squares from five squares in two moves." In contrast to the original task only two matches may be moved in this task. The arrows show the solution.

Although our subject has attempted to give her method a *regularity* (rules), the successes she obtained were always a surprise to her and occurred *without insight into the relations*. Wertheimer (1945), one of the leading Gestalt psychologists, spoke in this regard of "blind induction" – and that's the very point: How can we reduce the "blindness" of learning? What knowledge of inner *relations* (or connections) must be obtained to allow one to *learn* how to solve *all* match tasks?

18.3 The Path toward Insight and Understanding

From Blind Induction to Numeric Considerations

The match task presented here certainly demands a more systematic approach than our subject offered. Since the number of matches involved (16) is the same at all times, there must be some way to deduce *structural commonalities despite obvious differences in the spatial configurations* of the matches. Perhaps a few preliminary thoughts on the learning goal of this task are appropriate.

Squares have four sides. To make five squares, we thus need 20 matches. The father, however, is capable of doing this – without resorting to magic – with only 16 matches. The only conclusion is that four of the matches fulfill a *double function*. Figure 40 confirms this assumption.

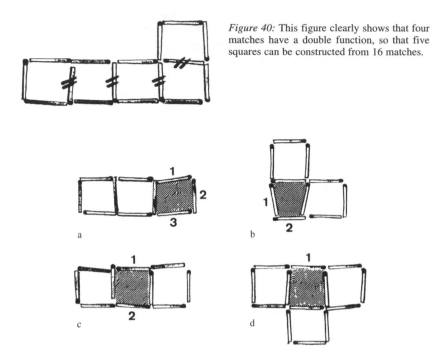

Figure 40: This figure clearly shows that four matches have a double function, so that five squares can be constructed from 16 matches.

Figure 41: Various types of squares: (a) wing squares formed from three matches; (b) corner squares formed from two matches; (c) middle squares formed from two matches; (d) embedded squares with only one match necessary.

If the task is to make four squares out of five, these four squares each have four (!) sides, that is, they must be free-floating squares that touch only on one corner. For this reason, all sides that have a double function must now become sides with just one single function. But strangely enough, this *mathematical approach* (also discussed by Katona, 1940) helps the subject little in such a test: Subjects tend not to employ this knowledge – or they are unable to employ it. Katona's formulation of the solution is *mathematically* correct, but *structurally* unfavorable. It is based on details, and these details (the sides) are less important than whole squares. It is certainly questionable whether the path leading from the details (the sides) to larger units actually leads to an understanding of the problem at hand (see Bergius, 1964, 306).

If we look again at the single starting situation, we can see that, on the one hand, the (number of) sides *are* important, since in the end one must move three of them to solve the problem. On the other hand, we are talking about the squares as *units*, with the object of constructing four from the five originally present. If we concentrate on the squares, we indeed find characteristic

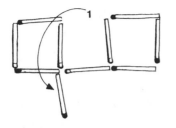

Figure 42: Any change at any place results in a change at another position: If match 1 is removed, the embedded square (cf. Figure 41c) is dismantled, albeit forming the basis for a new wing square.

differences (Figure 41): First, there are *wing squares* (Figure 41a) formed from only three matches. Then there are *corner squares* (Figure 41b) that are attached to other squares such that two matches suffice. Further, we find *middle squares* (Figure 41c) constructed of only two matches set opposite each other (compare these with the corner squares, (Figure 41b) built with the same amount of matches). Finally, we find *embedded squares* for which only one match is necessary (Figure 41d).

In the paragraph above, we said that a wing square could be constructed with three matches, a corner or middle square with two matches, and an embedded square with a single match. These numbers, however, are not valid for the act of *dismantling* squares, since one of the matches often remains in place, to form a new construction. Removing only a single match from a middle square suffices to dismantle it, as the remaining match being used as the basis for a new square with three matches (Figure 42).

From Numeric to Structural Considerations

Up to now we have considered only the purely numeric task of making free-standing squares from 16 matches, that is, four squares without common sides to them. But this does not tell us which of the squares have to be changed. For this, we need *structural information* to tell us something about single squares in their *figural context*. Depending on the particular context, one and the same square might become a totally different entity. This, in fact, is the *Gestalt character* of squares: They differ in *how they fit into the whole* – into the *overall Gestalt* – which determines the configuration of each individual square. Thus, we must grasp the *Gestalt or system character* of the task inherent to all configurations of the matches and their transformations. We are *not* dealing with simple mechanical learning or memorizing. *The overall task is not to memorize something, but to understand the organization of a whole and the transformations thereof.* These terms – *organizing* and *memorizing* – form the title of Katona's book (1940).

Transforming the setup of squares is done by removing individual matches and observing the consequences for the overall number of squares (which is a given in the task at hand). In our example, removing three matches breaks up more squares (exactly one more) than can later be reconstructed. Thus, we must learn the numeric workings (the *system*) present throughout all changes to the layout. The number of matches that may be moved dictates, on the one hand, the initial setup necessary before any matches are reinserted. If, as in the present example, three matches may be removed, then at least one must be initially available, since it is impossible to construct a new, free-standing square from only three matches.

If, however, the task requires moving only two matches (cf. the task posed in Figure 39), a twosome must be available (or remain untouched) for completing the task of building a four-sided square. The number of matches that can be moved thus also limits both the place and type of squares that can be (re)moved or transformed. In other words, one must break up two squares by moving two matches – and both cannot be middle ones, but must also include at least one corner square *(retrospection!)*. Yet, since I have only two matches for reconstruction, there must be two matches available for the square to be completed *(anticipation!)*. In addition, in this task more squares have to be dissolved than reconstructed.

If three matches are to be removed (as in the standard task: Figures 35–37), one may at best break up three embedded squares (Figure 41d). In the present configurations with five squares in the starting configuration, there is at best

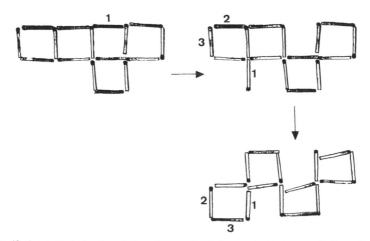

Figure 43: An example for the solution of the task. First, an embedded square is dismantled (1), then a wing square (2, 3). Thus, three matches are moved to make up a new wing square using one match from the just dismantled wing square to form the new one.

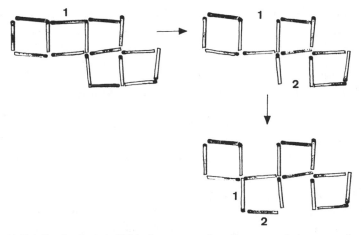

Figure 44: Solution for the task: "Make four squares from five squares in two moves."

one of this kind. This one and the middle square or a corner square (Figure 41c) can – and indeed *must* – be broken up to fulfill the rule that one square more be dissolved than rebuilt. But first a corner square must be *created* by moving a single match (denoted in Figure 43 by a 1).

If only two matches may be moved (Figure 44), and if the total number of squares is to be reduced by 1, the logical conclusion is to break up two middle squares so that one square each is lost, thereby reconstructing a single square with the help of the two available matches. A look at the figure shows that there is only a single middle square, but that perhaps changes could be made to other squares (e.g., corner squares) to make the necessary two matches available to construct a square from two existing sides. It is a matter of deliberately "tuning" out these actions in relation to one another.

Structural Considerations and Their Transferability

Learning this kind of coordinating ("tuning") of actions requires focusing on the number of squares to be constructed, which is determined not only by a certain number of match moves, but also by one's anticipation of the configuration, necessary to be completed eventually.

In the ears of a novice match-square problem solver, these thoughts surely seem rather complicated. Yet they constitute one's *understanding of the relations or connections,* the *system,* mentioned above – and this sort of understanding is, as opposed to things mechanically learned, transferable to *any and every* other configuration or task at hand. Katona explicitly stated the hypothesis that learning with understanding differs from mechanical memorizing in that the former permits an effective transfer of training and meaningful learning (see Bergius, 1964, 301).

Rote Learning vs. Insight or Understanding while Learning

The match-square tasks presented above clearly demonstrate the contrast between rote learning of rules and procedures and *insightful* learning, or learning based on *understanding*. In this case, "understanding" the workings of a comprehensive system implies at least three *process components: eliminating squares* by moving a limited number of matches, *preparing additions (anticipation),* and *completing the desired configuration*. (Compare in this respect my earlier comments on understanding text, mathematical operations, or geometric operations in Chapters 13, 15, and 16, respectively. Each case involves setting up *specific* systems!)

The contrast "rote learning vs. insight or understanding," which Katona as well as other Gestalt psychologists (e.g., Wertheimer, 1945) studied, plays an important role not only in situations such as our match-square example, but also in learning in school (from primary through vocational school to the university level). Many students, failing to have grasped the *meaning* of some event, logical connection, or principle, turn to *memorizing* to cover their tracks (cf. in Chapter 13, Section 13.2, on "Learning Goals").

18.4 Restructuring, the Construction of Dynamic Systems, and Insight

Gestalt psychologists such as Wertheimer (1945) or Duncker (1935) were intensely concerned with how people solve problems and how they go about *obtaining* such capabilities. They stressed the concept of *restructuring one's perceptual field*, i.e., reordering or rearranging the visual elements to form a new whole or totality (a Gestalt!), which in its wholeness is not only more than, but also different from the simple sum of the individual elements making up that whole.

This process of (re)organizing one's perceptual field is meant to influence how one "sees" the problem or its solution – one's very *insight* – since it occurs in interaction with memories already present and relevant to problem solving. (Recall that in Chapter 16 we already studied the problem of how we "see" elements and spatial relations while learning geometry. There we showed in some detail the prerequisites for "seeing" and the way restructuring may be described in terms of *cognitive learning theory*. These same require-ments pop up once again in the match problem at hand.)

Here, besides the restructuring of the perceptual field, we are concerned particularly with establishing an exact way of viewing the squares in their respective context, with grasping the *transformation processes* (that's where the restructuring comes in) with its various *prerequisites* (retrospection!) and *their predictable consequences*, in addition to *integrating* all of these process-es to form a coherent and dynamic system. All of this makes up what we call *insight into the match problem*. One could describe the system as a *dynamic action system*, similar to a *semantic network* with many feedback loops, the structure of which implies getting to know and coordinating the individual partial actions: in other words, eliminating squares, moving a set number of sides, preparing the final changes, and completing the configuration. In the terminology of the *expert–novice paradigm* well known to the field of cogni-tive psychology (see e.g., Chi, Glaser, & Rees, 1982, for an example from the field of physics), these latter skills indeed mark the expert: The expert is ahead of the novice by having the capability of integrating the individual actions to form a mental model for solving *all* such problems and using this model immediately to establish internal simulations of the respective changes to the configurations. The novice, on the other hand, depends on partial knowledge and individual behavior as well as the (often false) hypotheses or "rules" distilled from these, leading to improper actions or false solutions.

But how can we learn, and how can we teach, these principles? I am not aware of any studies on how such a coherent system arises (or even what its makeup might be) for solving our match-square problem – except those of Katona (1940), which did not focus, however, on the genetic or constructive aspect of learning. Duncker (1935), another Gestalt psychologist, touched on this theme only indirectly. In the future, we should concentrate on an analysis of these skills from the vantage point of developmental psychology or a dis-crete interventional study based on learning and precepts from developmental psychology directed toward raising such skills. Such studies would provide important information on exactly how partial skills may be integrated into a functioning dynamic system.

The readers should consider what is necessary to prepare them for solving any and all match problems thrown at them, i.e., what produces certain insight and what avoids harmful pitfalls.

Memo

1. The Gestalt psychologists were a group of psychologists in Berlin who were concerned with the problem of parts and wholes (the *Gestalten*) and the dynamic organization of behavior in various areas such as perception, thought, problem solving, intelligence, and the development of social relations. The main proponents were Wertheimer, Köhler, Duncker, Koffka and Lewin.
2. Match-square problems cannot be solved by trial and error and the respective reinforcement mechanisms. Rules derived from trial and error cannot be transferred at will to other tasks.
3. Learning to solve the match-square tasks means grasping the structure of the task at hand. A structural analysis leads to knowledge of both the characteristics of the material (the squares) and the relations or connections of the operations carried out on this material.
4. Any structural considerations of the task may be transferred to other configurations and problems.
5. Eliminating squares, moving a set number of matches, preparing the configurations for adjustment and completion, and actually making those completions are all operations that must be integrated into a dynamic system. With this, we understand the problem and gain insight into its solution.
6. Restructuring or reorganizing the whole (the *Gestalt*) is, according to Gestalt psychology, what the learner actually has to do – not rote learning of the successful solution. Katona's key idea was "Organize; don't memorize."
7. In terms of cognitive learning psychology, we might rephrase this as follows: To solve match-square problems, you first have to build up an active network of operations containing the reciprocal relations and interactions of the operations (cf. Point 4).

19. Learning to Play Chess: The Construction of Complex Operational and Goal Systems

19.1 Introduction

This final chapter does not contain a quick course on how to play chess and certainly includes no tips on becoming a master of the trade. Quite the opposite: The reader will quickly see just why he or she has *failed* to become a master and why this state of affairs has little chance of changing. Despite these poor prospects, let us nevertheless take a closer look at the fascinating game of chess.

Below, we will proceed through four sections covering the four stages of learning, from *novice* to *advanced beginner*, through being a *competent player*, to becoming an *expert* or even a *grand master*. We will concentrate especially on *changes that take place in the database* as well as the *type and organization of the elements* thereof during these transitions from one stage to the next.

The following terms are important to this chapter: *database; structural descriptions; condensing of the structural descriptions, patterns, or configurations; hierarchies of patterns and goals; novices and experts.*

Those readers interested in the details of the manifold strategies and tactics used in the stages of a chess game (e.g., openings, middle game, endgame) as well as the specific terminology (e.g., "KP opening," "Alekhine defense") should take a look in the rich literature available on this subject (see Unzicker, 1975).

19.2 Elementary Operations: What Novices Have to Learn

First let us consider the novice! The absolute necessities are *knowledge* of the *board layout* (its orientation), of the *pieces* (king, queen, knight, bishop, rook, pawn), of the way to set up the board, and of the *rules of possible moves*, i.e., the elementary operations possible and their effects. Figure 45a–g reviews

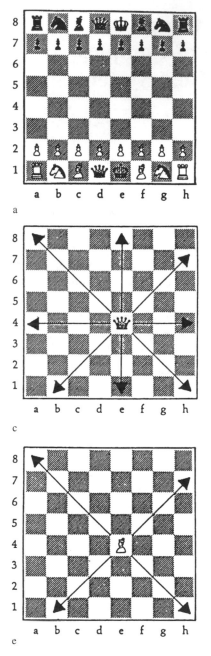
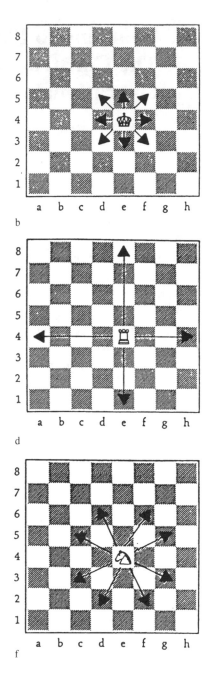

Figure 45a–f. For legend, see opposite.

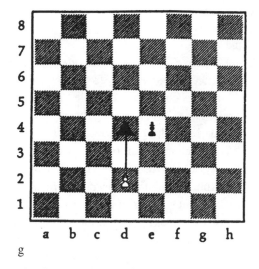

Figure 45: Setting up the pieces and the rules for the moves. (a) The board layout for the two sides. (b) The king can move in all directions – horizontally, vertically and diagonally – but only one square at a time. Kings should never land directly next to each other. (In time the beginner learns that the king is important above all at the end of a match and shows his "strengths" in that phase despite the limitations in movement.) (c) The queen, like the king, can move in all directions. But unlike the king she can move as far as the situation allows, i. e., more than one square at a time. (The beginner quickly learns that the queen is the strongest figure on the board, and that the loss of the queen is usually fatal to one's chances; cf. Figures 46 and 47 below.) (d) The rook may move horizontally and vertically but not diagonally. (The beginner soon learns that the rook's power lies in unfettered movement, i. e., when it is no longer contained by a closed row of pawns.) (e) The bishop may move only diagonally. The white bishop, as can be clearly seen, moves only on white squares, the black bishop on black squares. (The beginner here too learns that the bishop develops his power only when the line of pawns is opened up, whereupon he is like the queen or rook.) (f) The knight does not move, he jumps. The figure shows this better than any explanation can. (The beginner quickly learns that the knight can overcome closed rows of other figures and difficult situations. He also soon learns that the knight has no "extended" power, but rather is most useful in "thick action.") (g) The pawn moves in two ways: first, from the opening position one or two squares forward, thereafter only one square at a time – but always forward, never backward. The pawn is the only figure to capture not by moving in its basic direction, but diagonally. (We won't go into capturing here; the beginner soon learns that he should not move the pawns too carelessly, as they can never be moved backward.)

briefly the moves of the individual pieces – the *elementary operations* – without delving into great detail. Readers acquainted with the game of chess can skip this section.

The novice must first learn that the board is turned such that a white field is at the bottom right. This leads to the rule "white queen – white field" and its counterpart "black queen – black field." The other pieces can be set up once the proper position for the queen has been determined. The novice will notice that the two players' pieces mirror each other (axially, that is, not radially), and that the position of the queen and king depends on the color.

Rule Knowledge with and without Context

We earlier called the moves of the individual pieces *elementary operations.*
These are based on a certain *knowledge of the rules*, gathered from *explanations* of a more experienced chess player, from *literature* on the subject, or
from experience with a chess computer. The rule "The king may move either
diagonally or in a straight line (both horizontally and vertically), but only one
square at a time" can be learned, i.e., encoded *verbally*. Of course, one can
also encode it *visually* as the movement on the board, or *statically* as a result
(see Figure 45b). In fact, all moves can be visually perceived and encoded.
Yet, the moves of the knight are best *carried out directly* to help remember
them: Carrying out the knight's jumps oneself (two squares horizontally plus
one square vertically, or vice versa) best imprints them on a novice's memory.
Bruner (1964, 1966) would speak of an initially *enactive* representation,
which eventually becomes an *iconic* representation after corresponding practice (cf. Chapters 13 and 16, which deal with Bruner's modes of representation).

When someone first learns to play chess, the rules are context-free; i.e., the
novice learns and recalls them much as they are depicted in Figure 45b–g.

Yet, new knowledge soon follows. First, the novice learns that, as soon as
the pieces take their place in the overall environment, employment of the rules
is limited by certain spatial limitations. Above all, the novice is confronted
with *operational limitations* when contact is first made with one's opponent
after a few moves. The abstract rules must now be adapted (and thus extended)
to both the spatial and operational contexts. Novices quickly become aware
of the fact that they are indeed strongly caught by their knowledge of the rules,
that they have no overview of the whole happening, and that they are continually overlooking important relations between their own pieces and those of
their opponent. It soon becomes apparent that to understand what is going on
in the game better one must obtain a fairly precise *structural description* of
the situation at hand. (We will return to this subject in the next section.) In
order for the game to remain fun to play despite these difficult beginnings, the
novice gets some advice in the form of elementary bits of chess knowledge
from a more advanced player, for example, how to protect certain pieces from
being taken, which pieces can be sacrificed in what situations, and which must
not be lost. Yet, such knowledge of elementary operations will be completely
understood only upon being integrated in the respective context of the game
at hand.

19.3 The Operations and Their Implications – the Advanced Beginner

The novice we once knew has now become an *advanced beginner.* Let us describe the advances in terms of cognitive learning, keeping in mind the lessons of earlier chapters such as the processes of constructing mental models or semantic networks (cf. Chapters 13–17).

The advanced beginner has now taken his first steps and gathered some knowledge of the *strength* or the power of the various pieces – and has *understood* what he was told initially, namely, that moves on the chess board consist of very diverse *operations* (or *functions*). Each move expresses very different *intentions* and thus also *goals*. These are the possible operations of any piece:

1. Simple *shifts*, affecting solely the presence of the piece at a particular spot (e.g., opening moves). Later, the chess player becomes acquainted with situations in which such shifts become *necessary* simply because it is one's turn; the move itself has no particular meaning, i.e., neither a goal nor an effect. However, such pure shifts tend to be rare in chess, as one usually has some *intention* in mind or is building up some constructional step within the game's operational system, which becomes more and more dynamic. But pure shifts of this nature do have consequences *at later points in time:* Certain areas (squares on the board) in the power zone of a particular piece may be "blocked" and thus become a "danger zone" for the opponent's pieces, or a "safe zone" or "attack zone" for one's own pieces. Simple shifts may also represent flight behavior (from being attacked, or exchanged, or checked), particularly in the final phases of a game. A shift may also clear space for another piece to assume a particular action (cf. the first example in this chapter, Figure 46).

2. The second operation of all pieces is the *blocking* (of fields or squares on the board). Every piece has its own peculiar danger zone, which comprises its constituent power, on the one hand, and makes the game interesting as well, challenging the players' vigilance, on the other hand. The pieces and their positions can be visually grasped, but their *influence* is indirect (e.g., in the above-mentioned "danger zone"): One has to *discern* or *construct* it. Such constructions (which even the novice makes) soon lead to the conclusion that the queen is the strongest piece on the board. Knowing that rooks, knights, and bishops are *relatively* strong, each in its own *specific* way and *depending on the situation* at hand, means taking the context into account: That is, further constructions are made in time by an advanced beginner.

3. If a move leads not just to an empty field, but to an enemy piece's entering the danger zone of one's own piece, then we are dealing with the operation of an *attack* or a *threat*, the highest form of which is giving *check* to the opponent's king. The major consequence of check (except when it becomes checkmate, discussed later) is that the opponent is forced to move the king from the "check zone" or otherwise protect him, a task which includes that one cannot effectively handle or counterattack other dangers. Being in check binds resources that will be missing elsewhere. A check attack may – but need not – be accompanied by the call "check." In any case, all other simultaneous attacks remain unremarked.

4. If the attack is a silent one and remains undiscovered by the enemy, the next step occurs, namely, the *capture*, i.e., the loss of a chessman for one of the players or an advantage for the other player. The advanced beginner will soon learn that such confrontations often do not end in a single capture but lead to an *exchange* of pieces or even to a series of exchanges. Capturing is the logical extension of an attack. (For more on capturing the king, see Point 6 below.)

5. But one can also threaten an opponent's piece *indirectly*: One's own piece does not attack directly, but rather *covers* or *protects* another piece, i.e., takes this piece into its "care," as it were, simultaneously representing the danger zone of an opponent's chessman. *Covering* or *protecting* is thus the fifth elementary operation we have met with. It is often used solely as a protective means for pieces suspected of being in particular danger of being captured by one's opponent now or at some later time. But one can also effect protection for a piece by placing it in the safe zone of another of one's own chessmen. The latter operation is a sort of combination with the first type of operation: moving a piece with the goal of *protecting* it. By actively covering or protecting a piece, or by moving it into a safe zone, one attempts to ward off an attack by the opponent or at least to force him to pay the cost of such an attack. Such tactics, however, imply a relatively high level of logic not yet present in the advanced beginner. More on that later.

6. The sixth elementary operation is *checkmate*, in principle only a special form of *capturing*. If the king is attacked by "checking," and if the king cannot be moved, and if the attacking chessman itself cannot be captured, and if the attack cannot be thwarted by placing some other piece in the path – then the king is ripe to be captured. Out of respect for the king, however, he is not captured, only "checkmated."

7. As the seventh operation one could construe what was already mentioned in Point 6 above: *moving a piece into the line* of fire to ward off a check

or checkmate or some other threat to one of one's own pieces. This operation is basically another form of shifting (see Point 1 above), albeit for a very specific purpose not mentioned there.

On even higher levels there are, of course, a number of other operations, for example, offering a sacrifice. More on that later on.

What interest us from a learning psychology point of view, of course, are the *implications* emerging from these elementary operations. Mastering these and being able to implement them are what differentiate the novice from the expert.

19.4 Constructing a Complex Operational System

Let us first try to determine the aspects of playing chess that are relevant to learning and cognitive psychology. We will accompany our advanced beginner awhile on his path toward expertise.

Our budding chess player learns that every move causes more or less major changes to the situation on the board. Depending on the *power* (or action potential) of the respective chessman, a *single* move may cause small or large modifications. Regardless of the case at hand (particularly when the game is in a more advanced stage), many more pieces are affected than the one making the move. Experienced chess players know that at times a move with a "weak" piece such as a pawn can change the situation more dramatically than a move with the more powerful queen. Thus, how a situation is changed does not depend solely on the respective strength of the piece, but equally on the overall context.

Structural Descriptions and the Limits of Memory Capacity

Thus, the first step in building up a complex structural system is for the player to recognize the implications mentioned above and order them into a *comprehensive structural description*. This, of course, must be done for both one's own pieces and those of one's opponent! Such a capability demands that one quickly *scan* the *field of power* of all of one's own pieces, *mentally grasp* the *structural characteristics* of the situation, and *store* them in a rather complicated form, namely, as a mixture of verbal and visuospatial information. Any beginner at chess knows just how difficult such cognitive operations indeed can be. During the process of describing the structural characteristics of the situation one realizes just how much of what one initially grasped mentally has in fact fled one's memory: The process must begin anew.

Actually, the whole matter is even more difficult than just described. Not only must chess players describe the structural characteristics, a process which takes time in itself; they must also develop and evaluate both their own *planning steps* and those of their opponent – processes that call for considerable processing capacities.

We can and should assume that there is a limit to the capacity of human memory, something we touched on already in Chapter 14. If information had to be saved only in short-term memory during a chess match, we could assume (like Miller, 1956) that 7 ± 2 information packages ("chunks") could be retained for a limited period of time. But the situation surrounding the storage and processing of information both on the chessboard and in the player's head is much more complicated. First, a major part of the information lies open before the player on the chessboard; here, nothing must be stored as it can be readily perceived. Second, the player must anticipate some moves, store them as ideas, and recall them at will. At the same time, however, he must observe the opponent, activate his own ideas of future moves on the basis of the opponent's actions, weigh the various alternatives, and then make a decision. Besides storing ideas and plans, one *processes* a great deal of information. To generate plans and alternatives, the chess player will rely on his own expert knowledge (e.g., tried and true strategies), thus activating and employing information from long-term memory. Long-term memory plays a very specific role within working memory, which even prompted Ericsson and Kintsch (1995) to speak of a "long-term working memory."

Miller's magic number "7 ± 2" mentioned above is of particular interest in one respect, for it does not tell us anything about the size and extent of the 7 (or at most 9) chunks that can be stored, only their number. This is for the learner (as well as for anyone who wants to better his chess game) a real chance! With each game played he discovers and experiences similar moves, so that he becomes intimately aware of the structural descriptions; over time he will retain such repeated situational facts, though in a shortened or condensed and thus "handier" form. This process of condensing, which corresponds more or less to the chunking process, is what really counts. We will demonstrate this by using the opening moves in a chess match.

An Important Learning Step: Condensing Structural Descriptions

The next move in the match (see Figure 46) is the third move of black, so there's not yet a great deal of "history" in the game, and the situation is rather transparent. The first moves were as follows: white pawn from e2 to e4, and black pawn from e7 to e5. The respective *structural description* for white is thus still rather simple: Only fields d5 and f5 as well as d4 and f4 are danger zones for the opponent, respectively. Through the shift of the white e-pawn, however, the white queen on d1 has become active – albeit without having done anything herself. She *blocks* the diagonal d1 to h5. The same is true for the other side for the king's bishop, who also blocks a diagonal (f8 to a3). Such implicit information also belongs to a structural description; though at the moment of no particular interest, it could be of great importance to the match after a few further moves.

Let's take a closer look at the second moves, taken by the knights: White moves from g1 to f3, black from b8 to c6. The structural description for white has thus changed: The knight on f3 *blocks* the fields d2, d4, g5, and h4, and he *threatens* above all the opponent's pawn on e5. At the same time, to complete the description, he is *protecting* the pawn on h2 as well as the king, though these facts are not relevant at the moment. The advanced beginner thus apparently has the duty as well to differentiate between the *relevant* and the *irrelevant* effects of his chessmen. The more important fact is that the knight on f3 is restricting the latitude of the power of the white queen, who no longer blocks the line from d1 to h5 but does *protect* the knight on f3 (diagonally) and thus strengthens his position. Here, the advanced beginner learns that simple or *multiple protection* of one of one's own pieces increases the security

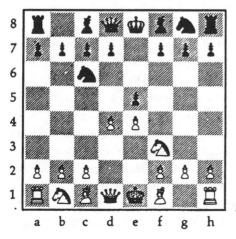

Figure 46: An example of an opening.

of that piece. What this means slowly becomes clear to the player, so that he will attempt to *secure* his own positions systematically in this manner. But we are now jumping ahead of ourselves on the learning process being studied here, namely, the *condensing of structural descriptions*. Finally, we should mention that the white queen is also protecting the pawn directly in front of her, though this is presently not of particular importance.

The return move by black (knight from b8 to c6) strengthens the position of the black pawn on e5; the black knight, now on c6, is being protected by a baseline's pawn (actually by two of them), much like the white knight on f3. Again, this is not yet important, but it is part of a complete structural description.

A situation has arisen in midfield for which our player (if he has been following the match closely) has a complete structural description. We may assume that this situation will crop up again in other matches, and that this *configuration* or a very similar one will reappear. The advanced beginner will not only *recognize* and register the identity or similarity of such configurations, he will note them as being typical whole *entities* or *structural patterns:* This helps him to react *more quickly* in new situations. Making a mental note of such *patterns*, as opposed to noting detailed structural descriptions, is a major step: The large mass of information present in the respective structural description has now been *condensed* into a pattern that can be retrieved and employed as a *new unit of higher-level information*. If necessary, one may query what details this piece of information *originally* contained – it can be "unfolded," the structural description "unpacked." Here, the parallels to our various conceptual constructions of Chapters 13 through 16 become clear. The most important thing is that the advanced beginner begin to note more and more of these patterns (condensed informational packages) and can recognize them in future matches.

These patterns – or the courses of action that lead up to such patterns – play a major role in the game of chess. This can be seen in the fact that many of them have, in the history of chess, become *well-known designations* that form a large part of the *database* of any good chess player, not just the experts. The opening described above, for example, is known as the beginning of the "Scottish" match. Any reasonably good chess player will immediately know what match is meant and be able to visualize the respective configuration as well as to describe the ramifications of the chessmen's effects stemming from this constellation and the consequences for the rest of the match.

Condensing or chunking is perhaps the most important skill any advanced beginner must attain. Without this ability he will literally have no chance of dealing with the ever larger amount of information available to him. One may adjudge whether a player has these skills by *how quickly* he is able to recognize configurations, whether he can "see it coming," i.e., easily predict and defuse upcoming events and plan in larger units. More on this below (cf. also Holding, 1985).

The player in our example will be able to anticipate that black will most likely exchange the white pawn on d4 with his pawn from e5. The player projects such an anticipation onto the board with all its patterns and subpatterns. At the same time, however, he also must continue to think, to anticipate alternatives – all of which makes great demands on the storage and processing capacity of his working memory. By learning to condense the information present on the board into patterns, the advanced beginner counters memory overload. He not only builds up a repertoire of patterns, but also enriches the patterns with new information, eventually allowing amazingly fast anticipation and planning.

Above I mentioned that this condensing of information occurs after *repeated moves* of the same kind. Indeed, seeing the configurations once or twice does not suffice, especially if the beginner still plays unsystematically, thus hindering, through his own inconsistency, the recognition of a structural description of the effects of the pieces or the condensing of descriptions into information packages. Recall the irregular movements of the beginning juggler, to which there are many parallels – the initial short movement segments that are slowly combined into larger units (chunks), only after a reasonable level of regularity has been reached. In juggling as in playing chess only intensive practice can lead to this level of regularity (cf. Chapter 12).

Not only the repetition of *identical configurations* leads to the construction of a condensed description available for retrieval in the form of a recognizable pattern; so does the appearance of *contrasting configurations*, which leads to comments such as "Oh, this time it's different!" In other words, different configurations are condensed into higher-level units at different points during the game(s). This is what determines the variety of available *patterns*.

If we recall that the number of chunks that can be held in *short-term* or *working memory* is limited, then it will come as no surprise that memory capacity can be better put to use by saving and retrieving the (condensed) *patterns* or *configurations* described above than through the employment of whole structural descriptions. The more comprehensive the patterns are, the greater the amount of information that can be processed simultaneously in memory during a single match.

Working Memory and Its Relation to Long-Term Memory

As mentioned above, modern memory researchers view short-term memory differently than Miller (1956) did. The short-term store is seen as part of the working memory (cf. Chapter 14), which allows both the storage (short-term storage) and – simultaneously – the processing of information. This processing consists of such processes as rehearsal, encoding and recoding of information (e.g., visual recoding of linguistic information in figural information, or vice versa), and more complex processes such as elaboration (cf. Chapter 14), categorization, construction of new information units (condensing or chunking), or hierarchical ordering of information. With chess, simple storage would not be of much use; we need the intensive processing of information all the more.

On the basis of present research we may assume that we use several different areas of memory capacity simultaneously. We use a visuospatial sketch pad to record the visual facts of the chessboard for later recall; how much of this is stored visually or spatially, respectively, we can only guess. At the same time, we can use a phonological loop to record verbal information about such configurations or other verbalizations, to the extent of what a person can say in about two seconds. A so-called central executive controls how these codings are distributed to the various subsystems of working memory as well as the processes doing the problem solving (e.g., Baddeley, 1986, 1990; Baddeley & Hitch, 1974; Baddeley & Liberman, 1977; Broadbent, 1981). Here, long-term memory plays a major role: First, in the chess match at hand, much information from long-term memory (configurations, details of the rules, etc.) is already active in working memory; second, a great deal of further information is held in "stand-by" in "long-term working memory," to be retrieved at the prompting of some particular cue (Ericsson & Kintsch, 1995). For this reason, chess experts can react extremely quickly to such cues in the board configuration, for example, a particular move by the opponent, by retrieving all information relevant to further planning or to one's next move. The better this skill has been developed, the greater the depth of the player's insight into what will follow (Charness, 1981).

It would appear that the processing capacity of working memory (as opposed to its storage capacity) can be increased enormously through training, without overloading the storage space, since one effectively changes the *quality* of the chunks. This renders irrelevant the question of exactly how much memory capacity is available for storing or processing configurations (though Miller's magical formula may provide the upper limit). An increase in learning in chess means the construction of broader, more complex information units through chunking (or condensing) and by development of the ability to reunfold condensed information whenever necessary.

Condensing as a General Cognitive Process

Condensing is not something new to us; we have touched on it several times in this volume. Condensing is the packing of a number of elements of a network (semantic, numeric, or some other type), including the relations that link them, into a new element of a higher order (Aebli, 1978, 1981, calls it objectification, i.e., building up a new "object" for further thinking). With chess we may assume, instead of a semantic network, a network of operations in which the pawns are the elements and the possible operations the relations that link them ("... protects ...," "... attacks ...," "... strengthens ...," etc.). Even when learning the course of a movement the beginner condenses movement segments, becoming ever better able to recall ever larger segments for controlling the course of action without having to retrieve the individual segments that were initially so laborious (cf. Chapter 3 on untangling the nails or Chapter 12 on juggling). Other researchers view this process as the compilation of knowledge (Anderson, 1987) or a process of chunking (Laird, Rosenbloom, & Newell, 1986).

19.5 The Hierarchy of the Patterns as a Basis for Further Planning: The Competent Chess Player

As we have seen, a chess player needs to learn to recognize quickly the patterns of the game and inject this knowledge into plans for the remainder of the match. In the current course of the game, he must expect to be confronted with any number of variations that do not or only partially correspond to his stored patterns. The amount of information thus increases, and the chess player must be able to deal with this situation. If our advanced beginner is able to combine the individual patterns already known to form larger patterns or to add partial patterns (game alternatives) to them or to integrate and subordinate them into existing patterns, then he effectively is constructing a *hierarchical system of patterns*. This system provides him with quick retrieval of information on many levels as well as a variety of detailed ways to plan the match. This is a major step forward for any advanced beginner on the road to becoming a competent player.

Viewing the situation from a different vantage point, we can say the following: The advanced beginner has started to develop and evaluate his own and his opponent's moves or series of moves as larger planning steps. The progress of the competent player may be described as follows: Besides an ever larger number of alternative planning steps, he develops an ever larger repertoire of creative alternatives and simultaneously integrates those of the opponent. Such anticipatory steps can be presented in hierarchical "tree diagrams" that correspond to the patterns we have discussed. The more competent a player is, the more depth his tree will have, i.e., the more hierarchical levels his planning steps will be embedded in (cf. Holding, 1985; Newell & Simon, 1972). This sort of hierarchical organization of patterns or planning steps may also be found in the hierarchy of goals, presented below.

Hierarchy of Goals

The hierarchical arrangement of patterns, however, is not the only way an advanced beginner becomes a competent player. Up to now we have concentrated on the necessary individual cognitive processes; now let us turn our attention the counterpart – the game itself and its structural demands. This is the second area that determines the competence of a good chess player.

The concrete goal of chess is not to advance the player's cognitive skills, but to checkmate the opponent's king! This is the highest goal in the game. Directly below this goal level is that of approaching the opponent's king, something that is possible (and that is the next lower goal level) only by weakening the other side's defenses. In other words, one wants systematically to remove those chessmen who could attack one's own or who protect the opponent's king. These, however, are very broadly formulated goals! Of utmost importance is to exchange those pieces of the opponent which have the strongest position or the highest power in the respective situation: queen, rooks, and so forth. And this can be done only through use of careful planning. Besides very concrete goals ("The rook on a5 has got to go so that I get my bishop to a6!"), the competent player must develop some higher-level goals such as sacrificing pieces in order to gain a more long-term advantage, for example, in order to advance to a particularly advantageous position. Other partial goals might be setting a trap or obtaining a "free pawn."

Hierarchy of Patterns and Goals and Their Interdependence

Such goals (on whatever level of the hierarchy) are very closely associated with the hierarchically organized patterns, i.e., with the elements of the now

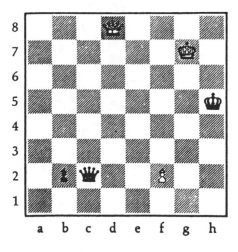

Figure 47: The situation toward the end of a match with a specific goal: to capture the black queen.

very complex database the competent player has built up. They tell him when they are activated in his working memory, and under what conditions a particular goal is relevant and realistic. *The competent and experienced chess player makes plans:* Cued by a well-known and recognized pattern, he calls up other patterns or subpatterns to reach intermediate goals (e.g., exchanging or taking some particular piece or gaining an advantage through a series of clashes with the opponent).

The competent player has learned that there are many advantages in developing parallel strategies: If he can attack two pieces at the same time, he may succeed in taking the more valuable one; or if he can check the king *and* at the same time endanger some other piece, he may force the opponent to take care of the king and lose the other piece. Below we demonstrate such a hierarchical goal that contains plans to reach an intermediate goal (here, to take the queen). The start position is shown in Figure 47.

The intermediate goal is obviously only a stop along the route to checkmating the black king! But that end goal is not our concern here; rather, we want to observe the fate of the black queen. Thus, the reader should first study Figures 47 and 48 intensely before proceeding.

Because of the overall situation and the goal of white, black cannot react as desired: He must act under pressure with only a limited number of alternatives. At this point of the match, the opponent's moves are relatively easy to predict, and the patterns are determined by the hierarchy of goals.

There is at least one alternative to the resolution shown (cf. the caption to Figure 48), from the third move onwards: (3) Qh1–g2 + Kg4–h5 or h4 (4) Qg2–h2 + Kg5 or g4 (5) f2–f4 + or f2–f3 + Kg4/K×P (6) Q×Q.

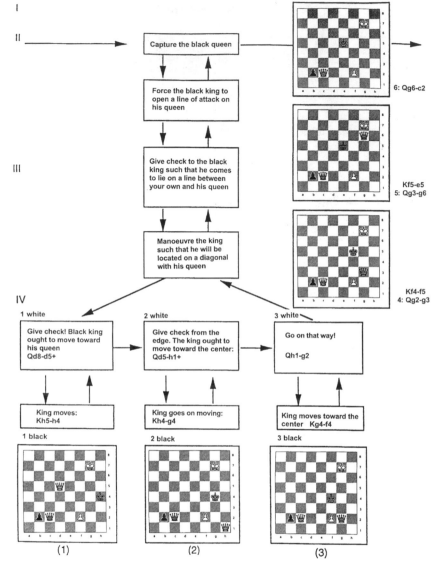

Figure 48: The goal hierarchy to attain the intermediate goal of "capturing the black queen," which in turn is part of the partial goal of "weakening" the enemy to reach the main goal of "checkmating the black king." The roman numerals at the left show the level of goals in the goal hierarchy: I, denotes the highest goal of checkmating the black king; II, the capture of the black queen; III, the intermediate goals necessary to the higher goals; and IV, as it were the "small stuff" without which the intermediate goals could not be reached. From top to bottom the goals become increasingly more specific. An intermediate goal is reached whenever the goals below it are reached. The arrows pointing downward always mean "do first," whereas the arrows pointing to the side or up mean "do next." The arabic numerals shows the moves for white (w) and black (b). They are as follows: (1) Queen d8–d5+ (+ means check), king h5–h4; (2) queen d5–h1+, king h4–g4; (3) queen h1–g2+, king g4–f4; (4) queen g2–g3+, king f4–f5; (5) queen g3–g6+, king f5–e5 or f5–f4; (6) White queen captures black queen (Q × Q). The depiction of a goal strategy as shown in this figure was constructed post hoc based on the protocol of a real match. We cannot be totally sure that the depiction actually shows the *goals* of the white player, but it cannot be too far off base.

It would also be possible that an earlier phase of the match corresponding to goal level IV (Figure 48) would develop more complexly and take more overall moves; or that the situation would arise (perhaps through some mistake) hindering white from returning to goal level III. In these cases the envisioned goal (level II or I) would have to be surrendered for a new one.

Even such purely theoretical constructions show that the chess player who is better off is the one whose competence is based on a broad and clearly hierarchically ordered repertoire of patterns and goals. It is nearly impossible to describe such a repertoire for any single moment in a particular match. The structural descriptions of the opening moves, as presented above, and the description of the goal hierarchy in our example for the phase in which the black queen is taken (Figures 47 and 48) were already very complicated. Further, such a repertoire is different for each individual (at least at the higher levels of the hierarchy) and is used differently by each individual. It is this "employment" of one's own repertoire of patterns that reveals the range of one's creative planning – and that determines how inventive and shrewd one's actions really are. Therein also lies the ability to calculate the risk of rather uncertain moves. Much is to be learned from studying the matches of the experts!

When our chess player has made the advances mentioned above, he has reached a level we earlier designated as that of mastery. He is indeed an excellent player, but, alas, compared to the professional world of chess still an amateur.

19.6 "Intuition" in Chess: The Expert

What our player is missing, and what crowns the experts *(grand masters)* of the game, giving them a completely different style from all others, is intuition. What we call intuition in an expert chess player is, from the vantage point of modern cognitive psychological knowledge, the high level of automatization and the extreme speed with which the expert recognizes the respective situation and activates the relevant patterns and subpatterns to plan and set goals for the rest of the match. Because of this very high-speed information processing going on within the expert, an observer has the feeling as if the master is referring to a revelation, an intuition. However, we may assume that the expert chess player needs only very few cues indeed from the board to recall a broad array of patterns that point him toward the goal. The individual moves, on the other hand, are part of a very carefully orchestrated planning routine (cf. level IV in Figure 48), albeit one that takes place much quicker than in even a good amateur. Even when playing simultaneous matches the expert can maintain this obvious sovereignty and "smoothness," enough to conquer up to 20 opponents in parallel.

On the Dimensions of the "Vocabulary" of Chess Patterns

What are the prerequisites to obtaining these skills and becoming a chess master? Newell and Simon (1972, 782) had some very interesting things to say about just this matter. Using computer simulations, they calculated that a complete vocabulary of chess configurations would have to contain between 10,000 and 100,000 different patterns (i.e., units consisting of groups of one's own and one's opponent's pieces and their respective power). This would appear to be such a great number that no one would believe it to be possible that someone could be in the position to store and retrieve that many different patterns. But, as the authors noted, if we recall that a very well-educated person has a vocabulary of perhaps 50,000 words, then it does not appear completely ridiculous that someone could learn and store that many different chess patterns. Indeed, the authors think that a chess master must be able to resort to about 50,000 patterns. And if one remembers how long it takes for someone to build up a word vocabulary of that dimension, how much daily work and training is necessary, then it is easy to understand that becoming a grand master of chess means beginning to play the game as a child and practicing daily for many, many years (cf. De Groot 1965, 1966). The "professional" chess player has a vocabulary of patterns that lies some two orders of magnitude (decimal places) above that of the average amateur!

19.7 Do Experts Have a Better Memory? Experimental Evidence

Are Visual Images the Crucial Processes?

Do the planning and anticipation of upcoming moves rest on visual images? And do competent chess players thus have a better visual imagination than others? Leaving aside the chess grand masters who can simultaneously play several blind matches, during a normal match the board is indeed a visual fact lying in front of the player. If the player plans his moves or thinks through possible moves of his opponent, visual images (i.e., inner visuospatial transformations) may indeed play a role. Nevertheless, the most important things are the structural descriptions and the condensations thereof that change with every anticipated move. From experimental studies we know about how the inner processes probably function in such situations, especially what divides the novices from the experts. This, then, forms the basis for answering the questions stated above on the role of visual images.

A number of studies compared novices and experts in their behavior when confronted with a certain chess situation (e.g., Chase & Simon, 1973). Both novices and experts were presented with the same board configuration for 5 seconds, a sort of "snapshot" from a longer match. They then had to reconstruct this situation on an empty board. Whereas the masters were able to complete this task without difficulty, both beginners and even more advanced players could locate few pieces in their proper positions. The interesting finding was that this skill of the masters did not stem from a superior memory, for example, a higher level of imagination or visualization: When the same pieces were placed on the board in a random fashion and shown to both novices and masters, both now showed the same (relatively poor) ability to reconstruct the configuration! (See in this regard the earlier studies of De Groot, 1965, 1966, which represent pioneering efforts in the study of the psychological background of chess.)

But in a real match the chessmen *are* in a meaningful and realistic position on the board, and the chess master registers the elements (the pieces) and their relations to one another on the basis of fewer characteristics in much larger units than the novice. For this reason, he is able to reconstruct the overall situation without difficulty. Since he had to grasp the situation within 5 seconds, we may assume that the reconstruction was already available in working memory. According to recent work (Holding, 1985), it is safe to assume that verbal codings play as large a role as do visuospatial or figural ones!

Our present knowledge of the quantitative aspect of working memory does not allow us to say exactly how much knowledge a master must have available in any one situation. We can't even adopt Miller's (1956) magic number of 7 ± 2, since it is now known that one can raise memory capacity by training. But we may assume that we are dealing with chunks, some of which are currently handled, some of which are accessible to be retrieved and put to use, whereas others are principally available and may be reconstructed should the situation demand it. The expert reconstructs the large units, takes the details he needs from them by unfolding them (i.e., "unpacks" those information packages that contain hierarchically ordered partial information), and can see in them both his own plans as well as the plans of his opponent. The master, unlike the beginner, does not orient himself to the situation surrounding the individual pieces.

In summary, a comparison: The master is like someone who can understand a long text sectionwise after only a short perusal; he can describe and use the text as well, whereas the novice is still plagued by the individual letters of the various words and thus never gets much beyond reconstructing individual words.

Memo

1. The chess novice first learns the elementary operations (the rules of chess) and their consequences on the chessboard. His database initially consists of structural descriptions of the operations of his own pieces and those of his opponent as well as the implications thereof.
2. Determining the implications of the operations on the chessboard can be viewed as a parallel to the discovery of implicit facts stemming from conceptual–linguistic information (inference processes).
3. The major step for the novice is learning to condense structural descriptions into higher-level elements – into patterns (configurations) that are stored in long-term memory and can be activated in working memory.
4. Condensing is a general cognitive process that allows one to resort to a large amount of information while also reducing the load on working memory.
5. Working memory provides, on the one hand, short-term storage of a number of elements (chunks) as well as, on the other hand, sufficient capacity for simultaneous information processing, i.e., for encoding and recoding, categorizing, hierarchically structuring or elaborating, condensing, or unpacking information.
   Processing capacity can be greatly expanded through intensive training (experts!), to the extent that it does not harm the storage capacity of working memory. There are no exact data available on the partial capacities of working memory, which depend, first, on the quality of the information to be stored and processed and, second, on the degree of expertise of the individual in question.
6. A pattern contains information on not only the spatiofigural arrangement of the pieces, but also on their respective action potentials. It is assumed that in addition to visuospatial (figural) encodings, verbal encodings in memory play a larger role than previously assumed.
7. The elements of an advanced beginner's database consist of patterns of typical chess configurations and their links to an initially simple and, over time, more elaborate operational system.
8. The major learning steps of the advanced beginner lie in the hierarchical ordering of all available patterns and the linking thereof with goal hierarchies. This is what makes a competent chess player out of a beginner.
9. The competent chess player may be characterized by his fluid and individual employment of pattern and goal hierarchies, i.e., by his ease of use of own operational and goal systems.
10. The expert may be seen in his "intuition" during a chess match, i.e., by the high level of automatization in his perception and judgment of situations as well as his planning and execution of further steps – by the high speed with which he works with his operational and goal systems. The expert has at his disposal approximately 50,000 patterns.
11. Learning to play chess is in many respects a typical higher-level learning process: It is complex; it can only initially be learned via simple algorithms; it implies that

further progress will entail a great number of heuristic moments; every learning situation is characterized by the careful weighing of facts and a very broad number of possible solutions with a varying amount of risks and uncertainties involved. This learning process is, for the most part, self-regulating; i.e., once correctly started, it proceeds, at least in part, via an inherent logic. The task is to learn to recognize the structures present in any one situation – to understand their meaning and to plan and react accordingly (cf. Resnick, 1987).

Bibliography

Abelson, R.P. (1976). Script processing in attitude formation and decision-making. In J.S. Carroll & J.W. Payne (Eds.), *Cognition and social behavior.* Hillsdale, NJ: Erlbaum.

Abramson, L.Y., Seligman, M.E.P., & Teasdale, J.D. (1978). Learned helplessness in humans: Critique and reformulation. *Journal of Abnormal Psychology, 87*(1), 49–74.

Adams, J.A. (1984). Learning movement sequences. *Psychological Bulletin, 96*(1), 3–28.

Aebli, H. (1969). Die geistige Entwicklung als Funktion von Anlage, Reifung, Umwelt und Erziehungsbedingungen. In H. Roth (Ed.), *Begabung und Lernen* (pp. 151–192). Stuttgart: Klett.

Aebli, H. (1978). Von Piagets Entwicklungspsychologie zur Theorie der kognitiven Sozialisation. In G. Steiner (Ed.), *Die Psychologie des 20. Jahrhunderts. Vol. 7: Piaget und die Folgen.* Munich: Kindler, 604–627.

Aebli, H. (1980, 1981). *Denken: Das Ordnen des Tuns* (Volumes I and II). Stuttgart: Klett-Cotta.

Aeschbacher U. (1986). *Unterrichtsziel: Verstehen.* Stuttgart: Klett.

Alloy, L., & Abramson, L.Y. (1979). Judgment of contingency in depressed and non-depressed students: Sadder but wiser? *Journal of Experimental Psychology: General, 108,* 441–485.

Allport, G.W. (1961). *Pattern and growth of personality.* New York: Holt, Rinehart & Winston.

Alschuler, C.F., & Alschuler, A.S. (1984). Developing healthy responses to anger: The counselor's role. *Journal of Counseling and Development, 63*(1), 26–29.

Anderson, J.R. (1987). Skill acquisition: Compilation of weak-method problem solutions. *Psychological Review, 94,* 192–210.

Aronfreed, J. (1969). The concept of internalization. In D.A. Goslin (Ed.), *Handbook of socialization theory and research* (pp. 263–324). Chicago: Rand McNally.

Atkinson, R.C. (1972). Optimizing the learning of a second language vocabulary. *Journal of Experimental Psychology, 96,* 124–129.

Atkinson, R.C. (1975). Mnemotechnics in second-language learning. *American Psychologist, 30,* 821–828.

Atkinson, R.C., & Raugh, M.R. (1975). An application of the mnemonic key word method to the acquisition of a Russian vocabulary. *Journal of Experimental Psychology: Human Learning and Memory, 1,* 126–133.

Austin, H. (1974). *A computational view of the skill of juggling.* Unpublished report. Artificial Intelligence Laboratory, MIT, Cambridge, MA.

Ausubel, D.P. (1968). *Educational psychology – A cognitive view.* New York: Holt, Rinehart & Winston.

Averill, J.R. (1982). *Anger and aggression. An essay on emotion.* New York: Springer-Verlag.

Azrin, N.H., & Holz, W.C. (1966). Punishment. In W.K. Honig (Ed.), *Operant behavior: Areas of research and application* (pp. 380–447). New York: Appleton-Century-Crofts.

Baddeley, A. (1986). *Working memory.* Oxford: Clarendon Press.

Baddeley, A. (1990). *Human memory. Theory and practice.* Hillsdale, NJ: Erlbaum.

Baddeley, A. (1992). Working memory. *Science, 255*(1), 556–559.

Baddeley, A., & Hitch, G.J. (1974). Working memory. In G.H. Bower (Ed.), *The psychology of learning and motivation.* (Vol. 8, pp. 47–84). New York: Academic Press.

Baddeley, A., & Hitch, G.J. (1994). Developments in the concepts of working memory. *Neuropsychology, 8*(4), 485–492.

Baddeley, A., & Liberman, K. (1977). Spatial working memory. In R. Nickerson (Ed.), *Attention and performance* (Vol. VIII). Hillsdale, NJ: Erlbaum.

Bahrick, H.P. (1983). The cognitive map of a city: Fifty years of learning and memory. *The Psychology of Learning and Motivation, 17,* 125–163.

Ballstaedt, S.-P., Mandl, H., Schnotz, W., & Tergan, S. (1981). *Texte verstehen, Texte gestalten.* Munich: Urban & Schwarzenberg.

Ballstaedt, S.-P., Molitor, S., & Mandl, H. (1987). *Wissen aus Text und Bild.* Forschungsbericht No. 40. Deutsches Institut für Fernstudien an der Universität Tübingen.

Bandura, A. (1977). *Social learning theory.* Englewood Cliffs, NJ: Prentice Hall.

Bandura, A. (1982). Self-efficacy mechanisms in human agency. *American Psychologist, 37,* 227–247.

Bandura, A. (1986). *Social foundations of thought and action: A social-cognitive theory.* Englewood Cliffs, NJ: Prentice Hall.

Bandura, A. (1989). Self-regulation of motivation and action through internal standards and goal systems. In L.A. Pervin (Ed.), *Goal concepts in personality and social psychology* (pp. 19–38). Hillsdale, NJ: Erlbaum.

Bandura, A. (1991). Self-regulation of motivation through anticipatory and self-reactive mechanisms. In R.A. Dienstbier (Ed.), *Perspectives on motivation: Nebraska Symposium on Motivation* (Vol. 38, pp. 69–164). Lincoln: University of Nebraska Press.

Bandura, A., & Schunk, D.H. (1981): Cultivating competence, self-efficacy, and intrinsic interest through proximal self-motivation. *Journal of Personality and Social Psychology, 41,* 586–598.

Bandura, A., & Walters, R.H. (1963). *Social learning and personality development.* New York: Holt, Rinehart & Winston.

Bartlett, F.C. (1932). *Remembering. A study in experimental social psychology.* Cambridge: Cambridge University Press.

Beek, P.J., & Turvey, M.T. (1992). Temporal patterning in cascade juggling. *Journal of Experimental Psychology, 18*(4), 934–947.

Bergius R. (1964). Übungsübertragung und Problemlösen. In R. Bergius (Ed.), *Handbuch der Psychologie* (Vol. 1, 2. Halbband, pp. 284–325). Göttingen: Hogrefe.

Berry, D.C., & Dienes, Z. (1993). *Implicit learning: Theoretical and empirical issues.* Hove, UK: Erlbaum.

Biaggio, M.K. (1987). Therapeutic management of anger. *Clinical Psychology Review, 7,* 663–675.

Bjork, R.A. (1988). Retrieval practice and the maintenance of knowledge. In M.M. Gruneberg, P.E. Morris & R.N. Sykes (Eds.), *Practical aspects of memory: Current research and issues. Vol. 1: Memory in everyday life* (pp. 396–401). Chichester, UK: Wiley.

Bower, G.H. (1970). Organizational factors in memory. *Cognitive Psychology, 1,* 28–46.

Bower, G.H. (1972). Mental imagery and associative learning. In L.W. Gregg (Ed.), *Cognition in learning and memory* (pp. 51–88). New York: Wiley.

Bower, G.H., & Hilgard, E.R. (1981). *Theories of learning*, revised edition. New York: Prentice Hall.

Bower, S.A., & Bower, G.H. (1976). *Asserting yourself. A practical guide for positive change.* Reading, MA: Addison-Wesley.

Bridges, K. (1932). Emotional development in infancy. *Child Development, 3,* 324–341.

Broadbent, D.E. (1981). From the percept to the cognitive structure. In L. Long & A. Baddeley (Eds.), *Attention and performance* (Vol. IX, pp. 1–24). Hillsdale, NJ: Erlbaum.

Bronfenbrenner, U., & Ceci, S.J. (1994). Nature–nurture reconceptualized in developmental perspective: A bioecological model. *Psychological Review, 10*(4), 568–586.

Brooke, M. (1970). *Tricks, games, and puzzles with matches.* New York: Dover.

Brown, A.L. (1978). Knowing when, where and how to remember – A problem of meta-cognition. In R. Glaser (Ed.), *Advances in instructional psychology* (pp. 77–165). Hillsdale, NJ: Erlbaum.

Brown, A.L., & Day, J.D. (1983). Macrorules for summarizing texts: The development of expertise. *Journal of Verbal Learning and Verbal Behavior, 22,* 1–14.

Brown, A.L., & Palincsar, A.S. (1989). Guided, cooperative learning and individual knowledge acquisition. In L.B. Resnick (Ed.), *Knowledge, learning and instruction. Essays in honor of Robert Glaser* (pp. 393–451). Hillsdale, NJ: Erlbaum.

Brown, A.L., Palincsar, A.S., & Armbruster, B. (1984). Instructing comprehension-fostering activities in interactive learning situations. In H. Mandl, N. Stein & T. Trabasso (Eds.), *Learning and comprehension of text* (pp. 255–286). Hillsdale, NJ: Erlbaum.

Bruner, J.S. (1964). The course of cognitive growth. *American Psychologist, 19,* 1–14.

Bruner, J.S. (1966). *Toward a theory of instruction.* Cambridge, MA: Harvard University Press.

Bruner, J.S., Olver, R.R., & Greenfield, P.M. (1966). *Studies in cognitive growth.* New York: Wiley.

Brunnhuber, P., & Czinczoll, B. (1974). *Lernen durch Entdecken.* Donauwörth: Auer.

Cameron, J., & Pierce, W.D. (1994). Reinforcement, reward, and intrinsic motivation: A meta-analysis. *Review of Educational Research, 64*(3), 363–423.

Canter, D., & Tagg, S. (1975). Distance estimation in cities. *Environment and Behavior, 7,* 59–80.

Charness, N. (1981). Search in chess: Age and skill differences. *Journal of Experimental Psychology: Human Perception and Performance, 7,* 476.

Chase, W.G. (1973). *Visual information processing.* New York: Academic Press.

Chase, W.G., & Simon, H.A. (1973). The mind's eye in chess. In W.G. Chase (Ed.), *Visual information processing* (pp. 215–282). New York: Academic Press.

Chi, M.T.H., Glaser, R., & Rees, E. (1982). Expertise in problem solving. In R. Sternberg (Ed.), *Advances in the psychology of human intelligence* (pp. 7–70). Hillsdale, NJ: Erlbaum.

Claparède, E. (1903). La faculté lointaine (sens de direction, sens de retour). *Archives de Psychologie, 2,* 133–180.

Cleeremans, A. (1993). *Mechanisms of implicit learning: Connectionist models of sequence processing.* Cambridge, MA: MIT-Press.

Collins, A., Brown, J.S., & Larkin, K.M. (1980). Inference in text understanding. In R.J. Spiro, B.C. Bruce & W.F. Brewer (Eds.), *Theoretical issues in reading comprehension* (pp. 385–407). Hillsdale, NJ: Erlbaum.

Copei, F. (1950). *Der fruchtbare Moment im Unterricht.* Heidelberg.

Csikszentmihalyi, M. (1975). *Beyond boredom and anxiety.* San Francisco: Jossey-Bass.

Csikszentmihalyi, M. (1978). Intrinsic rewards and emergent motivation. In M.R. Lepper & D. Greene (Eds.), *The hidden costs of rewards* (pp. 205–216). Hillsdale, NJ: Erlbaum.

Dansereau, D.F. (1988). Cooperative learning strategies. In C.E. Weinstein, E.T. Goetz & P.A. Alexander (Eds.), *Learning and study strategies* (pp. 103–120). New York: Academic Press.

Darwin, C. (1859). *On the origin of species by means of natural selection. Dt. Die Entstehung der Arten durch natürliche Zuchtwahl.* Stuttgart: Reclam, 1976.

de Charms, R. (1968). *Personal causation: The internal affective determinants of behavior.* New York: Academic Press.

Deci, E.L. (1971). Effects of externally mediated rewards on intrinsic motivation. *Journal of Personality and Social Psychology, 18*(1), 105–115.

Deci, E.L. (1972). Intrinsic motivation, extrinsic reinforcement, and inequity. *Journal of Personality and Social Psychology, 26,* 113–120.

Deci, E.L., & Ryan, R.M. (1985). *Intrinsic motivation and self-determination in human behavior.* New York: Plenum.

De Groot, A.D. (1965). *Thought and choice in chess.* The Hague, Netherlands: Mouton Publishers.

De Groot, A.D. (1966). Perception and memory versus thought: Some old ideas and recent findings. In B. Kleinmuntz (Ed.), *Problem solving.* New York: Wiley.

De Kleer, J., & Brown, J.S. (1983). Assumptions and ambiguities in mechanistic mental models. In D. Gentner & A.L. Stevens (Eds.), *Mental models* (pp. 155–190). Hillsdale, NJ: Erlbaum.

Detterman, D.K., & Sternberg, R.J. (Eds.) (1993). *Transfer on trial: Intelligence, cognition and instruction.* Norwood, NJ: Ablex.

Diekhoff, G.M., Brown, P.J., & Dansereau, D.F. (1982). A prose learning strategy training. *Experimental Education, 50,* 180–184.

Doise, W., & Mugny, G. (1984). *The social development of the intellect.* New York: Pergamon.

Dollard, J., & Miller, N.E. (1950). *Personality and psychotherapy.* New York: McGraw-Hill.

Downs, R.M., & Stea, D. (1973). *Image and environment.* Chicago: Aldine.

Downs, R.M., & Stea, D. (1977). *Maps in mind. Reflections on cognitive mapping.* New York: Harper & Row.

Duncker, K. (1935). *Zur Psychologie des produktiven Denkens.* Berlin: Springer-Verlag (Reprint 1974).

Ebbinghaus, H. (1979). *Grundzüge der Psychologie* (4th edition, K. Bühler, ed.). Leipzig: Veit.

Edwards, A.E., & Acker, L.E. (1962). A demonstration of the long-term retention of a conditional galvanic skin response. *Psychosomatic Medicine, 24,* 459–463.

Ellison, K.W., & Genz, J.L. (1983). *Stress and the police officer.* Springfield, IL: Charles C. Thomas.

Ericsson, K.A. (1985). Memory skill. *Canadian Journal of Psychology, 39,* 188–231.

Ericsson, K.A., & Kintsch, W. (1995). Long-term working memory. *Psychological Review, 102*(2), 211–245.

Eysenck, M.W., & Keane, M.T. (1990). *Cognitive psychology. A student's handbook.* Hillsdale, NJ: Erlbaum.

Fillmore, C.J. (1968). The case for case. In E. Bach & R.T. Harms (Eds.), *Universals of linguistic theory.* New York: Holt, Rinehart & Winston.

Fischer, P.M., Mandl, H. (1983). Förderung von Lernkompetenz und Lernregulation. Zentrale Komponenten der Steuerung und Regulation von Lernprozessen. In L. Koetter & H. Mandl (Eds.), *Kognitive Prozesse und Unterricht. Jahrbuch der Empirischen Erziehungswissenschaft* (pp. 263–317). Düsseldorf: Schwann.

Flavell, J.H. (1963). *The developmental psychology of Jean Piaget.* New York: Van Nostrand.

Flavell, J.H. (1978). Metacognitive development. In J.M. Scandura & J.C. Brainerd (Eds.), *Structural process theory of complex human behavior.* New York: Wiley.

Flavell, J.H. (1985). *Cognitive development* (2nd ed.). Englewood Cliffs, NJ: Prentice Hall.

Flavell, J.H., Botkin, P.T., Fry, C.L., Wright, J.W., & Jarvis, P.E. (1968). *The development of role-taking and communication skills in children.* New York: Wiley.

Frey, R.L. (1981). *Wirtschaft, Staat und Wohlfahrt. Eine Einführung in die Nationalökonomie.* Basel: Helbing & Lichtenhahn.

Fricke, A. (1970). Operative Lernprinzipien. In A. Fricke & H. Besuden, *Mathematik – Elemente einer Didaktik und Methodik.* Stuttgart: Klett.

Galton, F. (1872). *On finding the way. The art of travel or: Shifts and contrivances available in wild countries.* London: John Murray.

Gantt, W.H. (1966). Reflexology, schizokinesis, and autokinesis. *Conditional Reflex, 1,* 57–68.

Gärling, T., Böök, A., & Lindberg, E. (1984). Cognitive mapping of large-scale environments. The interrelationship of action plans, acquisition, and orientation. *Environment and Behavior, 16*(1), 3–34.

Glaser, R. (1984). Education and thinking: The role of knowledge. *American Psychologist, 39,* 93–104.

Gordon, A.D., Jupp, P.E., & Byrne, R.W. (1989). The construction and assessment of mental maps. *British Journal of Mathematical and Statistical Society, 42,* 169–182.

Gordon, T. (1977). *Leader effectiveness training. L.E.T.* New York: Peter H. Wyden.

Graesser, A.C. (1981). *Prose comprehension beyond the word.* New York: Springer-Verlag.

Gréco, P. (1963). Le progrès des inférences itératives et des notions arithmétiques chez l'enfant et l'adolescent. In J. Piaget (Ed.), *La formation des raisonnements récurrentiels. Études d'épistémiologie génétique* (pp. 143–281). Paris: Presses Universitaires de France.

Greeno, J.G., Smith, P.R., & Moore, J.L. (1993). Transfer of situated learning. In D.K. Detterman & R.J. Sternberg (Eds.), *Transfer on trial: Intelligence, cognition and instruction* (pp. 99–166). Norwood, NJ: Ablex.

Gulliver, E.P. (1908). Orientation of maps. *Journal of Geography, 7,* 55–58.

Guthrie, E.R. (1935). *The psychology of learning.* New York: Harper & Row.

Guthrie, E.R. (1959). Association by contiguity. In S. Koch (Ed.), *Psychology: A study of science* (Vol. 2, pp. 158–195). New York: McGraw-Hill.

Guthrie, E.R. (1960). *The psychology of learning* (rev. ed.). Gloucester, MA: Peter Smith.

Harris, B. (1979). Whatever happened to Little Albert. *American Psychologist, 34*(2), 151–160.

Heckhausen, H. (1969). Förderung der Lernmotivierung und der intellektuellen Tüchtigkeiten. In H. Roth (Ed.), *Begabung und Lernen* (pp. 193–228). Stuttgart: Klett.

Hiroto, D.S., & Seligman, M.E.P. (1975). Generality of learned helplessness in man. *Journal of Personality and Social Psychology, 31,* 311–327.

Hirtle, S.C., & Jonides, J. (1985). Evidence of hierarchies in cognitive maps. *Memory & Cognition, 13,* 208–217.

Hoffman, M.L. (1976). Empathy, role-taking, guilt and the development of altruistic motives. In T. Lickona (Ed.), *Moral development and behavior.* New York: Holt, Rinehart & Winston.

Holding, D.H. (1985). *The psychology of chess skill.* Hillsdale, NJ: Erlbaum.

Holland, J.G., & Skinner, B.F. (1961). *The analysis of behavior: A program for self-instruction.* New York: McGraw-Hill.

Holley, C.D., & Dansereau, D.F. (1984). *Spatial learning strategies: Techniques, applications, and related issues.* New York: Academic Press.

Holt, R.R. (1970). On the interpersonal and intrapersonal consequences of expressing or not expressing anger. *Journal of Counseling and Clinical Psychology, 35*(1), 8–12.

Hull, C.L. (1943). *Principles of behavior.* New York: Appleton-Century-Crofts.

Johnson-Laird, P.N. (1980). Mental models in cognitive science. *Cognitive Science, 4,* 71–115.

Johnson-Laird, P.N. (1983). *Mental models: Towards a cognitive science of language, inference and consciousness.* Cambridge: Cambridge University Press.

Johnston, J.M. (1972). Punishment of human behavior. *American Psychologist, 27,* 1033–1054.

Kant, I. (1781). *Kritik der reinen Vernunft* (Vol. 1). Frankfurt: Suhrkamp 1974.

Katona, G. (1940). *Organizing and memorizing.* New York: Columbia University Press.

Keller, F.S. (1969). *Learning: Reinforcement theory* (2nd ed.). New York: Random House.

Kintsch, W. (1988). The use of knowledge in discourse processing: A construction-integration model. *Psychological Review, 95,* 163–182.

Kintsch, W. (1992). A cognitive architecture for comprehension. In H.L. Pick, P. van den Broek & D.C. Kuill (Eds.), *The study of cognition: Conceptual and methodological issues* (pp. 143–164). Washington, DC: APA.

Kintsch, W. (1994). Text comprehension, memory, and learning. *American Psychologist, 49*(4), 294–303.

Koedinger, K.R., & Anderson, J.R. (1990). Abstract planning and perceptual chunks: Elements of expertise in geometry. *Cognitive Science, 14,* 511–550.

Koffka, K. (1935). *Principles of Gestalt psychology.* New York: Harcourt, Brace & World.

Köhler, W. (1929). *Gestalt psychology.* New York: Lifesight.

Kosslyn, S.M. (1980). *Image and mind.* Cambridge, MA: Harvard University Press.

Kosslyn, S.M., Ball, T., & Reiser, B. (1978). Visual images preserve metric spatial information: Evidence from studies of image scanning. *Journal of Experimental Psychology: Human Perception and Performance, 4,* 47–60.

Kozlowski, L.T., & Bryant, K.J. (1977). Sense of direction, spatial orientation, and cognitive maps. *Journal of Experimental Psychology,* 590–598.

Krebs, D. (1975). Empathy and altruism. *Journal of Personality and Social Psychology, 32,* 1134–1146.

Krohne, H.W. (1975). *Angst und Angstverarbeitung.* Stuttgart: Kohlhammer.

Krohne, H.W. (1981). *Theorien zur Angst* (2nd ed.). Stuttgart: Kohlhammer.

Krohne, H.W. (1985). Das Konzept der Angstbewältigung. In H.W. Krohne (Ed.), *Angstbewältigung in Leistungssituationen* (pp. 1–13). Weinheim: VCH Verlagsgemeinschaft.

Kuhl, J. (1984). Volitional aspects of achievement motivation and learned helplessness: Toward a comprehensive theory of action control. In B.A. Maher & W.B. Maher (Eds.), *Progress in experimental personality research* (pp. 99–171). New York: Academic Press.

Kuhl, J. (1988). Volitional mediators of cognition-behavior consistency: Self-regulatory processes and action versus state orientation. In J. Kuhl & J. Beckmann (Eds.), *Action control: From cognition to behavior.* Berlin: Springer-Verlag.

Kuhl, J., & Kraska, K. (1989). Self-regulation and metamotivation: Computational mechanisms, development, and assessment. In R. Kanfer, L. Ackerman & K. Cudek (Eds.), *Abilities, motivation, and methodology* (pp. 343–374). Hillsdale, NJ: Erlbaum.

Laird, J.E., Rosenbloom, P.S., & Newell, A. (1986). Chunking in soas: The anatomy of general learning mechanisms. *Machine Learning, 1,* 11–46.

Lashley, K.S. (1929). *Brain mechanisms and intelligence.* Chicago: University of Chicago Press.

Lashley, K.S. (1951). The problem of serial order in behavior. In L.A. Jeffress (Ed.), *Cerebral mechanisms in behavior. The Hixon Symposium* (pp. 112–130). New York: Wiley.

Laux, H. (1981). Psychologische Stresskonzeptionen. In H. Thomae (Ed.), *Handbuch der Psychologie. Vol. II: Motivation* (2nd ed.). Göttingen: Hogrefe.

Lazarus, R.S. (1966). *Psychological stress and the coping process.* New York: McGraw-Hill.

Lazarus, R.S., & Launier, R. (1978). Stress-related transactions between person and environment. In L.A. Pervin & M. Lewis (Eds.), *Perspectives in interactional psychology.* New York: Plenum.

Lee, T.D., & Magill, R.A. (1983). The locus of contextual interference in motor-skill acquisition. *Journal of Experimental Psychology: Learning, Memory, and Cognition, 9,* 730–746.

Lepper, M.R. (1973). Dissonance, self-perception, and honesty in children. *Journal of Personality and Social Psychology, 25,* 65–74.

Lepper, M.R. (1981). Intrinsic and extrinsic motivation in children: Detrimental effects of superfluous social controls. In W.A. Collins (Ed.), *Aspects of the development of competence: The Minnesota Symposia on Child Psychology* (Vol. 14, pp. 155–214). Hillsdale, NJ: Erlbaum.

Lepper, M.R., & Greene, D. (1975). Turning play into work: Effects of adult surveillance and extrinsic rewards on children's intrinsic motivation. *Journal of Personality and Social Psychology, 31,* 479–486.

Lepper, M.R., & Greene, D. (1978). Overjustification research and beyond: Towards a means-end analysis of intrinsic and extrinsic motivation. In M.R. Lepper & D. Greene (Eds.), *The hidden costs of reward* (pp. 109–148). Hillsdale, NJ: Erlbaum.

Lepper, M.R., Greene, D., & Nisbett, R.E. (1973). Undermining children's intrinsic interest with extrinsic reward: A test of the overjustification hypothesis. *Journal of Personality and Social Psychology, 28*(1), 129–137.

Levin, J.R. (1981). On functions of pictures in prose. In F.J. Pirozzolo & M.C. Wittrock (Eds.), *Neuropsychological and cognitive processes in reading* (pp. 203–228). New York: Academic Press.

Levin, J.R. (1982). Pictures as prose learning devices. In A. Flammer & W. Kintsch (Eds.), *Discourse processing* (pp. 412–444). Amsterdam: North-Holland.

Levin, J.R., & Mayer, R.E. (1993). Understanding illustrations in text. In B.K. Britton, A. Woodward & M. Binkley (Eds.), *Learning from textbooks* (pp. 95–113). Hillsdale, NJ: Erlbaum.

Lewin, K. (1935). *A dynamic theory of personality.* New York: McGraw-Hill.

Liddell, H.S. (1934). The conditioned reflex. In F.A. Moss (Ed.), *Comparative psychology.* New York: Prentice Hall.

Lindsay, P.H., & Norman, D.A. (1972). *Human information processing. An introduction to psychology.* New York: Academic Press.

Lübke, H. (1975, 1983). *Emploi des mots* (9th ed.). Dortmund: Lambert Lensing.

Lynch, K. (1960). *The image of the city.* Cambridge, MA: MIT Press.

Maccoby, E.E. (1980). *Social development. Psychological growth and the parent–child relationship.* New York: Harcourt, Brace & Jovanovich.

Magill, R.A., & Hall, K.G. (1990). A review of the contextual interference effect in motor skill acquisition. *Human Movement Science, 9,* 241–289.

Mandl, H., & Friedrich, H.F. (1986). Förderung des Wissenserwerbs im Kindes- und Erwachsenenalter. *Unterrichtswissenschaft, 1,* 10–24.

Mandl, H., & Schnotz, W. (1985). *New directions in text processing.* Deutsches Institut für Fernstudien an der Universität Tübingen, Forschungsbericht No. 36.

Mandl, H., Stein, N.L., & Trabasso, T. (1984). *Learning and comprehension of text.* Hillsdale, NJ: Erlbaum.

McGraw, K.O. (1978). The detrimental effects of reward on performance: A literature review and a prediction model. In M.R. Lepper & D. Greene (Eds.), *The hidden costs of reward* (pp. 33–60). Hillsdale, NJ: Erlbaum.

McNamara, D.S., Kintsch, E., Butler-Songer, N., & Kintsch, W. (1996). Are good texts always better? Interaction of text coherence, background knowledge, and levels of understanding in learning from text. *Cognition & Instruction, 14,* 1–43.

Meichenbaum, D. (1977). *Cognitive behavior modification.* New York: Plenum.

Meichenbaum, D.H., & Cameron, R. (1974). The clinical potential of modifying what clients say to themselves: A means of developing self-control. In M.J. Mahoney & C.E. Thoreson (Eds.), *Self-control: Power to the person.* Monterey, CA: Brooks/Cole.

Meichenbaum, D., & Novaco, R.W. (1978). Stress inoculation: A preventive approach. In C.D. Spielberger & I.G. Sarason (Eds.), *Stress and anxiety* (Vol. 5, pp. 317–330). New York: Halstead.

Menzel, E.W. (1973). Chimpanzee spatial memory organization. *Science, 182,* 943–945.

Menzel, E.W. (1978). Cognitive mapping in chimpanzees. In S.H. Hulse, H. Fowler & W.K. Honig (Eds.), *Cognitive processes in animal behavior* (pp. 375–422). Hillsdale, NJ: Erlbaum.

Merton, R.K. (1948). The self-fulfilling prophecy. In E.P. Hollander & R.G. Hunt (Eds.), *Classic contributions to social psychology* (pp. 260–266). London: Oxford University Press.

Meyer, W.U. (1984). *Das Konzept der eigenen Begabung.* Bern: Huber.

Meyer, W.-U., & Hallermann, B. (1974). Anstrengungsintention bei einer leichten und schweren Aufgabe in Abhängigkeit von der wahrgenommenen eigenen Begabung. *Archiv für Psychologie, 124,* 85–89.

Miller, G.A. (1956). The magical number seven, plus or minus two. *Psychological Review, 63,* 81–97.

Miller, G.A., Galanter, E., & Pribram, C. (1960). *Plans and the structure of behavior.* New York: Holt, Rinehart & Winston.

Minsky, M. (1975). A framework for representing knowledge. In P. Winston (Ed.), *The psychology of computer vision.* New York: McGraw-Hill.

Minsky, M., & Papert, S. (1972). *Perceptrons.* Cambridge, MA: MIT Press.

Mischel, W., & Patterson, C.J. (1978). Effective plans for self-control in children. In W.A. Collins (Ed.), *Minnesota Symposium on Child Psychology* (Vol. XI, pp. 199–230). Hillsdale, NJ: Erlbaum.

Mischel, W., & Staub, E. (1965). Effects of expectancy on working and waiting for larger reward. *Journal of Personality and Social Psychology, 2,* 625–633.

Mischel, W., & Underwood, B. (1974). Instrumental ideation in delay of gratification. *Child Development, 45,* 1083–1088.

Neber, H. (Ed.) (1973). *Entdeckendes Lernen.* Weinheim: Beltz.

Neisser, U. (1967). *Cognitive psychology.* New York: Appleton-Century-Crofts.

Neisser, U. (1976). *Cognition and reality.* San Francisco: Freeman.

Nesher, P. (1989). Microworlds in mathematical education: A pedagogical realism. In L.B. Resnick (Ed.), *Knowing, learning, and instruction. Essays in honor of Robert Glaser* (pp. 187–216). Hillsdale, NJ: Erlbaum.

Newell, A., & Simon, H.A. (1972). *Human problem solving.* Englewood Cliffs, NJ: Prentice Hall.

Nolen-Hoeksma, S., Girgus, J.S., & Seligman, M.E.P. (1986). Learned helplessness in children: A longitudinal study of depression, achievement, and explanatory style. *Journal of Personality and Social Psychology, 51*(2), 435–442.

Norman, D.A. (1976). *Memory and attention.* New York: Wiley.

Norman, D.A., & Rumelhart, D.E. (1975). *Explorations in cognition.* San Francisco: Freeman.

Pailhous, J. (1970). *La représentation de l'espace. L'exemple du chauffeur de taxi.* Paris: Presses Universitaires de France.

Paivio, A. (1971). *Imagery and verbal processes.* New York: Holt.

Paivio, A. (1983). The empirical case for dual coding. In J.C. Yuille (Ed.), *Imagery, memory, and cognition.* Hillsdale, NJ: Erlbaum.

Paivio, A. (1986). *Mental representations: A dual coding approach.* New York: Oxford University Press.

Paivio, A. (1991). *Images in mind: The evolution of a theory.* New York: Harvester Wheatsheaf.

Pavlov, I.P. (1927). *Conditional reflexes.* London: Clarendon Press.

Pavlov, I.P. (1928). *Lectures on conditioned reflexes* (translated by W.H. Gantt). New York: International Publishers.

Peters, T.J., & Waterman, R.H. Jr. (1982). *In search of excellence.* New York: Harper & Row.

Pflugradt, N. (1985). *Förderung des Verstehens und Behaltens von Textinformation durch "mapping."* Deutsches Institut für Fernstudien an der Universität Tübingen, Forschungsbericht No. 34.

Piaget, J. (1936). *La naissance de l'intelligence chez l'enfant.* Neuchâtel: Delachaux & Niestlé.

Piaget, J. (1947). *Die Psychologie der Intelligenz.* Zürich: Rascher.

Piaget, J., & Inhelder, B. (1948). *La représentation de l'espace chez l'enfant.* Neuchâtel: Delachaux & Niestlé.

Piaget, J., & Szeminska, A. (1941). *La genèse du nombre chez l'enfant.* Neuchâtel: Delachaux & Niestlé.

Prystav, G. (1985). Der Einfluss der Vorhersagbarkeit von Stressereignissen auf die Angstbewältigung. In H.W. Krohne (Ed.), *Angstbewältigung in Leistungssituationen* (pp. 14–44). Weinheim: VCH Verlagsgemeinschaft.

Pylyshyn, Z.W. (1973). What tells the mind's eye to the mind's brain: A critique of mental imagery. *Psychological Bulletin, 80,* 1–24.

Reber, A.S. (1993). *Implicit learning and tacit knowledge: An essay on the cognitive unconscious.* New York: Oxford University Press.

Rescorla, R.A. (1988). Pavlovian conditioning. *American Psychologist, 43*(3), 151–160.

Resnick, L. (1985). *Cognition and the curriculum.* Paper delivered at the AERA Conference, 1985, in Chicago.

Resnick, L.B. (1987). Instruction and the cultivation of thinking. In E. De Corte, J.G.L.C. Lodewijks, R. Parmentier & P. Span (Eds.), *Learning and instruction. A publication of the European Association for Research on Learning and Instruction.* Oxford/Louvain: Pergamon Press/Louvain.

Revenstorf, D. (1982). *Psychotherapeutische Verfahren: Vol. 2: Verhaltenstherapie.* Stuttgart: Kohlhammer.

Rosenhan, D. (1969). Some origins of concern for others. In P.A. Mussen, J. Langer & M. Covington (Eds.), *Trends and issues in developmental psychology.* New York: Holt, Rinehart & Winston.

Rosenthal, R., & Jacobson, L. (1968). *Pygmalion in the classroom.* New York: Holt, Rinehart & Winston.

Rotter, J. (1966). Generalized expectancies of internal versus external control of reinforcement. *Psychological Monographs, 80*(1), Whole No. 609, 1–28.

Rumelhart, D.E. (1980). Schemata: The building blocks of cognition. In R. Spirao, B. Bruce & W. Bewer (Eds.), *Theoretical issues in reading comprehension* (pp. 33–58). Hillsdale, NJ: Erlbaum.

Rumelhart, D.E., & Norman, D.A. (1976). Accretion, tuning, and restructuring: Three modes of learning. In J.W. Cotton & R.L. Klatzki (Eds.), *Semantic factors in cognition* (pp. 37–53). Hillsdale, NJ: Erlbaum.

Rumelhart, D.E., & Ortony, A. (1976). *The representation of knowledge in memory.* Technical Report No. 55. Center for Human Information Processing. Department of Psychology. University of California, San Diego.

Salmoni, A.W., Schmidt, R.A., & Walter, C.B. (1984). Knowledge of results and motor learning: A review and critical appraisal. *Psychological Bulletin, 95,* 355–386.

Sanford, A.J., & Garrod, S.C. (1981). *Understanding written language: Exploration of comprehension beyond the sentence.* New York: Wiley.

Sarason, I.G., Johnson, J.H., Berberich, J.P., & Siegel, J.M. (1979). Helping police officers to cope with stress: A cognitive-behavioral approach. *American Journal of Community Psychology, 7,* 590–603.

Schank, R. (1980). Language and memory. *Cognitive Science, 4,* 243–284.

Schank, R., & Abelson, R.P. (1977). *Scripts, plans, goals, and understanding.* Hillsdale, NJ: Erlbaum.

Schimmel, S. (1979). Anger and its control in Graeco-Roman and modern psychology. *Psychiatry, 42,* 320–377.

Schmidt, R.A. (1988). *Motor control and learning: A behavioral emphasis* (2nd ed.). Champaign, IL: Human Kinetics.

Schmidt, R.A. (1991a). *Motor learning and performance: From principles to practice.* Champaign, IL: Human Kinetics.

Schmidt, R.A. (1991b). Frequent augmented feedback can degrade learning: Evidence and interpretation. In J. Requin & G.E. Stelmach (Eds.), *Tutorials in motor neuroscience* (pp. 59–75). Dordrecht, Holland: Kluwer.

Schneider, W., & Shiffrin, R.M. (1977). Controlled and automatic human information processing: I. Detection, search, and attention. *Psychological Review, 84*(1), 1–66.

Schnotz, W. (1985). *Elementarische und holistische Theorieansätze zum Textverstehen.* Forschungsbericht No. 35. Deutsches Institut für Fernstudien an der Universität Tübingen.

Schnotz, W., & Kulhavy, R.W. (Eds.) (1994). *Comprehension of graphics.* Amsterdam: North-Holland.

Sears, R.R., Whiting, J.W., Nowlis, V., & Sears, P.S. (1953). Some child rearing antecedents of aggression and dependency in young children. *Genetic Psychology Monographs, 47,* 135–234.

Seligman, M.E.P., Peterson, C., Kaslow, N.J., Tannenbaum, R.L., Alloy, L., & Abramson, L.Y. (1984). Attributional style and depressive symptoms among children. *Journal of Abnormal Psychology, 88,* 235–238.

Selz, O. (1913). *Über die Gesetze des geordneten Denkablaufs. Eine experimentelle Untersuchung.* Stuttgart: Spemann.

Sharan, S. (Ed.) (1990). *Cooperative learning: Theory and research.* New York: Praeger.

Shea, J.B., & Morgan, R.L. (1979). Contextual interference effects on the acquisition, retention and transfer of a motor skill. *Journal of Experimental Psychology: Human Learning and Memory, 5,* 179–187.

Simon, H.A. (1972). What is visual imagery? An information processing interpretation. In L. Gregg (Ed.), *Cognition in learning and memory* (pp. 183–204). New York: Wiley.

Skinner, B.F. (1938). *The behavior of organisms: An experimental analysis.* Englewood Cliffs, NJ: Prentice-Hall.

Skinner, B.F. (1953). *Science and human behavior.* New York: Macmillan.

Smith, S., & Guthrie, E.R. (1921). *General psychology in terms of behavior.* New York: Appleton-Century-Crofts.

Spielberger, C.D., & Sarason, I.G. (Eds.) (1978). *Stress and anxiety* (Vol. 5). Washington, DC: Hemisphere.

Stein, F.M. (1986). Helping young policemen cope with stress and manage conflict situation. In J.C. Yuille (Ed.), *Police selection and training: The role of psychology* (pp. 301–306). Dordrecht: Nijhoff.

Steiner, G. (1972). *The use of Cuisenaire rods as tools for mentally retarded children in learning elementary arithmetic.* Research Report (unpublished manuscript). University of Berne (Switzerland), Department of Educational Psychology.

Steiner, G. (1980). *Visuelle Vorstellungen beim Lösen von elementaren Problemen.* Stuttgart: Klett-Cotta.

Steiner, G. (1983). Number learning as constructing coherent networks by using Piaget-derived operative principles. In M. Zweng, T. Green, J. Kilpatrick, H. Pollak & M. Snydam (Eds.), *ICME Proceedings of the Fourth International Congress on Mathematical Education* (pp. 508–511). Boston: Birkhäuser.

Steiner, G. (1986). Leadership training and an integrated introduction to psychology. In J.C. Yuille (Ed.), *Police selection and training: The role of psychology* (pp. 285–290). Dordrecht: Nijhoff.

Steiner, G. (1987). Analoge Repräsentationen. In H. Mandl., & H. Spada (Eds.), *Wissenspsychologie.* Munich: Urban & Schwarzenberg.

Steiner, G. (1994). Piaget's constructivism, semantic network theory, and a new approach to mathematics education – A microanalysis. In R. Biehler, R.W. Scholz & B. Winkelmann (Eds.), *Mathematics didactics as a scientific discipline* (pp. 247–261). Dordrecht, Holland: Kluwer.

Steiner, G. (1997). Educational learning theory. In R. Tennyson, F. Schott, N. Seel & S. Dijkstra (Eds.), *Instructional design* (Chapter 6). Hillsdale, NJ: Erlbaum.

Steiner, G., & Stöcklin, M. (1997). Fraction calculation – A didactic approach to constructing mathematical networks. *Learning and Instruction, 7*(5), 211–233.

Tavris, C. (1982). *Anger: The misunderstood emotion.* New York: Simon & Schuster.

Tavris, C. (1984). On the wisdom of counting to ten. Personal and social dangers of anger expression. *Review of Personality and Social Psychology, 5,* 170–191.

Thorndike, E.L. (1911). *Animal intelligence.* New York: Macmillan.

Thorndike, E.L. (1913). *Educational psychology: The psychology of learning* (Vol. 2). New York: Teachers College.

Thorndike, E.L. (1931). *Human learning.* New York: Century. Paperback: Cambridge: MIT Press 1966.

Thorndyke, P.W. (1981). Spatial cognition and reasoning. In J.H. Harvey (Ed.), *Cognition, social behavior, and the environment* (pp. 137–149). Hillsdale, NJ: Erlbaum.

Thorndyke, P., & Stasz, C. (1980). Individual differences in procedures for knowledge acquisition from maps. *Cognitive Psychology, 12,* 137–175.

Tolman, E.C. (1948). Cognitive maps in rats and men. *Psychological Review, 55*(4), 189–208.

Tolman, E.C., Ritchie, B.F., & Kalish, D. (1946). Studies in spatial learning. *Journal of Experimental Psychology, 36,* 15–20.

Trowbridge, C.C. (1913). On fundamental methods of orientation and imagery maps. *Science, 38,* 888–897.

Tulving, E. (1972). Episodic and semantic memory. In E. Tulving & W. Donaldson (Eds.), *Organization of memory* (pp. 382–404). New York: Academic Press.

Tversky, B. (1981). Distortions in memory for maps. *Cognitive Psychology, 13,* 407–433.

Ulich, D., Mayring, P., & Strehmel, P. (1983). Stress. In H. Mandl & G.L. Huber (Eds.), *Emotion und Kognition* (pp. 183–216). Munich: Urban & Schwarzenberg.

Unzicker, W. (1975). *Knaurs neues Schachbuch.* Munich: Knaur Nachf.

Van Dijk, T.A. (1980). *Macrostructures.* Hillsdale, NJ: Erlbaum.

Van Dijk, T.A., & Kintsch, W. (1983). *Strategies of discourse comprehension.* New York: Academic Press.

Voss, J.F., Fincher-Kiefer, R.H., Greene, T.R., & Post, T.A. (1986). Individual differences in performance: The constructive approach to knowledge. In R.J. Sternberg (Ed.), *Advances in the psychology of human intelligence* (pp. 297–334). Hillsdale, NJ: Erlbaum.

Wagenschein, M., Banholzer, S., & Thiel, S. (1973). *Kinder auf dem Wege zur Physik.* Stuttgart: Klett.

Wainer, H. (1992). Understanding graphs and tables. *Educational Researcher, 21*(1), 14–23.

Walters, R.H., & Demkoff, L. (1963). Timing of punishment as a determinant of resistance to temptation. *Child Development, 34,* 207–214.

Watson, J. (1919). *Psychology from the standpoint of a behaviorist.* Philadelphia, PA: Lippincott.

Watson, J., & Rayner, R. (1930). Conditioned emotional reactions. *Journal of Experimental Psychology, 3,* 1–14.

Weiner, B. (Ed.) (1974). *Achievement motivation and attribution theory.* Morristown, NJ: General Learning Press.

Weiner, B. (1985). An attributional theory of achievement motivation and emotion. *Psychological Review, 92*(4), 548–573.

Weinert, F.E., & Kluwe, R.H. (1983). *Motivation und Lernen.* Stuttgart: Kohlhammer.

Wertheimer, M. (1945). *Produktives Denken.* Frankfurt: Kramer.

Wickelgren, W.A. (1974). *How to solve problems.* San Francisco: Freeman.

Winstein, C.J., & Schmidt, R.A. (1990). Reduced frequency of knowledge of results enhances motor skill learning. *Journal of Experimental Psychology: Learning, Memory and Cognition, 16,* 677–691.

Wippich, W. (1984). *Lehrbuch der angewandten Gedächtnispsychologie* (Vol. 1). Stuttgart: Kohlhammer.

Wolpe, J. (1958). *Psychotherapy by reciprocal inhibition.* Stanford: Stanford University Press.

Wulf, G. (1992a). The learning of generalized motor programs and motor schemata: Effects of knowledge of results, relative frequency and contextual interference. *Journal of Human Movement Studies, 23,* 53–76.

Wulf, G. (1992b). Neuere Befunde zur Effektivierung des Bewegungslernens. *Sportpsychologie, 92*(1), 12–16.

Yarrow, M.R., Scott, P.M., & Waxler, L.Z. (1973). Learning concern for others. *Developmental Psychology, 8,* 240–260.

Zahn-Waxler, C., Radke-Yarrow, M., & King, R.A. (1979). Child rearing and children's prosocial initiations toward victims of distress. *Child Development, 50,* 319–330.

Author Index

Subject Index